table of **MOODS**

D0107344

1001
BOOKS
for every
MOOD

Hallie Ephron, Ph.D.

△adamsmedia
Avon, Massachusetts

In memory of my mother, Phoebe Ephron,
who would have had lots of opinions
about what to put in this book.

. . .

Copyright © 2008 by Hallie Ephron, Ph.D.

Published by Adams Media, an F+W Publications Company
57 Littlefield Street
Avon, MA 02322
www.adamsmedia.com

ISBN-10: 1-59869-585-1
ISBN-13: 978-1-59869-585-4

Printed in Canada.

J I H G F E D C B A

Library of Congress Cataloging-in-Publication Data
is available from the publisher.

This publication is designed to provide accurate and authoritative information with regard to the subject matter covered. It is sold with the understanding that the publisher is not engaged in rendering legal, accounting, or other
professional advice. If legal advice or other expert assistance is required, the
services of a competent professional person should be sought.

—From a *Declaration of Principles* jointly adopted
by a Committee of the American Bar Association
and a Committee of Publishers and Associations

Many of the designations used by manufacturers and sellers to distinguish
their product are claimed as trademarks. Where those designations appear
in this book and Adams Media was aware of a trademark claim, the designations have been printed with initial capital letters.

This book is available at quantity discounts for bulk purchases.
For information, please call 1-800-289-0963.

So Many Books, So Little Time

Foreword by Susan Stamberg

The pink couch in my parent's living room was a refuge, growing up on 96th and Central Park West in Manhattan in the 1940s and 1950s. That couch was the launchpad for my adventures in literature. Now, as a journalist it behooves me to inform you that in truth the couch color was more rose than pink. And it was more a loveseat than a couch. But since someday I intend to tattoo the motto "Never Let Facts Get In the Way of a Good Story" on a bicep, the small couch was pink because that's how I remember it.

As a little girl I fit it neatly—head to toe, lying flat, shoes off, throw pillow under my head. Perfectly prone, I would read. And read. And read. First, after staggering home with a wobbly tower of slim hardcovers, on the pink couch I went through the entire children's section of the New York Free Circulating Library at Amsterdam Avenue and 100th Street. And when I finished the children's section, I moved on—the tower of books getting heavier, and wobblier—to two of the day's real steamers, *A Rage to Live* and *Forever Amber.* The librarian noticed I'd strayed too far from *The Five Little Peppers and How They Grew*, and prevented any further checkouts of "adult" literature. Eventually, I moved out of my parents' house, away from the couch. But my reading habits were by then ingrained, and I could turn a stiff wooden chair, an airplane seat, a park bench into that pink reading place.

Hallie Ephron is like the best, friendliest, hippest librarian you ever met. Her taste is exquisite, her writing's a hoot, she's done her homework, and it's very clear that she loves, loves, loves books. She knows obscure ones like Dori Sander's novel *Clover*, and prompts us back to classics we haven't considered in years—Katherine Anne Porter's *Pale Horse, Pale Rider*, or W. Somerset Maugham's *Of Human Bondage*. Hallie has fine factoids, too. Is it really possible that *Bridges of Madison County* eventually outsold *Gone With the Wind*? Or that Flaubert and his editors were put on trial because *Madame Bovary* was, in the mid-nineteenth century, deemed morally offensive? How quaint! How current!

I bet there's a pink couch in Hallie Ephron's background. It probably sits in her Milton living room right now. And for her, as it was for me (and will be for you, thanks to this book), that couch is less about literature and more about transportation—a passport out of the house and into the Dust Bowl or West Egg, Long Island or the Edmont Hotel in 1950s New York where Holden Caulfield took refuge after being thrown out of Pency Prep. Hallie's 1001 books not only are grouped to suit an array of moods; they also take us into other lives, other experiences that are often more vivid—certainly more crafted—than our own. Wonderful books always do this. And the one you're holding in your hands right now is arranged to help with navigation. It's a menu designed to slake our insatiable story hungers.

Acknowledgments

Readers feel passionately about their favorites. Many thanks to these prodigious readers for their recommendations: Ellen Bassuk, Lorraine Bodger, John Brady, Lora Brody, Maggie Bucholt, Michelle Chambers, Ceilidh Charleson-Jennings, Delia Ephron, Diane Fassino, Melanie Kaernan Ford, Barbara Fournier, Victoria Golden, Roberta Isleib, Pat Kennedy, Joe Kennedy, Naomi Rand, Hank Phillippi Ryan, Donna Tramontozzi, Molly Touger, Naomi Touger, Jerry Touger, and Leslie Tuttle, and to fellow writers Jan Brogan, Floyd Kemske, and Barbara Shapiro. "Emphatic" thanks to Lorraine Bodger, for strategic advice on how to tackle this monster; to Pat Kennedy for going above and beyond; to Adams Media editor extraordinaire Paula Munier; and to my smart and patient agent, Gail Hochman.

And finally, deep gratitude to the brilliant Susan Stamberg—I couldn't have asked for a more delightful and generous foreword.

Introduction

What are you in the mood for? Let the answer direct you to your next great read.

Feeling anxious? The right book can cheer you up, calm you down, or help you appreciate how much worse things could be. Bored and blah? A book can astound you, give you hope, or scare your socks off. Feeling nostalgic? Let a book take you on a stroll down memory lane.

In the pages that follow, you'll find 1001 wonderful books—fiction and nonfiction, old and new, classic and iconoclastic—chosen to suit your every mood. Think of it as mood therapy in a book and your personal guide to the outstanding, funny, sad, thrilling, inspiring, mind-bending . . . books of our time.

A Word about How the Books Were Selected

My goal was to compile an eclectic list that mixes fiction with nonfiction, books for adults with books designed for younger readers, and to organize them thematically by mood. I included my personal favorites plus titles culled from books recommended by readers, librarians, booksellers, and reviewers. I set out to limit one title per author, but occasionally I couldn't keep an extra title or two from a single author from sneaking in.

The Rating System

Each emotion-charged entry is rated using the following method of highlighting the book's notable characteristics. Look for what you like, try something new, or find a book that has an interesting combination of both. . . .

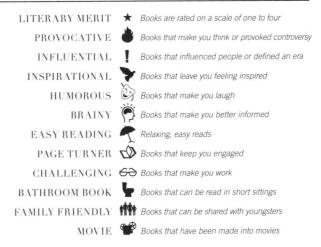

LITERARY MERIT	★	Books are rated on a scale of one to four
PROVOCATIVE		Books that make you think or provoked controversy
INFLUENTIAL	!	Books that influenced people or defined an era
INSPIRATIONAL		Books that leave you feeling inspired
HUMOROUS		Books that make you laugh
BRAINY		Books that make you better informed
EASY READING		Relaxing, easy reads
PAGE TURNER		Books that keep you engaged
CHALLENGING		Books that make you work
BATHROOM BOOK		Books that can be read in short sittings
FAMILY FRIENDLY		Books that can be shared with youngsters
MOVIE		Books that have been made into movies

Awards

Also included with each entry is a list of these highlighted awards that that particular book won. The noted annual book awards are:

For adult fiction and nonfiction:

American Book Award for outstanding literary achievement by contemporary American authors; to acknowledge multicultural diversity of American writing; awarded by the Before Columbus Foundation.

Booker Prize for best original novel, written in English, by a citizen of the Commonwealth of Nations or Ireland; awarded by the Booker Prize Foundation.

Hemingway Foundation/PEN Award for a novel or book of short stories by a first-time American author; administered by the Hemingway Society and PEN New England.

National Book Award for fiction, nonfiction, poetry, and young people's fiction by American authors; sponsored by American Book Publisher's Council, the Book Manufacturers' Institute, and the American Booksellers' Association.

National Book Critics Circle Award for the finest books published in English as voted by NBCC professional book review editors and book reviewers.

PEN/Faulkner Award for fiction by an American; awarded by the PEN/Faulkner Foundation.

Pulitzer Prize for fiction, biography, nonfiction, history, and poetry published in the United States by an American author.

For science fiction:

Hugo Award for best science fiction or fantasy work; voted annually by World Science Fiction Convention attendees and sponsored by the World Science Fiction Society.

Nebula Award for best science fiction or fantasy fiction published in the United States; awarded by Science Fiction and Fantasy Writers of America.

For crime fiction:

Edgar Award for best mystery fiction nor nonfiction; awarded by Mystery Writers of America.

For fantasy:

World Fantasy Award voted by attendees at the annual World Fantasy Conference.

For literature for younger readers:

Alex Award for books written for adults that have special appeal to young adults; awarded by the Young Adult Library Services Association (YALSA).

Newbery Medal for author of the outstanding American book for children; awarded by the American Library Association.

Caldecott Medal for the illustrator of the outstanding American children's book; awarded by the American Library Association.

Quizzes, Fun Facts, and More

In addition to the 1001 wonderful tomes picked to suit any mood, throughout you'll find interesting facts and challenging quizzes to supplement and test your literary prowess. It's all here—1001 of the books to read when you're in (or want to be in) a particular mood, and all the interesting highlights and sidenotes, trivia, and insight you could ever want.

...for a **Good Laugh**

LITERARY MERIT ★

PROVOCATIVE 🔥

INFLUENTIAL ❗

INSPIRATIONAL 🕊

HUMOROUS 😃

BRAINY 🧠

EASY READING ☂

PAGE TURNER 📖

CHALLENGING 👓

BATHROOM BOOK 🚽

FAMILY FRIENDLY 👪

MOVIE 🎥

1.

LITERARY MERIT

★ ★ ★

archy and mehitabel by Don Marquis

Archy is a beat poet reincarnated as a cockroach who eschews capitalization and punctuation— "i see things from the under side now"—his friend Mehitabel, a mangy alley cat who was once Cleopatra, is determined to be the belle of the ball. Originally published as newspaper columns, this satirical classic written in free verse has remained in print since 1916. The verses are full of eye-popping turns of phrase ("but wotthehell wotthehell") and grim humor; the staccato pen-and-ink drawings by George Herriman, the cartoonist who created the comic character Krazy Kat, are enchanting. *Cheerio my deario!*

2.

LITERARY MERIT

★ ★ ★ ★

A Confederacy of Dunces by John Kennedy Toole
Pulitzer 1981

This comic masterpiece of sloth and misadventure is set in New Orleans. The protagonist is a fat, lying, selfish, self-centered blowhard. Still living at home at the age of thirty, this miscreant sets out to get a job. And his ensuing mishaps are guaranteed not to raise your social consciousness. Published eleven years after Toole's 1969 suicide, attempts to adapt it into a movie have been ill-fated—John Belushi was set to star in it before he died in 1982; John Candy was cast in the lead before he died in 1994. The latest cancelled version would have starred Will Ferrell.

> **Department of Memorable Characters**
>
> "A green hunting cap squeezed the top of the fleshy balloon of a head. The green earflaps, full of large ears and uncut hair and the fine bristles that grew in the ears themselves, stuck out on either side like torn signals indicating two directions at once."
>
> —Ignatius J. Reilly,
> *A Confederacy of Dunces*

3.

LITERARY MERIT

★

Dave Barry's Complete Guide to Guys
by Dave Barry

For all of us who don't get it, find out the scientific reasons why guys act like jerks. At last, discover answers to life's great mysteries, including why guys don't write things down (like thank-you notes) or ask for directions, and above all, how they decide which urinal to use. Mind you, this is from an author who takes great pride in making booger jokes. His weekly humor column was syndicated for twenty-two years in newspapers across the country.

If Life Is a Bowl of Cherries, What Am I Doing in the Pits? by Erma Bombeck

The beloved syndicated columnist of the '60s and '70s, Bombeck was an original, and her observations on parenting, housecleaning, kids moving out, and kids moving back in, still resonate. She was the doyenne of the wisecrack in gentler times. The chapter "Who Killed Apple Pie," her take on the speed bumps on the way to women's lib, is priceless.

4.

LITERARY MERIT
★

I'll Always Have Paris by Art Buchwald

Art Buchwald fell in love with Paris in 1948. At twenty-two, he booked himself a one-way ticket on a "rusty, battered World War II troopship" and arrived, speaking no French ("the French took pity on me"). He talked his way into a job as a restaurant and nightclub reviewer for the Paris *Herald Tribune*. This is the humorous and heartwarming second installment of Buchwald's memoirs, and a journey back to a golden era after the war when oysters were cheap, Americans were heroes, and being in Paris meant you could rub shoulders with luminaries like Gertrude Stein and Ernest Hemingway.

5.

LITERARY MERIT
★ ★ ★

Naked by David Sedaris

Autobiographical essays by a hapless narrator will have you in stitches. Sedaris's tales of growing up in a dysfunctional (to put it mildly) family, hitchhiking trips, and deadly jobs are wickedly funny. Though at times the stories go very dark, they are never mean-spirited. Warning: Do not attempt eating while reading this book as it provokes helpless laughter.

> **Department of Great Opening Lines**
>
> "When the teacher asked if she might visit my mother, I touched my nose eight times to the surface of my desk."
> —*Naked*

6.

LITERARY MERIT
★ ★

Scoop by Evelyn Waugh

A scathingly funny send-up of the British tabloid press of the 1930s from one of the great satirists of the twentieth century. *The Beast* mistakenly sends columnist William Boot, instead of his war correspondent brother John, to "Ishmaelia" to cover a civil war. Bumbling ensues. Corker, a wire reporter whom Boot hooks up with on his travels, expresses Waugh's contempt for the press: "News is what a chap who doesn't care much about anything wants to read. And it's only news until he reads it. After that it's dead."

7.

LITERARY MERIT
★ ★ ★

8.

LITERARY MERIT

★

Sick Puppy by Carl Hiaasen

This comedic, wacky, absurd mystery novel is set in (where else?) South Florida. It features a dog-napping, thousands of singing toads, and a Republicans-only hooker. Eco-terrorist Twilly Spree tortures littering lobbyist and political fixer Palmer Stoat with dung beetles and glass eyeballs. Take that, you corrupt politicians and greedy, unscrupulous developers! At the heart of this novel, as in all Hiaasen's work, there's a plea for ecological sanity as serious, in its way, as Al Gore's.

> **Author's Insight**
>
> "Some novelists say they envy those of us who live in South Florida because our source material is so wondrously weird. True enough, but the toll on our imaginations is draining. On many days, fiction seems like a futile mission."
>
> —Carl Hiaasen,
> *Writers on Writing*

9.

LITERARY MERIT

★ ★ ★ ★

The Thurber Carnival by James Thurber

Surreal and funny, this is a classic collection of essays, short stories, and cartoons from the great humorist. It includes inspired versions of Aesop's fables; also the hilarious "The Night the Bed Fell" (people knew it by heart the way many of us know all the words to "Alice's Restaurant"); and "More Alarms at Night" in which our hero wakes up and can't remember Perth Amboy: "I thought of every other town in the country, as well as words and names and phrases as terra cotta, Walla Walla, bill of lading, vice versa, hoity toity. . . ."

10.

LITERARY MERIT

★

Your Disgusting Head: The Darkest, Most Offensive—and Moist—Secrets of Your Ears, Mouth and Nose by Dr. and Mr. Doris Haggis-On-Whey

The secrets of ear wax, the uvula, and "The roof of your mouth through history." Find out what horrors await, should you misplace your face, told with tongue planted firmly in cheek. You'll find great gobs of wit and irreverence in this second volume of the Haggis-on-Whey World of Unbelievable Brilliance books.

...for a *Good Cry*

LITERARY MERIT ★

PROVOCATIVE 🔥

INFLUENTIAL ❗

INSPIRATIONAL 🕊

HUMOROUS 😄

BRAINY 🧠

EASY READING ☂

PAGE TURNER 📖

CHALLENGING 👓

BATHROOM BOOK 🚽

FAMILY FRIENDLY 👪

MOVIE 🎥

11.

LITERARY MERIT

★ ★ ★ ★

Annie John by Jamaica Kincaid

After an idyllic childhood in paradise in Antigua, doted on by her parents, twelve-year-old Annie John's relationship with her mother turns bitter and estranged, torn between love and hate. Told with lilting prose and in interlocking short stories originally published in *The New Yorker*, this painful coming-of-age novel explores the narrow divide between mothering and smothering.

12.

LITERARY MERIT

★ ★ ★ ★

Beach Music by Pat Conroy

Weep your way through 800-plus pages of tragedies, small and large, in this novel about love and loss, guilt and redemption. Narrator Jack McCall comes back from Italy where he's lived in self-imposed isolation since his wife's suicide. He returns to his family's home in South Carolina where his mother is dying of leukemia. "Guilt is my mainstream. The central theme of my life," he says. The novel moves back and forth in time, spanning generations. Conroy's prose resonates as he movingly examines the human condition and the pall cast by war. And though it's not a food book, the food writing in this will make you hungry.

13.

LITERARY MERIT

★ ★ ★ ★

Beloved by Toni Morrison

Pulitzer 1988, American Book Award 1988

Handprints appear in birthday cake icing and mirrors shatter as the angry spirit of a murdered baby girl, "Beloved," haunts her mother Sethe's home and drives the family apart. This novel, set in Ohio at the terrible time of Reconstruction after the Civil War, makes the horror of slavery a palpable truth. It's one of those books that burrows its way in and takes up residence in a dark place in your soul.

14.

LITERARY MERIT

★ ★

Bridge to Terabithia by Katherine Paterson

Newbery Medal 1978

It's supposed to be a boys-only race, but tomboy Leslie Burke runs anyway, beating artistic loner, Jesse Oliver Aarons, Jr. Jesse gets over it, and the two outsiders become fast friends. They build a fantasyland in the woods where they escape the torment of peers and family. To get there, they have to swing across the creek on a rope, and thereby hangs the tale. This is a heartbreaking story about friendship, grief, and courage—and, of course, building bridges.

Bury My Heart at Wounded Knee: An Indian History of the American West

15.

by Dee Brown

LITERARY MERIT

★ ★ ★

First published in 1970, this extraordinary national bestseller was the first book to tell of the systematic destruction of the American Indian during the nineteenth century. Each chapter tells the tragedy of another tribe, from the Long Walk of the Navahos, to the Cheyenne

Did You Know It Means . . .

Wounded Knee: The Wounded Knee Massacre occurred on December 29, 1890. U.S. Cavalry surrounded a Sioux encampment with orders to disarm the Sioux and take them to the railroad for transport to Omaha Nebraska. Gunfire broke out. By the end, 150 Sioux lay dead.

Exodus, to the massacre of Lakota Sioux at Wounded Knee. Single-handedly, this book changed how Americans viewed the "heroic" winning of the West and challenged the notion of Manifest Destiny.

House of Sand and Fog by Andre Dubus III

16.

LITERARY MERIT

★ ★ ★ ★

A house in the California hills, mistakenly seized for back taxes, is the object of desire. For the former owner, recovering alcoholic Kathy Niccolo, who has lost everything else, it represents a last hope for the future. For struggling refugee from the Shah's Iran, Massoud Amir Behrani, who buys the house at auction, it represents his family's dignity. Wills collide with heartbreak for all. This page-turner is a full-blown tragedy and a cautionary tale for our greedy times.

Love Story by Erich Segal

17.

LITERARY MERIT

★ ★

Jenny Cavilleri and Oliver Barrett IV are opposites who attract. He's privileged and wealthy. She's working-class and witty. And by the end of the book she's dead. Remember Ali McGraw and Ryan O'Neal as the tragic lovers in the film version? This

Department of Memorable Lines

"Love means never having to say you're sorry."
    —Love Story

story captured the imagination of a generation. Proof: Jennifer became the most popular name for baby girls in the United States from 1970 to 1984.

18.

LITERARY MERIT

★ ★ ★ ★

Mama Day by Gloria Naylor

Ophelia (Cocoa) brings her New York citified husband George home to the isolated black community where she grew up on the Georgia sea island of Willow Springs. George spent his childhood in a homeless shelter in Harlem and worked his way through school. Mama Day is nearly a hundred years old and still a presence to be reckoned with. She knows the secrets of herbal healing and lightning does her bidding. She senses danger for Cocoa—only a great sacrifice can save her as cultures, belief systems, and just about everything else collide. Get through the beginning of this book and find yourself transported to a world of ritual and mysticism, and finally to a devastating ending that will leave you weeping.

19.

LITERARY MERIT

★ ★ ★ ★

A Map of the World by Jane Hamilton

This novel opens with unbearable tragedy. Farm wife Alice Goodwin looks away for a few moments and a little girl drowns in a pond. And that's just the first bad thing. Once that boundary between Alice's safe life and unthinkable tragedy has been breached, her life spins out of control. The "map of the world" is an imaginary Arcadia that Alice creates to escape from depression, but it provides no protection from the witch hunt that targets her. Read this book to understand how we bear the unbearable.

20.

LITERARY MERIT

★ ★ ★ ★

Of Human Bondage by W. Somerset Maugham

In this 1915 autobiographical novel, Maugham paints a portrait of orphan Philip Carey, born with a club foot. Carey grows up with a religious aunt and uncle. He tries becoming an artist in Paris, then pursues medicine in London where he meets Mildred, a beautiful, vulgar tea room waitress who torments him. Carey's obsessive love of this woman who stands for everything he detests is a fascinating counterpoint to Maugham's own closeted homosexuality. This is an enduring masterpiece.

21.

LITERARY MERIT

★ ★ ★ ★

Pale Horse, Pale Rider by Katherine Anne Porter

"Pale rider" is the figure of death that accompanies protagonist Miranda Rhea in her dreams in this collection of three long stories. In "Old Mortality," Miranda is a child, home from boarding school with her sister, Maria, and fascinated by a beautiful young cousin. In "Noon Wine," a Texas family is torn apart when the father murders a man. In "Pale Horse, Pale Rider," a disillusioned Miranda returns against the backdrop of World War I and the vividly portrayed great flu epidemic of 1918. Miranda survives, only to discover that the man she loves died. Thick with symbolism, Porter's distilled writing has been called Proustian.

The Pilot's Wife by Anita Shreve

22.

It's an airplane pilot's wife's worst nightmare: a knock on the door in the middle of the night. Kathryn Lyons gets the news of her husband's death in an explosion in the skies off the coast of Ireland, and soon she's on a journey to discover who her husband really was. This novel delivers loss, betrayal, and grief, in abundance.

LITERARY MERIT

★ ★ ★

Sophie's Choice by William Styron

23.

National Book Award 1980

Set in 1947 and told from the point of view of struggling, twenty-two-year-old writer Stingo (based on Styron himself), this novel tells of his friendship with his upstairs neighbors—the volatile Nathan Landau and his lover, the beautiful Polish immigrant Sophie. She survived a Nazi concentration camp in body but not in spirit, after having to make the most unbearable choice a mother can.

LITERARY MERIT

★ ★ ★ ★

The Spirit Catches You and You Fall Down by Anne Fadiman

24.

National Book Critics Circle 1997

In this true anthropological study that reads like a novel, a baby girl suffers seizures. To western doctors, the diagnosis is epilepsy, a malfunction of the brain. Medication is the answer. However, to her Hmong (mountain people from Laos) parents who speak no English, the problem isn't medical. Spirits have caught her and made her fall down. Only ritual and animal sacrifice can persuade these demons to give back her soul. Cultures collide with tragic consequences. This story will stay with you.

LITERARY MERIT

★ ★ ★ ★

25.

LITERARY MERIT

★ ★ ★ ★

Things Fall Apart by Chinua Achebe

This novel traces Nigerian tribal leader Okonkwo's fall from grace, his exile, and ultimate ruin on the eve of colonialism. Achebe makes Okonkwo cruel but sympathetic, a classic tragic hero who is a victim of his own belief that he is in control. First published in 1958, the book provides a fascinating, unflinching look at life in pre-colonial Nigeria. Achebe has been called the father of modern African literature, and in 2007 he was awarded the Booker International Prize.

> **Department of Memorable Characters**
>
> "He was tall and huge, and his bushy eyebrows and wide nose gave him a very severe look. He breathed heavily, and it was said that when he slept, his wives and their children in their outhouses could hear him breathe. When he walked, his heels hardly touched the ground and he seemed to walk on springs as if he was going to pounce on somebody. And he did pounce on people quite often."
>
> —Okonkwo,
> *Things Fall Apart*

26.

LITERARY MERIT

★ ★

True Notebooks: A Writer's Year at Juvenile Hall by Mark Salzman

Alex Award 2004

This story is from a teacher's diaries: The teacher is a writer, his students are juvenile felons incarcerated at Central Juvenile Hall in Los Angeles. Included are remarkable examples of students' writing as these young men come to terms with their crimes and face a grim future. No clichés here. *True Notebooks* is filled with unexpected moments, like when Salzman's cello-playing moves his prison audience to tears.

27.

LITERARY MERIT

★ ★ ★ ★

Wuthering Heights by Emily Brontë

Stock up on Kleenex before you start this classic tale about thwarted lovers, moody-broody Mr. Heathcliff, and passionately repressed Catherine Earnshaw. Back in the mid-nineteenth century, this book and *Jane Eyre* moved gothic romance squarely into the mainstream. All the fantasy and supernatural events of the book are rooted in the reality of daily life. Tragedy on tragedy, Emily Brontë died of consumption a year after the book was published.

> **Author's Insight**
>
> "One of the most perfect and marvelous endings in literature—it raises my hair now—is the little boy at the end of *Wuthering Heights*, crying that he's afraid to go across the moor because there's a man and a woman walking there."
>
> —Katherine Anne Porter

...for a *Wallow in a Slough of Despond*

LITERARY MERIT	★
PROVOCATIVE	🔥
INFLUENTIAL	!
INSPIRATIONAL	🕊
HUMOROUS	😊
BRAINY	🧠
EASY READING	☂
PAGE TURNER	📖
CHALLENGING	👓
BATHROOM BOOK	🚽
FAMILY FRIENDLY	👪
MOVIE	🎥

28.

LITERARY MERIT

★ ★ ★ ★

Barney's Version by Mordecai Richler

Bernard Panofsky needs to set the record straight. In this fictional memoir, the pathologically forgetful, adulterous, abrasive, loud-mouthed Canadian Jew tells his version of how he didn't drive his first wife, the feminist saint Clara, to suicide. What went wrong with his marriage to the "Second Mrs. Panofsky" wasn't his fault, either. Three turns out not to be the charm when he marries "Miriam, my heart's desire." This was Richler's last book published before his death, the only one written in the first person and possibly his best.

29.

LITERARY MERIT

★ ★ ★ ★

Bastard Out of Carolina by Dorothy Allison

Ruth Anne "Bone" Boatwright is one of the most original and unforgettable characters in literature. With "illegitimate" stamped on her birth certificate in red letters, she grows up in a desolate world of poverty, violence, and sexual abuse. Strong stuff. The book gives "stand by your man" a whole new level of tragic meaning. Hard to believe, this was a debut novel.

30.

LITERARY MERIT

★ ★ ★ ★

The Bell Jar by Sylvia Plath

In this autobiographical novel, Sylvia Plath takes a sad and scathingly honest look at depression and mental breakdown. Esther Greenwood, full of aspiration and prodigious talent, arrives in Manhattan for her dream job at a magazine. And comes to realize, she can't cope. This was first published in 1963 under the pseudonym Victoria Lucas. It came out again in 1971 under Plath's name after her suicide.

> **Department of Memorable Characters**
>
> "I knew something was wrong with me that summer, because all I could think about was the Rosenbergs and how stupid I'd been to buy all those uncomfortable, expensive clothes, hanging limp as fish in my closet, and how all the little successes I'd totted up so happily at college fizzled to nothing outside the slick marble and plate-glass fronts along Madison Avenue."
>
> —Esther Greenwood,
> *The Bell Jar*

Bowling Alone by Robert D. Putnam

"Bowling alone" is Putnam's metaphor for the disintegration of civil society in America. "Fewer and fewer of us find that the League of Women Voters, or the United Way, or the Shriners, or the monthly bridge club, or even a Sunday picnic with friends fits the way we have come to live our lives." A fascinating if depressing read, this nonfiction blames television for creating a culture of isolation.

LITERARY MERIT

★

Christ Stopped at Eboli: The Story of a Year by Carlo Levi

Levi's memoir tells of his year spent imprisoned in a remote village, a last outpost for civilization in southern Italy. A physician, writer, and painter exiled for opposing fascism, he was sought out by the local peasants for medical advice. Local doctors became jealous. He survived in a miasma of malaria, poverty, ignorance, and superstition, and when he was finally released, he found it hard to leave. This was one of the great works published after Italians were released from fascist censorship.

LITERARY MERIT

★ ★ ★ ★

The God of Small Things by Arundhati Roy

Booker Prize 1997

In 1960s Kerala, India, small things have marked Rahel, her twin brother Estha, and their colorful extended family with tragedy. The breathtaking novel, with its ruminations on life, death, and human nature, unfolds with sensuous prose and dreamlike storytelling. Roy faced obscenity charges in India for this award-winning novel's graphic depiction of inter-caste lovemaking.

LITERARY MERIT

★ ★ ★ ★

The Heart Is a Lonely Hunter
by Carson McCullers

Deep in the South in the depths of the Depression, deaf-mute John Singer and tomboy/aspiring pianist Mick Kelly live in a small Georgia town. The characters try to reach out from their isolation but can't. Humane, powerful, sad, and ultimately hopeful, the novel was published when McCullers, who once hoped to study music at Juilliard, was just twenty-three.

Department of Great Opening Lines

"In the town, there were two mutes and they were always together."

—*The Heart Is a Lonely Hunter*

LITERARY MERIT

★ ★ ★ ★

35.

LITERARY MERIT

★ ★ ★ ★

Herzog by Saul Bellow

National Book Award 1965

Herzog is a middle-aged, intellectual historian contemplating suicide. He believes that brotherhood is "what makes a man human," but his wife has left him for his best friend and he came of age at a time when six million of his fellow Jews were being killed. Failed as a father, lover, and academic, he wonders if he's going off the deep end. In an extended journey of self-discovery, Herzog revisits his past and churns out unsent letters to friends and enemies and famous people, living and dead. In 1965, this was the first novel by an American to win the International Literary Prize.

36.

LITERARY MERIT

★ ★ ★ ★

The Hours by Michael Cunningham

Pulitzer 1999, PEN/Faulkner Award 1999

The prologue begins with Virginia Woolf wading into water, her pockets loaded with stones. The note she leaves behind for Leonard begins, "I feel certain I am going mad again." Her suicide casts a shadow over a novel composed of the interwoven narratives of three women: Clarissa Vaughn, a book editor in present-day Greenwich Village; Laura Brown, an unhappy housewife in postwar California; and Virginia Woolf herself, at work on *Mrs. Dalloway*. This work is widely acknowledged as a tour de force. For added insight, try reading it after you've waded through *Mrs. Dalloway*.

37.

LITERARY MERIT

★ ★ ★ ★

Interpreter of Maladies by Jhumpa Lahiri

Pulitzer 2000, Hemingway Foundation/PEN Award 1999

Lahiri seduces her reader with unhappy marriages in this wondrous collection of nine short stories. Couples face stillborn children, exhaustion, infidelity, and mismatched passions and habits. The stories are laced with the intricacies of Indian domesticity; endings are bittersweet.

38.

LITERARY MERIT

★ ★ ★

Miss Lonelyhearts by Nathanael West

Miss Lonelyhearts is an advice columnist for a New York City paper during the Depression, only she's a he, and the column is supposed to be a goof. But the more letters he reads from desperate New Yorkers, the more deeply depressed he becomes. Sadly for Miss L, at least one reader takes his advice seriously. Very dark. This novella, published in 1933, has been made into two films, a Broadway play, and an opera.

Mister Sandman by Barbara Gowdy

39.

LITERARY MERIT

★ ★ ★

Joan Canary was dropped on her head at birth and can't speak. But the tiny girl is a musical genius, a mimic, and eerily wise. Little Joan is only one of the Canary family's many closeted secrets. Though Gowdy revels in her characters' eccentricities, she never turns them into caricatures. With this, her third novel, Gowdy gained critical acclaim and became one of Canada's literary stars.

> **Department of Extraordinary Events**
>
> "Joan Canary was the Reincarnation Baby. Big news at the time, at least in the Vancouver papers. Joan was the newborn who supposedly screamed, 'Oh, no, not again!' at a pitch so shrill that one of the woman attending the birth clawed out her hearing aid. The other old woman fainted. She was the one who grabbed the umbilical cord and pulled Joan head-first onto the floor."
> —*Mister Sandman*

Mrs. Dalloway by Virginia Woolf

40.

LITERARY MERIT

★ ★ ★ ★

Written in stream of consciousness and published three years after James Joyce's *Ulysses*, this novel is a day in two lives. Clarissa Dalloway is buying flowers for a party she will give that night; Septimus Warren Smith, a shell-shocked World War I veteran, is in the park listening to sparrows he believes are singing to him in Greek. This study of sanity and suicide explores the subjectivity of truth. The dense prose makes this a challenging but rewarding read.

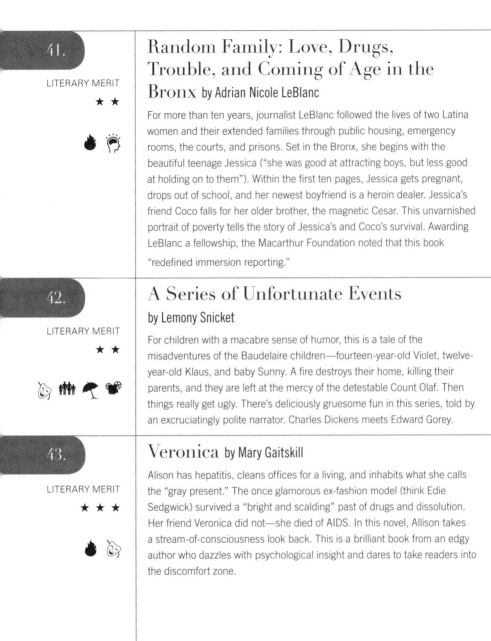

41.

LITERARY MERIT

★ ★

Random Family: Love, Drugs, Trouble, and Coming of Age in the Bronx by Adrian Nicole LeBlanc

For more than ten years, journalist LeBlanc followed the lives of two Latina women and their extended families through public housing, emergency rooms, the courts, and prisons. Set in the Bronx, she begins with the beautiful teenage Jessica ("she was good at attracting boys, but less good at holding on to them"). Within the first ten pages, Jessica gets pregnant, drops out of school, and her newest boyfriend is a heroin dealer. Jessica's friend Coco falls for her older brother, the magnetic Cesar. This unvarnished portrait of poverty tells the story of Jessica's and Coco's survival. Awarding LeBlanc a fellowship, the Macarthur Foundation noted that this book "redefined immersion reporting."

42.

LITERARY MERIT

★ ★

A Series of Unfortunate Events

by Lemony Snicket

For children with a macabre sense of humor, this is a tale of the misadventures of the Baudelaire children—fourteen-year-old Violet, twelve-year-old Klaus, and baby Sunny. A fire destroys their home, killing their parents, and they are left at the mercy of the detestable Count Olaf. Then things really get ugly. There's deliciously gruesome fun in this series, told by an excruciatingly polite narrator. Charles Dickens meets Edward Gorey.

43.

LITERARY MERIT

★ ★ ★

Veronica by Mary Gaitskill

Alison has hepatitis, cleans offices for a living, and inhabits what she calls the "gray present." The once glamorous ex-fashion model (think Edie Sedgwick) survived a "bright and scalding" past of drugs and dissolution. Her friend Veronica did not—she died of AIDS. In this novel, Allison takes a stream-of-consciousness look back. This is a brilliant book from an edgy author who dazzles with psychological insight and dares to take readers into the discomfort zone.

...to *behave*

LITERARY MERIT ★

PROVOCATIVE 🔥

INFLUENTIAL !

INSPIRATIONAL 🕊

HUMOROUS 😄

BRAINY 💡

EASY READING ☂

PAGE TURNER 📖

CHALLENGING 👓

BATHROOM BOOK 🚽

FAMILY FRIENDLY 👪

MOVIE 🎥

44.

LITERARY MERIT

★

Better Than Beauty: A Guide to Charm
by H. Valentine

In 1938, this was *the* guide to being perfectly charming. One's appearance was considered the "priming coat." It advises: "Apply rouge lightly to the cheeks. Never mind all the confusing planes and angles. This isn't a mural for the Louvre, it's your face." It includes everything anyone needs to know about how to stand, how to sit, what to wear, how to lose weight, and how to be kind to atrocious people.

45.

LITERARY MERIT

★

The Book of Household Management
by Isabella Beeton

Back in the 1860s, Mrs. Beeton was the era's Martha Stewart. This 1,100-page tome was the authoritative guide to running a middle-class home in Victorian England. It includes 900 pages of recipes and, should you need to know, reveals the ins and outs of the duties of the butler, footman, coachman, and groom.

> **Department of Memorable Lines**
>
> "As with the Commander of an Army, or the leader of any enterprise, so it is with the mistress of the house. Her spirit will be seen through the whole establishment; and just in proportion as she performs her duties intelligently and thoroughly, so will her domestics follow in her path."
> —*The Book of Household Management*

46.

LITERARY MERIT

★ ★

Domestic Manners of the Americans
by Frances Milton Trollope

Fanny Trollope (Anthony's mom) traveled through America in the 1820s. Through her beady little eyes, we see our flaws. Here's her impression of an afternoon gathering: "The gentlemen spit, talk of elections and the price of produce, and spit again. The ladies look at each other's dresses till they know every pin by heart; talk of Parson Somebody's last sermon . . . till the 'tea' is announced, when they all console themselves together for whatever they may have suffered in keeping awake, by taking more tea, coffee, hot cake and custard, hoe cake, johnny cake, waffle cake, and dodger cake, pickled peaches, and preserved cucumbers, ham, turkey, hung beef, apple sauce, and pickled oysters than ever were prepared in any other country of the known world." She was a sharp observer and talented writer; read this for a less than flattering snapshot of an era. Fanny and Miss Manners would have been best buds.

Etiquette in Society, in Business, in Politics, and at Home by Emily Post

47.

LITERARY MERIT

★

"According to Emily Post. . . ." The original version, published in 1922, is tart, funny, philosophical, and usually sensible. In a chapter on "The Bore" she admits that, alas, it's true: "Be polite to bores and so shall you have bores always around you." Also included is an indispensable guide to etiquette at balls.

! &) 🎤 🚽

How to Be a Jewish Mother by Dan Greenburg

48.

Take heart, you don't have to be Jewish or a mother to be a Jewish mother, says Greenburg in this classic from 1965. Heck, you don't even have to be a woman to learn the art of the noodge and the sigh and the proper way to breed guilt in your offspring.

LITERARY MERIT

★

! &) ♟♟♟ 🚽

I Like You: Hospitality Under the Influence by Amy Sedaris

49.

LITERARY MERIT

★ ★

Etiquette for the new millennium, HA! "This is not a joke cookbook," Sedaris cautions her readers in the introduction. Actually, the recipes look just fine in this standup comic routine in a cookbook. The photos are a hoot, Sedaris as 1950s happy homemaker, and her advice for throwing a party is solid: "Have toilet paper."

&) ☂ 🚽

Mary Poppins by P. L. Travers

50.

The children living at Number Seventeen Cherry Tree Lane (the smallest house on the street and much in need of a coat of paint) require a nanny. An East wind blows in Mary Poppins. She's austere, with piercing blue eyes, and controls her charges with a regal sniff. Much tarter than the movie version, the book is full of lovely satire of British middle-class life.

LITERARY MERIT

★ ★ ★

🔥 ! ♟♟♟ 🎥

51.

LITERARY MERIT

★

Miss Manners' Guide to Excruciatingly Correct Behavior by Judith Martin

This is a book of etiquette for our time with a nod to the past. In vaguely Victorian sotto voce, advice columnist Miss Manners addresses her "Gentle Readers" and tries to coax acceptable behavior from us. She urges us to be "unfailingly polite" even in the face of boors. Mistress of the arch aside, she offers sensible, pointed advice on getting along in civilized society, such as it is.

52.

LITERARY MERIT

★

Modern Manners: An Etiquette Book for Rude People by P. J. O'Rourke

O'Rourke is a survivor of *National Lampoon*, which gives you an idea where he's coming from. Gloriously irreverent, this guide includes tips for "cultivating the right sort of well-bred stupidity," and instructions for "when to stand up, when to sit down, and when to roll over and play dead." This book is the antidote to some of the other books in this section.

Department of Odds and Ends

"Those who have mastered etiquette, who are entirely, impeccably right, would seem to arrive at a point of exquisite dullness."

—Dorothy Parker

...to **Misbehave**

LITERARY MERIT ★

PROVOCATIVE 🔥

INFLUENTIAL !

INSPIRATIONAL 🕊

HUMOROUS 😄

BRAINY 💡

EASY READING ☂

PAGE TURNER 📖

CHALLENGING 👓

BATHROOM BOOK 🚽

FAMILY FRIENDLY 👪

MOVIE 🎥

53.

LITERARY MERIT

★ ★ ★

Fear of Flying by Erica Jong

This exuberantly bawdy novel caused a sensation when first published in 1973. Jong's sexually liberated Isadora Wing yearns for freedom and, most infamously, for uncommitted "zipless" sex, put rather more profanely. The author insisted that the novel was only a tad autobiographical, but parallels between Jong and her protagonist abound. It's still *the* novel about women's sexual liberation.

54.

LITERARY MERIT

★ ★ ★

The Ginger Tree by Oswald Wynd

At the start of this sprawling, epistolary novel spanning 40 years and set against a backdrop of Japan, Russia, and China vying for Manchuria, Scotswoman Mary McKenzie bridles under the yoke of a disastrous marriage to a British army officer. Innocent and chaste, and eager not to be, she drifts into an affair with a Japanese nobleman and becomes pregnant. She follows her lover to Japan where she must live as his concubine and loses her infant son. A BBC dramatization of this epic novel in 1989 brought it back into print. Try reading it after *The Makioka Sisters*.

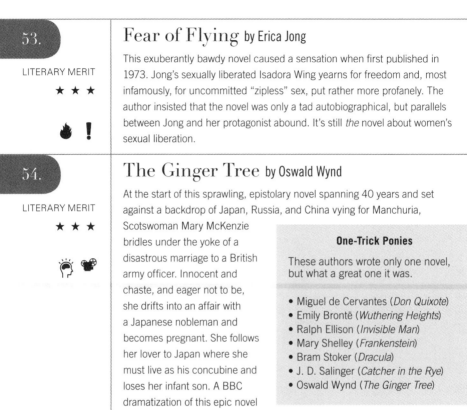

One-Trick Ponies

These authors wrote only one novel, but what a great one it was.

- Miguel de Cervantes (*Don Quixote*)
- Emily Brontë (*Wuthering Heights*)
- Ralph Ellison (*Invisible Man*)
- Mary Shelley (*Frankenstein*)
- Bram Stoker (*Dracula*)
- J. D. Salinger (*Catcher in the Rye*)
- Oswald Wynd (*The Ginger Tree*)

55.

LITERARY MERIT

★

Miss Julia Speaks Her Mind by Ann B. Ross

Narrating this novel in a ladylike, southern drawl, Julia Springer tries to come to terms with her husband's death after 44 years of marriage. "I thought I'd never get over the shock of finding Wesley Lloyd, dead as a doornail, slumped over the steering wheel of his Buick Park Avenue. Steel gray with plush upholstery, parked right out there in the driveway." The church wants to appropriate her inheritance for their building fund. And then there's shifty Uncle Vern and the little matter of her husband's son, the product of a secret decade-long affair. By the novel's end, Julia speaks her mind. This is utterly audacious and great fun for uppity women.

56.

LITERARY MERIT

★ ★ ★

Moll Flanders by Daniel Defoe

Poor Moll. In this racy, cautionary tale by the man who wrote *Robinson Crusoe*, Moll is born to a convict in Newgate Prison, abandoned and raised by a foster mother. She then sets off determined to make something of herself. Her weapons: artful thievery, conniving, sex, and marriage. Narrated with wit and élan by a heroine who refuses to give her real name. Virginia Woolf, who was a tough critic, called this one of the "few English novels which we can call indisputably great."

Puppetry of the Penis: The Ancient Australian Art of Genital Origami
by Simon Morley and David Friend

Two Australian buddies learned how to tie themselves up in knots and get paid for it. They have performed their genital origami in Australia, at the Edinburgh Festival, and on Broadway. This book definitely pushes the boundaries of how one can misbehave in public. Move over, balloon animals.

57.

LITERARY MERIT

★

Running with Scissors by Augusten Burroughs

In this memoir of life-as-disaster, the protagonist and his family make the Portnoys look tame. Meet Burroughs's horrifyingly dysfunctional family (his mother is "crazy as in a gas oven, toothpaste sandwich, I am God sort of way"), and the scatalogically obsessed psychiatrist his mother signs him over to. Guaranteed to provoke a strong reaction.

58.

LITERARY MERIT

★ ★

Steal This Book by Abbie Hoffman

Hoffman's late 1960s rant about what's wrong with "Amerika" begins, appropriately enough, with a "Table of Discontents." His messages: SURVIVE! FIGHT! LIBERATE! It includes practical advice on growing marijuana, stealing food, and getting free buffalo from the Department of the Interior. He was the archetypal politically radical hippie ("Yippie")—not so terrifying by today's standards.

> **Department of Memorable Opening Lines**
>
> "In a country such as Amerika, there is bound to be a hell-of-a-lot of food lying around just waiting to be ripped off."
> —*Steal This Book*

59.

LITERARY MERIT

★

Wicked: The Life and Times of the Wicked Witch of the West
by Gregory Maguire

Here's what happened before Dorothy and Toto got picked up by a tornado and tossed over the rainbow. Now you can hear the other side of the story from Elphaba, the little green girl with sharp teeth and an aversion to water, who grew up to become the Wicked Witch of the West. Aside from being funny and imaginative, this satirical allegory is also a commentary on our times.

> **Department of Great Characters**
>
> "[She] sat clumplike, her green hands on her green toes, curiosity on her sharp pinched face."
> —Elphaba, *Wicked*

60.

LITERARY MERIT

★ ★ ★

61.

LITERARY MERIT

★ ★

!

Where the Wild Things Are

by Maurice Sendak

Caldecott Medal 1964

A naughty little boy is sent to bed without his supper. In his room, "a forest grows," and off he sails to where Wild Things roar terrible roars and gnash terrible teeth. Little Max tames them with a magic trick and is crowned their king. A lovely picture book for naughty children and their grownups.

The Author Explains the Title

"At first the book was to be called 'Where the Wild Horses Are,' but when it became apparent to my editor I could not draw horses, she kindly changed the title to 'Wild Things,' with the idea that I could at the very least draw 'a thing.' So I drew my relatives. They're all dead now, so I can tell people."

—Maurice Sendak

...to **Go Over the Edge**

LITERARY MERIT ★

PROVOCATIVE

INFLUENTIAL !

INSPIRATIONAL

HUMOROUS

BRAINY

EASY READING

PAGE TURNER

CHALLENGING

BATHROOM BOOK

FAMILY FRIENDLY

MOVIE

62.

LITERARY MERIT

★ ★

American Psycho by Bret Easton Ellis

Patrick Bateman earns his living by day on Wall Street. By night he pursues torture and murder. With this satirical novel, Ellis pushed every boundary and everyone's buttons. The *Washington Post* called it the "literary equivalent of a snuff flick." So, reader beware, this one is definitely "over the edge."

63.

LITERARY MERIT

★ ★ ★

Bright Lights, Big City by Jay McInerney

In this debut novel that defined 1980s Manhattan, the cocaine-addicted protagonist is a self-absorbed New Yorker. He's a magazine fact checker working for a woman with a "mind like a steel mousetrap and a heart like a twelve-minute egg." In short order he loses his job, buys a ferret, tries to kill himself, and takes a limo ride with a cocaine magnate. This is one of the few successful novels written in the second person.

64.

LITERARY MERIT

★ ★ ★ ★

The Curious Incident of the Dog in the Night-Time by Mark Haddon

Alex Award 2004

Christopher John Francis Boone is an autistic fifteen-year-old who finds his neighbor's dog impaled with a garden fork. In his detached, oddly affecting way, he tries to work it out: ". . . the dog was probably killed with the fork because I could not see any other wounds in the dog and I do not think you would stick a garden fork into a dog after it had died for some other reason." Christopher decides to write a Sherlock Holmes-style story about finding the dog's killer. This novel is written with great empathy for a character who can rattle off prime numbers and square roots but can't distinguish sarcasm from happiness.

65.

LITERARY MERIT

★ ★ ★

Girl, Interrupted by Susanna Kaysen

In 1967, eighteen-year-old Susanna Kaysen was voluntarily committed to McLean Hospital after trying to kill herself. The diagnosis: borderline personality disorder. In this book, published 26 years later, the McLean becomes "Claymore." With humor and irony, Kaysen tells of two years she spent there. This is a moving, angry, coming-of-age story, and an illuminating insider's view of a venerable psychiatric hospital during a period of turmoil and transition.

The Author Explains the Title

"The title is taken from the title of a Vermeer painting: "Interrupted at her music: As my life had been interrupted in the music of being seventeen, as her life had been snatched and fixed on canvas: one moment made to stand still and to stand for all other moments, whatever they would or might have been. What life can recover from that?"

—Susanna Kaysen

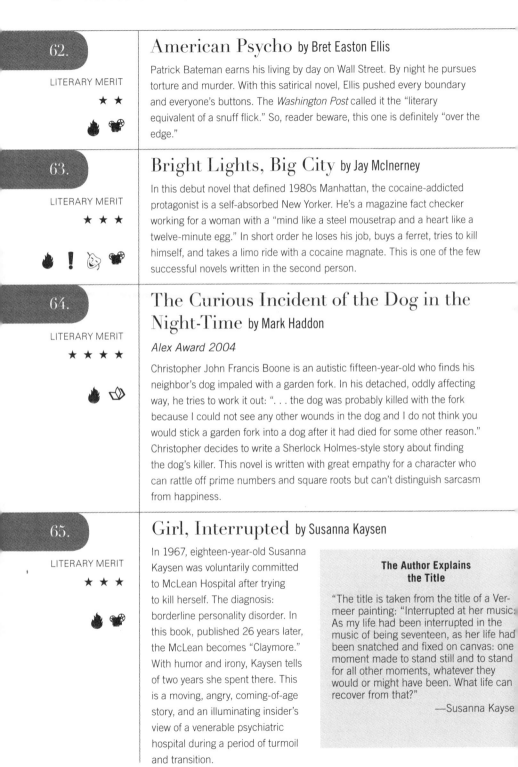

The Golden Notebook

66.

by Doris Lessing

LITERARY MERIT

★ ★ ★ ★

Like multiple narrators, divorced writer Anna Wulf reveals different aspects of her life in separate notebooks. In a black one, she writes of an experience in Africa that led her to write her first novel. In a blue one, she examines her problems with men. The yellow one contains bits of her professional writing. In the eponymous golden notebook, she attempts to pull the narratives (and herself) together and trace a journey to emotional breakdown. In awarding Lessing the 2007 Nobel Prize in Literature, the Swedish academy cited this, her breakthrough novel: "The burgeoning feminist movement saw it as a pioneering work and it belongs to the handful of books that inform the twentieth-century view of the male-female relationship."

! ➤ ◍

Gracefully Insane: The Rise and Fall of America's Premier Mental Hospital

67.

by Alex Beam

LITERARY MERIT

★ ★

Before there was *DSM-IV*, there was the McLean. Beam takes us from McLean Hospital's founding in the early nineteenth century, through its heyday as the healing grounds of the rich and crazy, up to today and the strictures of managed care. The history of the place is mixed with the history of psychiatry. The past of this single institution speaks volumes about the painful changes American healthcare institutions are undergoing. *The Bell Jar* and *Girl, Interrupted* were written about their authors' experiences here.

◍ 👁

Department of Odds and Ends

Famous former inmates of McLean, Harvard's psychiatric hospital in Belmont, Massachusetts:

- Mathematician John Forbes Nash
- Musicians Ray Charles and James Taylor
- Landscape architect Frederick Law Olmsted
- Poets Robert Lowell, Sylvia Plath, and Anne Sexton
- The father of American psychology, William James

I Never Promised You a Rose Garden

68.

by Joanne Greenberg

LITERARY MERIT

★

This is an autobiographical novel of mental illness, told from the patient's side of the bed. In it, a sixteen-year-old schizophrenic is helped by a caring doctor. Greenberg wrote it under the pseudonym Hannah Green. It was a must-read for teenagers when it was published in 1964, and grew into a cult novel.

◍ 🎞 !

➤ 📖

69.

LITERARY MERIT

★ ★

The Man Who Loved Only Numbers: The Story of Paul Erdos and the Search for Mathematical Truth by Paul Hoffman

He was a brilliant mathematician whose odd, peripatetic life (he lived out of a plastic bag) made him legendary. He authored nearly 1,500 scholarly papers, lived with friends, and gave away his money. He did math all day, every day of his life. This affectionate portrait grew out of an article Hoffman wrote for *The Atlantic* and won a National Magazine Award. You don't have to be a mathematician to enjoy it.

70.

LITERARY MERIT

★ ★

The Man Who Mistook His Wife for a Hat, and Other Clinical Tales
by Oliver Sacks

Read about Dr. P, a music teacher whose visual perceptions are so skewed that he mistakes his wife's head for a hat. Or Jimmie G, who remembers events from four decades ago but can't remember something that happened four minutes ago. The fascinating case studies are compassionate and told with the insight of a great psychologist who makes the neurological intricacies of the human brain riveting reading.

71.

LITERARY MERIT

★

Memoirs of Extraordinary Popular Delusions and the Madness of Crowds (Volumes I, II, and III)
by Charles Mackay

How easily the masses are led astray. Remember alchemy? The South Sea bubble? Tulipomania? This classic treatment of shared delusions and irrational fears was first published in 1841. It makes a strong case that human nature makes us easy prey for fortune tellers, charismatic politicians, and religious leaders. "Men . . . think in herds; it will be seen that they go mad in herds, while they only recover their senses slowly, and one by one."

One Flew Over the Cuckoo's Nest by Ken Kesey

Defiant, charming Korean War veteran R. P. McMurphy makes the erroneous assumption that it's easier to serve time for an assault conviction in a mental hospital than on a prison farm. He locks horns with the tyrannical Nurse Ratched and quickly discovers that the system has lost its mind. The book became the rebel's manifesto for the 1960s.

72.

LITERARY MERIT

★ ★ ★ ★

Spider by Patrick McGrath

Welcome to the macabre. Like a character from an Edward Gorey cartoon, gaunt, delusional Dennis "Spider" Clege has been released from a psychiatric hospital. He unravels in a halfway house in a squalid London neighborhood. The novel is Spider's diary, and the world as Spider sees it is suffused with wicked humor and creepiness: "I cut into my potato, and dead in the middle of the halved potato there was a . . . thick, slow discharge I recognized as blood." And for dessert, jellied eels.

73.

LITERARY MERIT

★ ★

An Unquiet Mind by Kay Redfield Jamison

This one's written from both sides of the bed—a psychiatrist who is a world authority on manic depression examines her own manic depression. She talks about denying and ultimately accepting that medication and psychotherapy will always be part of her life. For anyone who's ever struggled with depression, this is a must-read.

74.

LITERARY MERIT

★

LITERARY MERIT

★ ★ ★

The Yellow Wallpaper and Other Stories by Charlotte Perkins Gilman

In the short story "The Yellow Wallpaper," written at the turn of the century, a new mother is advised to abandon her intellectual life and avoid stimulating company. She finds herself marooned in the nursery of a rented house with only yellow wallpaper to contemplate. Alone, she descends into madness. Gilman wrote the story when she was on bed rest for her depression. It has become a feminist classic.

Department of Memorable Lines

"The color is repellent, almost revolting: a smoldering unclean yellow, strangely faded by the slow-turning sunlight. It is a dull yet lurid orange in some places, a sickly sulphur tint in others."

—"The Yellow Wallpaper"

...to *Love*

LITERARY MERIT ★

PROVOCATIVE ♨

INFLUENTIAL ❗

INSPIRATIONAL 🕊

HUMOROUS 😀

BRAINY 🧠

EASY READING ☂

PAGE TURNER 📖

CHALLENGING ∞

BATHROOM BOOK 🚽

FAMILY FRIENDLY 👪

MOVIE 🎥

76.

LITERARY MERIT

★ ★ ★ ★

Cold Mountain by Charles Frazier

National Book Award 1997

In this extraordinary debut novel, Inman is a seriously wounded Confederate soldier. Disillusioned, he leaves the Civil War and takes the long lonely walk home to Cold Mountain in North Carolina, hoping to be reunited with his love Ada. She, meanwhile, is struggling to maintain her family farm. This is a great love story wrapped around a Homeric journey.

> **Department of Memorable Opening Lines**
>
> "At the first gesture of morning, flies began stirring."
> —*Cold Mountain*

77.

LITERARY MERIT

★ ★ ★

The End of the Story by Lydia Davis

Sometimes that guy you dumped looks a whole lot better in the rearview mirror. This is a novel about the obsessive aftermath of a short-lived love affair between a woman and a man twelve years younger. The loosely structured, fluid prose is more an extended essay than a story, and the sentences swirl like poetry.

78.

LITERARY MERIT

★ ★ ★

Endless Love by Scott Spencer

It's 1967 and seventeen-year-old David Axelrod falls in love, overwhelmingly in love with sixteen-year-old Jade Butterfield. He narrates an anguished tale of love turned to obsession after Jade's father banishes him. Desperate, he plans to set fire to the Butterfield's home so he can rescue Jade and return to her family's good graces: "In full obedience to my heart's most urgent commands, I stepped far from the pathway of normal life and in a moment's time ruined everything I loved." This impassioned novel, by an author who's been called the contemporary American master of the love story, contains amazing sex and a heartbreaking ending.

79.

LITERARY MERIT

★ ★ ★ ★

A Farewell to Arms
by Ernest Hemingway

Nobel laureate Hemingway tells a tender tale of love and loss. It's World War I and the doomed lovers are Lieutenant Frederic Henry and nurse Catherine Barkley. He's a wounded American ambulance driver assigned to a unit in Italy; she works at the army hospital in Milan where Frederic is sent for treatment. He returns to the war, barely escapes with his life, and returns to find Catherine. Exquisite writing, of course, from an author considered the most influential of his generation. Like Henry, Hemingway was an American Red Cross ambulance driver in Italy during World War I and was severely wounded on the Austrian front.

The Feast of Love by Charles Baxter

Love between ordinary people is rendered by an extraordinary writer. On the novel's page one, Charlie (the author) has insomnia. He's sitting on his front step when his neighbor, Bradley, comes by walking his dog, also named Bradley. Soon what's happening in the fictional present merges with the novel Baxter is writing. Bradley suggests Charlie call his book *The Feast of Love* and that he write about real people. And that's when we're off into a novel that breaks just about every literary boundary while exploring the many splendid, horrifying, and hilarious sides of love.

LITERARY MERIT

★ ★ ★ ★

The History of Love by Nicole Krauss

This complex novel intertwines the stories of an unlikely pair who make an astonishing connection. Leo Gursky, a retired locksmith living in Brooklyn, spends his days terrified that no one will notice when he dies. Alma Singer, named after one of the characters in a novel her mother translated, is a bright fourteen-year-old who misses her dead father and tries to comfort her emotionally distant, widowed mother. While Leo yearns for the woman he's always loved, watches from afar a son he cannot acknowledge, and mourns his lost novel, Alma becomes convinced that the only way to help her mother is to unravel the mysteries of her novel and track down its characters. Poignant, beautifully written, and surprising.

LITERARY MERIT

★ ★ ★ ★

The Giant's House: A Romance
by Elizabeth McCracken

Just twenty-six and already considered a spinster, lonely librarian Peggy Cort recognizes a soul-mate in eleven-year-old Jason Carlson Sweatt. Already over six feet tall, he's destined to become the world's tallest man. This unusual and moving love story is told from Peggy's acerbic, often misanthropic viewpoint. "I do not love mankind" is her first message to the reader. Later she amends it: "I do not love mankind, but he was different."

LITERARY MERIT

★ ★ ★ ★

Gone With the Wind by Margaret Mitchell
Pulitzer 1937

It was a deadly triangle: Scarlett, Rhett, and the Civil War. Mitchell said of her book: "I wrote about the people who had gumption and the people who didn't." She created Scarlett O'Hara, one of literature's most spirited, flirtatious, and self-centered creatures, and Rhett Butler, a dashing scoundrel and one of literature's great hunks. In the opening chapter, Scarlett preens before her male admirers and declares, "There won't be any war and I'm tired of hearing about it." But of course there is, or there wouldn't have been any story. When you need a good escape, open the cover and crawl in.

LITERARY MERIT

★ ★ ★

80.

81.

82.

83.

84.

LITERARY MERIT

★ ★ ★

The Sterile Cuckoo by John Treadwell Nichols

The novel starts at a Friarsburg, Oklahoma bus depot. Jerry Payne is waiting for the bus. Pookie Adams saunters out of the restaurant and plops herself down beside him. Her pickup line: "Judging from the intense expression on your incredibly boyish face, you are thinking of either punching a gorgeous naked broad in her big white belly, or else catching a flock of tame canaries in a huge net just before they fall into the Mississippi River." Pookie is a one-off, and it takes Jerry a while to admit he's smitten. In 2003, Nichols was awarded the prestigious Stegner Award for his body of work.

85.

LITERARY MERIT

★ ★ ★ ★

Three Junes by Julia Glass

National Book Award 2002

Three interrelated stories, all taking place in the month of June, comprise this novel. First it's after World War II and Paul MacLeod travels to Greece, trying to get over his wife's death. The next June is six years later and Paul's son Fenno, a gay failed graduate student nearing middle age, opens a New York bookstore and must decide whether to donate sperm to help his brother's wife conceive a child. The final June is years later, and the protagonist is Fern, a pregnant widow who met Paul in Greece in the novel's first section. For readers who revel in rich prose, this debut novel delivers in brilliantly rendered moments.

...to Love Again

LITERARY MERIT ★

PROVOCATIVE

INFLUENTIAL !

INSPIRATIONAL

HUMOROUS

BRAINY

EASY READING

PAGE TURNER

CHALLENGING

BATHROOM BOOK

FAMILY FRIENDLY

MOVIE

86.

LITERARY MERIT

★ ★ ★ ★

The Accidental Tourist by Anne Tyler
National Book Critics Circle 1985

No one creates poignant, dysfunctional characters like Anne Tyler. Case in point: Macon Leary, the travel writer who hates to travel. When his wife leaves him, Macon pares his routine to the bare essentials. He launders his clothes underfoot while sloshing around in his evening shower, and sleeps in tomorrow's underwear so he won't have to wash pajamas. Not a moment too soon, he meets dog trainer Muriel Pritchett at the Meow-Bow Animal Hospital. With her "aggressively frizzy black hair that burgeoned to her shoulders like an Arab headdress" and her own brand of quirkiness, she reconnects him with life.

87.

LITERARY MERIT

★ ★ ★ ★

The Beginning of Spring by Penelope Fitzgerald

This comedy of manners is set in Moscow in 1913, on the eve of the Revolution. English-born Frank is a stolid, decent man whose life falls apart when his wife Nellie leaves him, taking their three children with her. He retrieves the kids, who only make it as far as the train station, and hires Lisa Ivanovna, a beautiful, serene shop girl as their new governess. The children in this novel are refreshing and intelligent creatures, far more clear-sighted than their father. Though Fitzgerald didn't begin her literary career until she was nearly 60, she is one of only a handful of authors who has had four novels, including this one, nominated for the Booker Prize.

88.

LITERARY MERIT

★

The Bridges of Madison County
by Robert James Waller

Fifty-two-year-old photographer Robert Kincaid is looking for a covered bridge. He asks an Iowa farm wife, Francesca Johnson, for directions. Four steamy days later, they move on. Is it "a mushy memorial to a brief encounter in the Midwest" as one critic claimed, or as another noted, "a quietly powerful and credible first novel"? Whatevah—it spent nearly 150 weeks on the *New York Times* bestseller list and in 1995 topped *Gone With the Wind* as the best-selling fiction book of all time.

Department of Odds and Ends

Is there a real bridge? In *The Bridges of Madison County,* the covered bridge that photographer Robert Kincaid is looking for, the bridge where Francesca Johnson leaves her note inviting him to dinner, is the Roseman Covered Bridge in Madison County, Iowa. According to Madison County lore, it's also known as the "haunted bridge"—in 1892 a sheriff's posse trapped a jail escapee there and supposedly he rose straight up through the roof of the bridge and disappeared forever.

Clover by Dori Sanders

89.

A widowed African American father marries a white woman. Hours after the ceremony, he dies in a tragic accident. "They dressed me in white for my daddy's funeral," says his ten-year-old daughter Clover, who disdainfully refers to the woman who will now raise her as "this woman." This is a novel about family, about learning to accept and to finally cherish again. The author is a peach farmer in South Carolina and says she found inspiration "observing the new South from my peach stand."

LITERARY MERIT

★ ★ ★

Cold Sassy Tree by Olive Ann Burns

90.

In this novel, Grandpa Rucker marries the town's milliner on July 5, 1906, three weeks after his wife's death, "three months after the big earthquake in San Francisco and about two months after a stranger drove through Cold Sassy in a Pope-Waverly electric automobile that got stalled trying to cross the railroad tracks." His new wife is a fraction of his age and a Yankee to boot. The parochial southern town is thrown into an uproar and fourteen-year-old Will Tweedy (Grandpa Rucker's grandson) goes into a tailspin. Read this one for pure pleasure.

LITERARY MERIT

★ ★ ★

Author's Insight

". . . I interviewed parents, aunts, and old cousins, and I took down what they said in their own words, using the rhythms of their own speech. What I was after was not just names and dates. I wanted stories and details that would bring the dead to life."

—Olive Ann Burns on how she wrote *Cold Sassy Tree*

Foreign Affairs by Alison Lurie

91.

Pulitzer 1985

Opposites attract, and a lonely ex-pat academic in London finds love in an unlikely place. Fifty-four-year-old spinster Vinnie Miner meets Chuck Mumpson on a plane trip. She dismisses the recently laid-off sewer supplier from Oklahoma in a cowboy hat as a "large stupid semiliterate man." But she keeps running into him. This smart, witty novel is a comic masterpiece.

LITERARY MERIT

★ ★ ★ ★

High Fidelity by Nick Hornby

92.

British pop music maven Rob Fleming has just been dumped by his latest girlfriend, Laura. He licks his wounds in his record store, Championship Vinyl, and wiles away the hours making top five lists (top five songs to play at a funeral, top five films, top five dream jobs) until "top five breakups" has him revisiting each of his failed relationships. Who says you can't turn back the clock?

LITERARY MERIT

★ ★ ★ ★

93.

LITERARY MERIT

★ ★ ★ ★

Hotel Du Lac by Anita Brookner
Booker Prize 1984

Middle-aged Edith Hope is a "serious woman" who writes romance novels. When her life takes a sharp turn that resembles the plot of one of her novels, her scandalized, buttoned-down friends banish her to the Hotel du Lac to regain her good sense and respectability. She finds herself riveted by other guests injured in love. When she draws the attentions of the worldly, enigmatic Mr. Neville, she must decide what it is in life that really matters to her. This novel asks a question: Does a woman really need a man in her life?

94.

LITERARY MERIT

★ ★ ★

Jane Eyre by Charlotte Brontë

In this classic Gothic romance, the plain, plucky orphaned Jane Eyre is raised like Cinderella by callous, hateful relatives who pack her off to the aptly named Lowood boarding school. (Brontë and her sisters were sent off to a similar institution where two of them died.) Jane becomes a teacher, but she yearns for a life beyond the school's cloistered walls. Barely eighteen, she posts an advertisement: "A young woman accustomed to tuition is desirous of meeting with a situation in a private family. . . ." Off she goes to Thornfield Manor where she meets Edward Rochester, twenty years her senior, and falls passionately in love. But he and the house harbor a secret that stands in the way of her happiness. This is the book that added "the mad woman in the attic" to the Gothic vocabulary.

95.

LITERARY MERIT

★ ★ ★ ★

Love in the Time of Cholera
by Gabriel García Márquez

This is a tale of thwarted love that finally flourishes after fifty-one years, nine months, and four days. Second in a trilogy of autobiographical novels by the great Colombian writer and Nobel laureate, the book seethes with unrequited, youthful passions that turn to deep love, seasoned by experience and grief in old age. Thomas Pynchon, reviewing the novel for the *New York Times*, called the voice "classical and familiar, opalescent and pure, able to praise and curse, laugh and cry. Fabulate and sing and when called upon, take off and soar."

96.

LITERARY MERIT

★ ★ ★ ★

Madame Bovary by Gustave Flaubert

An unhappy woman tries to escape the emptiness of her married life. She falls in love with a cad, then a coward, all the while ignoring her boring, stolid, well-meaning husband and young daughter. Things end badly. The novel is now considered a poetic masterpiece, but that wasn't always so. After it was serialized in 1856 in the *Revue de Paris*, its editors and Flaubert were put on trial for the novel's moral offensiveness.

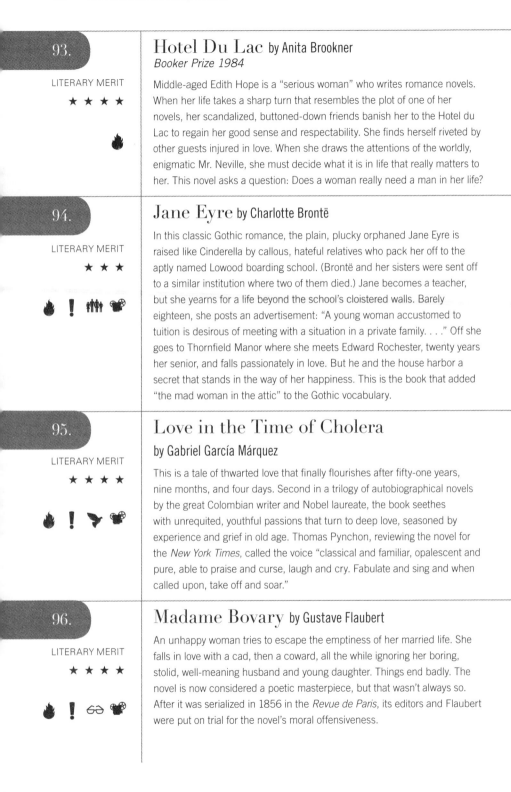

Mrs. Palfrey at the Claremont by Elizabeth Taylor

97.

Mrs. Palfrey, a widow, lives at London's once elegant Claremont Hotel, among other elderly residents (their informal motto: We Aren't Allowed to Die Here). She's caught in a pall of boredom and loneliness. One day, she falls down and is rescued by Ludovic Meyer, a struggling young writer. A friendship forms. The eccentricities of aging and falling in love again make a lovely combination.

LITERARY MERIT

★ ★ ★

Rebecca by Daphne Du Maurier

98.

Narrated as an extended flashback by the nameless bride of Maxim de Winter, this novel combines Gothic romance, murder, and taut suspense. With shades of *Jane Eyre*, the book tells of a plucky young governess who comes to work for an older man with a dark secret. Rebecca was his first wife who mysteriously drowned, and now her spirit holds Manderlay estate and the new bride in her icy grip. And as if a haunting ex-wife isn't enough for the young bride, Mrs. Danvers, the housekeeper, is a most formidable villain. This novel made Du Maurier one of the most popular authors of her day and still holds us captive.

LITERARY MERIT

★ ★ ★ ★

The Time Traveler's Wife by Audrey Niffenegger

99.

Alex Award 2004

Henry is a time traveler. His wife and the love of his life, Clare, is not. He repeatedly visits her through her childhood and adolescence. When she meets him "for the first time" in her time continuum, he doesn't recognize her but she knows him well. They marry and, after many miscarriages, have a child who possesses his father's genetic gift for time travel. This is a soaring love story with a twelve-hankie ending.

LITERARY MERIT

★ ★ ★ ★

Waiting by Ha Jin

100.

National Book Award 1999, Hemingway Foundation/PEN Award 1999

Physician Lin Kong is tired of waiting for his compliant, devoted wife Shuyu to grant him a divorce. For seventeen years he's been secretly and passionately in love with Manna Wu. Lin Kong finally gets his wish, with poignant and ironic results. This novel captures the reader, and reveals a fascinating portrait of Chinese society during and since the Cultural Revolution.

LITERARY MERIT

★ ★ ★ ★

...to Celebrate Friends

LITERARY MERIT	★
PROVOCATIVE	🔥
INFLUENTIAL	!
INSPIRATIONAL	🕊
HUMOROUS	😊
BRAINY	💡
EASY READING	⛱
PAGE TURNER	📖
CHALLENGING	👓
BATHROOM BOOK	🚽
FAMILY FRIENDLY	👪
MOVIE	🎥

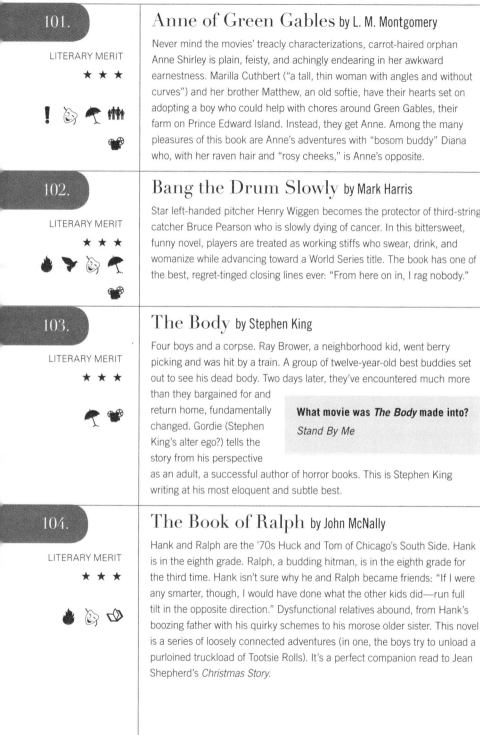

101.

LITERARY MERIT

★ ★ ★

Anne of Green Gables by L. M. Montgomery

Never mind the movies' treacly characterizations, carrot-haired orphan Anne Shirley is plain, feisty, and achingly endearing in her awkward earnestness. Marilla Cuthbert ("a tall, thin woman with angles and without curves") and her brother Matthew, an old softie, have their hearts set on adopting a boy who could help with chores around Green Gables, their farm on Prince Edward Island. Instead, they get Anne. Among the many pleasures of this book are Anne's adventures with "bosom buddy" Diana who, with her raven hair and "rosy cheeks," is Anne's opposite.

102.

LITERARY MERIT

★ ★ ★

Bang the Drum Slowly by Mark Harris

Star left-handed pitcher Henry Wiggen becomes the protector of third-string catcher Bruce Pearson who is slowly dying of cancer. In this bittersweet, funny novel, players are treated as working stiffs who swear, drink, and womanize while advancing toward a World Series title. The book has one of the best, regret-tinged closing lines ever: "From here on in, I rag nobody."

103.

LITERARY MERIT

★ ★ ★

The Body by Stephen King

Four boys and a corpse. Ray Brower, a neighborhood kid, went berry picking and was hit by a train. A group of twelve-year-old best buddies set out to see his dead body. Two days later, they've encountered much more than they bargained for and return home, fundamentally changed. Gordie (Stephen King's alter ego?) tells the story from his perspective as an adult, a successful author of horror books. This is Stephen King writing at his most eloquent and subtle best.

What movie was *The Body* made into?

Stand By Me

104.

LITERARY MERIT

★ ★ ★

The Book of Ralph by John McNally

Hank and Ralph are the '70s Huck and Tom of Chicago's South Side. Hank is in the eighth grade. Ralph, a budding hitman, is in the eighth grade for the third time. Hank isn't sure why he and Ralph became friends: "If I were any smarter, though, I would have done what the other kids did—run full tilt in the opposite direction." Dysfunctional relatives abound, from Hank's boozing father with his quirky schemes to his morose older sister. This novel is a series of loosely connected adventures (in one, the boys try to unload a purloined truckload of Tootsie Rolls). It's a perfect companion read to Jean Shepherd's *Christmas Story*.

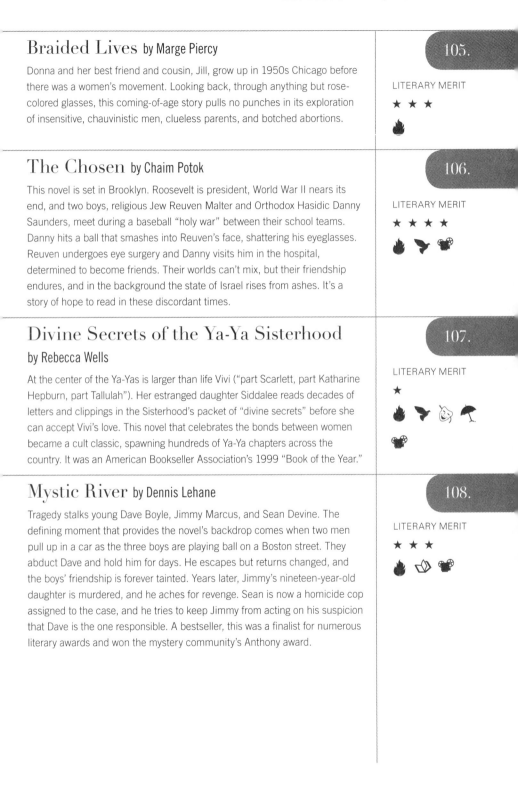

Braided Lives by Marge Piercy

Donna and her best friend and cousin, Jill, grow up in 1950s Chicago before there was a women's movement. Looking back, through anything but rose-colored glasses, this coming-of-age story pulls no punches in its exploration of insensitive, chauvinistic men, clueless parents, and botched abortions.

105.

LITERARY MERIT

★ ★ ★

The Chosen by Chaim Potok

This novel is set in Brooklyn. Roosevelt is president, World War II nears its end, and two boys, religious Jew Reuven Malter and Orthodox Hasidic Danny Saunders, meet during a baseball "holy war" between their school teams. Danny hits a ball that smashes into Reuven's face, shattering his eyeglasses. Reuven undergoes eye surgery and Danny visits him in the hospital, determined to become friends. Their worlds can't mix, but their friendship endures, and in the background the state of Israel rises from ashes. It's a story of hope to read in these discordant times.

106.

LITERARY MERIT

★ ★ ★ ★

Divine Secrets of the Ya-Ya Sisterhood
by Rebecca Wells

At the center of the Ya-Yas is larger than life Vivi ("part Scarlett, part Katharine Hepburn, part Tallulah"). Her estranged daughter Siddalee reads decades of letters and clippings in the Sisterhood's packet of "divine secrets" before she can accept Vivi's love. This novel that celebrates the bonds between women became a cult classic, spawning hundreds of Ya-Ya chapters across the country. It was an American Bookseller Association's 1999 "Book of the Year."

107.

LITERARY MERIT

★

Mystic River by Dennis Lehane

Tragedy stalks young Dave Boyle, Jimmy Marcus, and Sean Devine. The defining moment that provides the novel's backdrop comes when two men pull up in a car as the three boys are playing ball on a Boston street. They abduct Dave and hold him for days. He escapes but returns changed, and the boys' friendship is forever tainted. Years later, Jimmy's nineteen-year-old daughter is murdered, and he aches for revenge. Sean is now a homicide cop assigned to the case, and he tries to keep Jimmy from acting on his suspicion that Dave is the one responsible. A bestseller, this was a finalist for numerous literary awards and won the mystery community's Anthony award.

108.

LITERARY MERIT

★ ★ ★

109.

LITERARY MERIT

★ ★ ★ ★

Reading Lolita in Tehran by Azar Nafisi

Azar Nafisi and seven Iranian women, her former students, gathered Thursday mornings in Nafisi's home in Tehran and read forbidden works of Western literature. For their courage, they were warned, arrested, and even beaten. In this retelling, the stories of *Pride and Prejudice*, *Lolita*, *The Great Gatsby*, and other classics become intertwined with the stories of the women's lives. This harrowing portrait of life inside the Islamic Revolution was an American Bookseller Association's 2004 "Book of the Year."

> **Department of Memorable Lines**
>
> "For nearly two years, almost every Thursday morning, rain or shine, they came to my house, and almost every time, I could not get over the shock of seeing them shed their mandatory veils and robes and burst into color."
>
> —*Reading Lolita in Tehran*

110.

LITERARY MERIT

★ ★

Sideways by Rex Pickett

This is a hilarious, autobiographical buddy story in which Miles Raymond, a depressed, divorced, unpublished writer with an "undying passion for wine," takes his closest friend and ex-college roommate, a womanizer who's about to get married, on a prenuptial tour of wine country. A main difference between author Pickett and his alter ego Miles: Miles never gets his book published.

111.

LITERARY MERIT

★

The Sisterhood of the Traveling Pants

by Ann Brashares

They're just a pair of thrift-shop jeans, but they miraculously fit four girls. It's the first summer the best friends have spent apart from each other. Lena goes to Greece to stay with her grandparents; Bridget attends soccer camp in Mexico; Carmen visits her father in South Carolina; and Tibby stays home. Each girl takes a personal journey and the pants keep them emotionally bonded. This was the first in a series of bestselling young adult novels—young girls still respond to feel-good stories of romance and friendship.

112.

LITERARY MERIT

★ ★ ★ ★

The Van by Roddy Doyle

A pair of aging, out of work Dubliners—Jimmy Rabbitte and his best buddy Bimbo—go into business together. They spiff up a rusting van and turn it into a rolling restaurant serving fish, chips, and burgers without the benefit of Health Department certification. Things go well, sort of, for a while. This rowdy novel of Irish working-class life is the third in Doyle's much-lauded Rabbitte family series, after *The Commitments* and *The Snapper*.

...to *Celebrate*
Siblings

LITERARY MERIT ★

PROVOCATIVE 🔥

INFLUENTIAL !

INSPIRATIONAL 🕊

HUMOROUS 😄

BRAINY 💡

EASY READING ☂

PAGE TURNER 📖

CHALLENGING 👓

BATHROOM BOOK 🚽

FAMILY FRIENDLY 👪

MOVIE 🎥

113.

LITERARY MERIT

★

Born to Rebel: Birth Order, Family Dynamics, and Creative Lives by Frank Sulloway

If you've got older sibs, then according to Sulloway, you're born to rebel. Based on a ton of research, his conclusions fly in the face of conventional wisdom. In a nutshell, firstborn children are conformers. They identify with power and authority. Their younger siblings are likely to be more adventurous, rebellious, and generally in your face. Fascinating stuff, and an awfully good argument for having an only child.

114.

LITERARY MERIT

★ ★ ★

Chang and Eng by Darin Strauss

Alex Award 2001

This daring debut novel is a fictionalized account of the two brothers for whom the term *Siamese twins* was coined. The real brothers were born in 1811, fused at the chest. As young men they wowed audiences from Europe to the United States with their acrobatic feats. They married sisters and retired to father twenty-one children between them. They died in the same bed, within hours of one another. Strauss fuses fact and fantasy in an intensely humane story of two brothers who can't live with and can't live without one another.

115.

LITERARY MERIT

★ ★ ★ ★

East of Eden by John Steinbeck

A combination novel and memoir, this tells the story of two families, the Trasks and the Hamiltons, spanning three generations from the Civil War to World War I. Steinbeck called the book "a sort of autobiography of the Salinas Valley," a story about families and how one lives with human suffering. Steinbeck draws on his own life, and even appears as a minor character. Stories from the past and present are interwoven, and often cast as allegorical retellings of the story of Cain and Abel from Genesis. This was the "big book" that Steinbeck promised himself he'd write after *The Grapes of Wrath*.

116.

LITERARY MERIT

★ ★ ★

Founding Brothers: The Revolutionary Generation by Joseph J. Ellis

Pulitzer 2001

How a "band of brothers"—John Adams, Thomas Jefferson, George Washington, James Madison, Alexander Hamilton, and Aaron Burr—came together in the 1790s to found a nation. Fractious, competitive, often with dramatically different visions, these leaders are examined by the Pulitzer-winning historian through six crucial events in their shared lives. Read his account, and you'll marvel that a nation ever emerged whole from the American Revolution.

Having Our Say by Sarah L. Delany
and A. Elizabeth Delany with Amy Hill Hearth

LITERARY MERIT

★

Sisters Bessie and Sadie, pioneering African American professionals, have been around for more than a hundred years. Bessie was the only black female member of her Columbia University Dental School class in the 1920s. Her older sister Sadie became the first black home economics teacher in the New York City high schools. *New York Times* contributing reporter Hearth tells their story using their own words. Bessie and Sadie are warm, funny, feisty, and plenty opinionated as they offer a leavened but serious commentary on class and race.

The Author Explains the Title

Having Our Say: "I never thought I'd see the day that the world would want to hear what two old Negro women have to say."
—Bessie Delany

Housekeeping by Marilynne Robinson

LITERARY MERIT

★ ★ ★ ★

Hemingway Foundation/PEN Award 1981

Sisters Ruth and Lucille are abandoned by their mother on their grandmother's front porch in Fingerbone, Idaho. Mom drives her car into a nearby lake and leaves Grandma to care for the girls. Aunt Sylvie, their mother's sister, appears and takes over. Sylvie's notions of childrearing and housekeeping are eccentric in the extreme, and soon the house is overrun with newspapers, small animals, and leaves. This eloquent novel challenges the virtues of domestic order, and suggests that homelessness isn't necessarily about not having a home.

The Hundred Brothers by Donald Antrim

LITERARY MERIT

★ ★ ★

In the moldy library of their father's estate, ninety-nine brothers gather to find and bury their father's ashes. The youngest is in his twenties and the oldest in his nineties. One is an architect who designs "radically unbuildable buildings," another channels "spirits who speak across time," another is famous for his work on the sexual language of social insects. Only George, the urban planner, is missing, having recently vanished "with a girl named Jane and an overnight bag packed with municipal funds in unmarked hundreds." Prepare to be dazzled by an author who really can juggle 100-plus characters. Read, think, laugh. Read, think, laugh. Repeat until all the pages are turned.

120.

LITERARY MERIT

★ ★ ★

Little Women by Louisa May Alcott

Spend a presentless Christmas morning with the four March sisters (Meg, Jo, Amy, and Beth) and their mother Marmee. The girls, especially the boyish rebel Jo who inspired many girls to become writers, bridle against nineteenth century society's expectations that they behave like "little women."

> **Department of Great Opening Lines**
>
> "'Christmas won't be Christmas without any presents,' grumbled Jo, lying on the rug."
>
> —*Little Women*

The story, in all its sentimental splendor and based heavily on Alcott's life, has captivated generations.

121.

LITERARY MERIT

★ ★ ★

The Makioka Sisters by Junichiro Tanizaki

In this epic novel, set in wartime Osaka, Japan, older married sisters, Tsuruko and Sachiko, desperately try to arrange a marriage for shy Yukiko while Taeko, the youngest, waits her turn. Impatient, Taeko throws herself into affairs with disastrous results. This story of a venerable family's extinction is Tanizaki's masterpiece and reveals a myriad of tiny, exquisite details of everyday life.

122.

LITERARY MERIT

★ ★

My Sister's Keeper by Jody Picoult

Alex Award 2005

Anna was conceived as a bone marrow donor match for her sister Kate, sick with leukemia. Anna endures operations, blood transfusions, and shots, but when a kidney transplant is imminent, she balks. Meanwhile, her neglected older brother Jesse is out setting fires. Provocative is the key word here as this novel presents an unflinching, compelling look at the devastating effect of a sick child on a family.

A River Runs Through It and Other Stories by Norman Maclean

123.

LITERARY MERIT

★ ★ ★ ★

In this novella/memoir about fathers, sons, and brothers, and their often futile attempts to find common ground, the narrator reminisces about fly fishing and God. "In our family," he says, "there was no line between religion and fly fishing." Many compare the tightly written prose to poetry.

Department of Great Lines

"As the heat mirages on the river in front of me danced with and through each other, I could feel patterns from my own life joining with them. It was here, while waiting for my brother, that I started this story, although, of course, at the time I did not know that stories of life are often more like rivers than books."

—*A River Runs Through It*

A Summer Bird-Cage by Margaret Drabble

124.

LITERARY MERIT

★ ★ ★

This was the British author's stunning 1963 debut novel, and a great place to start reading her work. In it, older sister Louise is glamorous, sophisticated, and cold. Her plain younger sister, Sarah, has come home from Paris to be in Louise's wedding. The reader sees the marriage through Sarah's critical eyes. Laced with humor and cutting insights, the novel explores the choices women make.

The Tale of Peter Rabbit by Beatrix Potter

125.

LITERARY MERIT

★ ★

In this cautionary children's tale, naughty Peter Rabbit defies his mother and ventures into Mr. MacGregor's garden. Potter's illustrations are lovely. This remains one of the best read-to books of all time.

A Thousand Acres by Jane Smiley

126.

Pulitzer 1992, National Book Critics Circle 1991

LITERARY MERIT

★ ★ ★ ★

A domineering father decides to divide his Iowa farm among his three daughters. The youngest, a lawyer who is the only one who's left home, hesitates to accept. Peremptorily her father cuts her from the will. With shades of Shakespeare's King Lear, this novel explores the tragedy of America's disappearing family farm.

Quiz Time!
Match each literary character with his or her sibling.

1. Flopsy	**a.** Holden
2. Beth	**b.** Faramir
3. Lucy	**c.** Peter
4. Tita	**d.** Edmund
5. Sherlock	**e.** Lecia
6. Boromir	**f.** Rosaura
7. Phoebe	**g.** Mycroft
8. Mary	**h.** Jo

Answers: 1-c, 2-h, 3-d, 4-f, 5-g, 6-b, 7-a, 8-e

...to Remember Mama

LITERARY MERIT ★

PROVOCATIVE 🔥

INFLUENTIAL !

INSPIRATIONAL 🕊

HUMOROUS 🎭

BRAINY 💡

EASY READING ☂

PAGE TURNER 📖

CHALLENGING 👓

BATHROOM BOOK 🚽

FAMILY FRIENDLY 👪

MOVIE 🎥

127.

LITERARY MERIT

★ ★

All Over but the Shoutin' by Rick Bragg

Alex Award 1998

In this memoir of a hardscrabble youth, a poor southern white boy pays tribute to his mother who picked cotton and cleaned houses to keep her children fed. Bragg recalls, "Of all the lessons my mother tried to teach me, the most important was that every life deserves a certain amount of dignity, no matter how poor or damaged the shell that carries it." This book will have you laughing between the sobs.

128.

LITERARY MERIT

★ ★ ★

Anywhere But Here by Mona Simpson

Ann's mother Adele is larger than life, theatrical, maddening, and manipulative. Hungry for the kind of men and money that have eluded her, she uproots Ann from Wisconsin and moves her to Southern California with big plans to turn her into a child star. But instead of studio backlots, they end up in bleak motel rooms and desolate strip mall parking lots that smell of dusty bougainvillea—a spot-on portrait of the dark side of Tinsel Town. This was Simpson's splashy literary debut, a complex exploration of the claustrophobic bonds between mother and daughter.

129.

LITERARY MERIT

★ ★

The Color of Water by James McBride

Black musician, composer, and writer McBride's mother was the daughter of an Orthodox rabbi who grew up in a violently racist and anti-Semitic southern town. She broke away to marry a black preacher. As her son, McBride was confused about his racial identity. When he asks her, "Is God black or white?" she answers: "God is the color of water. Water doesn't have a color." This is an extraordinary biographical and autobiographical work.

130.

LITERARY MERIT

★ ★ ★

Growing Up by Russell Baker

Pulitzer 1983

With gentle wit and fondness, the great satirical commentator remembers his life, and especially his mother. He tells us, "At the age of eighty my mother had her last bad fall, and after that her mind wandered free through time." He follows the meanderings of her mind and recalls her efforts to make something of her son.

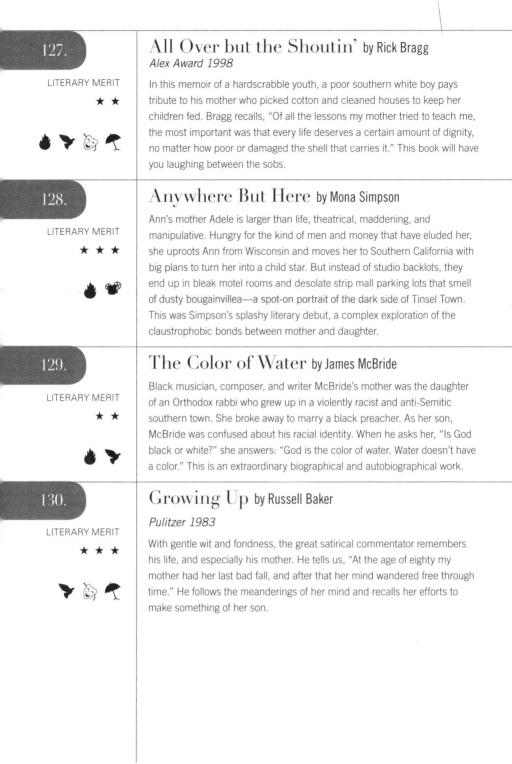

The Joy Luck Club by Amy Tan

Nominated for the National Book Award in 1989, this novel celebrates the joys and frustrations of an age and culture gap through the lives of four Chinese immigrants and their first-generation Chinese American daughters. When Suyuan Woo dies, her daughter June reluctantly takes her place in the Joy Luck Club and at the mahjong table with her mother's three friends. June discovers a tragic secret from her mother's past, and with the help of the Joy Luck Club, she journeys to China to complete a mission her mother could not.

Mama Makes Up Her Mind: And Other Dangers of Southern Living by Bailey White

This sweetly funny anthology of stories is from the NPR storyteller with the gravelly southern voice. In the title story, Mama decides she wants smoked mullet, so it's off to Rosey's, a "tough juke joint" where "you never know if you're drunk or not because the floors wave up and down anyway." In every essay, along with the colorful characters and gentle wit, there's a mini-epiphany and a nugget of truth.

The Probable Future by Alice Hoffman

Each Sparrow woman has a special witchy power, and each discovers it on her thirteenth birthday. Stella's grandmother Elinor detects lies; her mother Jenny sees other people's dreams. Stella turns thirteen and discovers she can see how people will die. When she predicts a murder, her mother becomes fearful that the murderer will try to kill Stella, so she whisks her off to their ancestral home in Unity, where grandmother Elinor is dying of cancer and yearning for family. Hoffman's novels are crowd pleasers with their alchemy of fairy tale and magic.

Sarah, Plain and Tall by Patricia MacLachlan

Newbery Medal 1986

In this classic novel for children, Sarah is a plain, tall, spinster schoolteacher from Maine. She responds to an advertisement for a mail-order bride, placed by a widowed midwestern farmer raising two young children. Sarah promises to visit and stay a month. She arrives with her cat Seal, a seashell for young Caleb, and sea stone for his sister Anna. The children are delighted to find Sarah can sing. If only she'll stay. This is one of the best books ever about yearning for a mother.

131.

LITERARY MERIT

★ ★ ★ ★

132.

LITERARY MERIT

★ ★

133.

LITERARY MERIT

★ ★ ★

134.

LITERARY MERIT

★ ★

135.

LITERARY MERIT

★ ★ ★

The Secret Life of Bees by Sue Monk Kidd

Fourteen-year-old Lily Owens is forced to kneel on piles of Martha White grits as punishment by an abusive father she can't bring herself to call "Daddy." He also has her convinced that she shot her mother to death when she was four years old. Feeling unloved and unwanted, Lily runs away with Rosaleen, the family servant. Together they set off in search of Lily's mysterious mother. They find the "black Madonna" and an eccentric trio of beekeeping sisters. Lily is a one-off, and nothing about this plot is expected. This was an American Bookseller Association's "Book of the Year" for 2002.

136.

LITERARY MERIT

★ ★ ★

Then She Found Me by Elinor Lipman

Quiet high school Latin teacher April Epner's adoptive parents die, and into her life walks Bernice Graverman (Bette Midler in the movie version), the larger-than-life, flamboyant host of a Boston morning TV show, *Bernice G!* Bracelets jangling, Bernice claims she's April's birth mother. This novel is Lipman at her comedic best.

137.

LITERARY MERIT

★ ★ ★ ★

The Stone Diaries by Carol Shields

Pulitzer 1995, National Book Critics Circle 1994

Masquerading as memoir/diary, complete with period photos and a family tree, this novel tells of Daisy's life. Her food-obsessed mother dies when she's an infant and Daisy goes to live with Clarentine Flett, a botanist as obsessed with the western ladyslipper as Daisy's mother was with Malvern pudding. The diary leaps forward in decade-wide bounds, and Daisy's home-centered life is lovingly told in gorgeous prose, and through the accretion of vivid detail.

Author's Insight

"I didn't think there were enough novels about women who didn't make the historical record."

—Carol Shields

138.

LITERARY MERIT

★ ★ ★ ★

A Yellow Raft in Blue Water by Michael Dorris

This forty-year-long family saga is told, *Rashomon*-style, from the perspective of three Native American women: daughter Rayona, mother Christine, and fierce great-aunt Ida. Rayona is abandoned by her mother, and in turn abandons Ida. Bitter rifts are explained when a terrible secret is revealed. Dorris was of Native American ancestry, which may explain his exquisite sensitivity to these characters and their stories.

...to REMEMBER DEAR OL' DAD

LITERARY MERIT ★

PROVOCATIVE

INFLUENTIAL !

INSPIRATIONAL

HUMOROUS

BRAINY

EASY READING

PAGE TURNER

CHALLENGING

BATHROOM BOOK

FAMILY FRIENDLY

MOVIE

139.

LITERARY MERIT

★ ★ ★

About Schmidt by Louis Begley

Albert Schmidt is a bigoted, prickly, recently widowed retired lawyer ("last of the WASPs"), knocking around in a big empty house in the Hamptons. His daughter Charlotte is an entitled yuppie who handles PR for tobacco firms. When Charlotte announces that she's going to marry a buttoned-down Jewish lawyer Albert detests, he unravels. Soon he falls for a scheming Puerto Rican waitress who perks him up and moves into his house with her drug-dealing boyfriend. This novel delivers a complex character who shows us that old dogs can be taught new tricks.

140.

LITERARY MERIT

★ ★ ★ ★

Burger's Daughter by Nadine Gordimer

Rosa Burger grows up white and South African. Her Communist, anti-apartheid, activist father dies in prison. Her mother has died too. Rosa becomes a physiotherapist and tries to numb herself to the horrors around her and steer clear of politics. But a scene of cruelty in the streets of Soweto drives her from the country. In self-imposed exile in France, she analyzes her relationship to her father. She finds herself and the strength to return to her homeland and fight back. Like so many of the books in this category, this one explores the inescapable power exerted by parentage.

141.

LITERARY MERIT

★ ★ ★

Chasing Hawk: Looking for My Father, Finding Myself by Andrew Sheehan

An emotionally neglected son, Sheehan remembers his father, a well-known physician who wrote a syndicated column on running and who abandoned his family for his career. "I had always chased [him], chased after his love, chased him through his many changes. I chased him even when I thought I was running in the other direction. Today, even though he is gone, I chase him still. I know he is the key to my freedom." After surviving a downward spiral of alcohol and drugs, Sheehan began work on this honest, moving memoir.

142.

LITERARY MERIT

★

Finding Our Fathers: How a Man's Life Is Shaped by His Relationship with His Father by Samuel Osherson

Coming to terms with "unfinished business" can free a man to be a better dad. Just because your father was emotionally cold and aloof doesn't mean you're doomed to be a cold and aloof parent, too. Dr. Osherson delivers this advice in one of the first self-help books to look at men's relationships with their fathers.

Galileo's Daughter: A Historical Memoir of Science, Faith and Love

by Dava Sobel

LITERARY MERIT

★ ★ ★ ★

Galileo's argument for a sun-centered cosmos threatened the very core of Christian dogma. But to his illegitimate daughter, Suor Maria Celeste, a cloistered nun, he "remained a good Catholic who believed in the power of prayer and endeavored always to conform his duty as a scientist with the destiny of his soul." This hit number 1 on the *New York Times* bestseller list. It is based on 124 letters Galileo's daughter wrote him from 1623 to 1634, before she died of dysentery at the age of 33, and reveal the great physicist in a new light.

The Godfather by Mario Puzo

It's hard to read this without hearing Brando's raspy Don Vito Corleone voice—did you remember that the reason the character talks like that is because he was shot in the throat? Corleone has three sons: Sonny ("so generously endowed that it was common knowledge that his wife feared the marriage bed as unbelievers once feared the rack"), Fredo ("Dutiful, loyal, always at the service of his father"), and Michael ("the only child who had refused the great man's direction"). This is the book that spawned an entire genre of mobster lit. Puzo's portrayal was so authentic that he repeatedly had to deny that he had ties to the mob.

LITERARY MERIT

★ ★ ★

Department of Great Opening Lines

"Amerigo Bonasero sat in New York Criminal Court Number 3 and waited for justice; vengeance on the men who had so cruelly hurt his daughter, who had tried to dishonor her."

—*The Godfather*

Independence Day by Richard Ford

Pulitzer 1996, PEN/Faulkner Award 1996

In this novel, forty-four-year-old Frank Bascombe finds his life at a "turning or at least a curving point." He's divorced and sells real estate in suburban New Jersey where he's just showed a couple their forty-sixth potential home. July 4th, he picks up his troubled son for a trip to two sports halls of fame. At a baseball field, he's struck by a lightning bolt and everything changes. This tour de force was the first book ever to win both the Pulitzer and the PEN/Faulkner awards, and critics put Bascombe in the pantheon of great American fictional characters with Nick Carraway and Augie March.

LITERARY MERIT

★ ★ ★ ★

146.

LITERARY MERIT

★ ★ ★ ★

Liar's Club by Mary Karr

"Of all the men in the Liar's Club, Daddy told the best stories," Mary Karr says in this memoir of a harrowing childhood. "No matter how many tangents he took or how far the tale flew from its starting point before he reeled it back, he had this gift: he knew how to be believed." Her father's whoppers were easier to bear than a family life replete with alcoholism, squalor, rape, and illness in an East Texas oil town. Karr was a terror, a fearless score-settler who needed her every ounce of meanness in order to survive. After this powerful book's huge success, the market for literary memoir exploded.

> **Department of Memorable Characters**
>
> "I was small-boned and skinny, but more than able to make up for that with sheer meanness. Lecia still holds that I would have jumped a buzz saw. Daddy had instructed me in the virtues of what he called equalizers, which meant not only stick, boards, and rocks, but having one hell of a long memory for mistreatment."
> —Mary Karr

147.

LITERARY MERIT

★ ★ ★ ★

The Mosquito Coast by Paul Theroux

Misanthropic Allie Fox is disillusioned with America. He howls at the price of gas and rants against newspaper "crapsheets." Schools and religion are useless. It infuriates him that they sell ice. "Those dingbats are selling water!" With his grandiose dream of utopia and confidence that he can invent anything, he packs his family off to the Honduran jungle. Ironically, it's his invention of "Fat Boy," an ice machine, combined with his own hubris that leads to his tragic downfall. This novel from the prolific travel writer was nominated for the American Book Award.

> **Who played Allie and Charlie Fox in the movie adaptation of *The Mosquito Coast*?**
>
> Harrison Ford and River Phoenix

148.

LITERARY MERIT

★ ★ ★ ★

Ordinary Wolves by Seth Kantner

The memorable, conflicted hero of this novel is Cutuk Hawdy. His father, like misanthropic idealist Allie Fox of *Mosquito Coast*, drags his family to the edge of existence on the harsh Alaska tundra. The Hawdys live by traditional Iñupiaq ways, while the real Iñupiaq live in villages with TVs and snowmobiles. Cutuk feels marooned between the white and the native cultures, his greatest fear: "Something is missing in me—that feels like being born a wolf and choosing a dog's life." Like his protagonist, author Kantner grew up in a remote Alaskan wilderness. This is one of the great Alaskan novels (it won the Whiting Writers Award); read it with Jack London's *Call of the Wild*.

The Risk Pool by Richard Russo

149.

In this tale of fractured families, Ned Hall's mother disappears into a Librium-induced fugue after an affair with a priest. The boy's father drops back into his life and whisks him away from a relatively ordered, antiseptic suburban existence. The two live in a squalid apartment, and Ned learns to shoot pool, play cards, pilfer, and lie. Then he falls in love with a girl from a privileged home who, like him, is damaged goods and terrified of turning out like her dad. This book is an excellent introduction to Russo, a modern master at capturing flawed characters in a blue-collar landscape.

LITERARY MERIT

★ ★ ★

The Story of My Father by Sue Miller

150.

It sounds grim, caring for a father in decline from Alzheimer's. Somehow Sue Miller, award-winning fiction writer who has always written about family relationships (*The Good Mother*), manages to sidestep despair without sugarcoating her story. Set in the painful present as she witnesses the cruel indignity of a relentless disease, leavened with reflections from a poignant past, Miller celebrates her father. He died in 1991 and for ten years after, she struggled to write this story.

LITERARY MERIT

★ ★ ★ ★

...*to* **Blame Your Genes**

LITERARY MERIT ★

PROVOCATIVE 🔥

INFLUENTIAL !

INSPIRATIONAL 🕊

HUMOROUS 😄

BRAINY 🧠

EASY READING ☂

PAGE TURNER 📖

CHALLENGING 👓

BATHROOM BOOK 🚽

FAMILY FRIENDLY 👪

MOVIE 🎥

151.

LITERARY MERIT

★ ★

The Beak of the Finch: A Story of Evolution in Our Time by Jonathan Weiner

Pulitzer 1995

Charles Darwin spent five weeks in the Galapagos studying fourteen species of finch, similar except for their beaks. He reasoned that while all were descended from a common ancestor, their beaks evolved to adapt to foods in their different environment. Voilà—the theory of natural selection. Evolutionary biologists Peter and Rosemary Grant spent twenty years in the Galapagos, banding and tracking generations of tens of thousands of the finches. Journalist Weiner writes about their work, and the discovery that evolution happens far more rapidly than Darwin imagined. Read this to appreciate the elegance of evolution and the drama of groundbreaking scientific research.

152.

LITERARY MERIT

★

The Cartoon Guide to Genetics

by Larry Gonick and Mark Wheelis

No, this is not by Watson and Crick. Larry Gonick is a cartoonist and Wheelis is a bona fide UC Davis microbiologist. First published in 1983, this is the real stuff, Genetics 101—it's the talking peas and fruit flies with attitude that make it so digestible.

153.

LITERARY MERIT

★

The Double Helix by James D. Watson

In 1953, the world first heard about DNA. The image of spiraling, twisted, interconnected strands became a modern icon. In this fascinating, first-person account of one of the major scientific discoveries of all time, Watson recalls how he and Francis Crick raced other scientists to make the breakthrough. His candor offended colleagues and controversy surrounds his unflattering portrayal of collaborator Rosalind Franklin. But there's no better book for understanding the sheer hubris and ruthless determination it takes to become a great scientist. If this whets your appetite, try Watson's brash 2007 autobiography, *Avoid Boring People*.

154.

LITERARY MERIT

★

Genome: The Autobiography of a Species in 23 Chapters by Matt Ridley

Each chapter of this book focuses on a newly discovered gene in each of twenty-three pairs of chromosomes in the human genome. Take a fascinating journey through the human genome through this jargon-free narrative.

The Author Explains the Title

"In a funny way, the genome is a book. I mean, that's one of the great discoveries, is that there is an instruction manual—a recipe, if you like—written inside ourselves."

—Matt Ridley

In My Blood: Six Generations of Madness and Desire in an American Family
by John Sedgwick

LITERARY MERIT

★ ★

John Sedgwick's family's fame and notoriety stretches from George Washington (an early John Sedgwick was a Revolutionary War general) to Andy Warhol (cousin Edie was Warhol's drugged-out muse). The family legacy included brilliance, hypomania, self-absorption, manic-depression, and suicide. In the wake of his breakdown and failed marriage, John Sedgwick examines the branches of his family tree. There's something endlessly fascinating about the mercurial, Boston Brahmin Sedgwicks, a family steeped in privilege and dysfunction.

The Origin of Species by Charles Darwin

Published in 1859, this still readable tome tells of Darwin's five-year, round-the-world voyage, observing and collecting specimens. He left England a creationist. On the voyage, he studied fossils, finches, and the great Galapagos tortoise, and returned convinced that life evolves from previously existing forms. This is a book that changed the way we think about life.

LITERARY MERIT

★

Department of Odds and Ends

Charles Darwin's grandfather Erasmus Darwin (1703–1802) was a physician and a leading intellectual who developed one of the first formal theories on evolution in his book *Zoonomia: Or, the Laws of Organic Life.*

The Selfish Gene by Richard Dawkins

We cut in line, exploit our assets to get ahead, lie to protect our children. Now we can blame a gene. The selfish gene, sociobiologist Dawkins argues, is the one we should credit for self-serving behaviors that ensure our survival and the survival of those we care about. No, he argues, evolution does not work for the good of all. This was Dawkins' first big book; he's gone on to become religion's modern gadfly.

LITERARY MERIT

★

Department of Great Opening Lines

"Intelligent life on a planet comes of age when it first works out the reason for its own existence."
—*The Selfish Gene*

158.

LITERARY MERIT

★

The Source: A Guidebook of American Genealogy

edited by Loretto Dennis Szucs and Sandra Hargreaves Luebking

So you think your parents passed through Ellis Island back in 1937? Think your great-grandfather had a twin brother back in Walla Walla? This book is your guide to finding out. Ship's manifests, census records, church records, death notices—they're all out there waiting to be uncovered. This guidebook has been called the genealogist's bible.

...to Celebrate the Season

LITERARY MERIT ★

PROVOCATIVE 🔥

INFLUENTIAL !

INSPIRATIONAL 🕊

HUMOROUS 😀

BRAINY 💡

EASY READING ☂

PAGE TURNER 📖

CHALLENGING 👓

BATHROOM BOOK 🚽

FAMILY FRIENDLY 👪

MOVIE 🎥

159.

LITERARY MERIT

★ ★ ★ ★

A Child's Christmas in Wales by Dylan Thomas

There's a reason this short story, written in 1955 for radio, has become a classic. The voice of a small child wonders: Could Christmas really have been so different years and years ago? The narrator answers: "Our snow was not only shaken from white wash buckets down the sky, it came shawling out of the ground and swam and drifted out of the arms and hands and bodies of the trees; snow grew overnight on the roofs of the houses like a pure and grandfather moss, minutely white-ivied the walls and settled on the postman, opening the gate, like a dumb, numb thunder-storm of white, torn Christmas cards." That prose cries out to be read aloud.

160.

LITERARY MERIT

★ ★ ★ ★

A Christmas Carol by Charles Dickens

Read the original story of Ebenezer Scrooge, and how the cold-hearted miser was transformed in a glorious overnight of visitations. Ghosts of Christmas Past, Christmas Present, and Christmas Yet to Come grab the old geezer by the collar and shake him good. The character of Scrooge most certainly inspired the great Grinch of Dr. Seuss (proof: Jim Carrey was cast as Scrooge in an upcoming production). First published in 1843, back then the novel sold 6,000 copies in a single week.

161.

LITERARY MERIT

★ ★

Christmas Story by Jean Shepherd

You've seen the movie; the book is even funnier. You'll hear the voice of the inimitable Jean Shepherd as you read the adventures of Ralphie Parker who yearns for a "Red Ryder carbine action two-hundred-shot range model air rifle" and his father whose heart's desire is a lamp with "a monstrous, barrel-shape bulging tube of a shade, a striking lingerie pink in color, topped by a glittering cut-crystal orb."

162.

LITERARY MERIT

★ ★

Holidays on Ice by David Sedaris

This wonderfully twisted collection of Christmas stories includes the hilarious "Santaland Diaries" in which Sedaris takes a job as a Macy's Christmas elf named Crumpet. Follow Sedaris in his work uniform ("green velvet knickers, a yellow turtleneck, a forest-green velvet smock, and a perky stocking cap decorated with spangles") through training and out into Christmas hell. Hopefully you won't see yourself as any of those parents he skewers. When you start getting a toothache from too many candy canes and gumdrops, read this.

An Idiot Girl's Christmas: True Tales from the Top of the Naughty List
by Laurie Notaro

These essays offer another twisted take on the holiday. Novato's Christmas wish list includes a "Travis the Singing Trout," bath crystals "so I could use them when I take a shower because I don't have a bathtub," and "a scrumptious delicacy from my mother's favorite Wax Candle Baked Goods store." Read this and you'll wonder if the Notaro family are related to the Sedarises.

Miracle on the 17th Green
by James Patterson and Peter de Jonge

Mystery author Patterson takes a swing at a Christmas fantasy. This is the perfect novel for anyone whose idea of a great Christmas morning is one spent on the green instead of wearing it. Advertising copywriter Travis McKinley's career and family are on the rocks when, with Zen-like clarity, he can "see the line" and learns how to putt. Soon he's on the PGA senior tour. Move over Trevino.

The Physics of Christmas: From the Aerodynamics of Reindeer to the Thermodynamics of Turkey
by Roger Highfield

For those of us who always wanted to look at Christmas lights through a mass spectrometer, this is a trivia-filled collection of facts that every self-respecting celebrant needs to know. British journalist Highfield claims he's been investigating Christmas for more than a decade. "Take those flying reindeer, Santa's red and white color scheme, and his jolly disposition, for example. They are all probably linked to the use of a hallucinogenic toadstool in ancient rituals."

Did You Know . . .

The sad truth about reindeer: "Rudolph, Dasher, Prancer, and the rest of the crew are so well adapted to the cold that they would probably find loafing around chimneys and firesides with Santa too warm to be comfortable."
—*The Physics of Christmas*

166.

LITERARY MERIT

★ ★

Polar Express by Chris Van Allsburg

In this children's story, a little boy who still believes in Santa hops aboard the Polar Express. It speeds him and other youngsters to the North Pole. When the boy is chosen to receive the first gift, anything that his heart desires, he picks a silver bell from Santa's sleigh. This is an allegorical tale about Christmas magic that only children can hear.

167.

LITERARY MERIT

★ ★ ★

The Stupidest Angel by Christopher Moore

Here's a Christmas farce with shades of horror. In the California town of Pine Cove, a man in a Santa suit is accidentally murdered by his ex-wife, also dressed as Santa. Visiting angel Raziel, who's been sent to earth to perform a Christmas miracle, tries to set things right. But, as the title promises, he's not the brightest bulb on the tree. But then neither is the giant talking fruit bat. Not your typical Christmas book, this is one goofy read.

Department of Great Opening Lines

"Christmas crept into Pine Cove like a creeping Christmas thing: dragging garland, ribbon, and sleigh bells, oozing eggnog, reeking of pine, and threatening festive doom."

—*The Stupidest Angel*

...to Hug Your Dog

LITERARY MERIT	★
PROVOCATIVE	🔥
INFLUENTIAL	!
INSPIRATIONAL	🕊
HUMOROUS	😄
BRAINY	💡
EASY READING	☂
PAGE TURNER	📖
CHALLENGING	👓
BATHROOM BOOK	🚽
FAMILY FRIENDLY	👪
MOVIE	🎥

168.

LITERARY MERIT

★

Cesar's Way by Cesar Milan with Melissa Jo Peltier

TV's Dog Whisperer, Cesar Milan, can tame even the most recalcitrant pooch. More human/animal psychologist than dog trainer, he argues for exercise, discipline, and affection, in that order. "Just like children, dogs need rules, boundaries and limitations in order to be properly socialized." In this guide, he demonstrates using celebrity's dogs like Oprah's cocker spaniel Sophie and Jada Pinkett-Smith's rottweilers. This is a pretty interesting read, even if you don't own a dog.

169.

LITERARY MERIT

★ ★ ★

Colter: The True Story of the Best Dog I Ever Had by Rick Bass

"The best dog I ever had," Rick Bass calls his pointer Colter. The dog was a walking companion, bird dog, and "raging genius" of the hunt. Bass writes of the intensely personal, physical, and emotional bond between man and dog. For those of us who've always been baffled, this book sheds some light on why people love to hunt (it's not always about killing).

170.

LITERARY MERIT

★ ★

The Cruelest Miles: The Heroic Story of Dogs and Men in a Race Against an Epidemic
by Gay Salisbury and Laney Salisbury

1925. Ice-bound Nome, Alaska, is threatened with a diphtheria outbreak. In what reads like a thriller, this is a true story of how twenty men and more than two hundred dogs took a harrowing 624-mile dogsled journey through gales and blizzards, "ice fog," and treacherous ice floes in a race against time to deliver life-saving serum. An amazing saga of heroism and perseverance.

171.

LITERARY MERIT

★

Fay by William Wegman

William Wegman loves his Weimaraners. His amazing photographs and affectionate storytelling turned his pet pooch Man Ray into a media star (*The Village Voice* named the dog "Man of the Year" in 1982). After Man Ray died, Wegman turned his lens on Fay, six months old with "the eyes of a jungle cat," as his new muse. He photographed her through puppyhood, through motherhood, bewigged and costumed or posed seductively au naturel.

Hank the Cowdog by John R. Erickson

172.

Youngsters find this scruffy "Head of Ranch Security" hilarious as he gets himself in deep doo every time he investigates another crime. "Well, you know me, I'm no dummy," he says. "There's a thin line between heroism and stupidity, and I try to stay on the south side of it." Hank's so popular he's been registered as a trademark.

LITERARY MERIT

★

Lad: a Dog by Albert Payson Terhune

173.

Before Lassie there was Lad. First published in 1919, this collection of stories pays tribute to an extraordinary collie, "thoroughbred in spirit as well as in blood." Lad shows off his heroism fighting off burglars and saving a crippled child from a venomous snake. Terhune based Lad on his first collie, and went on to write many books about the collies he raised at his farm, now Terhune-Sunnybank Park, where picnickers can visit graves of the dogs the books made famous.

LITERARY MERIT

★ ★

Marley & Me: Life and Love with the World's Worst Dog by John Grogan

174.

A wondrously neurotic yellow Lab, Marley caroms off walls, chews the furniture, drools on visitors, and flunks out of obedience school. This part dog story, part touching memoir about the pangs and pleasures of having not dogs but children, is a reader favorite.

LITERARY MERIT

★ ★ ★

Merle's Door: Lessons from a Freethinking Dog

by Ted Kerasote

175.

LITERARY MERIT

★ ★

An award-winning nature writer turns his attention to a ten-month-old stray that shows up while the author is on a camping trip. "He came out of the night, appearing suddenly in my headlights. . . ." The Labrador mix turned out to be the dog Kerasote has been looking for. When Ted throws a stick, Merle watches it go and gives a look the author interprets to mean: "I don't fetch." A great dog story, but more than that, a fascinating introduction to dog genealogy and the evolution of the human-dog nexus.

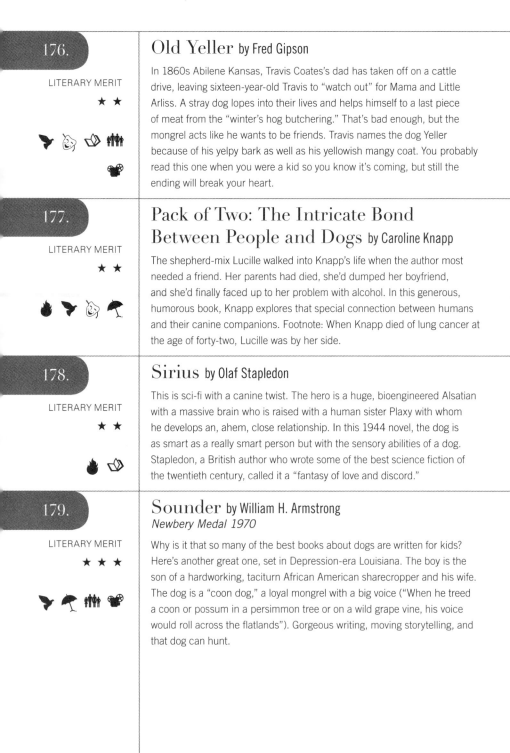

176.

LITERARY MERIT

★ ★

Old Yeller by Fred Gipson

In 1860s Abilene Kansas, Travis Coates's dad has taken off on a cattle drive, leaving sixteen-year-old Travis to "watch out" for Mama and Little Arliss. A stray dog lopes into their lives and helps himself to a last piece of meat from the "winter's hog butchering." That's bad enough, but the mongrel acts like he wants to be friends. Travis names the dog Yeller because of his yelpy bark as well as his yellowish mangy coat. You probably read this one when you were a kid so you know it's coming, but still the ending will break your heart.

177.

LITERARY MERIT

★ ★

Pack of Two: The Intricate Bond Between People and Dogs by Caroline Knapp

The shepherd-mix Lucille walked into Knapp's life when the author most needed a friend. Her parents had died, she'd dumped her boyfriend, and she'd finally faced up to her problem with alcohol. In this generous, humorous book, Knapp explores that special connection between humans and their canine companions. Footnote: When Knapp died of lung cancer at the age of forty-two, Lucille was by her side.

178.

LITERARY MERIT

★ ★

Sirius by Olaf Stapledon

This is sci-fi with a canine twist. The hero is a huge, bioengineered Alsatian with a massive brain who is raised with a human sister Plaxy with whom he develops an, ahem, close relationship. In this 1944 novel, the dog is as smart as a really smart person but with the sensory abilities of a dog. Stapledon, a British author who wrote some of the best science fiction of the twentieth century, called it a "fantasy of love and discord."

179.

LITERARY MERIT

★ ★ ★

Sounder by William H. Armstrong
Newbery Medal 1970

Why is it that so many of the best books about dogs are written for kids? Here's another great one, set in Depression-era Louisiana. The boy is the son of a hardworking, taciturn African American sharecropper and his wife. The dog is a "coon dog," a loyal mongrel with a big voice ("When he treed a coon or possum in a persimmon tree or on a wild grape vine, his voice would roll across the flatlands"). Gorgeous writing, moving storytelling, and that dog can hunt.

Travels with Charley by John Steinbeck

In September of 1960, late in his career, John Steinbeck packed up a customized three-quarter-ton pickup (christened "Rocinante" in honor of Don Quixote's horse) and took a three-month, 10,000 mile journey across America with his pet poodle, Charley. He left, determined to "try to rediscover this monster land." Steinbeck's charming, rueful chronicle of their adventures turned out to be one of his most commercially successful books.

LITERARY MERIT

★ ★

Walking in Circles Before Lying Down
by Merrill Markoe

181.

Sure, everyone talks to their pets. But how many of us have pets that talk back? Angelena Dawn Tarnauer is unlucky in love. After her latest boyfriend Paxton, a radio DJ, dumps her, her dog Chuck asks, "Couldn't you smell her on his pants?" Angelena goes through the usual chick-lit schtick until the dog runs away and things get interesting. The author is a TV writer and a standup comic and it shows (in a good way).

LITERARY MERIT

★

Watchers by Dean Koontz

182.

On his thirty-sixth birthday, Travis Cornell is hiking in a California canyon when a mangy dog with matted fur bursts from the dry brush. "It stopped in front of him, sat, cocked his head, and looked up at him with an undeniably friendly expression." But this isn't any dog. It's one that can open the glove compartment with his foreleg and seems to understand everything Travis says. Author Koontz, a master of horror, suspense and mystery, combines all three genres here with a heavy dose of the supernatural to keep readers riveted.

LITERARY MERIT

★ ★

Quiz Time!
Match each canine's description with the pooch's name.

1. "A big ugly slick-haired" food-stealing mongrel
2. A chocolaty female Weimaraner
3. A yellow lab
4. A huge Alsatian crossbreed with an oversized brain
5. A standard poodle "of a color called bleu"
6. A mysterious dog with human-like intelligence

a. Charley, aka Charles le Chien (*Travels with Charley*)
b. Fay Wray (*Fay*)
c. Marley (*Marley & Me*)
d. Old Yeller (*Old Yeller*)
e. Einstein (*Watchers*)
f. Sirius (*Sirius*)

Answers: *1-d, 2-b, 3-c, 4-f, 5-a, 6-e*

...to **SIFT THROUGH CLUES**

LITERARY MERIT ★

PROVOCATIVE 🔥

INFLUENTIAL ❗

INSPIRATIONAL ➥

HUMOROUS 😃

BRAINY 💡

EASY READING ☂

PAGE TURNER 📖

CHALLENGING 👓

BATHROOM BOOK 🚽

FAMILY FRIENDLY 👨‍👩‍👧

MOVIE 🎥

183.

LITERARY MERIT

★ ★

The Big Sleep by Raymond Chandler

A dying millionaire hires Philip Marlowe to deal with his daughter's blackmailer. This is the book that introduced the world to Marlowe, one of the first hardboiled private dicks. In his "powder-blue suit, with dark blue shirt, tie and display handkerchief, black brogues, black wool socks with dark blue clocks on them," only the attitude resembles Bogey's portrayal on the silver screen.

> **Department of Great Opening Lines**
>
> "It was about eleven o'clock in the morning, mid October, with the sun not shining and a look of hard wet rain in the clearness. . . ."—*The Big Sleep*

184.

LITERARY MERIT

★ ★ ★

The Black Dahlia by James Ellroy

In postwar LA, burnt-out New York cop and former prizefighter Bucky Bleichert becomes obsessed with the real (and to this day) unsolved 1947 Black Dahlia torture-murder case. This book gives you all the gory details of the actual crime. Bleichert cracks the case, but in the process he loses his job and much more. In spare, powerful prose, Ellroy machine-guns his story at the reader. A poignant afterword discloses that his own mother was the victim of an unsolved murder.

185.

LITERARY MERIT

★

The Circular Staircase by Mary Roberts Rinehart

The first line says it all: "This is the story of how a middle-aged spinster lost her mind, deserted her domestic gods in the city, took a furnished house for the summer out of town, and found herself involved in one of those mysterious crimes that keep our newspapers and detective agencies happy and prosperous." Soon our girl's up to her corset in ghosts, stolen securities, and murder. This 1908 novel was the first from the prolific author and invented the mystery subgenre "fem jep," in which a heroine is in jeopardy and has to be rescued (in modern versions, she rescues herself).

186.

LITERARY MERIT

★ ★

The Concrete Blonde by Michael Connelly

LAPD detective Hieronymus "Harry" Bosch has killed a man he thinks is a serial killer of prostitutes and porn stars. Then a similar murder occurs. Did Bosch kill an innocent man? Many feel Connelly is our best living American mystery writer, and this is considered one of his best novels.

The Daughter of Time by Josephine Tey

Scottish author Tey explores one of the greatest unsolved mysteries of all time: the murder of Richard III's two young nephews and heirs to the throne. In this enduring novel written in 1951, a painting of Richard III catches the interest of Scotland Yard Inspector Alan Grant while he's laid up in a hospital and bored to tears. The inspector, something of an expert on faces, "lay a long time looking at that face, at those extraordinary eyes." He muses, "I can't remember any murderers, either in my own experience, or in case-histories, who resemble him." As he tries to solve the murders, Tey provides readers with an enthralling blend of fact and fiction.

187.

LITERARY MERIT

★ ★ ★

The Deep Blue Good-by by John D. MacDonald

This first of twenty-one Travis McGee novels (published between 1964 and 1985) launched the much beloved salvager of lost causes who lives on the *Busted Flush*, a 52-foot houseboat docked in Fort Lauderdale, drives a blue Rolls-turned-truck he calls "Miss Agnes," and has a soft spot for a desperate woman. In this one, the dame is Cathy Kerr, "a brown-eyed blonde, with the helpless mournful eyes of a basset hound" who seeks his help recovering gems belonging to her deceased father.

188.

LITERARY MERIT

★ ★

> **Department of Great Characters**
>
> "I am tall, and I gangle. I look like a loose-jointed, clumsy hundred and eighty. . . . As far as clumsiness and reflexes go, I have never had to use a fly swatter in my life."
>
> —Travis McGee,
> *The Deep Blue Good-by*

Devil in a Blue Dress
by Walter Mosley

It's 1948 in a Los Angeles where there's "still a large stretch of farmland between Los Angeles and Santa Monica." Black, World War II army vet Ezekiel "Easy" Rawlins is out of work. He accepts $100 from a white thug to find Daphne Monet, a missing white woman who's been seen partying in black nightspots. "That girl is the devil, man. She got evil in every pocket," he says after friends of the missing woman start turning up dead and Rawlins becomes the prime suspect. This first novel won Mosley critical acclaim for the unique voice and post-war setting.

189.

LITERARY MERIT

★ ★

190.

LITERARY MERIT

★ ★ ★

Eight Million Ways to Die by Lawrence Block

Matthew Scudder is not just another hardboiled private investigator, though he certainly fits the mold—an alcoholic ex-cop, divorced and estranged from his family, guilt-ridden by a holdup he couldn't stop and a little girl's murder he couldn't prevent. He's also one of life's sardonic observers. A twenty-three-year-old hooker comes to him for help getting out of "the life." She's murdered. Scudder is determined to find her killer. Block, one of today's most prolific and widely read mystery authors, is a writer's writer who does dark, claustrophobic New York to a tee.

191.

LITERARY MERIT

★ ★ ★

The Hard Way by Lee Child

Raymond Chandler meets Hemingway in Child's spare prose. In this tenth series novel, tough-guy Jack Reacher is in a New York café, minding his own business, when he sees a man get into a Mercedes Benz and drive off. Turns out he's witnessed a ransom payoff. Twenty-four hours later, the kidnappers haven't released millionaire Edward Lane's wife and daughter, and Reacher gets recruited to find them. Child may be a Brit, but he nails American macho.

192.

LITERARY MERIT

★ ★

The Hound of the Baskervilles
by Sir Arthur Conan Doyle

Holmes, Watson, Lestrade, and the legend of a hell hound of Dartmoor. Was Sir Charles Baskerville killed by the infamous Hound of the Baskervilles, a demonic dog believed responsible for killing his ancestor Sir Hugo Baskerville hundreds of years earlier? As Holmes and Watson journey to investigate, they encounter an "enormous coal-black hound, but not such a hound as mortal eyes have ever seen." If you've never read a legendary Holmes book, here's a good place to start. Read it for pure fun, then read the version annotated by Leslie S. Klinger for fascinating insights.

193.

LITERARY MERIT

★ ★ ★

The Last Good Kiss by James Crumley

Here's a tough, ex-army investigator who lives in Montana and has a name you can't pronounce: C. W. Sughrue. He's hired to find Abraham Trahearne, a boozing author. When he tracks Trahearne down, he's "drinking beer with an alcoholic bulldog named Fireball Roberts in a ramshackle joint just outside of Sonoma California, drinking the heart of a fine spring afternoon." Wow—can this guy channel Chandler or what?

Looking for Rachel Wallace by Robert B. Parker

In this series novel, PI Spenser is hired to protect a woman author who has rattled a few cages with her tell-all book. She fires him for being too "macho" (he is); but when she's abducted he comes to her rescue. Parker is a master minimalist. Boston's his beat, and deadpan dialogue is his winning game. He's at his best in this one.

194.

LITERARY MERIT

★ ★ ★

❗ 📗

Mallory's Oracle by Carol O'Connell

NYPD Sgt. Kathy Mallory was once a child thief. Now she keeps company with computers. When her adoptive father, who rescued her from a life on the streets and tried to tame her, is found murdered, Mallory forces herself to deal with humans to solve the crime. Mallory stalks into scenes with preternatural grace ("She moved on the boy in the shutter blink of the old man's eyes") and with a cold, otherworldly ability to sense what others miss. O'Connell told an interviewer: "Yes, she's a deliberately sociopathic creation, and perhaps a strong response to more politically correct characters in books by other authors." It's definitely one for readers who like their protagonists (and authors) prickly.

195.

LITERARY MERIT

★ ★

🔥 📗

The Maltese Falcon by Dashiell Hammett

Private investigator Sam Spade is out to avenge the death of his partner, Miles Archer. Sinister Joel Cairo offers Spade $500 to retrieve a black figurine. Beautiful Brigid O'Shaughnessy throws herself at Spade ("I want you to save me—from it all"). Turns out she wants the statue, too. But tough, ruthless, single-minded Spade is immune to her feminine wiles. Hammett wrote only this one novel featuring Spade, but with it he created the mold for the hardboiled private investigator who follows his own moral compass.

196.

LITERARY MERIT

★ ★ ★

🔥 ❗ 🎥

Motherless Brooklyn by Jonathan Lethem

National Book Critics Circle 1999

Lionel Essrog, the narrator of this hybrid hardboiled crime-slash-literary fiction, has Tourette syndrome, and his verbal pyrotechnics turn the novel into an extended rap. The murder victim is a small-time mobster who is also Essrog's mentor and his boss at a car service/detective agency. Essrog, armed with tics and screams, infiltrates Brooklyn's "secret system" to hunt down the killer. Another neurologically impaired detective? He's anything but. The genre may be familiar, but the territory Lethem explores with it is unique.

197.

LITERARY MERIT

★ ★ ★ ★

🔥 📗 👓

198.

LITERARY MERIT

★ ★

Murder Must Advertise by Dorothy L. Sayers

Dorothy L. Sayers set the standard for Britain's golden age of mystery with her fourteen novels and a passel of short stories starring wealthy, witty Lord Peter Wimsey. In this one, Peter assumes the name "Death Bredon" and goes undercover at Pym's Publicity to investigate the mysterious death of a copywriter in their employ. Sayers writes a sharply satirical view of the advertising world, which she knew well—she worked in a London advertising agency for seven years.

199.

LITERARY MERIT

★

The Murder of Roger Ackroyd
by Agatha Christie

The apparent suicide of wealthy widow Mrs. Ferrar looks like murder when her fiancé Roger Ackroyd is found dead, too. Hercule Poirot, the diminutive and oh-so-precise Belgian detective, investigates. When Poirot tells the narrator, Dr. Sheppard, that his life's work is "the study of human nature," Sheppard concludes that Poirot is a retired hairdresser. Sheppard becomes Poirot's helpmate in the investigation. There was a great hue and cry about the ending of this novel. No doubt Dame Agatha chuckled all the way to the bank.

200.

LITERARY MERIT

★ ★

The No. 1 Ladies' Detective Agency
by Alexander McCall Smith

Prolific author Alexander McCall Smith struck gold when he conjured Precious Ramotswe, the only lady detective in Botswana. She takes proceeds of the sale of cattle she inherits after her father's death and sets out to do as he directed: "I want you to have your own business." She sets up office on the edge of town with a brightly painted sign promising "SATISFACTION GUARANTEED," brews a pot of red bush tea, and settles in to wait for clients. Hold the noir, hold the violence; this is a wry, delightful mystery series with a wise female sleuth.

201.

LITERARY MERIT

★ ★

The Postman Always Rings Twice
by James M. Cain

In this hardboiled/noir classic, young drifter Frank Chambers stops at the Twin Oaks Tavern. He takes one look at the owner's wife Cora and he's a goner: "Except for the shape, she really wasn't any raving beauty, but she had a sulky look to her, and her lips stuck out in a way that made me want to mash them in for her." Cora talks Frank into helping her kill her husband, but things go awry. Greed, lust, and plenty of kinky moments. The book was banned in Boston.

Presumed Innocent by Scott Turow

202.

LITERARY MERIT

★ ★ ★

Kindle County prosecutor Rusty Sabich is assigned to investigate the rape and murder of a woman colleague. He fails to disclose that he and the victim had had an affair. Compelling physical evidence makes Sabich the prime suspect. This novel defined the legal thriller genre, but it has the kind of characters you expect from a literary novel and an infamous surprise ending that most of us don't see coming.

The Science of Sherlock Holmes: From Baskerville Hall to the Valley of Fear, the Real Forensics Behind the Great Detective's Greatest Cases by E. J. Wagner

203.

LITERARY MERIT

★

Edgar Award 2007
"When you have eliminated the impossible, whatever remains, however improbable, must be the truth." Sherlock Holmes delivered that famous line in *The Sign of Four*; Wagner calls it "the first great building block of the science of Sherlock Holmes." Using the Holmes stories as a jumping off point, the author traces the major advances in forensic science—anatomy, toxicology, blood chemistry, and more—through the nineteenth and twentieth centuries. It's an excellent antidote to the pseudo-science dished out on *CSI*.

A Thief of Time by Tony Hillerman

204.

LITERARY MERIT

★ ★

An anthropologist vanishes. Navajo Tribal Policemen Lt. Joe Leaphorn and Officer Jim Chee investigate the ravaged ancient burial site where she was last seen. One of Hillerman's best novels, the mystery is woven into a tapestry of earth-tone landscape and shot through with the convincing detail of Native American life.

Whip Hand by Dick Francis

205.

LITERARY MERIT

★ ★

Edgar Award 1981
Dick Francis was jockey to Queen Elizabeth from 1953 to 1957. Lucky for us, he had to retire from racing after a serious fall and took up writing. His prodigious body of work combines horseracing with action-packed mystery. In this one, ex-jockey and private investigator Sid Halley looks into allegations of foul play at a stable. Francis, a master of the opening line, begins *Whip Hand* with this eye-popping opener: "I took the battery out of my arm and fed it into the recharger, and only realized I'd done it when ten seconds later the fingers wouldn't work."

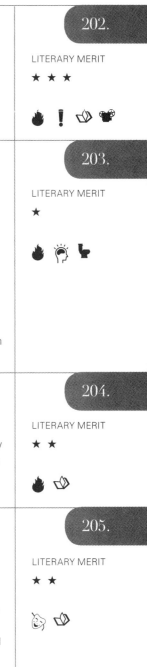

The Woman in White by Wilkie Collins

LITERARY MERIT

★ ★

! 💡 👓 🎥

On Hampstead Heath on a moonlit night, drawing teacher Walter Cartwright encounters a "solitary Woman, dressed from head to foot in white garments, her face bent in grave inquiry on mine, her hand pointing to the dark cloud over London, as I faced her." He helps her, and later discovers that she escaped from a nearby asylum. This complicated tale of murder, madness, and mistaken identity is narrated from multiple viewpoints and was inspired by a true crime. One of the most popular novels of the nineteenth century, this was also one of the first true mystery novels.

Mystery Writers *Rank Them*

Many of the books in this section were ranked among the "Top 100 Mystery Novels of All Time" by professional mystery writers in Mystery Writers of America. To see the complete list, visit their Web site: *http://www .mysterywriters.org/pages/resources/Top100.pdf.*

Rank out of 100	Title
1.	*The Complete Sherlock Holmes (Hound of the Baskervilles)*
2.	*The Maltese Falcon*
4.	*The Daughter of Time*
5.	*Presumed Innocent*
8.	*The Big Sleep*
12.	*The Murder of Roger Ackroyd*
14.	*The Postman Always Rings Twice*
32.	*The Woman in White*
40.	*The Circular Staircase*
53.	*A Thief of Time*
56.	*Murder Must Advertise*
92.	*Devil in the Blue Dress*

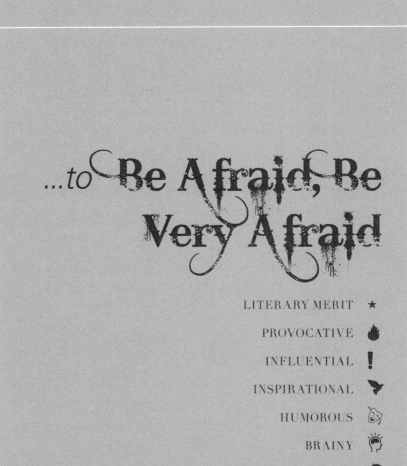

...to Be Afraid, Be Very Afraid

LITERARY MERIT	★
PROVOCATIVE	
INFLUENTIAL	!
INSPIRATIONAL	
HUMOROUS	
BRAINY	
EASY READING	
PAGE TURNER	
CHALLENGING	
BATHROOM BOOK	
FAMILY FRIENDLY	
MOVIE	

207.

LITERARY MERIT

★ ★ ★

The Collector by John Fowles

Creepy Frederick Clegg watches Miranda Grey, stalks her ("Seeing her always made me feel like I was catching a rarity, going up to it very careful, heart-in-mouth as they say"), and captures and imprisons her like one of his butterfly specimens. A master of self-delusion, Frederick's fantasy is that Miranda will fall in love with him once she gets to know him. This novel, told both from the collector's viewpoint and through the pages of Miranda's diary, will make you claustrophobic in the extreme.

208.

LITERARY MERIT

★

The Exorcist by William Peter Blatty

Before the movie, there was this book, a horror classic. Eleven-year-old Regan is possessed by a powerful demon. The first hint of trouble comes after Regan has been playing all day with a Ouija board and starts talking to "Captain Howdy." Her mother dismisses it as a "fantasy playmate." Soon even Mom smells fire and brimstone and it's seriously downhill from there. Believe it or not, Blatty started his career writing comedies (*A Shot in the Dark* and *Which Way to Mecca, Jack*).

209.

LITERARY MERIT

★ ★ ★

The Haunting of Hill House by Shirley Jackson

Anthropological scholar Dr. John Mortimer rents the house, determined to get to the bottom of its psychic phenomena. He invites Eleanor Vance, a shy vulnerable loner, and two others to join him in a ghost watch. Eleanor ends up seduced by the house. This novel was published in 1959, and it's right up there with *The Turn of the Screw* as one of the most haunting and enduring ghost stories ever.

> **Department of Memorable Opening Lines**
>
> "No live organism can continue for long to exist sanely under conditions of absolute reality; even larks and katydids are supposed, by some, to dream. Hill House, not sane, stood by itself against its hills, holding darkness within it; it had stood so for eighty years and might stand for eighty more."
> —*The Haunting of Hill House*

210.

LITERARY MERIT

★ ★ ★

The Historian by Elizabeth Kostova

A motherless teenaged girl, living in Amsterdam, discovers in her father's library some letters and a mysterious book—the pages are blank except for a dragon woodcut and the word *Drakulya*. Her father explains that the empty book belonged to his former professor who mysteriously disappeared after he became convinced that Dracula still lives. When the girl's father disappears, she goes on a quest that takes her through Europe and into the past to find him. Just when you thought the last drops of blood had been wrung from the Dracula legend, along comes this thoroughly creepy, intricately plotted, literary blockbuster of suspense.

The Hot Zone: A Terrifying True Story

211

by Richard Preston

LITERARY MERIT

In 1989, Ebola virus broke out in a quarantine unit of wild monkeys that had been imported for research. Preston tells how the U.S. Veterinary Corps spotted Ebola at Reston and brought in a secret SWAT team to contain the outbreak. He traces the evolution of the disease, its gruesome course, and the scientists' race to contain it. This nonfiction is scarier than fiction— popular science writing at its best.

★

Pan's Garden by Algernon Blackwood

212.

This collection of fifteen short stories illustrates what happens when nature is anything but benign. "The Man Whom Trees Loved" opens with: "He painted trees as by some special divining instinct of their essential qualities. He understood them." By the end, the man's wife has lost him to the trees and, during a cataclysmic storm, "The Forest bellowed out its victory to the winds; the winds in turn proclaimed it to the Night." Blackwood was a master of the supernatural, and this volume contains some of his best.

LITERARY MERIT

★ ★ ★ ★

Rosemary's Baby by Ira Levin

213.

Poor Rosemary Woodhouse. She's pregnant, alone, and her neighbors are decidedly odd and entirely too helpful. No one can explain the strange burning odor she smells, or the terrifying dreams she's

> **Who played Rosemary Woodhouse in the movie adaptation of *Rosemary's Baby*?**
>
> Mia Farrow

having, or why she finds herself "chewing on a raw and dripping chicken heart in the kitchen one morning at four-fifteen." This is a modern, Faustian tale in which a struggling young actor makes a deal with the devil. Moral: Never marry an actor. It was made into an iconic 1968 horror film.

LITERARY MERIT

★ ★

Something Wicked This Way Comes

214.

by Ray Bradbury

In this fantasy classic, a pair of thirteen-year-old lads hang out at Cooger and Dark's Pandemonium Shadow Show, a mysterious carnival that's sprung up overnight in Green Town. They

> **Where does the title *Something Wicked This Way Comes* come from?**
>
> A quote from *Macbeth*

meet Mr. Dark, the tattooed carnival leader ("His picture crowds flooded raw upon his flesh"), and learn, when it's almost too late, that each tattoo represents a person who traded his soul for a chance to live out a secret fantasy.

LITERARY MERIT

★ ★

215.

LITERARY MERIT

★ ★

The Thirteenth Tale by Diane Setterfield

Alex Award 2007

In this modern-day Gothic novel, famous recluse Vida Winter sends a letter asking biographer Margaret Lea to write her life story before she dies. Margaret, who has never read any of Miss Winter's many novels, digs out her father's rare copy of Miss Winter's *Thirteen Tales of Change and Desperation.* She's surprised and intrigued to discover that the book contains only twelve stories. She agrees to become Miss Winter's biographer. For both women, the collaboration dredges up turbulent secrets from the past. Readers compare this debut novel to the great Gothic triumvirate: *Jane Eyre, Wuthering Heights,* and *Rebecca.*

216.

LITERARY MERIT

★ ★

The Turn of the Screw by Henry James

Considered the classic ghost story, this novella, originally published in 1898, tells of an impressionable young governess hired by a disinterested uncle to care for his orphaned niece and nephew. She is left alone in the great house to tend to Flora and Miles. Things only the governess sees go bump in the night, and she has to admit the possibility that former governess Miss Jessel and her lover are controlling the children from their graves. James laces this tale with repressed sexuality and psychological ambiguity. He plays his cards close to the vest, leaving readers still arguing today about whether the ghosts are real. The best movie made from this was *The Innocents* in 1961 with luminous Deborah Kerr as the young governess.

...to *Dream*

LITERARY MERIT	★
PROVOCATIVE	🔥
INFLUENTIAL	❗
INSPIRATIONAL	🕊
HUMOROUS	😂
BRAINY	💡
EASY READING	☂
PAGE TURNER	📖
CHALLENGING	👓
BATHROOM BOOK	🚽
FAMILY FRIENDLY	👪
MOVIE	🎥

217.

LITERARY MERIT

★ ★ ★

The Alchemist: A Fable About Following Your Dream by Paulo Coelho

A shepherd boy follows his dream of finding buried treasure at an Egyptian pyramid, and eventually the quest leads him home again. Supposedly, Coelho wrote this slim volume, retelling a fable from *A Thousand and One Nights*, in just two weeks.

Not a bad ROI—it's been translated from Portuguese into more than sixty languages and sold more than 20 million copies. President Clinton was photographed carrying a copy.

Department of Great Lines

"It is the possibility of having a dream come true that makes life interesting."
    —*The Alchemist*

218.

LITERARY MERIT

★ ★

Goodnight Moon by Margaret Wise Brown

This beloved children's book is the best ever for putting kids (or yourself) to sleep. The book, with its bold green, red, blue, and yellow illustrations by Clement Hurd, is a deceptively simple and simply exquisite book. The slight verse is hypnotic. "Goodnight clocks/And goodnight socks." It was first published in 1947. Brown died of appendicitis just five years later at the age of forty-two.

219.

LITERARY MERIT

★ ★ ★

The House of Sleep by Jonathan Coe

Can you tell dreams from reality, and are you sure you want to? Can you become addicted to dreams? Is sleep a disease that robs people of half their lives? This complicated novel with a comic edge (Coe has been compared to Wodehouse and Waugh) explores these questions as a mad psychologist tries to eliminate the need for slumber while his narcoleptic ex-girlfriend struggles to separate dream fantasies from life. The novel is divided into the stages of sleep: "Awake," "'Stage One" through "Stage Four," and finally "REM Sleep."

220.

LITERARY MERIT

★

The Interpretation of Dreams
by Sigmund Freud

This work, one of the most influential of the twentieth century, was largely ignored when it was first published in 1900. Freud set out to "demonstrate that there is a psychological technique which makes it possible to interpret dreams." Dreams, he argued, are not random events. Read it and see if you agree.

The Mind at Night: The New Science of How and Why We Dream by Andrea Rock

221.

LITERARY MERIT

★

Fast-forwarding from Freud, the history of dream science begins in the 1950s when Eugene Aserinsky created the first sleep lab, a makeshift affair in the bowels of the University of Chicago where he hooked his sleeping son up to electrodes and discovered the REM phase of sleep. Since then, neuroscientists have done much to shake the veil from the mystery of what exactly is going on when we dream. This fascinating book chronicles the history of the science of dreaming and will help you sort through all that hoo-ha about dream symbology and self-actualization through dreams.

The Promise of Sleep
by William C. Dement and Christopher Vaughn

222.

LITERARY MERIT

★

"When dreaming, the mind takes on a different consciousness, inhabits a new world that is as real as the world it experiences when awake." The authors corral decades of sleep research and deliver it up in highly readable packets, culminating with some ways to change your lifestyle in order to sleep better.

> **Did You Know . . .**
>
> "Even people who are blind from birth experience REM sleep, though the content of their dreams does not contain visual images."
>
> —*The Promise of Sleep*

The Sandman by Neil Gaiman

223.

LITERARY MERIT

★ ★

Okay, so it's not really a book. *The Sandman* is a series of seventy-five comic books published in the 1990s that tell a complete story. The collection set a new standard for the industry. Now available as a multi-volume set, let's call them graphic novels. The protagonist is Dream (aka Morpheus), a god-like character (but not a god because gods die when men stop believing in them) who is the personification of dreams and storytelling. Fantasy, horror, and plenty of suspense—Gaiman has been called the Shakespeare of comics.

224.

White Light by Rudy Rucker

Lucid dreaming and "fuzz weed"—burnt out mathematics professor Felix Rayman combines the two in hopes of gaining insight into the continuum hypothesis, a genuine but unproven mathematical theory. "Bad dream" doesn't begin to describe what Rayman gets instead. He loses his body and journeys to Cimon, a planet an "infinite" distance from earth, where he encounters Donald Duck's nephews, among others, living in a hotel based on Hilbert's paradox of the Grand Hotel. Oh yeah, he also falls in love with a talking beetle. You'll have to read this hallucinatory novel, considered a cyberpunk classic, to decide if you want what he's smoking.

...to BE ASTOUNDED

LITERARY MERIT ★

PROVOCATIVE 🔥

INFLUENTIAL !

INSPIRATIONAL 🕊

HUMOROUS 😄

BRAINY 💡

EASY READING ☂

PAGE TURNER 📖

CHALLENGING 👓

BATHROOM BOOK 🚽

FAMILY FRIENDLY 👪

MOVIE 🎥

225.

LITERARY MERIT

★ ★

Anansi Boys by Neil Gaiman

Alex Award 2006

"Fat Charlie" Nancy's humdrum life in London is upended when his estranged father dies. First, he discovers that his father was a human form of Anansi, an African trickster god. Second, he discovers that he has a brother, Spider, who inherited Dad's magical powers. Spider descends on Charlie, jolts him out of his comfortable passivity, and wreaks havoc on every aspect of his life. This novel, voted top honors by fantasy and sci-fi organizations, comes from a dazzling writer who bends genres, combining romantic comedy, crime drama, and fantasy.

> **Department of Memorable Opening Lines**
>
> "When Fat Charlie's dad named something, it stuck. Like calling Fat Charlie 'Fat Charlie.'"
> —*Anansi Boys*

226.

LITERARY MERIT

★ ★

Carter Beats the Devil by Glenn David Gold

This debut novel is based on the real life of magician Charles Carter (Carter the Great), a superstar illusionist from the turn of the century and a contemporary of Harry Houdini. The whirlwind plot has President Warren Harding appearing in a death-defying stunt in Carter's act and, hours later, dying unexpectedly in a San Francisco hotel room. The death echoes a tragedy from years earlier when Carter's wife died in a magic trick gone wrong. Enlightening and astounding, this novel pays loving tribute to magic's golden age.

227.

LITERARY MERIT

★ ★ ★

Grendel by John Gardner

This story is written from the point of view of the poor, beleaguered monster of *Beowulf*. "Ah, the unfairness of everything," he cries out to the heavens, and is terrified by the sound of his own huge voice. This version of the Old English beast is eloquent, funny, and filled with existential angst. When he isn't battling Danish King Hrothgar, he's observing humans, and finding them unfathomable.

228.

LITERARY MERIT

★ ★ ★ ★

The Handmaid's Tale by Margaret Atwood

The Republic of Gilead, once called the United States, is an oppressive, underpopulated theocracy ruled by men. The narrator, known only by the cipher Offred, has been enslaved in order to bear children. Like all other women in the society, she's forbidden to learn to read. This cautionary tale is controversial for its forthright feminism. What's most terrifying is that every scenario in the novel has been played out at some time in history. Tuck it on the shelf between *1984* and *The Stepford Wives*.

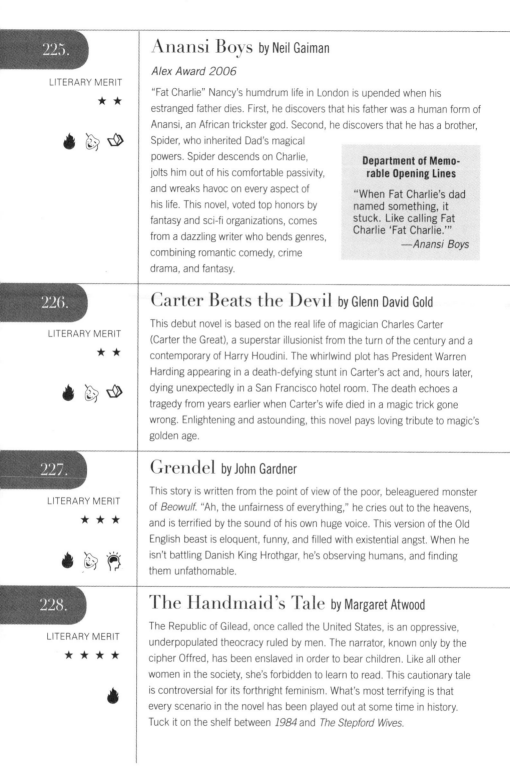

Harry Potter and the Sorcerer's Stone

by J. K. Rowling

229.

LITERARY MERIT

★ ★

In case you've been living under a rock, this is the book that introduced the world to Harry Potter. It's even been translated into Urdu. Meet the small, skinny eleven-year-old orphan with a mysterious scar on his forehead who lives in a dark cupboard in the home of his ghastly human family. That is, until he's whisked off to Hogwarts magic school where he tries to finish his parents' battle with arch-villain Voldemort.

Holes by Louis Sachar

230.

National Book Award 1998, Newbery Medal 1999

LITERARY MERIT

★ ★ ★ ★

Poor Stanley Yelnats, unfairly accused of stealing the used sneakers of baseball great Clyde Livings (actually they fell from the sky and landed on his head), is sent off to Camp Green Lake to serve out an eighteen-month sentence. It's a "dry, flat wasteland," a lakebed where nothing is green and there's no water. Stanley and

> **Department of Odds and Ends**
>
> Louis Sachar knew he wanted to name the main character in *Holes* Stanley, but he didn't want to have to figure out a last name. So he just spelled the character's first name backwards to get Yelnats.

his fellow inmates are roused before dawn each day to dig five-by-five-by-five holes in the desert. Only Warden seems to know what they're looking for. Sounds grim but it's very funny, and particularly satisfying when the plot's jigsaw pieces fit together at the end.

Invisible Cities by Italo Calvino

231.

LITERARY MERIT

★ ★ ★

More meditation than story, this surreal fantasy finds Venetian traveler Marco Polo inventing mythical cities to entertain Emperor Kublai Khan. "Already the Great Khan was leafing through his atlas, over the maps of the cities that menace in nightmares and maledictions: Enoch, Babylong, Yahooland, Butua, Brave New World." Praising the work of this great Italian writer, Salman Rushdie said: "Reading Calvino, you're constantly assailed by the notion that he is writing down what you have always known, except that you've never thought of it before."

232.

LITERARY MERIT
★ ★

Jonathan Strange & Mr. Norrell

by Susanna Clarke

Hugo Award 2006, World Fantasy Award 2005

In early nineteenth-century England, fussy old Gilbert Norrell and his pupil, the handsome and charming Jonathan Strange, dust off their wands and revive the dark arts to aid the British in the Napoleonic Wars. They go on to have a falling out over a prophecy by the Raven King: "Two magicians will appear in England. The first shall fear me; the second long to behold me." There are 800 pages of magic in this vast début fantasy novel with long, witty footnotes that give it the eerie feeling of nonfiction.

233.

LITERARY MERIT
★ ★

The Last Unicorn by Peter S. Beagle

In this beloved post-Tolkien fantasy novel, "The unicorn lived in a lilac wood, and she lived all alone. She was very old, though she did not know it. . . ." She also does not know that she's the last of her kind until she overhears a hunter say, "Unicorns are long gone." She asks a passing butterfly, "Are there others like me?" They have been chased to the end of the earth by Red Bull, the butterfly tells her, but "You can find your people if you are brave." The unicorn is joined in her quest to save the unicorns by Schmendrick, a magician who can perform no magic, and Molly Grue who long ago had stopped looking for unicorns.

234.

LITERARY MERIT
★ ★

The Lion, the Witch, and the Wardrobe

by C. S. Lewis

Four children evacuated from World War II London explore an old country house. The youngest, Lucy, steps into a wardrobe in an otherwise empty room and sequesters herself among fur coats. Stepping further in, she finds another row of coats, and another. Then she finds herself standing in a snow-filled forest. A faun, who addresses her as "Daughter of Eve," tells her she's in Narnia. Soon, Lucy's sister Susan and brothers Peter and Edmund follow her into the magical land, and Edmund is put to the test as the White Witch lures him into betraying his siblings. A children's classic.

235.

LITERARY MERIT
★ ★ ★

Little, Big by John Crowley

World Fantasy Award 1982

Somewhere in New England, Smoky Barnable falls in love with Daily Alice Drinkwater. Her home is in Edgewood, a place not on any map. But Smoky believes that because he loves her, he will find it. Edgewood turns out to be a folly of a house, much larger on the inside than seems possible from the outside. From there, this novel, considered a fantasy masterpiece, tells an epic tale, the family saga of six generations of Drinkwaters.

Lord of Light by Roger Zelazny

Hugo Award 1968

The Earth has long since died, and a perverted form of Hinduism dukes it out with Buddhism on a colonized planet. The original starship crew have gained extra-human powers and learned to transfer their minds to new, cloned bodies. With the help of technology, they've become despots, lording over descendants of the ship's passengers. One of the original crew opposes this tyranny. Considered a classic, this novel is recommended for readers who crave poetry and philosophy with their sci-fi.

LITERARY MERIT

★ ★

The Mists of Avalon by Marion Zimmer Bradley

Bradley imagines the legend of King Arthur from the point of view of its women. In her version, Gwynyfar (Guinevere) pushes toward the destruction of Camelot. Morgaine, usually portrayed as the distant evil sorceress, becomes the Fairy Queen. Bradley was a wildly prolific fantasy author (she wrote six Avalon novels and more than twenty Darkover series novels) and this is one of her best.

LITERARY MERIT

★

One Hundred Years of Solitude

by Gabriel García Márquez

This novel follows one hundred years in the village of Macondo, focusing on its founder Jose Arcadio Buendia and generations of his descendants. Comedy and tragedy are suffused with magical realism as daisies fall on lovers from the sky, an entire town is struck with insomnia, a woman ascends to heaven while hanging laundry, and it rains for four years, eleven months, and two days. Published in 1968, critics put him in the pantheon with Faulkner.

LITERARY MERIT

★ ★ ★ ★

The Once and Future King by T. H. White

This fantasy novel is a modern retelling of the legend of King Arthur, from his education by Merlyn to his death and the end of the Round Table. When Harry Potter pulled the Sword of Gryffindor from the Sorting Hat, surely J. K. Rowling was paying homage to the moment when young Arthur pulls the magic sword from a stone, revealing himself to be the rightful king of England. The musical play and movie *Camelot* are based on this, and Disney adapted it into the movie *The Sword and the Stone*.

LITERARY MERIT

★ ★

240.

LITERARY MERIT

★ ★

The Prestige by Christopher Priest

World Fantasy Award 1996

Written in the guise of two autobiographical memoirs, this novel tells of an obsessive rivalry between two Victorian-era illusionists at the height of their powers. Rupert Angier and Alfred Borden crave each other's signature tricks. They try deception and sabotage with nearly lethal results, and the spitefulness between them reaches forward through generations. Priest is a notable, award-winning author who writes in fantasy and sci-fi with literary panache.

241.

LITERARY MERIT

★ ★

The Phantom Tollbooth by Norton Juster

Bored little Milo. "It seems to me almost everything is a waste of time," he reflects as he and his "unhappy thoughts" head home from school. Waiting for him in his room, he finds a gift and a card that reads "FOR MILO, WHO HAS PLENTY OF TIME." It's a miniature purple tollbooth. Magically it transports him to the Kingdom of Wisdom. From there, he journeys to the Land of Expectation, winds his way through the Doldrums, and leaps to the Isle of Conclusions. Clever wordplay and wry humor abound in this modern fairytale.

242.

LITERARY MERIT

★ ★

The Princess Bride: S. Morgenstern's Classic Tale of True Love and High Adventure (The 'Good Parts' Version)
by William Goldman

This is the tale of Buttercup who taunts young Westley who works on her parents land, and then realizes too late that he's her own true love. He's gone off to earn his fortune and is reported killed by a pirate. Bereft, Buttercup is betrothed to the odious Prince Humperdinck, kidnapped by criminals, and rescued only to have to endure the perils of the Fire Swamp and Rodents of Unusual Size. No, there never was an S. Morgenstern whose antiquated work Goldman claims he abridged. If he was stepping out of his comfort zone in writing this delightful book, it doesn't show—before writing this, Goldman had written screenplays for movies like *Butch Cassidy and the Sundance Kid*.

Redwall by Brian Jacques

The mice inhabitants of Redwall Abbey are blissfully unaware as Cluny the Scourge, a villainous one-eyed warlord rat, and his army prepare to fight a bloody battle. Exuberant young mouse Matthias, a novice at the abbey, is the unlikely hero who must find the lost sword of Martin the Warrior to defeat Cluny and his minions. A delightful *Wind-in-the-Willows*-y supporting cast includes the bold shrew Log-a-Log, the stalwart badger Constance, and the irascible Basil Stag Hare. Pure fun, this is the much praised first novel in a series of nineteen (and counting) Redwall books.

LITERARY MERIT

★ ★

Stranger Things Happen by Kelly Link

244.

A *Twilight Zone* for the new millennium, this book offers up eleven cautionary tales with ghosts and giant dogs, amnesiacs, honeymooners, and a man with no nose. "In actual fact, Mr. Rook did have a nose, which was carved out of what appeared to be pine" which "nestled, delicate as a sleeping mouse between the two lenses of his glasses." The final story is a tour de force about a "girl detective" (aka Nancy Drew) adrift in the underworld. A rare beast, this book started life self-published.

LITERARY MERIT

★ ★

Quiz Time!
Match these fantasy worlds with their fantastic novels.

1. Republic of Gilead
2. Hrothgar's Meadhall
3. Hogwarts
4. The Isle of Gramarye

5. Dictionopolis
6. Florin

a. *The Phantom Tollbooth*
b. *The Handmaid's Tale*
c. *Once and Future King*
d. *Harry Potter and the Sorcerer's Stone*
e. *The Princess Bride*
f. *Grendel*

Answers: 1-b, 2-f, 3-d, 4-c, 5-a, 6-e

...to _Hit a Home Run_

LITERARY MERIT ★

PROVOCATIVE 🔥

INFLUENTIAL !

INSPIRATIONAL 🐦

HUMOROUS 😂

BRAINY 💡

EASY READING ☂

PAGE TURNER 📖

CHALLENGING 👓

BATHROOM BOOK 🚽

FAMILY FRIENDLY 👪

MOVIE 🎥

246.

LITERARY MERIT

★

Ball Four by Jim Bouton

It's fast and inside—this pitcher's 1969 diary stunned the baseball world with its frank honesty. Bouton was one of the Yankee's hardest throwing pitchers, but by 1969 his arm was gone and he was a knuckleballer for Seattle in the Pacific Coast League. He writes about a season that was far from his best, naming names and revealing the petty jealousies, boozing, amphetamine use, and womanizing that was endemic to professional baseball. Commissioner Bowie Kuhn called the book "detrimental to baseball" and tried to get Bouton to take back his allegations.

247.

LITERARY MERIT

★ ★ ★

The Boys of Summer
by Roger Kahn of the Brooklyn Dodgers

The Brooklyn Dodgers, what a team. Jackie Robinson and Pee Wee Reese and Roy Campanella and and and. . . . *New York Herald Tribune* sports reporter Roger Kahn grew up in the '30s and '40s within throwing distance of Ebbets Field. In what some consider the best baseball book ever written, he writes about his own passion for the game, the mythic players that were in their prime at the time of the 1955 Dodgers' World Series victory, and what happened as they got older.

248.

LITERARY MERIT

★ ★ ★

The Kid from Tomkinsville by John R. Tunis

It's a grim, gripping story. The "Kid" is Roy Tucker and his father died when he was four, his mother when he was sixteen, and he went to live with his grandmother on a farm in Connecticut. He becomes a phenomenal pitcher his first season in the pros, starting for the Dodgers. Then, a devastating injury ends his pitching career. All the next winter, he's out in his grandmother's barn, whacking at a ball suspended by a string. Through sheer force of will he turns himself into a great hitter and the next season he roars back. The opening of Philip Roth's American Pastoral pays homage to this great young adult novel, first published in 1940.

249.

LITERARY MERIT

★ ★

Maybe I'll Pitch Forever
by Leroy "Satchel" Paige and David Lipman

Paige was a great raconteur. He was also one of the greatest pitchers in baseball. In this memoir crafted from interviews with Lipman, Paige recalls how, at 42, he was signed by Bill Veeck to the Cleveland Indians and became the first black pitcher in the American League. He was already a legend, dazzling crowds since 1926 in the Negro Baseball Leagues. All those years, he'd been listening to people say to him, "If you were only white. . . ." His first game for the Indians he pitched a shutout.

Men at Work: The Craft of Baseball

250.

by George Will

LITERARY MERIT

★

Is your game of life driven by the home-run or base-by-base strategy? Will reveals the essential elements in baseball—hitting, fielding, pitching, and managing—as embodied by stellar players. The lessons learned can be applied much more broadly: "If Americans made goods and services the way Ripken makes double plays, Gwynn makes hits, and La Russa makes decisions, you would hear no more about the nation's trajectory having passed its apogee."

Moneyball: The Art of Winning an Unfair Game

251.

by Michael Lewis

LITERARY MERIT

★ ★

How did the 2002 Oakland Athletics achieve a spectacular record with the smallest payroll of any major league baseball team, spending only $41M compared to the New York Yankees' $150M? They threw out the collective wisdom of baseball insiders and

Did You Know It Means . . .

Sabermetrics: The analysis of baseball through statistics in order to determine why teams win. The term, popularized by *Moneyball*, was coined by Bill James. "Saber" refers to the Society for American Baseball Research (SABR). Sabermetricians pay attention to numbers like "on-base plus slugging" (OPS)—a complicated formula that factors in hits, bases on balls, times hit by pitcher, at bats, sacrifice flies, and total bases.

focused on baseball statistical analysis (sabermetrics). But this isn't a dry book about baseball statistics. Lewis is a great storyteller, and he was there with the A's top management that summer as they wheeled and dealed and crunched the numbers and won.

The Natural by Bernard Malamud

252.

LITERARY MERIT

★ ★ ★ ★

To be "the best that there ever was" is Roy Hobbs's dream. The 34-year-old rookie's career was put on hold when he was shot by a girl in a hotel room. He can pitch, and with the help of a bat (Wonderboy) hewn from the wood of a tree struck by lightning, he can hit anything they throw at him. Hobbs signs on with the last-place New York Knights, and for the first time, the team has a shot at the pennant. This mythic, allegorical novel, published in 1952 was Malamud's first; he would go on to win a Pulitzer.

253.

LITERARY MERIT

★ ★

Pride of the Bimbos by John Sayles

This outrageous and funny first novel from the lauded filmmaker tells the story of a five-man circus sideshow softball team, the Brooklyn Bimbos, who play carnivals across the South. They're the "Darlings of the Diamond—those comical cuties—baseball's most beeyouteeful bonus babies . . .," and they play in drag. For readers who don't mind having their masculinity checked at the gate.

254.

LITERARY MERIT

★ ★

Shoeless Joe by W. P. Kinsella

One spring evening at dusk, Ray Kinsella is sitting out on the verandah of his eastern Iowa farm home when a ballpark announcer's voice booms out of nowhere, "If you build it, he will come." Immediately he knows "he" is Shoeless Joe Jackson, "the best left fielder of all time," the guy whose glove was "the place triples go to die." Ray builds a ballpark in the middle of a cornfield and sure enough, "he" comes. Here's another one that "takes you out" with myth and fantasy, but its exploration of love and memory takes it to another level.

255.

LITERARY MERIT

★

Veeck—As in Wreck by Bill Veeck with Ed Linn

Imagine sitting in a bar and knocking back drinks with one of the most fabled showmen in baseball history. At various times, Veeck owned the Cleveland Indians, the St. Louis Browns, and the Chicago White Sox. His stunts were legendary. He installed an exploding scoreboard at Chicago's Comiskey park, and in '51 signed a midget who was walked his only time at bat. He was also the visionary who signed 42-year-old rookie Satchel Paige.

256.

LITERARY MERIT

★ ★ ★

Wait Till Next Year by Doris Kearns Goodwin

This memoir of Goodwin's childhood pays tribute to the blind hope that rekindled itself each opening day at Ebbets Field. Her father was a rabid Brooklyn Dodgers fan. When she was six, he gave her a scorebook and she learned to record every play of a game. It's a lovely moment when young Doris gives Gil Hodges, the Dodger first baseman who'd been in a batting slump, her prized St. Christopher medal, blessed by the Pope. "He reached out in a gesture of gratitude, and my fingers disappeared in a palm four times the size of mine." The next day Hodges began to hit again.

257.

LITERARY MERIT

★ ★ ★

You Know Me, Al by Ring Lardner

Lardner was one of the great sportswriters of the early twentieth century, and this is the book that made his unique style of satirical humor famous. It's written as a collection of letters from pugnacious bush league ("busher") pitcher Jack Keefe to his hometown friend Al Blanchard. Lardner captures the players' clueless egotism.

...for

LITERARY MERIT ★

PROVOCATIVE 🔥

INFLUENTIAL !

INSPIRATIONAL ➤

HUMOROUS 😃

BRAINY 💡

EASY READING ☂

PAGE TURNER 📖

CHALLENGING 👓

BATHROOM BOOK 🚽

FAMILY FRIENDLY 👪

MOVIE 🎥

257.

LITERARY MERIT

★ ★

Captain Blood by Rafael Sabatini

It begins oddly for swashbuckling fiction: "Peter Blood, bachelor of medicine and several other things besides, smoked a pipe and tended the geraniums boxed on the sill of his window. . . ." Yes, the mild-mannered physician and English gentleman turns into the infamous pirate Captain Blood. He's forced into the life, but never loses his honor or nobility. This gripping pirate's tale was published in 1922 and made Sabatini an overnight success after twenty-five years of writing.

258.

LITERARY MERIT

★ ★

Ender's Game by Orson Scott Card

Hugo Award 1986

It takes place on earth in a violent future. Buggers, an aptly named alien species, have almost annihilated the human race. Youngsters like six-year-old Andrew "Ender" Wiggin are being bred and trained at Battle School. Ender is a genius among geniuses, and training takes the form of good-versus-bad games like "buggers and astronauts." From a predictable story line, Card launches a complex and unpredictable character who eventually asks, "Why are we fighting buggers?" The Ender series has developed a cult-like following.

259.

LITERARY MERIT

★ ★

King Solomon's Mines by H. Rider Haggard

Supposedly Haggard wrote this when his brother bet him that he couldn't write a ripping yarn half as good as *Treasure Island*. In it, Alan Quartermain leads a group deep into Africa's unexplored regions, looking for a man who disappeared after setting out to find the legendary King Solomon's mines. The novel was first published in 1885 with a huge fanfare more appropriate to modern than Victorian times. Posters put up in the dead of night in London greeted residents in the morning with the message THE MOST AMAZING BOOK EVER WRITTEN. It created what came to be known as the "lost world" genre.

260.

LITERARY MERIT

★ ★

The Professional by W. C. Heinz

This novel tells the story of middleweight contender Eddie Brown and his wise, cantankerous manager Doc Carroll's fight to make Eddie the champ. Hemingway called this novel, with its spare prose and powerful, authentic dialogue, "the only good novel I've ever read about a fighter." Surely Heinz's clean style owed a debt to Papa. Heinz paid it forward to Elmore Leonard who, as a kid, wrote his first fan letter to Heinz and years later penned the introduction to the 2001 reissue edition of this book.

Ice Station by Matthew Reilly

They don't get more action-packed than this. The excitement begins when a team of marines receives a distress call. A spacecraft has been discovered in the ice below an Antarctic research station. But the marines aren't the only ones who want to recover it. This was the Australian thriller writer's first published novel, written when he was twenty-three years old. He filled it with non-stop stunts and techno-wizardry.

261.

LITERARY MERIT

★

Pacific Vortex by Clive Cussler

Dirk Pitt's first deep-sea adventure takes the marine engineer deep into the Pacific Vortex, a fog enshrouded Bermuda triangle-like area where *Starbuck*, an American nuclear submarine, is the latest vessel to vanish without a trace. Ten, nine, eight. . . . Pitt must salvage the ship before the sea explodes. Considered one of the great modern adventure novelists, Cussler shows off his expertise as a diver and a recognized authority on shipwrecks.

262.

LITERARY MERIT

★

The Relic by Douglas Preston and Lincoln Child

Ever wonder what rooms are hidden in the New York Museum of Natural History? In this techno-thriller, Preston and Child's first collaboration, we descend into the museum's hidden corridors, crawlspaces, and Gothic chambers where artifacts are stored and where visitors are turning up murdered. The mayhem is connected to a relic about to be put on display that depicts the lizard god of the Kothoga tribe. These guys plumb our deepest fears and fascinations.

263.

LITERARY MERIT

★

Shogun by James Clavell

Great adventure in feudal Japan with all the trimmings. Bold English adventurer and ship's captain John Blackthorne, or Anjin-san as the Japanese call him, is shipwrecked in Japan and captured by the Kasigi samurai clan. Educated in Japanese culture and values, he gets caught up in a clash between samurai clans. This sweeping, passionate novel is based on the real adventures of British navigator Will Adams. Clavell undoubtedly drew from his own experiences as well. He was a captain with the British Royal Artillery in Southeast Asia during World War II and imprisoned in the infamous Japanese Changi prison.

264.

LITERARY MERIT

★ ★

Who played Major John Blackthorne in the *Shogun* TV miniseries?

Richard Chamberlan

265.

LITERARY MERIT

★ ★ ★

Treasure Island by Robert Louis Stevenson

This hugely successful novel, first published in England in 1883, set the standard for swashbuckling fiction with its buccaneers, treasure map, buried gold, mutiny at sea, and boy hero. Ever since its publication, readers have debated the moral ambiguity of tall, powerful, wily Long John Silver with his "timber leg," engaged as cook for the voyage but secretly a former mate of the infamous Captain Flint.

266.

LITERARY MERIT

★

Under the Black Flag: The Romance and the Reality of Life Among the Pirates
by David Cordingly

If you've ever harbored dreams of being a pirate, this will cure you. Historian Cordingly, former head of exhibitions at the National Maritime Museum in Greenwich, England, takes a hard look at the brutal reality of seventeenth-century pirate life. This book contains every bit of fascinating trivia you ever wanted to know about pirates—from their pets (yes, there were parrots and monkeys), to what it took to be a pirate leader (they were elected by their crew), to how they dispatched their victims (they didn't "walk the plank"), to equal opportunity pillaging (yes, there were women buccaneers).

...for GRAND ADVENTURE

LITERARY MERIT ★

PROVOCATIVE 🔥

INFLUENTIAL !

INSPIRATIONAL 🕊

HUMOROUS 😄

BRAINY 🧠

EASY READING ☂

PAGE TURNER 📖

CHALLENGING 👓

BATHROOM BOOK 🚽

FAMILY FRIENDLY 👪

MOVIE 🎥

267.

LITERARY MERIT

★

2001: A Space Odyssey by Arthur C. Clarke

Welcome to the past and the future, as Clarke conceived them back in 1968, a year before the first moon landing. In his version, a mysterious black crystalline monolith appeared among our ape-like ancestors three million years ago. In 1999 a similar monolith is excavated on the surface of the moon. It transmits radio signals to the alien world that left it there. Eighteen months later, Discovery One, with its psychotic sixth crew member, a computer named HAL 9000 (notice each letter of HAL directly precedes the ones in IBM), takes off for Saturn. The book and the landmark movie were written simultaneously.

268.

LITERARY MERIT

★

The Dangerous Book for Boys
by Conn Iggulden and Hal Iggulden

This delightful how-to book comes from two brothers who haven't forgotten the things boys loved to do in the days before video games, iPods, and MySpace. Learn how to tie knots, construct "the best paper airplane in the world," build a tree house, or find due north in the dark. The book was a huge hit in the U.K. before it was modified for American audiences, and was named the 2007 British Book of the Year.

269.

LITERARY MERIT

★ ★

The Eight by Katherine Neville

A historical tale intertwines with a modern-day quest for Charlemagne's chess set (the Montglane Service), which can unlock great power. Financial computer expert Catherine Velis, about to be sent to Algiers on a job, encounters an antique dealer who asks her to search for the missing chess pieces. Her path parallels that of Mireille de Remi, a young girl hiding the fabled chess pieces during the French Revolution. With its ciphers and codes, convoluted plot, high stakes, and nonstop action, this novel mines the same vein as *The Da Vinci Code* but with more literary panache.

270.

LITERARY MERIT

★ ★

Gulliver's Travels by Jonathan Swift

A traveler's tale replete with allegory and satire, this four-part novel has remained in print since 1726. It tells of the four voyages of Lemuel Gulliver ("first a surgeon, then a captain of several ships"). First, he's shipwrecked and taken hostage by the Lilliputians, a race of 6-inch tall people at war with the neighboring Blefuscudans (a feud his readers recognized as a satire of the conflict between England and France). On the second voyage, he's captured by a 72-foot giant farmer and sold to the Queen of Brobdingnag. A third voyage takes him to an assortment of odd destinations. And on his fourth voyage, a mutinous crew abandons him on Houyhnhnms where he finds a race of intelligent horses that rule over Yahoos, deformed creatures with perfect human faces. Turns out these "abominable animals" are actually humans.

The Hobbit by J. R. R. Tolkien

Bilbo Baggins is a hobbit who wants nothing more than to be left alone to sit contentedly by the fire, smoke his pipe, and sip a good beer. With great reluctance, he agrees to Gandalf the Grey's invitation to partake in a "great adventure." In the company of dwarves, he takes a perilous journey to the Lonely Mountains to reclaim a stolen fortune from the dragon Smaug. Of course this was only a prelude to *The Lord of the Rings*. Tolkien is the Homer of the twentieth century.

LITERARY MERIT

★ ★ ★

Into Africa: The Epic Adventures of Stanley and Livingstone by Martin Dugard

Explorer Dr. David Livingstone was a media celebrity of the nineteenth century, "so famous that one poll showed only Victoria herself was better known." He went in search of the source of the Nile and hadn't been heard from in five years. As a publicity stunt, the *New York Herald* sent journalist Henry Morton Stanley to find him. Ten months later Stanley did, and uttered the famous "Dr. Livingstone, I presume." To tell the story, historian Dugard unearthed factual material from unpublished diaries, newspapers of the time, and the archives of Britain's Royal Geographical Society, but he's not afraid to make grand leaps of fiction to bring these historical figures to life.

LITERARY MERIT

★ ★

Kon-Tiki by Thor Heyerdahl

Norwegian anthropologist Thor Heyerdahl undertook a great adventure, sailing 4,300 miles across the Pacific on a primitive raft made of balsa wood, in order to prove a theory—that ancient people from pre-Columbian times could have settled Polynesia in the South Pacific. He christened the vessel *Kon-Tiki*, after the Inca sun god. On April 28, 1937, he and five other men and a green parrot set sail from Peru. A hundred and one days later, the raft crash-landed on the Polynesian island of Raroia, proving his point.

LITERARY MERIT

★

Life of Pi by Yann Martel
Booker Prize 2002

This is one of literature's more profound novels. Piscine Molitor Patel, a boy in Pondicherry, India, fed up with the nickname "Pissing," christens himself "Pi." In Part One of the novel, Pi searches for God.

Department of Memorable Characters

"His head was the size of a lifebuoy, with teeth."
—Richard Parker,
a 450-pound Bengal tiger

LITERARY MERIT

★ ★ ★ ★

He becomes a devout disciple of Hinduism, Christianity, and Islam, until the pandit, the priest, and the imam get wise. When the zoo where Pi's father works closes, the family sets sail for Canada with the animals, which are destined for zoos around the world. Part Two begins, "The ship sank." Pi is cast adrift with a huge Bengal tiger named Richard Parker.

273.

LITERARY MERIT

★ ★ ★ ★

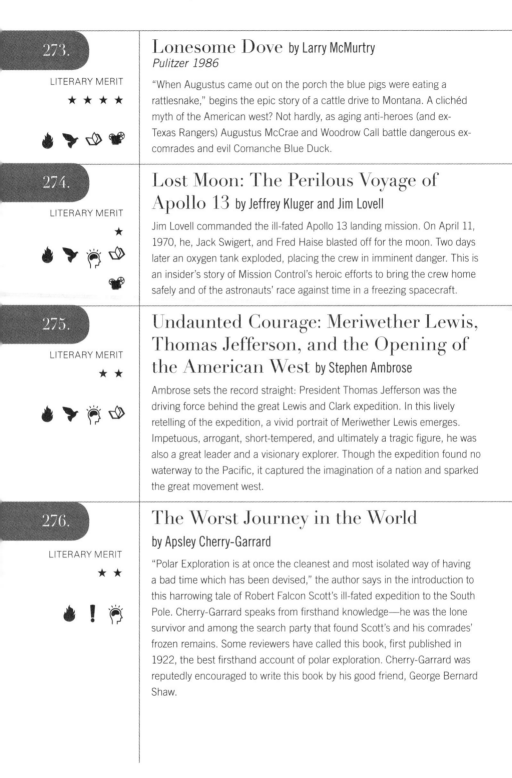

Lonesome Dove by Larry McMurtry
Pulitzer 1986

"When Augustus came out on the porch the blue pigs were eating a rattlesnake," begins the epic story of a cattle drive to Montana. A clichéd myth of the American west? Not hardly, as aging anti-heroes (and ex-Texas Rangers) Augustus McCrae and Woodrow Call battle dangerous ex-comrades and evil Comanche Blue Duck.

274.

LITERARY MERIT

★

Lost Moon: The Perilous Voyage of Apollo 13 by Jeffrey Kluger and Jim Lovell

Jim Lovell commanded the ill-fated Apollo 13 landing mission. On April 11, 1970, he, Jack Swigert, and Fred Haise blasted off for the moon. Two days later an oxygen tank exploded, placing the crew in imminent danger. This is an insider's story of Mission Control's heroic efforts to bring the crew home safely and of the astronauts' race against time in a freezing spacecraft.

275.

LITERARY MERIT

★ ★

Undaunted Courage: Meriwether Lewis, Thomas Jefferson, and the Opening of the American West by Stephen Ambrose

Ambrose sets the record straight: President Thomas Jefferson was the driving force behind the great Lewis and Clark expedition. In this lively retelling of the expedition, a vivid portrait of Meriwether Lewis emerges. Impetuous, arrogant, short-tempered, and ultimately a tragic figure, he was also a great leader and a visionary explorer. Though the expedition found no waterway to the Pacific, it captured the imagination of a nation and sparked the great movement west.

276.

LITERARY MERIT

★ ★

The Worst Journey in the World
by Apsley Cherry-Garrard

"Polar Exploration is at once the cleanest and most isolated way of having a bad time which has been devised," the author says in the introduction to this harrowing tale of Robert Falcon Scott's ill-fated expedition to the South Pole. Cherry-Garrard speaks from firsthand knowledge—he was the lone survivor and among the search party that found Scott's and his comrades' frozen remains. Some reviewers have called this book, first published in 1922, the best firsthand account of polar exploration. Cherry-Garrard was reputedly encouraged to write this book by his good friend, George Bernard Shaw.

...for Apocalyptic Vision

LITERARY MERIT ★

PROVOCATIVE 🔥

INFLUENTIAL !

INSPIRATIONAL 🕊

HUMOROUS 😄

BRAINY 💡

EASY READING ☂

PAGE TURNER 📖

CHALLENGING 👓

BATHROOM BOOK 🚽

FAMILY FRIENDLY 👪

MOVIE 🎥

279.

LITERARY MERIT

★ ★

Alas, Babylon by Pat Frank

Randolph Bragg receives a telegram from his brother, a high-ranking military officer: "Urgent you meet me at Base Ops McCoy noon today." He signs off, "Alas, Babylon." Bragg recognizes the code phrase the brothers have used since childhood for disaster. The news turns out to be seriously bad: an impending nuclear attack. The residents of Fort Repose in 1950s Florida struggle to survive nuclear winter, and Bragg turns into an unlikely hero. Published in 1959, this was one of the first post-apocalyptic novels of the nuclear age.

280.

LITERARY MERIT

★ ★ ★

Blindness by José Saramago

In this profound, allegorical novel from a Portuguese writer and Nobel Literature laureate, a car sits at a traffic light that's turned green, the driver shouting "I am blind." A good Samaritan helps the driver get home, then steals his car only to go blind himself. Soon there's an epidemic, and the blind are quarantined in an asylum while more go blind and civilization crumbles.

281.

LITERARY MERIT

★ ★

A Canticle for Leibowitz by Walter M. Miller

Hugo Award 1961

Civilization rebuilds itself after nuclear holocaust and repeats all the mistakes made the first time around. The novel follows an abbey of monks that was founded by survivor Isaac Edward Leibowitz. Over centuries, the monks dedicate themselves to preserving knowledge by hiding and memorizing surviving texts as society plunges into the dark ages. One of the more prosaic artifacts they save is a note Leibowitz scrawled on a scrap of paper: "pound pastrami, can kraut, six bagels—bring home for Emma." This novel is considered a sci-fi masterpiece as well as a meditation on world history and the Catholic church.

282.

LITERARY MERIT

★ ★ ★ ★

Cat's Cradle by Kurt Vonnegut

This darkly comedic, satirical, autobiographical 1963 novel catapulted Vonnegut from writer to literary icon. The narrator, who is working on a book about what people did on the day Hiroshima was bombed, is a practitioner of the fictional religion of Bokonism which espouses living fomas ("harmless untruths" that make one better able to face reality). Fomas are of little help as the narrator witnesses the destruction of the world by Ice-Nine, the "seed of doom," which turns all water to ice upon contact.

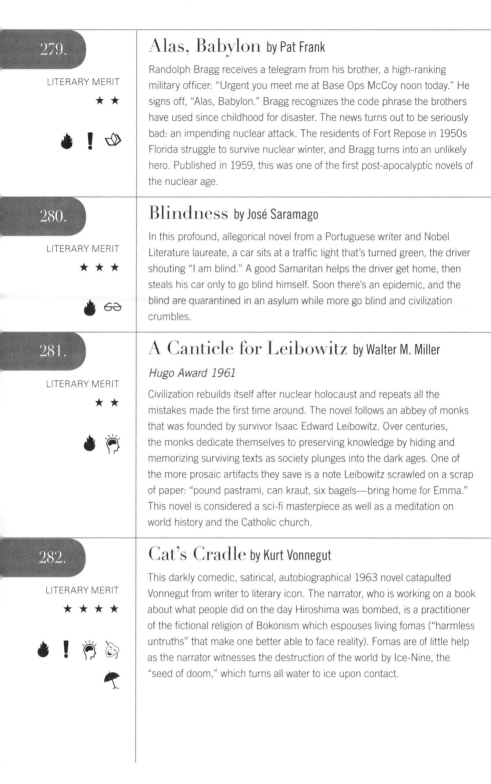

A Crack in the Edge of the World: America and the Great California Earthquake of 1906
by Simon Winchester

283.

LITERARY MERIT

★ ★ ★

Winchester examines the moment in 1906 when the earth "shrugged," and an earthquake registering 8.25 on the Richter Scale struck San Francisco, wrecking 290 blocks and toppling 25,000 buildings, leaving the city without water or power. Fires raged for three days after. He gives a potent lesson on the power of tectonic plates, and reminds us that "places like the mountains of Montana and Wyoming exist, and only by the planet's consent that all towns and all cities—New Madrid, Charleston, Anchorage, Banda Aceh—and San Francisco—survive for as long as they do."

Do Androids Dream of Electric Sheep?
by Philip K. Dick

284.

LITERARY MERIT

★ ★

In a fallout-shrouded San Francisco after "World War Terminus" has destroyed much of Earth, empathy boxes and mood organs keep the populace docile. "Electric sheep," robotic replicas of animals, are given to survivors who can't afford to own a real member of the endangered species. Bounty hunter Rick Deckard tracks down renegade androids, robots that look just like humans and were created to serve families emigrating to colonies on Mars. During his hunt, he has a crisis of consciousness. This classic cyberpunk novel was published in 1968, before the term was coined.

> **What movie was *Do Androids Dream of Electric Sheep?* made into?**
>
> *Blade Runner*

The Day of the Triffids by John Wyndham

285.

LITERARY MERIT

★ ★

There's no nuclear attack in this 1951 British sci-fi classic. Instead, a mysterious meteor shower blinds everyone on earth. Bill Masen is spared because he was in the hospital, his eyes bandaged after having been stung by a Triffid. Triffids are seven-foot-tall plants that can move about, eat rotting meat, and are being cultivated across the world for their extracts and oils. Masen wanders the streets of London and watches civilization collapse around him. As the unsighted gang up to enslave the sighted, Triffids seize their edge over humanity. Thoroughly believable; thoroughly terrifying.

286.

LITERARY MERIT

★ ★ ★

Hiroshima by John Hersey

Far more moving and horrifying than any post-apocalyptic fiction, this book tells the stories of six survivors of the atomic bomb dropped August 6, 1945, on Hiroshima, Japan. It is based on Hersey's interviews with survivors. The book was first published in *The New Yorker* a year after the attack, taking over an entire cartoonless issue.

287.

LITERARY MERIT

★ ★ ★

On the Beach by Nevil Shute

Innocent victims of an accidental war are living out their last days in Australia, making do with what they have, hoping for a miracle. As the deadly fallout moves ever closer, the world winds toward its inevitable end. Published in 1957, many Americans first grasped the threat of nuclear war by reading this book. Keep a box of tissues handy.

288.

LITERARY MERIT

★ ★ ★

The Road by Cormac McCarthy

Pulitzer 2007

The world after nuclear annihilation is filled with "creedless shells of men tottering down the causeways like migrants in a feverland." The novel follows two of the last survivors, a man and his son, as they forage in a charred wasteland and hide from starving gangs who have turned to cannibalism. There is nothing to live for, but still the man is driven by his need to shelter and protect his son. "Are we still the good guys?" the little boy asks. Bleak and surprisingly funny, read it with Saramago's *Blindness*.

289.

LITERARY MERIT

★ ★

The Stand by Stephen King

King called this an "American epic fantasy, set in a plague-decimated USA." He was tuned into a growing distrust of the powers-that-be when he came up with this plot about a deadly, government-engineered flu virus that is accidentally released and wipes out most of humanity. For many of his fans, this and *The Shining* are the prolific King's best novels.

290.

LITERARY MERIT

★ ★

War of the Worlds by H. G. Wells

In this classic sci-fi novella published way back in 1898, a huge cylinder from Mars lands in England creating a crater. Gigantic, tentacled creatures that glisten like leather emerge. Men approach the creatures, waving a white flag, and are incinerated. Not an auspicious start. Orson Welles's adaptation of the novel for radio on Halloween eve, 1938, terrified listeners who believed that a real Martian invasion was in progress.

...*for a* **Walk on the Wild Side**

LITERARY MERIT ★

PROVOCATIVE 🔥

INFLUENTIAL !

INSPIRATIONAL 🕊

HUMOROUS 😄

BRAINY 💡

EASY READING ☂

PAGE TURNER 📖

CHALLENGING 👓

BATHROOM BOOK 🚽

FAMILY FRIENDLY 👪

MOVIE 🎥

291.

LITERARY MERIT

★ ★ ★

Animal Farm by George Orwell

In this allegorical tale, pigs on Manor Farm revolt. They expel the humans from the farm and set up a Bolshevik-style commune. Their first commandment: "All animals are equal." A battle for leadership ensues and dictatorial Napoleon (Orwell's stand-in for Stalin) takes over. After many years the pigs learn to walk on two legs. They carry whips and their commandment becomes: "All animals are equal, but some animals are more equal than others." When this was published, critics compared Orwell's satire to Voltaire's *Candide* and Swift's *Gulliver's Travels*.

292.

LITERARY MERIT

★ ★

Blue Meridian: The Search for the Great White Shark by Peter Matthiessen

Swim with the sharks, anyone? Before Peter Benchley demonized the great white in *Jaws*, nature writer and novelist Peter Matthiessen sailed off with millionaire sportsman and filmmaker Peter Gimbel to find sharks and film them. They suspended underwater cages from commercially killed whales, and photographed sharks that gathered to feed off the carcasses. The book was written to hype the film *Blue Water, White Death*, but with its vivid writing and photographs it stands on its own.

293.

LITERARY MERIT

★

Born Free: A Lioness of Two Worlds
by Joy Adamson

Living in Kenya, naturalist Joy Adamson adopted Elsa, a tame lion cub. Adamson fed the tiny cub with a baby bottle, pushed her on a homemade swing, and treated her more like a child than a pet or wild animal. Then for two years, she and her husband trained Elsa to return to the wild. First published in 1960, it continues to raise awareness of the need to protect wildlife and conserve our remaining wild ecosystems.

294.

LITERARY MERIT

★ ★ ★

Brazzaville Beach by William Boyd

British ecologist Hope Clearwater, recovering from a failed marriage to a brilliant mathematician, is studying a band of chimps in an unnamed civil-war torn African nation, observing the intimate details of their lives. What she discovers flies in the face of orthodox thinking in the field and threatens her own career. This is an enthralling read from an underappreciated writer. Boyd won the McVitie Prize for Scottish Writer of the Year for this work.

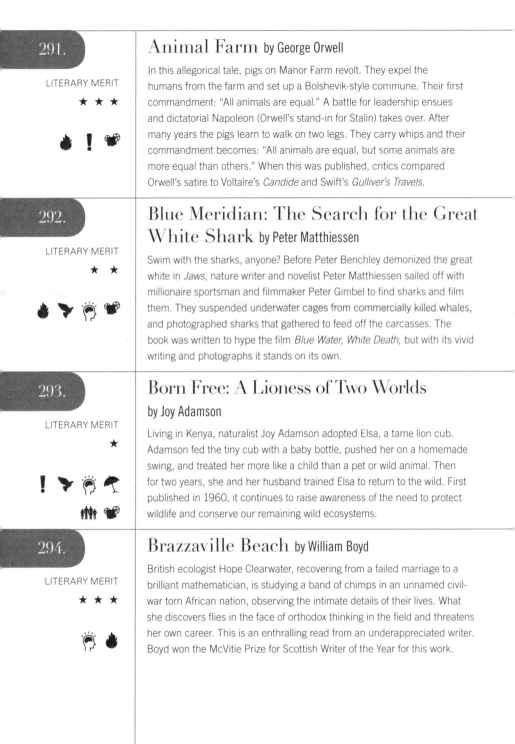

The Call of the Wild by Jack London

295.

When "men, groping the Arctic darkness," find gold, there's a rush northward. The Klondike strike needs strong, heavy dogs with thick coats to pull the sleds. Buck, a St. Bernard/Scotch shepherd mix, is snatched from his comfortable home in the Santa Clara Valley and shipped to the harsh frozen Yukon where he must fight for survival. The book ends with the unforgettable image of Buck, running wild, leading a wolf pack through pale moonlight. The book has remained in print for over a hundred years; Carl Sandburg called it "the greatest dog story ever written."

Department of Great Opening Lines

"Buck did not read the newspapers, or he would have known that trouble was brewing, not alone for himself, but for every tidewater dog, strong of muscle and with warm, long hair, from Puget Sound to San Diego."
—*The Call of the Wild*

The Complete Walker by Colin Fletcher

296.

Often called the "Backpacker's Bible," this book by the notoriously reclusive Fletcher is an exhaustive guide to the most basic form of outdoor travel. Lyrical, practical—when it was first published in 1968 it sent thousands of us striding off into mountains and deserts. The fourth update was published in 2002. Fletcher died in 2007 of injuries suffered from being struck by a car while walking near his home.

Jane Goodall: The Woman Who Redefined Man
by Dale Peterson

297.

This is the biography of the woman who revolutionized the way scientists study primates. At twenty-six and a secretarial school graduate, she was sent into the Gombe Stream Chimpanzee Reserve in Tanzania. Goodall observed that chimps ate meat and engaged in what amounted to organized warfare. When she reported to Louis Leakey that the chimps fashioned tools, he sent her a telegram: "Now we must redefine tool, redefine man, or accept chimpanzees as human." Peterson creates a fascinating portrait of a woman and a scientist.

298.

LITERARY MERIT

★ ★

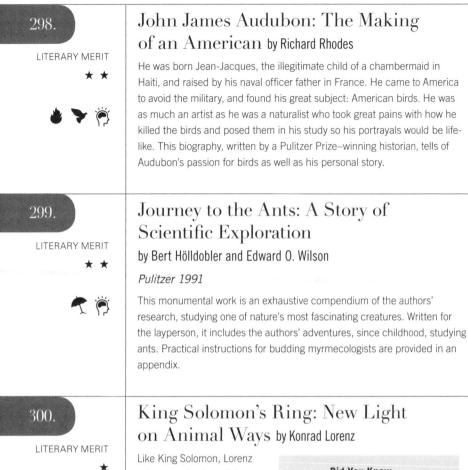

John James Audubon: The Making of an American by Richard Rhodes

He was born Jean-Jacques, the illegitimate child of a chambermaid in Haiti, and raised by his naval officer father in France. He came to America to avoid the military, and found his great subject: American birds. He was as much an artist as he was a naturalist who took great pains with how he killed the birds and posed them in his study so his portrayals would be life-like. This biography, written by a Pulitzer Prize–winning historian, tells of Audubon's passion for birds as well as his personal story.

299.

LITERARY MERIT

★ ★

Journey to the Ants: A Story of Scientific Exploration
by Bert Hölldobler and Edward O. Wilson

Pulitzer 1991

This monumental work is an exhaustive compendium of the authors' research, studying one of nature's most fascinating creatures. Written for the layperson, it includes the authors' adventures, since childhood, studying ants. Practical instructions for budding myrmecologists are provided in an appendix.

300.

LITERARY MERIT

★

King Solomon's Ring: New Light on Animal Ways by Konrad Lorenz

Like King Solomon, Lorenz talked to animals and they talked back. He studied all manner of creatures from the Eurasian jackdaw to tiny water-shrews. He

> **Did You Know . . .**
>
> Graylag geese mate for life and cannot be housetrained.

raised animals in and around his home, and then observed them. "Graylag goslings," he noted, "unquestioningly accept the first living being whom they meet as their mother and run confidently after him." Read about a brood that hatches, imprints upon him, and follows him everywhere. Solid science combined with rich anecdotes and great humor.

The Naked Ape: A Zoologist's Study of the Human Animal by Desmond Morris

301.

LITERARY MERIT

★

Evolutionary biologist Morris writes about humans with the same detachment naturalists reserve for their examination of animal behavior. He considers the human animal a naked ape, "marked off by his nudity from all the thousands of hairy, shaggy or furry land-dwelling mammalian species." What a letdown to discover that we owe our "sexual qualities" to our "fruit-picking, forest ape ancestors."

The Author Explains the Title

"There are one hundred and ninety-three living species of monkeys and apes. One hundred and ninety-two of them are covered with hair. The exception is a naked ape self-named *Homo sapiens.*"—*Desmond Morris*

Pigeons: The Fascinating Saga of the World's Most Revered and Reviled Bird

by Andrew D. Blechman

302.

LITERARY MERIT

★ ★

They're reviled for their droppings, but also raced, bred, and shown in pageants. Blechman traces the history of these gentle, intelligent birds. Read it to learn about the radical pro-pigeon underground in New York City, and meet pigeon-lover Mike Tyson: "Could there be a more classic dichotomy, a more unusual pairing, than Iron Mike Tyson, former heavyweight champion of the world, and his gentle birds?" Find out how one of man's most steadfast companions became regarded as a "rat of the sky."

Rats: Observations on the History and Habitat of the City's Most Unwanted Inhabitants by Robert Sullivan

303.

LITERARY MERIT

★

Alex Award 2005

Robert Sullivan stalked New York's alleyways with a night-vision monocular to spy on the nocturnal habits of rats. He calls it being out "ratting." One of his favorite haunts was a "filth-slicked alleyway" near City Hall. Through his study of these scurrying little creatures, he gives us a unique, rodent's-eye view of the history of the Big Apple.

304.

LITERARY MERIT

★ ★

The Secret Life of Lobsters by Trevor Corson

Journalist Corson thought he knew all about lobsters after spending two years working on a lobster boat in the Gulf of Maine. Then he started talking to an eccentric group of biologists who study them. Turns out lobsters are happiest in deep, dark places and most active at night. They engage in an elaborate and prolonged mating dance (males greet females by standing on tiptoe and waving their swimmerets). He hypothesizes that as long as there are plenty of dark crevices deep in the sea, lobsters will remain plentiful. *USA Today* and *Discover* magazine named this the best science book of 2004.

305.

LITERARY MERIT

★ ★

When Elephants Weep
by Jeffrey Moussaieff and Susan McCarthy

The authors offer rafts of anecdotal evidence to support the contention that animals do have emotions. This comes as no surprise to pet owners, but still it's fascinating to read about a giraffe that kicks a car that honks at him, or an aquarium whale that pins a diver who teased him to the floor of the tank, or baby African elephants who, after seeing their families killed by poachers, wake up in the middle of the night screaming. Can you spell "anthropomorphism" . . . or maybe not? Pretty compelling stuff.

...for Thrills

LITERARY MERIT	★
PROVOCATIVE	🔥
INFLUENTIAL	!
INSPIRATIONAL	🕊
HUMOROUS	😄
BRAINY	💡
EASY READING	☂
PAGE TURNER	📖
CHALLENGING	👓
BATHROOM BOOK	🚽
FAMILY FRIENDLY	👪
MOVIE	🎥

306.

LITERARY MERIT

★ ★

The Alienist by Caleb Carr

Written in period style, this thriller is set in vividly portrayed turn-of-the-century New York City. The police commissioner is Theodore Roosevelt. A serial killer's latest victim, a young male prostitute, has been found in a watchtower of the Williamsburg Bridge. Dr. Laszlo Kreizler, the "Alienist," is assigned to track down the killer. This had a 25-week run as a *Publishers Weekly* bestseller.

Did You Know It Means . . .

Alienist: A nineteenth-century term for psychiatrist, used more specifically to refer to a psychological profiler.

307.

LITERARY MERIT

★ ★ ★

American Tabloid by James Ellroy

Staccato sentences. Disembodied dialogue. Spare powerful prose. The characters include thugs, mobsters, spies, schemers, extortionists, John F. Kennedy, Bobby Kennedy, and J. Edgar Hoover, and not a single one of them is likeable. It ends with the Kennedy assassination. Ellroy's unique style influences a raft of modern thriller writers.

308.

LITERARY MERIT

★

The Bourne Identity by Robert Ludlum

He's the man without a past from the author who perfected the espionage thriller. This first entry in the Bourne trilogy opens with a gun battle at sea. Man overboard! A small fishing boat plucks a wounded man from the ocean. He has no memory of who shot him or who he is. From a piece of microfiche embedded in his thigh, he discovers a name, Jason Bourne, and a four-million-dollar Swiss bank account in Bourne's name. The minute he starts to withdraw money, assassins are on his tail.

309.

LITERARY MERIT

★ ★

Casino Royale by Ian Fleming

This is the book that introduced the world's best-loved secret agent, James Bond. "M," head of the British Secret Service, assigns Bond the task of bankrupting Monsieur Le Chiffre ("the cipher"), a Soviet agent with the assassination bureau SMERSH, in a game of baccarat. In the kind of logic you find only in a Bond novel, the Brits hope that SMERSH will then kill Le Chiffre because of his gambling debts. Bond's car is not yet an Aston Martin and he doesn't drink a vodka martini (shaken, not stirred). But he does introduce himself as "Bond, James Bond" and is already an unapologetic misogynist.

Department of Great Characters

"Her dress was black velvet, simple and yet with a touch of splendour that only a half-dozen couturiers in the world can achieve. There was a thin necklace of diamonds at her throat and a small diamond clip in the low vee which just exposed the jutting swell of her breasts."

—Vesper Lynd, the first "Bond girl" in *Casino Royale*

The Devil in the White City by Erik Larson

310.

An architect who built a shining white dreamscape and a murderer who lured victims to gas chambers and crematoriums—these characters' true stories are intertwined and read like a thriller in this retelling of events surrounding the 1893 Chicago World's Fair. This book was a finalist for the 2003 National Book Award.

LITERARY MERIT

★ ★ ★ ★

Drama City by George Pelecanos

311.

Down DC's stark, dark streets walks Lorenzo Brown and his probation officer, Rachel Lopez. He's just out from doing eight years on felony drug charges, trying to start over and working for the Humane Society. She's a cool professional who, by day, helps guys like Brown stay clean and sober. By night she cruises bars looking for rough sex. Inevitably, Lorenzo and Rachel get caught in crossfire. Pelecanos is considered one of today's best crime fiction writers, and this is one of his best.

LITERARY MERIT

★ ★ ★

Foucault's Pendulum by Umberto Eco

312.

The publication of this book in Italy provoked nearly as much frenzied media speculation as the seventh *Harry Potter* book. It's the story of three editors at a Milan publishing house who concoct an elaborate, imaginary, computerized plot to take over the world—only to discover that their plan comes true. For readers who didn't get enough Knights Templar in *The Da Vinci Code* and are up for a much more challenging read.

LITERARY MERIT

★ ★

The Great Escape by Paul Brickhill

313.

As a prisoner of the Germans, Brickhill witnessed the mass escape from Stalag Luft III in the spring of 1944. He writes of preparations that went on for months as more than 600 prisoners dug three tunnels ("Tom," "Dick," and "Harry"), forged papers, and created fake German uniforms and fake weaponry. He writes of the escape and the tragic ending. A gripping true story, this is one of the great escape narratives.

LITERARY MERIT

★ ★

Jaws by Peter Benchley

314.

Benchley creates a mythic monster, a white shark that terrorizes a Long Island seaside resort. Published in 1974, the image of "The great fish" moving "silently through the night water, propelled by short sweeps of its crescent tail" has become part of the zeitgeist. Benchley became an ardent conservationist and defender of sharks.

LITERARY MERIT

★ ★

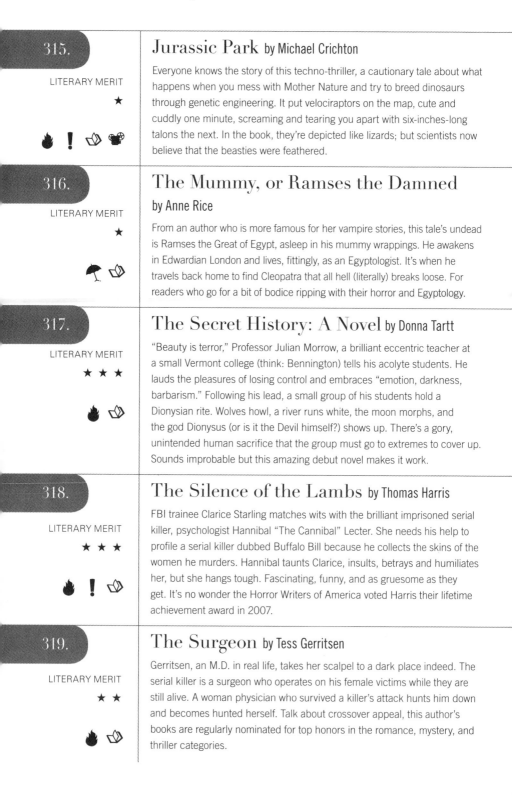

315.

LITERARY MERIT

★

Jurassic Park by Michael Crichton

Everyone knows the story of this techno-thriller, a cautionary tale about what happens when you mess with Mother Nature and try to breed dinosaurs through genetic engineering. It put velociraptors on the map, cute and cuddly one minute, screaming and tearing you apart with six-inches-long talons the next. In the book, they're depicted like lizards; but scientists now believe that the beasties were feathered.

316.

LITERARY MERIT

★

The Mummy, or Ramses the Damned
by Anne Rice

From an author who is more famous for her vampire stories, this tale's undead is Ramses the Great of Egypt, asleep in his mummy wrappings. He awakens in Edwardian London and lives, fittingly, as an Egyptologist. It's when he travels back home to find Cleopatra that all hell (literally) breaks loose. For readers who go for a bit of bodice ripping with their horror and Egyptology.

317.

LITERARY MERIT

★ ★ ★

The Secret History: A Novel by Donna Tartt

"Beauty is terror," Professor Julian Morrow, a brilliant eccentric teacher at a small Vermont college (think: Bennington) tells his acolyte students. He lauds the pleasures of losing control and embraces "emotion, darkness, barbarism." Following his lead, a small group of his students hold a Dionysian rite. Wolves howl, a river runs white, the moon morphs, and the god Dionysus (or is it the Devil himself?) shows up. There's a gory, unintended human sacrifice that the group must go to extremes to cover up. Sounds improbable but this amazing debut novel makes it work.

318.

LITERARY MERIT

★ ★ ★

The Silence of the Lambs by Thomas Harris

FBI trainee Clarice Starling matches wits with the brilliant imprisoned serial killer, psychologist Hannibal "The Cannibal" Lecter. She needs his help to profile a serial killer dubbed Buffalo Bill because he collects the skins of the women he murders. Hannibal taunts Clarice, insults, betrays and humiliates her, but she hangs tough. Fascinating, funny, and as gruesome as they get. It's no wonder the Horror Writers of America voted Harris their lifetime achievement award in 2007.

319.

LITERARY MERIT

★ ★

The Surgeon by Tess Gerritsen

Gerritsen, an M.D. in real life, takes her scalpel to a dark place indeed. The serial killer is a surgeon who operates on his female victims while they are still alive. A woman physician who survived a killer's attack hunts him down and becomes hunted herself. Talk about crossover appeal, this author's books are regularly nominated for top honors in the romance, mystery, and thriller categories.

...for CHILLS

LITERARY MERIT ★

PROVOCATIVE 🔥

INFLUENTIAL !

INSPIRATIONAL 🕊

HUMOROUS 😄

BRAINY 💡

EASY READING ☂

PAGE TURNER 📖

CHALLENGING 👓

BATHROOM BOOK 🚽

FAMILY FRIENDLY 👪

MOVIE 🎥

320.

LITERARY MERIT

★

Annapurna by Maurice Herzog

Maurice Herzog led an expedition of French climbers to the 26,000-foot Himalayan peak in 1950. The story of the ascent with no map is spellbinding; the story of the five-week descent is a spine-chilling nightmare of avalanche, frostbite, and snow-blindness. Read it cocooned before a cozy fire. Later books (*True Summit* by David Roberts, for example) raise questions about Herzog's version of events.

321.

LITERARY MERIT

★ ★

Endurance: Shackleton's Incredible Voyage by Alfred Lansing

Alex Award 1999

In 1914, Shackleton and his crew set off for Antarctica aboard the *Endurance*. A year later, their boat was trapped in ice and eventually crushed. Through the diaries of team members and interviews with survivors, Lansing tells the harrowing account of five months on drifting pack ice before setting sail in one of the ship's lifeboats. Amazingly, not one of Shackleton's 27 men was lost.

322.

LITERARY MERIT

★ ★ ★

The Ice Storm by Rick Moody

An affluent New England family falls apart in this novel. They share more than a fence with their neighbors, as the father pursues an affair with his neighbor's wife. Meanwhile, the kids are experimenting with drugs, alcohol, and sex. An apocalyptical winter storm approaches as tragic events unfold. This is a vivid portrait of '70s suburbia.

323.

LITERARY MERIT

★ ★ ★ ★

In Cold Blood by Truman Capote

The village of Holcomb, "on the high wheat plains of western Kansas, a lonesome area that other Kansans call 'out there,'" was the real-life setting for the brutal murder of the Clutter family. The flamboyant Capote journeyed to the town with the more outwardly conventional Harper Lee, and spent time there researching this crime. He wormed his charming way into the head of killer Perry Smith who told him: "I really admired Mr. Clutter, right up until the moment I slit his throat." Immersing himself in the setting, Capote pushed the bounds of journalism. Dramatizing the lives of real people, he pushed the bounds of nonfiction.

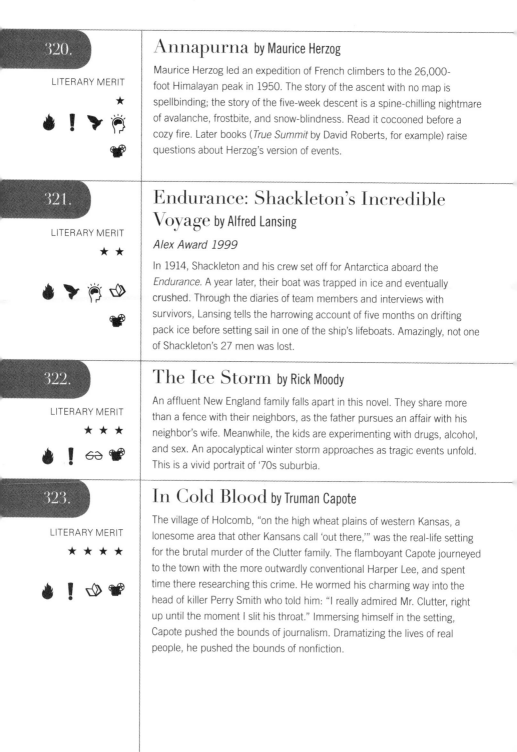

Into Thin Air: A Personal Account of the Mt. Everest Disaster by Jon Krakauer

LITERARY MERIT

★ ★

Alex Award 1998

Krakauer survived a 1996 expedition up Mount Everest in which eleven climbers died. Rob Hall, the leader of the Adventure Consultants expedition, had bragged that he could get almost any reasonably fit person to the summit. Even routine climbing in the "death zone" sounds like a version of hell: bone-chilling cold by night, blinding, skin-burning solar radiation by day, coupled with the risks of high-altitude pulmonary and cerebral edema. Engaging, thought-provoking, *Time* magazine named this a 1998 "Book of the Year."

Smilla's Sense of Snow by Peter Hoeg

LITERARY MERIT

★ ★ ★

The novel begins with a trail of small footprints in snow, leading off the edge of a rooftop. Smilla Jaspersen, half Danish, half Greenlander, investigates the

Department of Great Opening Lines

"It's freezing—an extraordinary 0° Fahrenheit—and it's snowing, and in the language that is no longer mine, the snow is qanik—big, almost weightless crystals falling in clumps and covering the ground with a layer of pulverized white frost."
—*Smilla's Sense of Snow*

boy who plunged to his death. Her journey takes her from the dark streets of Copenhagen to an icebreaker off Greenland's icy coast. Who knew the physics of icebergs could be so fascinating? With this breakout book, Hoeg won the 1992 Glass Key Award from the Crime Writers of Scandinavia.

Touching the Void by Joe Simpson

LITERARY MERIT

★ ★

This is the true story of British climbers Simpson and Simon Yates's ill-fated attempt to climb Siula Grande in the Peruvian Andes in 1985. They were the first to ascend via the nearly vertical icy west face. It was on the descent where they ran into trouble. Even for readers who have no desire to climb a glacier, this is a riveting (if excruciating) read.

327.

LITERARY MERIT

★ ★

Winterdance: The Fine Madness of Running the Iditarod by Gary Paulsen

When Paulsen first contemplated the 1,180-mile race by dogsled across Alaska from Anchorage to Nome, he was just a guy living in Minnesota who liked to hunt with his dogs. He writes of the training it took to prepare, and of a grueling 17-day race during which he braved moose attacks, frostbite, wind so fierce it blew his eyelids open and blinded his eyes with snow, and cold so intense that it wasn't possible to strike a match. Written with clarity and great humor.

Quiz Time!
Match the mountains to their books.

1. Himalayas   **a.** *Into Thin Air*
2. Mount Everest   **b.** *Annapurna*
3. Peruvian Andes   **c.** *Touching the Void*

Answers: 1-b, 2-a, 3-c

...for Intrigue

LITERARY MERIT	★
PROVOCATIVE	
INFLUENTIAL	!
INSPIRATIONAL	
HUMOROUS	
BRAINY	
EASY READING	
PAGE TURNER	
CHALLENGING	
BATHROOM BOOK	
FAMILY FRIENDLY	
MOVIE	

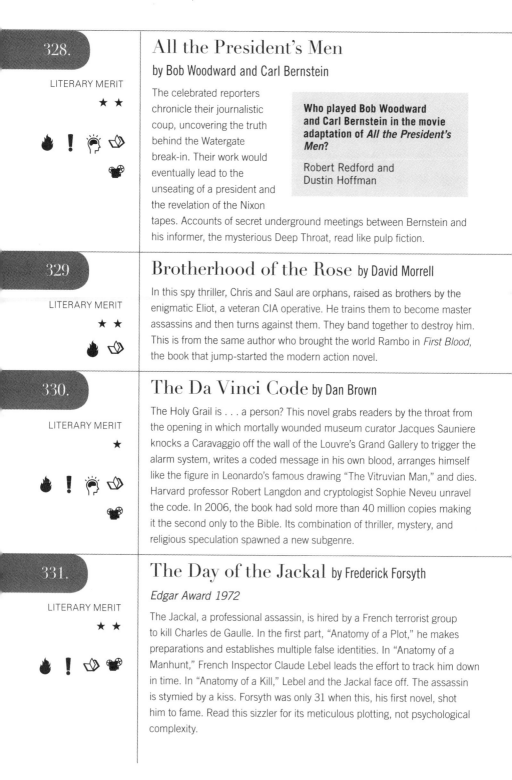

328.

LITERARY MERIT

★ ★

All the President's Men
by Bob Woodward and Carl Bernstein

The celebrated reporters chronicle their journalistic coup, uncovering the truth behind the Watergate break-in. Their work would eventually lead to the unseating of a president and the revelation of the Nixon tapes. Accounts of secret underground meetings between Bernstein and his informer, the mysterious Deep Throat, read like pulp fiction.

> **Who played Bob Woodward and Carl Bernstein in the movie adaptation of *All the President's Men*?**
>
> Robert Redford and Dustin Hoffman

329

LITERARY MERIT

★ ★

Brotherhood of the Rose by David Morrell

In this spy thriller, Chris and Saul are orphans, raised as brothers by the enigmatic Eliot, a veteran CIA operative. He trains them to become master assassins and then turns against them. They band together to destroy him. This is from the same author who brought the world Rambo in *First Blood*, the book that jump-started the modern action novel.

330.

LITERARY MERIT

★

The Da Vinci Code by Dan Brown

The Holy Grail is . . . a person? This novel grabs readers by the throat from the opening in which mortally wounded museum curator Jacques Sauniere knocks a Caravaggio off the wall of the Louvre's Grand Gallery to trigger the alarm system, writes a coded message in his own blood, arranges himself like the figure in Leonardo's famous drawing "The Vitruvian Man," and dies. Harvard professor Robert Langdon and cryptologist Sophie Neveu unravel the code. In 2006, the book had sold more than 40 million copies making it the second only to the Bible. Its combination of thriller, mystery, and religious speculation spawned a new subgenre.

331.

LITERARY MERIT

★ ★

The Day of the Jackal by Frederick Forsyth

Edgar Award 1972

The Jackal, a professional assassin, is hired by a French terrorist group to kill Charles de Gaulle. In the first part, "Anatomy of a Plot," he makes preparations and establishes multiple false identities. In "Anatomy of a Manhunt," French Inspector Claude Lebel leads the effort to track him down in time. In "Anatomy of a Kill," Lebel and the Jackal face off. The assassin is stymied by a kiss. Forsyth was only 31 when this, his first novel, shot him to fame. Read this sizzler for its meticulous plotting, not psychological complexity.

The Faithful Spy by Alex Berenson

332.

LITERARY MERIT

★ ★

Edgar Award 2006
Fast-forward three-plus decades from *The Day of the Jackal* and this
espionage novel is loaded with psychological complexity. John Wells is an
undercover CIA agent who infiltrated al-Qaeda in Afghanistan and converted
to Islam. Al-Qaeda sends him back to the United States on a terror mission.
Berenson gives us an eye-opening image of America, through the eyes of an
outsider.

The Good Soldier by Ford Madox Ford

333.

LITERARY MERIT

★ ★

Set just before World War I and published in 1915, this is the story of two
couples. Its tale of deceit and philandering is told by one of the husbands,
a profoundly unreliable narrator. It starts sad and ends even sadder as it
explores the boundary between reality and appearance. John Le Carré calls
this one of the finest, though neglected, novels of the twentieth century.

Gorky Park by Martin Cruz Smith

334.

LITERARY MERIT

★ ★ ★

Set in Cold War Moscow, the novel opens with an unforgettable image: "They
lay peacefully, even artfully, under their thawing crust of ice, the center one on
its back, hands folded as if for a religious funeral, the other two turned, arms
out under the ice like flanking emblems on embossed paper." All three victims
have been shot and had their faces and fingertips removed. Arkady Renko,
the taciturn homicide detective, must battle KGB, FBI, and New York police
to identify the victims and find the murderer. Critics compare Cruz Smith's
dense, atmospheric, carefully plotted thriller to the work of John Le Carré.

The Last Spymaster by Gayle Lynds

335.

LITERARY MERIT

★

For his latest trick, the legendary "last spymaster" and traitor Charles Jay Tice
escapes from his supposedly inescapable prison cell where he's serving a
life sentence. CIA hunter Elaine Cunningham tries to find out how and why,
and gets sucked into a world in which nothing is as it seems and no one can
be trusted. Lynds writes slam-bang action, and then more action, and then
more. This one was named "Novel of the Year" by the Military Writers Society
of America.

336.

LITERARY MERIT

★ ★

The Pelican Brief by John Grisham

Two Supreme Court Justices are assassinated and Tulane University law student Darby Shaw thinks she knows why. She compiles a brief outlining her conclusions, shares it with the wrong person, and soon she's running for her life. Grisham is a modern master of the intricately plotted legal thriller. In a 1998 profile, *Publishers Weekly* declared him "the bestselling novelist of the '90s." Like many of his other works, this one is un-putdownable.

337.

LITERARY MERIT

★ ★ ★

The Thirty-Nine Steps by John Buchan

Look in the rearview mirror of James Bond's Aston Martin and you'll see, fading in the distance, Richard Hannay, the mining engineer/British spy of *The Thirty-Nine Steps*. In this novel, Hannay meets an American journalist who tells of an international assassination plan. When the journalist is murdered and Hannay becomes the prime suspect, he realizes that only he can save the nation. Some of the plotting defies logic, and there's a nasty tinge of anti-Semitism, but this remains a fascinating period piece. Hitchcock made a memorable version of this for the screen in 1935.

338.

LITERARY MERIT

★ ★ ★

Tinker, Tailor, Soldier, Spy by John Le Carré

George Smiley is the anti-James Bond—middle-aged, shy, mild-mannered, and a genius at bureaucratic maneuvering. He's lured from retirement to work for M16 (the "Circus") to identify and destroy a double agent who has infiltrated the top echelons of British intelligence. This is considered a modern masterpiece—a spy novel populated by thoroughly human characters. Find out why "character-driven thriller" isn't necessarily an oxymoron.

> **Department of Memorable Characters**
>
> "Small, podgy, and at best middle-aged, he was by appearance one of London's meek who do not inherit the earth."—George Smiley, *Tinker, Tailor, Soldier, Spy*

339.

LITERARY MERIT

★ ★ ★

The Untouchable by John Banville

Through fictional journal entries, Irish novelist Banville re-imagines the adventures of Anthony Blunt, a distinguished English art historian, art curator, and real-life spymaster. Blunt worked for the Kremlin from the 1930s to the 1960s. Unmasked and publicly disgraced in 1979, he died of a heart attack in 1983. In the novel, Blunt is Victor Maskell, an aloof cynic and Soviet spy who thinks "Man is only loveable in the multitude and at a good distance." Fact and fiction do an intricate dance in this satisfying and thoroughly literary thriller.

...for THEATRICS

LITERARY MERIT ★

PROVOCATIVE 🔥

INFLUENTIAL !

INSPIRATIONAL 🕊

HUMOROUS 😄

BRAINY 💡

EASY READING ☂

PAGE TURNER 📖

CHALLENGING 👓

BATHROOM BOOK 🚽

FAMILY FRIENDLY 👪

MOVIE 🎥

340.

LITERARY MERIT

★ ★

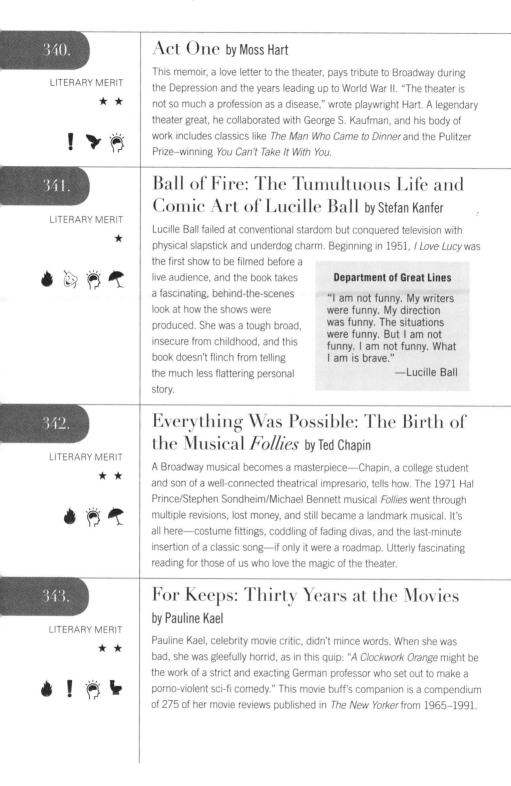

Act One by Moss Hart

This memoir, a love letter to the theater, pays tribute to Broadway during the Depression and the years leading up to World War II. "The theater is not so much a profession as a disease," wrote playwright Hart. A legendary theater great, he collaborated with George S. Kaufman, and his body of work includes classics like *The Man Who Came to Dinner* and the Pulitzer Prize–winning *You Can't Take It With You.*

341.

LITERARY MERIT

★

Ball of Fire: The Tumultuous Life and Comic Art of Lucille Ball by Stefan Kanfer

Lucille Ball failed at conventional stardom but conquered television with physical slapstick and underdog charm. Beginning in 1951, *I Love Lucy* was the first show to be filmed before a live audience, and the book takes a fascinating, behind-the-scenes look at how the shows were produced. She was a tough broad, insecure from childhood, and this book doesn't flinch from telling the much less flattering personal story.

Department of Great Lines

"I am not funny. My writers were funny. My direction was funny. The situations were funny. But I am not funny. I am not funny. What I am is brave."

—Lucille Ball

342.

LITERARY MERIT

★ ★

Everything Was Possible: The Birth of the Musical *Follies* by Ted Chapin

A Broadway musical becomes a masterpiece—Chapin, a college student and son of a well-connected theatrical impresario, tells how. The 1971 Hal Prince/Stephen Sondheim/Michael Bennett musical *Follies* went through multiple revisions, lost money, and still became a landmark musical. It's all here—costume fittings, coddling of fading divas, and the last-minute insertion of a classic song—if only it were a roadmap. Utterly fascinating reading for those of us who love the magic of the theater.

343.

LITERARY MERIT

★ ★

For Keeps: Thirty Years at the Movies
by Pauline Kael

Pauline Kael, celebrity movie critic, didn't mince words. When she was bad, she was gleefully horrid, as in this quip: "*A Clockwork Orange* might be the work of a strict and exacting German professor who set out to make a porno-violent sci-fi comedy." This movie buff's companion is a compendium of 275 of her movie reviews published in *The New Yorker* from 1965–1991.

The Ghost Light by Frank Rich

344.

An anxious, unhappy kid, marooned in a DC suburb, grows up to become the drama critic for the *New York Times*. This memoir focuses on his initiation as a young and naive viewer. He writes about the magic of watching lives acted out on stage and the thrill of being among the first to witness the creation of art.

Did You Know It Means . . .

Ghost light: According to theater superstition, a single bulb must be left burning onstage in an empty, dark house to prevent a ghost from moving in.

LITERARY MERIT

★ ★ ★

Hitchcock by Helen G. Scott and Francois Truffaut

345.

In the late 1960s the great young French film director Truffaut interviewed the usually private Hitchcock (Truffaut addressed him as "Mr. Hitchcock"). In this extended conversation, Hitchcock reflects on his childhood and Catholic upbringing that resulted in his "fear of being involved in anything evil." He talks about each of his films, the successful and the not so successful, and how he uses the camera and light to caress his actors and manipulate his audience. For every cinemaphile.

LITERARY MERIT

★ ★

Kate: The Woman Who Was Hepburn
by William J. Mann

346.

There have been many books about Hepburn, whose extraordinary career spanned seven decades, but this one is meticulously detailed and reveals the woman behind the façade. Mann writes, "The brilliance and singular devotion she gave to the creation and maintenance of her public image should inspire awe—especially when one sees all that went on behind it."

Who made this dramatic line famous? "The calla lilies are in bloom again."

Katherine Hepburn in *Stage Door*

LITERARY MERIT

★ ★

Lauren Bacall: By Myself by Lauren Bacall
National Book Award, 1980

"You know how to whistle, don't you, Steve?" Bacall was only nineteen in 1944 when she delivered that famous line in her first film, *To Have and Have Not*. By then she was already a successful model who had graced the cover of *Harper's Bazaar*. "Steve" was Humphrey Bogart. Bacall wrote this funny, vital, straightforward memoir in 1978.

347.

LITERARY MERIT

★ ★

348.

LITERARY MERIT

★

My Life in Art by Konstantin Stanislavsky

In this fascinating autobiography published in 1924, Stanislavsky says, "On the dramatic stage it is also necessary to know how to act differently from life on every portion of the stage, so that truth may pass over the footlights." In service of that truth, he rebelled against the stylized theater of the nineteenth century and founded the Moscow Art Theatre. This book provides an excellent introduction to his "method" taught to generations of actors.

> **Department of Great Lines**
>
> "There are no small parts, only small actors."
> —*My Life in Art*

349.

LITERARY MERIT

★ ★ ★

Profiles by Kenneth Tynan

This collection of fifty profiles from the most celebrated British theater critic of our time spans thirty years. With typical wit, Tynan sized up Orson Welles: "A superb bravura director, a fair bravura actor and a limited bravura writer; but an incomparable bravura personality." What Pauline Kael was to movies, Tynan was to the theater.

350.

LITERARY MERIT

★ ★ ★

Show Boat by Edna Ferber

None of its screen or stage adaptations truly capture this sprawling, colorful, heartbreaking novel of riverboat life, first published in 1926, and its courageous handling of the stigma of miscegenation. A defining moment is when Steve Baker, the white husband of biracial Julie Dozier, draws blood from her finger and then sucks it so that he too "becomes black" according to the "one-drop" rule.

351.

LITERARY MERIT

★

Scorsese on Scorsese by David Thomson

Thomson turned on the tape and just let it run. In an extended interview, Scorsese takes us from his childhood in Little Italy, through his developing sensibility as an artist, to his career and intense, often violent, always compelling style of filmmaking. Among the revelations: "Seeing *Citizen Kane* about the age of fourteen or fifteen . . . . made me aware for the first time of what a director did." Insight after insight for fans of this master of cinematic violence.

Tab Hunter Confidential by Tab Hunter

Hunter was molded by impresario Henry Willson into "The Sigh Guy," the handsome, studly reigning hunk of the 1950s. He was number-one in the movie theaters and on the pop charts, and his romance with Natalie Wood was concocted to hype his image. By 1959 he was on his way into eclipse with Troy Donahue in the ascendant. Written at the age of 74, after coming back and coming out, Hunter looks back with candor and wit.

352.

LITERARY MERIT

★

Tallulah: My Autobiography by Tallulah Bankhead

Her father was a U.S. congressman and her grandfather was a senator, but even that plus years in a convent school and lessons in how to be a southern belle couldn't tame her. Tallulah, a huge screen and legitimate stage star, was known as much for her recklessness and outrageous behavior as for her talent and wit. Read her version of filming one of her most famous movies, Alfred Hitchcock's *Lifeboat*, in which the entire action was confined to a 40-foot lifeboat and was filmed in the studio with Miss Bankhead wearing a mink coat. First published in 1952, she leaves us with our mouths gaping.

353.

LITERARY MERIT

★

True and False: Heresy and Common Sense for the Actor by David Mamet

The book contains a series of bracing, common-sense essays. Acting, according to the much-lauded playwright, ultimately relies on action. Forget the "method" of Stanislavsky. Learn your lines, hit your marks, speak up and speak clearly, and interact with the other characters on the stage. Repeat until mastered.

354.

LITERARY MERIT

★

Will in the World: How Shakespeare Became Shakespeare by Stephen Greenblatt

Greenblatt sets the life of young Will Shakespeare against the religion, politics, and society of Elizabethan times. Historical fact and material from the plays and sonnets are used to weave a tapestry of an enigmatic artist's life. This book, which was a finalist for the National Book Award, humanizes the myth.

355.

LITERARY MERIT

★ ★ ★ ★

...to Play the Game

LITERARY MERIT ★

PROVOCATIVE 🔥

INFLUENTIAL !

INSPIRATIONAL 🕊

HUMOROUS 😂

BRAINY 🧠

EASY READING ☂

PAGE TURNER 📖

CHALLENGING 👓

BATHROOM BOOK 🚽

FAMILY FRIENDLY 👪

MOVIE 🎥

356.

LITERARY MERIT

★ ★

About Three Bricks Shy . . . And the Load Filled Up by Roy Blount Jr.

In 1973, the Pittsburgh Steelers missed the bowl but were poised to dominate the NFL for years to come. *Sports Illustrated* writer and humorist Roy Blount Jr. spent the season with the team. He takes the reader inside—the players' homes, their bawdy humor, their psychology of aggression—as he explores the brutality and subtlety of the game.

The Author Explains the Title

"Craig Hanneman, a nose guard/defensive tackle out of Oregon State, told me that the guys on that team 'were crazy . . . so crazy that they were about three bricks shy of a load.' So, it was an apt title for [the book] because everyone was so eccentric on that team."

—Roy Blount Jr.

357.

LITERARY MERIT

★ ★

Big Game, Small World: A Basketball Adventure by Alexander Wolff

Another *Sports Illustrated* writer, Wolff spent a year traveling the world, chasing basketball. He visited sixteen different countries and ten states. In Bhutan, he visits the king with his own private basketball tutor. In Ontario, Canada, he visits a museum devoted to James Naismith, the inventor of the game. Just in case you thought basketball was a uniquely American sport.

358.

LITERARY MERIT

★ ★

The Blind Side: Evolution of a Game
by Michael Lewis

Alex Award 2007

Quiet sixteen-year-old Michael Oher, a 6'5", 330-odd pound mountain of a teenager, was struggling through Briarcrest Christian School in Memphis when he caught the attention of Sean Tuohy, a self-made millionaire and former star point-guard for Ole Miss. Tuohy recognized the makings of a perfect offensive left tackle, the pivotal position on a football team. More than a Cinderella story, this book deconstructs the game.

359.

LITERARY MERIT

★ ★ ★

End Zone by Don DeLillo

This 1970s comic literary novel set at "Logos College" in west Texas, inspired critical accolades. The *New York Times* compared it to "the fortuitous encounter of a football team and a poet on a rubdown table." On one level it's the story of a mouthy football-playing college kid; on another, it's about nuclear warfare and racism.

Friday Night Lights: A Town, a Team, and a Dream by H. G. Bissinger

360.

LITERARY MERIT

★ ★

Pulitzer-prize winning journalist Bissinger left his job at the *Philadelphia Inquirer* and spent 1988 in Odessa, Texas, a dying town obsessed with football. Odessa's Permian Panthers were in the running for the state championship. This is a book about a town's obsession with a team, and a chilling indictment of America's willingness to win at any cost.

Games People Play by Eric Berne, M.D.

361.

LITERARY MERIT

★

And then there are the games of life. Berne named and categorized them. There's blame games like "See What You Made Me Do," marital games like "If It Weren't For You," sexual games like "Perversion," and more. This pop psychology book lays out the basics of transactional analysis. It was a very big deal when it first appeared in 1965, back in the day when talk therapy ruled.

The Golf Omnibus by P. G. Wodehouse

362.

LITERARY MERIT

★ ★ ★

From the bloke who brought the world Jeeves and loved taking potshots at Britain's upper "clawses," this collection of thirty-one stories contains many holes-in-one. Wodehouse was, after all, from Scotland, a country that's mad about golf, though reputedly he was terrible at it. There's much inspired silliness, as when beautiful Celia tries to murder George Mackintosh with her niblick.

A Good Walk Spoiled: Days and Nights on the PGA Tour by John Feinstein

363.

LITERARY MERIT

★ ★

Washington Post sports reporter Feinstein went on the 1994 PGA Tour. He relates the experiences of stars like Greg Norman and Nick Price, and of non-stars for whom there's no salary, no guaranteed appearance fee, and lots of expenses. Even "the greatest players alive wake up most mornings having no idea whether the day will produce a 65 or a 75." This won the 1995 British William Hill Sports Book of the Year Award.

Harvey Penick's Little Red Book
by Harvey Penick with Bud Shrake

364.

LITERARY MERIT

★ ★

This is a compendium of anecdotes and tips from a legendary golf instructor. From the hand position to the grip to the swing, Shrake doesn't pretend it's science. On the waggle: "I think the main value of the waggle is that it turns on your juice and gets your adrenaline flowing." This little book of wisdom is one of the bestselling sports books ever.

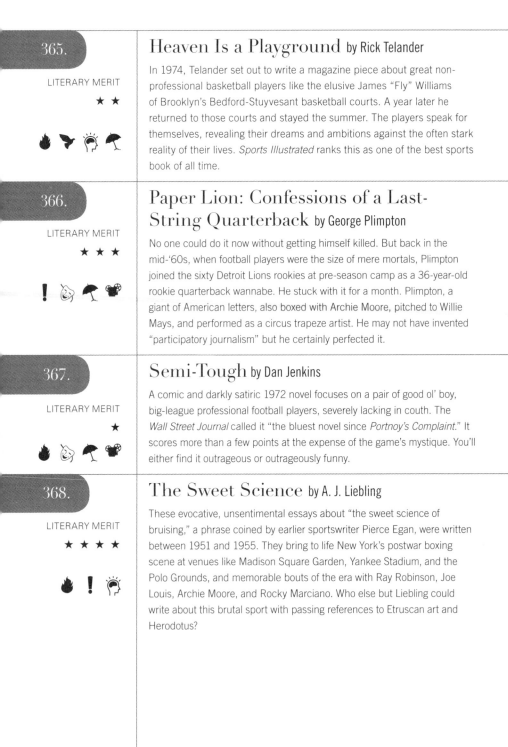

365.

LITERARY MERIT

★ ★

Heaven Is a Playground by Rick Telander

In 1974, Telander set out to write a magazine piece about great non-professional basketball players like the elusive James "Fly" Williams of Brooklyn's Bedford-Stuyvesant basketball courts. A year later he returned to those courts and stayed the summer. The players speak for themselves, revealing their dreams and ambitions against the often stark reality of their lives. *Sports Illustrated* ranks this as one of the best sports book of all time.

366.

LITERARY MERIT

★ ★ ★

Paper Lion: Confessions of a Last-String Quarterback by George Plimpton

No one could do it now without getting himself killed. But back in the mid-'60s, when football players were the size of mere mortals, Plimpton joined the sixty Detroit Lions rookies at pre-season camp as a 36-year-old rookie quarterback wannabe. He stuck with it for a month. Plimpton, a giant of American letters, also boxed with Archie Moore, pitched to Willie Mays, and performed as a circus trapeze artist. He may not have invented "participatory journalism" but he certainly perfected it.

367.

LITERARY MERIT

★

Semi-Tough by Dan Jenkins

A comic and darkly satiric 1972 novel focuses on a pair of good ol' boy, big-league professional football players, severely lacking in couth. The *Wall Street Journal* called it "the bluest novel since *Portnoy's Complaint*." It scores more than a few points at the expense of the game's mystique. You'll either find it outrageous or outrageously funny.

368.

LITERARY MERIT

★ ★ ★ ★

The Sweet Science by A. J. Liebling

These evocative, unsentimental essays about "the sweet science of bruising," a phrase coined by earlier sportswriter Pierce Egan, were written between 1951 and 1955. They bring to life New York's postwar boxing scene at venues like Madison Square Garden, Yankee Stadium, and the Polo Grounds, and memorable bouts of the era with Ray Robinson, Joe Louis, Archie Moore, and Rocky Marciano. Who else but Liebling could write about this brutal sport with passing references to Etruscan art and Herodotus?

...for a *Musical Interlude*

LITERARY MERIT ★

PROVOCATIVE 🔥

INFLUENTIAL !

INSPIRATIONAL 🕊

HUMOROUS 😄

BRAINY 💡

EASY READING ☂

PAGE TURNER 📖

CHALLENGING 👓

BATHROOM BOOK 🚽

FAMILY FRIENDLY 👪

MOVIE 🎥

369.

LITERARY MERIT

★ ★ ★ ★

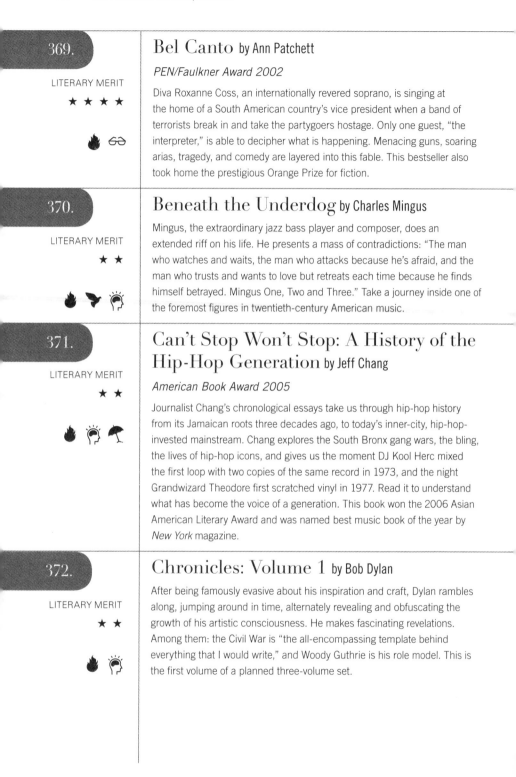

Bel Canto by Ann Patchett

PEN/Faulkner Award 2002

Diva Roxanne Coss, an internationally revered soprano, is singing at the home of a South American country's vice president when a band of terrorists break in and take the partygoers hostage. Only one guest, "the interpreter," is able to decipher what is happening. Menacing guns, soaring arias, tragedy, and comedy are layered into this fable. This bestseller also took home the prestigious Orange Prize for fiction.

370.

LITERARY MERIT

★ ★

Beneath the Underdog by Charles Mingus

Mingus, the extraordinary jazz bass player and composer, does an extended riff on his life. He presents a mass of contradictions: "The man who watches and waits, the man who attacks because he's afraid, and the man who trusts and wants to love but retreats each time because he finds himself betrayed. Mingus One, Two and Three." Take a journey inside one of the foremost figures in twentieth-century American music.

371.

LITERARY MERIT

★ ★

Can't Stop Won't Stop: A History of the Hip-Hop Generation by Jeff Chang

American Book Award 2005

Journalist Chang's chronological essays take us through hip-hop history from its Jamaican roots three decades ago, to today's inner-city, hip-hop-invested mainstream. Chang explores the South Bronx gang wars, the bling, the lives of hip-hop icons, and gives us the moment DJ Kool Herc mixed the first loop with two copies of the same record in 1973, and the night Grandwizard Theodore first scratched vinyl in 1977. Read it to understand what has become the voice of a generation. This book won the 2006 Asian American Literary Award and was named best music book of the year by *New York* magazine.

372.

LITERARY MERIT

★ ★

Chronicles: Volume 1 by Bob Dylan

After being famously evasive about his inspiration and craft, Dylan rambles along, jumping around in time, alternately revealing and obfuscating the growth of his artistic consciousness. He makes fascinating revelations. Among them: the Civil War is "the all-encompassing template behind everything that I would write," and Woody Guthrie is his role model. This is the first volume of a planned three-volume set.

Devil's Dream by Lee Smith

373.

This fictionalized portrait of the roots of country music tells of four generations of Baileys, echoing the history of the Carter music dynasty, all of them God-fearing and passionate about country music. The story begins at a Christmas family reunion at the Opryland Hotel. Smith tells the family saga while tracing the country music back to primitive Baptist hymns and fiddle-playing, in gospel and on to rockabilly and contemporary country western. *Publishers Weekly* called this a "rollicking hillbilly saga."

LITERARY MERIT

★ ★

The Land Where the Blues Began

by Alan Lomax

374.

National Book Critics Circle 1993

Armed with a tape recorder and thousands of questions, Lomax and his father searched the Mississippi Delta in the 1940s for the beginnings of American Blues. Legendary figures, they founded the Archive of American Folk Song at the Library of Congress and preserved the recordings of blues icons like Leadbelly, Woody Guthrie, and Jelly Roll Morton. Lomax captures the call and response of spirituals, sermons, blues, play songs, and work songs. Fire up the Victrola and listen while you read Lomax conjuring the sounds of music's storied past.

LITERARY MERIT

★ ★ ★

The Mambo Kings Play Songs of Love

by Oscar Hijuelos

375.

Pulitzer 1990

Triumphs and tragedies play out in this novel set against the backdrop of émigré Cuban life. Cesar and Nestor Castillo, Cuban-born musicians, form a band in New York. They play dance halls, nightclubs, and quince parties, and appear on an *I Love Lucy* episode playing Ricky's cousins. These colorful, flawed heroes are loaded with musical talent, Latin melancholy, and a consuming interest in sex. Hijuelos was the first Hispanic writer to win the Pulitzer for fiction.

LITERARY MERIT

★ ★ ★ ★

Music Is My Mistress by Duke Ellington

376.

This memoir of the jazz great contains prose that is nearly as lush as his compositions. Writing of New York, he said: "Night Life is cut out of a very luxurious, royal-blue bolt of velvet. It sparkles with jewels, and it sparkles in tingling and tinkling tones." Some would say that Ellington himself was cut from the same cloth.

LITERARY MERIT

★ ★

377.

LITERARY MERIT

★ ★

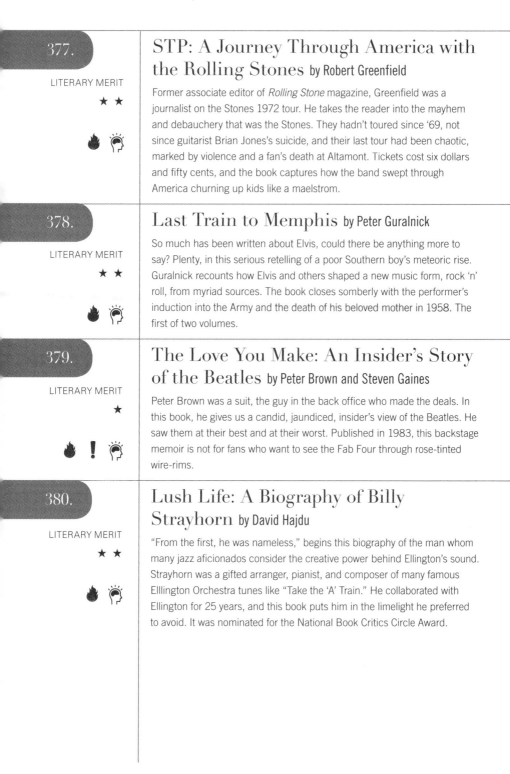

STP: A Journey Through America with the Rolling Stones by Robert Greenfield

Former associate editor of *Rolling Stone* magazine, Greenfield was a journalist on the Stones 1972 tour. He takes the reader into the mayhem and debauchery that was the Stones. They hadn't toured since '69, not since guitarist Brian Jones's suicide, and their last tour had been chaotic, marked by violence and a fan's death at Altamont. Tickets cost six dollars and fifty cents, and the book captures how the band swept through America churning up kids like a maelstrom.

378.

LITERARY MERIT

★ ★

Last Train to Memphis by Peter Guralnick

So much has been written about Elvis, could there be anything more to say? Plenty, in this serious retelling of a poor Southern boy's meteoric rise. Guralnick recounts how Elvis and others shaped a new music form, rock 'n' roll, from myriad sources. The book closes somberly with the performer's induction into the Army and the death of his beloved mother in 1958. The first of two volumes.

379.

LITERARY MERIT

★

The Love You Make: An Insider's Story of the Beatles by Peter Brown and Steven Gaines

Peter Brown was a suit, the guy in the back office who made the deals. In this book, he gives us a candid, jaundiced, insider's view of the Beatles. He saw them at their best and at their worst. Published in 1983, this backstage memoir is not for fans who want to see the Fab Four through rose-tinted wire-rims.

380.

LITERARY MERIT

★ ★

Lush Life: A Biography of Billy Strayhorn by David Hajdu

"From the first, he was nameless," begins this biography of the man whom many jazz aficionados consider the creative power behind Ellington's sound. Strayhorn was a gifted arranger, pianist, and composer of many famous Elllington Orchestra tunes like "Take the 'A' Train." He collaborated with Ellington for 25 years, and this book puts him in the limelight he preferred to avoid. It was nominated for the National Book Critics Circle Award.

Pet Sounds (33 1/3) by Jim Fusilli

This slim volume—part biography, part autobiography—explores the beauty and the despair behind the pop sounds of Brian Wilson and the Beach Boys in their seminal work *Pet Sounds*. "All the songs are personal statements about love, about what it means and where it fits in a man's life—whether it defines a man's life and what happens when love goes." Fusilli, music critic for the *Wall Street Journal*, gives the Beach Boys' music the empathy and attention it deserves.

381.

LITERARY MERIT

★ ★

This Is Your Brain on Music by Daniel J. Levitin

Eating chocolate, experiencing an orgasm, and listening to music release the same chemicals that stimulate the brain. As a rock producer, Levitin can tell you all about recording sessions and how sounds are committed to tape. But as a neuroscientist, he can also examine why music makes the spirit soar. What other book can boast blurbs from both Oliver Sacks and Stevie Wonder? It was a finalist for the 2006 Los Angeles Times' Book Prize.

Department of Great Lines

"Does our innate love of music serve an evolutionary purpose? You decide. In *This Is Your Brain on Music*, Daniel Levitin reveals research that shows that if women could choose whom they'd like to be impregnated by, they'd choose a rock star."

—*This Is Your Brain on Music*

382.

LITERARY MERIT

★ ★

White Bicycles: Making Music in the 1960s by Joe Boyd

Barely out of college in 1965, Boyd was stage manager for the Newport Folk Festival where Bob Dylan played his groundbreaking electric set. In London, Boyd was one of the founders of the UFO club, at Britain's Fillmore. He booked early shows by Pink Floyd and the Soft Machine. This autobiography is a clear, lucid account of an insider's trip (he didn't do the drugs). He traces his music life through jazz, blues, folk, and rock. The CD of musical accompaniment to this book won best compilation of the year at the Mojo awards.

The Author Explains the Title

White bicycles were left throughout Amsterdam for free use by citizens. "In Amsterdam almost all the white bicycles by the end of 1967 had been stolen and repainted. So white bicycles became a kind of symbol of the spirit of that age, and that inevitable doom for that innocence and naïveté."

—Joe Boyd

383.

LITERARY MERIT

★ ★

384.

LITERARY MERIT

★ ★

Woody Guthrie: A Life by Joe Klein

This is the authorized biography of the legendary folk singer and composer/political radical whose body of work includes "Hard Travelin" and "This Land Is Your Land." His life was marked by tragedy and he died of a hereditary wasting disease, Huntington's Chorea. He influenced generations of musicians—like young Robert Zimmerman who remade himself in Woody's image and renamed himself Bob Dylan. This is an unsentimental account of the life of one of the great geniuses of our time. Klein, who would go on to become an award-winning journalist and bestselling political novelist, wrote this early in his career.

...for Romance

LITERARY MERIT ★

PROVOCATIVE 🔥

INFLUENTIAL ❗

INSPIRATIONAL 🕊

HUMOROUS 😄

BRAINY 💡

EASY READING ☂

PAGE TURNER 📖

CHALLENGING 👓

BATHROOM BOOK 🚽

FAMILY FRIENDLY 👪

MOVIE 🎥

385.

LITERARY MERIT

★ ★ ★

A Cup of Tea by Amy Ephron

It's New York, 1917, and on a dark rainy night, "A young woman stood under a street lamp." She's observed there by Rosemary Fells, a woman with great wealth and too much time on her hands, who takes pity on the creature and brings her in for a cup of hot tea. There, the street urchin, if that's what she is, exchanges a furtive look with Rosemary's handsome fiancé. It's the old "no good deed goes unpunished." The novel received a *Booklist* Best Fiction of the Year award in 2005.

386.

LITERARY MERIT

★ ★ ★ ★

The Blue Flower by Penelope Fitzgerald

National Book Critics Circle 1998

Long a favorite of British critics and writers, Fitzgerald became familiar to American readers with this novel. In it, Friederich "Fritz" von Hardenberg (based on a real historical figure) is a young man who will become a leading German Romantic poet of the eighteenth century. The novel imagines him in his twenties, as a university student, falling disastrously in love with a plain, simple, twelve-year-old girl. His family is shocked by his hopeless romanticism.

387.

LITERARY MERIT

★ ★

Dirty Girls Social Club
by Alisa Valdes-Rodriguez

"Twice a year, every year, the sucias show up," this novel begins. *Sucias* is Spanish for "dirty girls," and there are six of them, Latina women who became fast friends while students at Boston University. Now they're out in the world, looking for love and falling for losers. Lively and humorous, this is chick lit with characters that defy stereotypes.

388.

LITERARY MERIT

★ ★ ★ ★

The English Patient by Michael Ondaatje

Booker Prize 1992

The English patient is Count Ladislaus, a Hungarian explorer. In braided accounts, the novel tells of his love affair with the wife of another explorer, and of the grieving young Canadian nurse who later cares for him as he lies dying of burns sustained in a plane crash. As she pours calamine over his chest, he whispers to her and drags "the listening heart of the young nurse beside him to wherever his mind is, into that well of memory he kept plunging into during the months before he died."

The Great Fire by Shirley Hazzard

National Book Award 2003

Love in a time of chaos. The "great fire" of the title is World War II, and the story is set in its aftermath. War hero Alfred Leith walks across China to discover the effects of the war. He comes to Japan to see the aftermath of the atomic bomb, and there he is smitten by seventeen-year-old Helen, a "little mermaid" of a girl, who has nursed her older brother Benedict through debilitating illness. This novel wanders back and forth in time. Reviewers proclaim it a masterpiece, a "tapestry in clear and elegant prose."

389.

LITERARY MERIT

★ ★ ★ ★

I Capture the Castle by Dodie Smith

390.

LITERARY MERIT

★ ★ ★

Romance is all in your viewpoint, as seventeen-year-old Cassandra Mortmain, daughter of a famous writer with a

Department of Great Opening Lines

"I write this sitting in the kitchen sink."—*I Capture the Castle*

terminal case of writer's block, notes in her journal: "I have just remarked to Rose that our situation is really rather romantic, two girls in this strange and lonely house. She replied that she saw nothing romantic about being shut up in a crumbling ruin surrounded by a sea of mud." This delightful, enduring coming-of-age story with a charismatic narrator's voice was published in 1948 by the author who gave us *101 Dalmatians*.

Message in a Bottle by Nicholas Sparks

391.

LITERARY MERIT

★ ★

Theresa Osborne has given up on love. Three years after her divorce from a philandering husband, she's jogging on a Cape Cod beach and finds a bottle with a message in it. "I miss you my darling . . ." it begins, and is signed "Garret." Smitten by the romantic message, Theresa tracks Garret down. Complications ensue as the two try to unload old baggage. As with most love stories, this one deals in tragedy, too. When it came out, reviewers called it "this summer's *Bridges of Madison County*."

The Remains of the Day by Kazuo Ishiguro

392.

LITERARY MERIT

★ ★ ★ ★

Booker Prize 1989

The propriety-bound, emotionally repressed narrator of this novel is Mr. Stevens, venerable butler at Darlington Hall. He travels to the West Country on the pretext of persuading the former housekeeper to return. Though he's an expert on being a butler, he's clueless in affairs of his own heart and blind to his employer's imperfections. The writing is sublime. Before he became Hannibal Lecter to a generation of moviegoers, Anthony Hopkins gave a perfectly nuanced Oscar-nominated performance as Stevens in the movie version.

393.

LITERARY MERIT

★ ★ ★ ★

The Sea, The Sea by Iris Murdoch

Booker Prize 1978

Charles Arrowby, a great man of London's theater world, retires and sequesters himself at his seaside home on the South English coast. As he begins his memoir, intending to "abjure magic and become a hermit," he is haunted by a strange sea monster, obsessed by the woman who was his first love who happens to live in the nearby town, and visited by a steady stream of friends and former lovers. Considered the prolific British novelist's major work, read it to understand why her writing is held in such high esteem.

394.

LITERARY MERIT

★ ★ ★ ★

Sentimental Education: The Story of a Young Man by Gustave Flaubert

Passion for an older woman drives this last novel published in the great French novelist's lifetime. Set in Paris in the 1840s, law student Frederic Moreau becomes besotted by the beautiful Madame Arnoux. He befriends her husband so he can be near her. Written with Flaubert's signature irony and pessimism, the novel draws on his own experiences. This is considered the most influential French novel of the nineteenth century.

395.

LITERARY MERIT

★ ★

Waiting to Exhale by Terry McMillan

Four smart black women share a mutual obsession: men. They find them at leisure and get rid of them in style. Savannah Jackson says in her prayer, "Could you send me a decent man? Could he be full of zest, and please, a slow, tender, passionate lover—and could he already be what he aspired to?" This book spawned a whole subgenre of female-buddy fiction.

Quiz Time!

Match these characters who were oh-so-wrong for one another. Extra points if you know the novel!

1. Catherine Earnshaw
2. Mildred Rogers
3. Lydia Bennet
4. Scarlett O'Hara
5. Madame Arnoux

a. George Wickham
b. Edgar Linton
c. Ashley Wilkes
d. Frederic Moreau
e. Philip Carey

Answers: *1-b (*Wuthering Heights*); 2-e (*Of Human Bondage*); 3-a (*Pride and Prejudice*); 4-c (*Gone with the Wind*); 5-d (*Sentimental Education*)*

...*for* **Revenge**

LITERARY MERIT ★

PROVOCATIVE 🔥

INFLUENTIAL ❗

INSPIRATIONAL 🕊

HUMOROUS 😂

BRAINY 💡

EASY READING ☂

PAGE TURNER 📖

CHALLENGING 👓

BATHROOM BOOK 🚽

FAMILY FRIENDLY 👪

MOVIE 🎥

396.

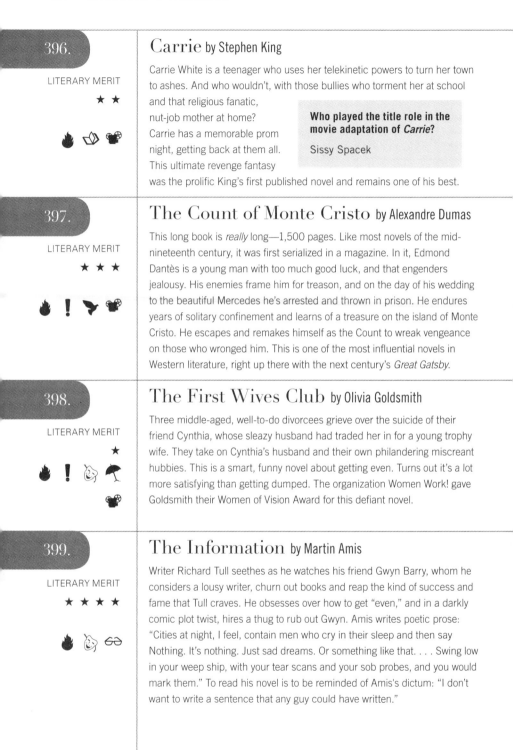

LITERARY MERIT

★ ★

Carrie by Stephen King

Carrie White is a teenager who uses her telekinetic powers to turn her town to ashes. And who wouldn't, with those bullies who torment her at school and that religious fanatic, nut-job mother at home? Carrie has a memorable prom night, getting back at them all. This ultimate revenge fantasy was the prolific King's first published novel and remains one of his best.

Who played the title role in the movie adaptation of *Carrie*?

Sissy Spacek

397.

LITERARY MERIT

★ ★ ★

The Count of Monte Cristo by Alexandre Dumas

This long book is *really* long—1,500 pages. Like most novels of the mid-nineteenth century, it was first serialized in a magazine. In it, Edmond Dantès is a young man with too much good luck, and that engenders jealousy. His enemies frame him for treason, and on the day of his wedding to the beautiful Mercedes he's arrested and thrown in prison. He endures years of solitary confinement and learns of a treasure on the island of Monte Cristo. He escapes and remakes himself as the Count to wreak vengeance on those who wronged him. This is one of the most influential novels in Western literature, right up there with the next century's *Great Gatsby*.

398.

LITERARY MERIT

★

The First Wives Club by Olivia Goldsmith

Three middle-aged, well-to-do divorcees grieve over the suicide of their friend Cynthia, whose sleazy husband had traded her in for a young trophy wife. They take on Cynthia's husband and their own philandering miscreant hubbies. This is a smart, funny novel about getting even. Turns out it's a lot more satisfying than getting dumped. The organization Women Work! gave Goldsmith their Women of Vision Award for this defiant novel.

399.

LITERARY MERIT

★ ★ ★ ★

The Information by Martin Amis

Writer Richard Tull seethes as he watches his friend Gwyn Barry, whom he considers a lousy writer, churn out books and reap the kind of success and fame that Tull craves. He obsesses over how to get "even," and in a darkly comic plot twist, hires a thug to rub out Gwyn. Amis writes poetic prose: "Cities at night, I feel, contain men who cry in their sleep and then say Nothing. It's nothing. Just sad dreams. Or something like that. . . . Swing low in your weep ship, with your tear scans and your sob probes, and you would mark them." To read his novel is to be reminded of Amis's dictum: "I don't want to write a sentence that any guy could have written."

Les Miserables by Victor Hugo

Played out against the backdrop of the Napoleonic wars, the story of Jean Valjean ties together plots and scores of vivid characters, many drawn from the desolate fringes of French society. Valjean is a starving orphan who steals a loaf of bread and gets caught. Sentenced to five years of hard labor, he tries to escape, only to have fourteen years added to his sentence. Released at last, in middle age, he is shunned and denied shelter. He is bent on wreaking revenge until he is taken in by the saintly bishop of Digne (Monsieur Bienvenu). Since it was first published in French in 1862, this 1,200-page morality play of revenge turned into redemption has captured generations.

400.

LITERARY MERIT

★ ★ ★ ★

The Life and Loves of a She-Devil
by Fay Weldon

401.

LITERARY MERIT

★ ★ ★

Ruth is fed up with her life. "I want revenge. I want power. I want money. I want to be loved and not love in return," she announces after her husband leaves her for a woman who is slender and beautiful. Ruth's weapon isn't so much magic as plastic surgery and malice with which she stirs up trouble in her ex's life. This biting satire was published in 1983, years before reality TV was invented and shows like *The Swan* made this British feminist author look clairvoyant. Hard to believe, this is the same author who wrote the first episode of the BBC's *Upstairs, Downstairs*.

Department of Great Characters

"I am six feet two inches tall, which is fine for a man but not for a woman. I . . . have one of those jutting jaws that tall, dark women often have, and eyes sunk rather far back in my face, and a hooked nose."
—Ruth in *Life and Loves of a She Devil*

Extra points if you know who played her in the movie?
Roseanne Barr

The Lovely Bones by Alice Sebold

402.

LITERARY MERIT

★ ★

The novel opens: "My name was Salmon, like the fish; first name Susie. I was fourteen when I was murdered on December 6, 1973." Her killer dismembers her body; only her elbow is found. Now she watches from heaven as her parents, her sister, her friends, and her killer get on with their lives. From there she finds the love and revenge that life denied her. This runaway bestseller captured readers with its narrator's distinctive voice. It was an American Bookseller Association's "Book of the Year" for 2002, won the Bram Stoker Award from the Horror Writers Association, and its success fueled a spate of books narrated by the dead.

403.

LITERARY MERIT

★ ★ ★ ★

Moby Dick by Herman Melville

The narrator of this iconic 1851 novel, Ishmael, signs on to crew the whaling vessel the *Pequod*. On the voyage, tyrannical and increasingly erratic Captain Ahab exhorts his crew to search for "the white-headed whale with a wrinkled brow and a crooked jaw." It's the whale that took Captain Ahab's leg, and the voyage is his doomed attempt to wreak vengeance. The epilogue begins with a quote from Job: "And I only am escaped alone to tell thee." Not sure how influential this book was? Read it with Peter Benchley's *Jaws* and Ernest Hemingway's *The Old Man and the Sea.*

404.

LITERARY MERIT

★

The Nanny Diaries
by Emma McLaughlin and Nicola Kraus

Turns out royalty aren't the only ones who have to watch whom they hire. The authors claim to have worked for more than thirty New York families, and they were taking careful notes. The heroine is named Nanny; the self-obsessed Park Avenue parents are the high-powered Wall Streeter Mr. X, who is usually out, and the passive-aggressive Mrs. X, who sends Nanny a steady stream of condescending notes on pale-blue Tiffany stationery. Writing, in this case, is the best revenge in this wonderfully bitchy insider's look at family life among the Upper East Side's cosseted rich.

...for Heartbreak

LITERARY MERIT ★

PROVOCATIVE 🔥

INFLUENTIAL !

INSPIRATIONAL 🕊

HUMOROUS 😄

BRAINY 💡

EASY READING ☂

PAGE TURNER 📖

CHALLENGING 👓

BATHROOM BOOK 🚽

FAMILY FRIENDLY 👪

MOVIE 🎥

405.

LITERARY MERIT

★ ★ ★ ★

Anna Karenina by Leo Tolstoy

This tragic story of passionate love and disastrous infidelity takes place in imperial Russia. Beautiful Anna Karenina defies convention and leaves her cold bureaucrat husband to live with Count Vronsky. She's shunned by polite society and alienated from Vronsky by her own

> **Department of Memorable Opening Lines**
>
> "Happy families are all alike; every unhappy family is unhappy in its own way."
> —*Anna Karenina*

jealousy as she moves toward a tragic end. The counterpoint to her story is Konstantin Levin's search for fulfillment through marriage, family, and hard work. Published in the 1870s, this novel continues to influence authors. In an interview with *Vanity Fair*, Norman Mailer named Anna Karenina as "the protagonist from whom I learned the most."

406.

LITERARY MERIT

★ ★ ★

The Beans of Egypt, Maine by Carolyn Chute

Earlene Pomerleau's daddy warned her: "If it runs, a Bean will shoot it! If it falls, a Bean will eat it. Earlene, don't go over to the Bean's side of the right-of-way. Not ever!" But Earlene can't stay away. She ends up marrying one. This dark, disturbing portrait of rural poverty swings from funny to sad. File it beside *To Kill a Mockingbird* for its courage, luminous prose, spare storytelling, and because the author hasn't written anything in the same league since.

407.

LITERARY MERIT

★ ★ ★ ★

The Bluest Eye by Toni Morrison

Nobel laureate Morrison's first novel tells the poignant story of an eleven-year-old black girl named Pecola Breedlove who yearns for the blondest hair and the bluest eye. ". . . It was as though some mysterious all-knowing master had given each one a cloak of ugliness to wear, and they had each accepted it without question." Morrison's writing is jazz-like, more poetry than prose, with multiple voices and themes that intertwine.

408.

LITERARY MERIT

★ ★ ★ ★

Empire of the Sun by J. G. Ballard

This luminous novelistic memoir begins with events in wartime China, following the Pearl Harbor bombing, and seen through the eyes of an eleven-year-old British boy. It continues through a vividly told story of survival in World War II concentration camps. The boy sees a brilliant flash in the sky—the atomic bomb has destroyed Nagasaki, five hundred miles away—and he recognizes it as the rebirth of Japan, a new empire of the sun. The novel was shortlisted for the Booker Prize.

The Famished Road by Ben Okri

409.

Booker Prize 1991

LITERARY MERIT

★ ★ ★ ★

Azaro is an "abiku," a child condemned to die and be reborn endlessly. He's born into a Nigerian family on the eve of independence. "Tired of coming and going," he breaks his pact with his fellow unborn spirits and fights death. The spirits pursue him but he persists, even though the life he's been born to is painful and death would provide release. In this novel of African-style magical realism, the "famished road" of the title is Nigeria's independence, beset by hunger and often devouring its own people.

The French Lieutenant's Woman by John Fowles

410.

Sarah Woodruff stands at the end of a breakwater, gazing out at the sea. Is she yearning for the French lover who has forsaken her? Charles Smithson, an amateur paleontologist engaged to another woman, becomes obsessed with the mysterious figure and eventually succumbs. This enigmatic novel is written in Victorian style, but with the modern conceit of the author himself as a character.

LITERARY MERIT

★ ★ ★ ★

It presents three different endings and asks the reader to choose. Fowles is considered one of the English-speaking world's first postmodern novelists.

Who played both Rachel Samstat in the movie adaptation of *Heartburn* and Sarah Woodruff in the adaptation of *The French Lieutenant's Woman*?

Meryl Streep

Kate Vaiden by Reynolds Price

411.

National Book Critics Circle 1986

LITERARY MERIT

★ ★ ★ ★

Kate Vaiden is surrounded by severed ties. Her mother's mother died in childbirth. Kate feels she's responsible for her father's death, too. At seventeen, she abandons her newborn son. In middle age, she reaches out for him. This is a rich Southern tale about a woman who yearns for love; but when it's within reach, she can't accept it. The *New York Times* reviewer called this "the product of a storyteller working at the full height of his artistic powers."

Heartburn by Nora Ephron

412.

This was Nora Ephron's roman a clef after her breakup with Watergate reporter Carl Bernstein. Nora becomes Rachel Samstat, a pregnant cookbook writer. Carl's Mark is a philandering cad who doesn't even bother to hide his incriminating MasterCard bills. Ephron manages to make real heartbreak hilarious and laugh all the way to the bank.

LITERARY MERIT

★ ★ ★

413.

LITERARY MERIT

★ ★ ★ ★

Middlemarch by George Eliot

In this novel about Victorians who marry unwisely, beautiful Dorothea Brooke is stuck in the provincial town of Middlemarch. She's seething with ideas with no outlet in upper-class society. She makes a disastrous marriage to an aged academic who fortuitously dies, but his will forbids her to marry the man she loves.

> **Department of Memorable Characters**
>
> "She had that kind of beauty which seems to be thrown into relief by poor dress."
> —Dorothea Brooke, *Middlemarch*

Meanwhile, Dorothea's friend, physician Tertius Lydgate, marries the frivolous Rosamund whose pursuit of wealth and status brings them both to the brink of ruin. Dorothea Brooke inspires us, as one of English literature's first aspiring intellectual women. Virginia Woolf called the novel "one of the few . . . written for grown-up people." During its first year in print (1871), it sold an amazing 20,000 copies.

414.

LITERARY MERIT

★ ★ ★ ★

Of Mice and Men by John Steinbeck

It's the Great Depression and two drifters are following a path along a river bank in California's Salinas Valley. One is "small and quick, dark of face, with restless and sharp, strong features." The other is "a huge man, shapeless of face, with large, pale eyes, with wide sloping shoulders; and he walked heavily, dragging his feet a little, the way a bear drags his paws." These outsiders dream of a better life, but too much goes awry in the world they inhabit. This iconic novel of the Depression was first published in 1937.

Quiz Time!

Match each author's pen name with their real name.

1. Isak Dinesen
2. Mark Twain
3. Josephine Tey
4. George Eliot
5. John Le Carré
6. George Orwell
7. Augusten Burroughs
8. Victoria Lucas

a. Samuel Longhorn Clemens
b. David John Moore Cornwell
c. Sylvia Plath
d. Baroness Karen Blixen
e. Mary Ann Evans
f. Christopher Robison
g. Elizabeth Mackintosh
h. Eric Arthur Blair

Answers: *1-d, 2-a, 3-g, 4-e, 5-b, 6-h, 7-f, 8-c*

...*for* Heartburn

LITERARY MERIT ★

PROVOCATIVE 🔥

INFLUENTIAL !

INSPIRATIONAL ➤

HUMOROUS 😄

BRAINY 💡

EASY READING ☂

PAGE TURNER 📖

CHALLENGING 👓

BATHROOM BOOK 🚽

FAMILY FRIENDLY 👨‍👩‍👧

MOVIE 🎥

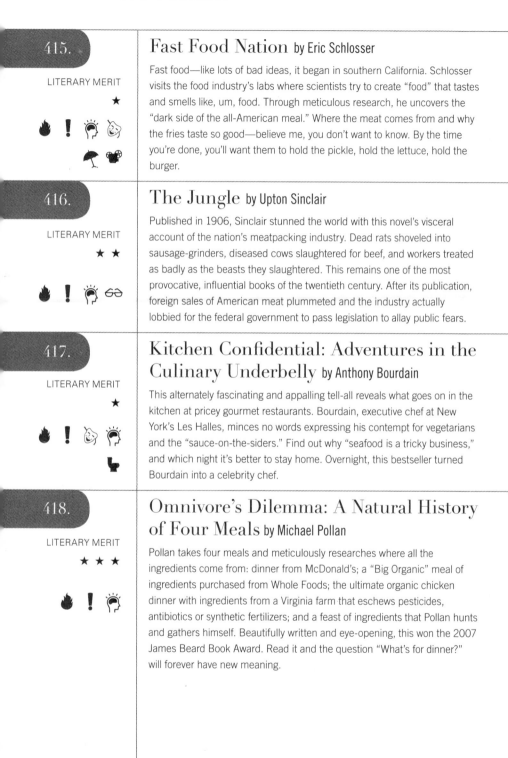

415.

LITERARY MERIT

★

Fast Food Nation by Eric Schlosser

Fast food—like lots of bad ideas, it began in southern California. Schlosser visits the food industry's labs where scientists try to create "food" that tastes and smells like, um, food. Through meticulous research, he uncovers the "dark side of the all-American meal." Where the meat comes from and why the fries taste so good—believe me, you don't want to know. By the time you're done, you'll want them to hold the pickle, hold the lettuce, hold the burger.

416.

LITERARY MERIT

★ ★

The Jungle by Upton Sinclair

Published in 1906, Sinclair stunned the world with this novel's visceral account of the nation's meatpacking industry. Dead rats shoveled into sausage-grinders, diseased cows slaughtered for beef, and workers treated as badly as the beasts they slaughtered. This remains one of the most provocative, influential books of the twentieth century. After its publication, foreign sales of American meat plummeted and the industry actually lobbied for the federal government to pass legislation to allay public fears.

417.

LITERARY MERIT

★

Kitchen Confidential: Adventures in the Culinary Underbelly by Anthony Bourdain

This alternately fascinating and appalling tell-all reveals what goes on in the kitchen at pricey gourmet restaurants. Bourdain, executive chef at New York's Les Halles, minces no words expressing his contempt for vegetarians and the "sauce-on-the-siders." Find out why "seafood is a tricky business," and which night it's better to stay home. Overnight, this bestseller turned Bourdain into a celebrity chef.

418.

LITERARY MERIT

★ ★ ★

Omnivore's Dilemma: A Natural History of Four Meals by Michael Pollan

Pollan takes four meals and meticulously researches where all the ingredients come from: dinner from McDonald's; a "Big Organic" meal of ingredients purchased from Whole Foods; the ultimate organic chicken dinner with ingredients from a Virginia farm that eschews pesticides, antibiotics or synthetic fertilizers; and a feast of ingredients that Pollan hunts and gathers himself. Beautifully written and eye-opening, this won the 2007 James Beard Book Award. Read it and the question "What's for dinner?" will forever have new meaning.

Twinkie, Deconstructed: My Journey to Discover how the Ingredients Found in Processed Foods Are Grown, Mined (Yes Mined), and Manipulated Into What America Eats by Steve Ettlinger

419.

LITERARY MERIT

★

There's no cream in the "cream" filling and no egg in the yellow spongy cake. So what is in a Twinkie? Ettlinger travels to plants, mines, and refineries to find out. The book's table of contents is the Twinkies ingredients list. How about a little Soy Protein Isolate with your Cellulose Gum? No value judgments here, Ettlinger just tells it like it is and leaves you to decide. Guaranteed to change the way you look at packaged foods.

The Whole Beast: Nose to Tail Eating
by Fergus Henderson

420.

LITERARY MERIT

★ ★

Doesn't it just kill you that so much of each animal slaughtered goes to waste? Pig spleen. Lamb heart. Quarts and quarts of perfectly good blood. Henderson is the chef at London's popular St. John's restaurant and his recipes show you how to cook the parts people skip. The recipes must be good—the book won the Andre Simon Award for the best food book of 1999.

...for **ADOLESCENT ANGST**

LITERARY MERIT ★

PROVOCATIVE 🔥

INFLUENTIAL !

INSPIRATIONAL 🕊

HUMOROUS 😄

BRAINY 🗣

EASY READING ☂

PAGE TURNER 📖

CHALLENGING 👓

BATHROOM BOOK 🚽

FAMILY FRIENDLY 👪

MOVIE 🎬

421.

LITERARY MERIT

★ ★ ★ ★

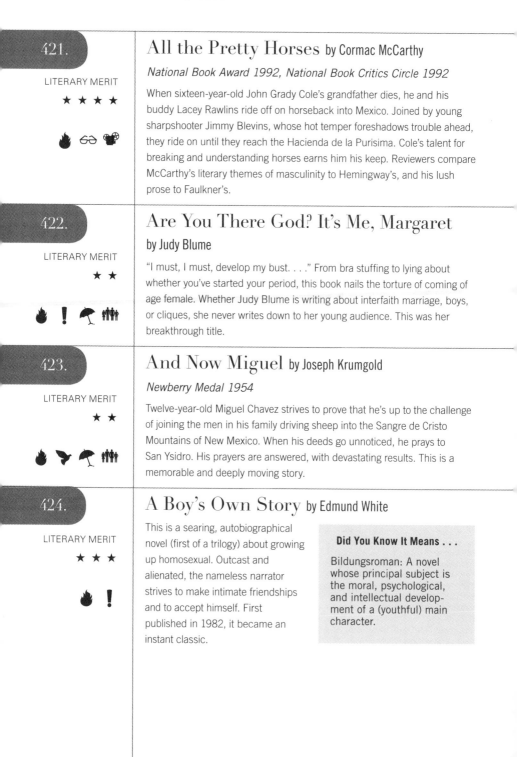

All the Pretty Horses by Cormac McCarthy

National Book Award 1992, National Book Critics Circle 1992

When sixteen-year-old John Grady Cole's grandfather dies, he and his buddy Lacey Rawlins ride off on horseback into Mexico. Joined by young sharpshooter Jimmy Blevins, whose hot temper foreshadows trouble ahead, they ride on until they reach the Hacienda de la Purisima. Cole's talent for breaking and understanding horses earns him his keep. Reviewers compare McCarthy's literary themes of masculinity to Hemingway's, and his lush prose to Faulkner's.

422.

LITERARY MERIT

★ ★

Are You There God? It's Me, Margaret
by Judy Blume

"I must, I must, develop my bust. . . ." From bra stuffing to lying about whether you've started your period, this book nails the torture of coming of age female. Whether Judy Blume is writing about interfaith marriage, boys, or cliques, she never writes down to her young audience. This was her breakthrough title.

423.

LITERARY MERIT

★ ★

And Now Miguel by Joseph Krumgold

Newberry Medal 1954

Twelve-year-old Miguel Chavez strives to prove that he's up to the challenge of joining the men in his family driving sheep into the Sangre de Cristo Mountains of New Mexico. When his deeds go unnoticed, he prays to San Ysidro. His prayers are answered, with devastating results. This is a memorable and deeply moving story.

424.

LITERARY MERIT

★ ★ ★

A Boy's Own Story by Edmund White

This is a searing, autobiographical novel (first of a trilogy) about growing up homosexual. Outcast and alienated, the nameless narrator strives to make intimate friendships and to accept himself. First published in 1982, it became an instant classic.

Did You Know It Means . . .

Bildungsroman: A novel whose principal subject is the moral, psychological, and intellectual development of a (youthful) main character.

The Buddha of Suburbia by Hanif Kureishi

425.

The narrator of this punk-rock infused novel is Karim Amir—a culturally and sexually conflicted "Englishman born and bred, almost"—growing up and living in London amid squalor and racism. The "Buddha" of the title is his father, Haroon, who becomes a guru dispensing Buddhist wisdom and falls in love with the arty Eva. This autobiographical first novel from the screenwriter of *My Beautiful Laundrette* is about much more than coming of age. It won the Whitbread Best First Novel Award in 1990.

LITERARY MERIT

★ ★ ★ ★

The Catcher in the Rye by J. D. Salinger

426.

If you haven't heard the cynical, jaded voice of seventeen-year-old Holden Caulfield telling this story from a California psychiatric hospital, now's the time—if only to understand what's the big deal. The novel is one of the most influential and most frequently banned books of the last century. It was never made into a movie or play; Salinger has refused all offers to sell the rights.

Department of Opening Lines

"If you really want to hear about it, the first thing you'll probably want to know is where I was born and what my lousy childhood was like, and how my parents were occupied and all before they had me, and all that David Copperfield kind of crap, but I don't feel like going into it, if you want to know the truth. In the first place, that stuff bores me, and in the second place, my parents would have about two hemorrhages apiece if I told anything pretty personal about them."

—*The Catcher in the Rye*

LITERARY MERIT

★ ★ ★ ★

Dicey's Song by Cynthia Voigt

427.

Newbery Medal 1983

Dicey is the fixer, the caretaker, the one who gets herself and her three siblings to Gram's farm after Momma disappears. A new home, new friends, a new school, and at last Dicey can let down her guard—only she knows better because "big troubles had little beginnings, just like little troubles." Loving and caring are the themes of this moving sequel to another young adult classic, *Homecoming*.

LITERARY MERIT

★ ★

428.

LITERARY MERIT

★ ★

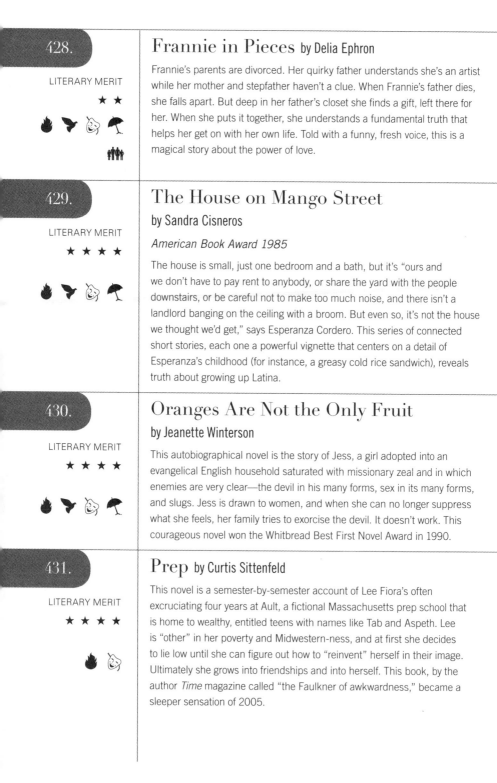

Frannie in Pieces by Delia Ephron

Frannie's parents are divorced. Her quirky father understands she's an artist while her mother and stepfather haven't a clue. When Frannie's father dies, she falls apart. But deep in her father's closet she finds a gift, left there for her. When she puts it together, she understands a fundamental truth that helps her get on with her own life. Told with a funny, fresh voice, this is a magical story about the power of love.

429.

LITERARY MERIT

★ ★ ★ ★

The House on Mango Street
by Sandra Cisneros

American Book Award 1985

The house is small, just one bedroom and a bath, but it's "ours and we don't have to pay rent to anybody, or share the yard with the people downstairs, or be careful not to make too much noise, and there isn't a landlord banging on the ceiling with a broom. But even so, it's not the house we thought we'd get," says Esperanza Cordero. This series of connected short stories, each one a powerful vignette that centers on a detail of Esperanza's childhood (for instance, a greasy cold rice sandwich), reveals truth about growing up Latina.

430.

LITERARY MERIT

★ ★ ★ ★

Oranges Are Not the Only Fruit
by Jeanette Winterson

This autobiographical novel is the story of Jess, a girl adopted into an evangelical English household saturated with missionary zeal and in which enemies are very clear—the devil in his many forms, sex in its many forms, and slugs. Jess is drawn to women, and when she can no longer suppress what she feels, her family tries to exorcise the devil. It doesn't work. This courageous novel won the Whitbread Best First Novel Award in 1990.

431.

LITERARY MERIT

★ ★ ★ ★

Prep by Curtis Sittenfeld

This novel is a semester-by-semester account of Lee Fiora's often excruciating four years at Ault, a fictional Massachusetts prep school that is home to wealthy, entitled teens with names like Tab and Aspeth. Lee is "other" in her poverty and Midwestern-ness, and at first she decides to lie low until she can figure out how to "reinvent" herself in their image. Ultimately she grows into friendships and into herself. This book, by the author *Time* magazine called "the Faulkner of awkwardness," became a sleeper sensation of 2005.

Reviving Ophelia by Mary Pipher

Depression, eating disorders, self-cutting, addiction, and suicide—is this what adolescence has come to mean in today's "girl poisoning" society? The author is a clinical psychologist with twenty years of experience treating troubled girls, and she shares what she's learned from listening. One typical patient, a bulimic young gymnast, tells her: "Appearance was all we talked about. I tried not to get caught up in it, but I couldn't help it. I wanted to be pretty like everyone else." This was a groundbreaking book.

The Author Explains the Title

"The book's title comes from *Hamlet*. Ophelia was mentally intact and happy until she fell in love with Hamlet. She was torn between her desire to please him and to please her father. She grows confused, depressed, and eventually, she kills herself. Her experience is a good metaphor for what happens to many girls in early adolescence. They become confused by others' expectations and their true selves are lost."
—Mary Pipher

LITERARY MERIT
★

A Separate Peace by John Knowles

Explore the dark side of adolescence in this story of two boys. It takes place less than a year after the 1941 bombing of Pearl Harbor, and the war casts a shadow over the lives of alienated, introverted, intellectual Gene and brash, daredevil athlete Finny. This was Knowles's first novel, published in 1959, and is based on his experiences as a student at Phillips Exeter Academy (called "Devon" in the book). It became a classic the moment it was published.

LITERARY MERIT
★ ★ ★

Sloppy Firsts by Megan McCafferty

Here's chick lit, set in an angst-ridden New Jersey high school. Jessica Darling is sixteen years old and her best friend since forever moves to Tennessee. But "I'm still here. You're still here," Jessica says in her letter to Hope. Jessica is cheerful, funny, painfully honest, and not very polite (she sounds a lot like a real kid.) This is the novel that Harvard undergraduate wunderkind and first-time author Kaavya Viswanathan claimed she inadvertently "memorized."

LITERARY MERIT
★ ★

435.

LITERARY MERIT

★ ★ ★ ★

Waiting for Snow in Havana: Confessions of a Cuban Boy
by Carlos Eire

National Book Award 2003

This memoir of boyhood, growing up privileged in Havana in the idyllic 1950s, is a modern *Paradise Lost*. It begins "The world changed while I slept, and much to my surprise, no one had consulted me." Castro had swept into power and being prosperous became dangerous. Eire and his brother were among fourteen thousand children shipped out of Cuba without their parents and delivered to Miami. Eire never saw his father again. It's a sad irony that this book, though it's been translated into Spanish, is banned in Cuba.

436.

LITERARY MERIT

★ ★ ★

White Oleander by Janet Fitch

In another fall from grace, twelve-year-old Janet Astrid's world implodes when her mother, Ingrid, a brilliant poet ("her beauty was like the edge of a sharp knife") is sent to jail for murdering her former lover. She poisoned him with white oleander flowers. Astrid's six year journey from foster family to foster family is a Dickensian descent into hell. A captivating narrative, this novel grew out of Fitch's short story published in *Best American Short Stories 1994*.

...to Indulge Your Inner Child

LITERARY MERIT ★

PROVOCATIVE 🔥

INFLUENTIAL ❗

INSPIRATIONAL 🕊

HUMOROUS 😂

BRAINY 💡

EASY READING ☂

PAGE TURNER 📩

CHALLENGING 👓

BATHROOM BOOK 🚽

FAMILY FRIENDLY 👪

MOVIE 🎥

437.

LITERARY MERIT

★ ★ ★ ★

An American Childhood by Annie Dillard

Dillard recalls her 1950s Pittsburgh childhood: "Every woman stayed alone in her house . . . like a coin in a safe." She writes lovingly of her quirky, caring parents. Her father helped make the movie *Night of the Living Dead* and read Kerouac's *On the Road* "approximately a million" times, as did the author. Her mother reveled in words and gave her "the freedom of the streets as soon I could say our telephone number." This meditation on growing up and growing aware comes thirty years after Dillard's meditations on the natural world were published in the Pulitzer-winning *Pilgrim at Tinker Creek*. Reading it is like eating a favorite comfort food.

438.

LITERARY MERIT

★ ★

Amphigorey by Edward Gorey

The fifteen illustrated tales in this book have luminous titles like "The Listing Attic" and "The Fatal Lozenge." Then there's "The Gashlycrumb Tinies"— "an appalling Alphabet which introduces a Gallery of enchanting tots and produces a Gasp of involuntary mirth when they attain their Dreadful Demises." Droll, macabre pen-and-ink drawings combine with oddball verse and surreal stories, many involving untimely deaths and dreadful accidents. Gorey has the unique ability to make you laugh while making your hair stand on end.

439.

LITERARY MERIT

★

Eloise by Kay Thompson, illustrated by Hilary Knight

The incomparable illustrator Hilary Knight brings the six-year-old with her loose limbs, jelly-bean body, and insouciant smirk to life along with Nanny, Eloise's nurse and "mostly companion," Weenie her "dog that looks like a cat," and Skipperdee the turtle that "eats raisins and wears sneakers." This is an enduring classic.

440.

LITERARY MERIT

★

Harriet the Spy by Louise Fitzhugh

Harriet M. Welch is a creature of habit. Every day at school, the sixth-grader eats a tomato and mayonnaise sandwich. After school she follows her spy route, taking careful notes. She spies on the rich old lady who never gets out of bed and the man with twenty-five cats. She also jots down unvarnished observations about the kids with whom she goes to school: "IF MARION HAWTHORNE DOESN'T WATCH OUT SHE'S GOING TO GROW UP TO BE A LADY HITLER." Harriet never dreams how humiliating it will be when the kids she skewers get a load of what she's been writing. This book broke new ground with its gutsy, more realistic portrayal of less than likable characters. In 1964 it won the *New York Times* Outstanding Book of the Year Award.

Horton Hears a Who by Dr. Seuss

441.

In this favorite from the great oeuvre of Dr. Seuss (Theodor Geisel), kindhearted Horton the Elephant responds to a call for help from "a small speck of dust blowing past through the air." It's

Department of Great Lines

"A person's a person, no matter how small."
—*Horton Hears a Who*

LITERARY MERIT

★ ★

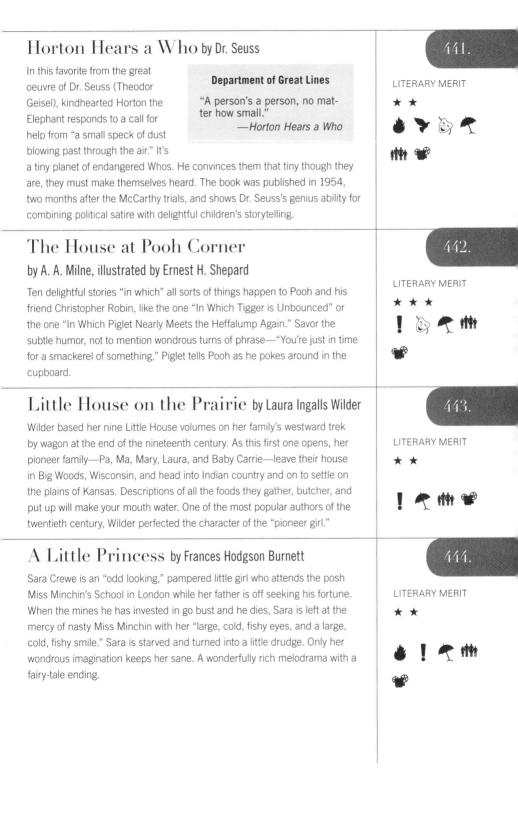

a tiny planet of endangered Whos. He convinces them that tiny though they are, they must make themselves heard. The book was published in 1954, two months after the McCarthy trials, and shows Dr. Seuss's genius ability for combining political satire with delightful children's storytelling.

The House at Pooh Corner

442.

by A. A. Milne, illustrated by Ernest H. Shepard

Ten delightful stories "in which" all sorts of things happen to Pooh and his friend Christopher Robin, like the one "In Which Tigger is Unbounced" or the one "In Which Piglet Nearly Meets the Heffalump Again." Savor the subtle humor, not to mention wondrous turns of phrase—"You're just in time for a smackerel of something," Piglet tells Pooh as he pokes around in the cupboard.

LITERARY MERIT

★ ★ ★

Little House on the Prairie by Laura Ingalls Wilder

443.

Wilder based her nine Little House volumes on her family's westward trek by wagon at the end of the nineteenth century. As this first one opens, her pioneer family—Pa, Ma, Mary, Laura, and Baby Carrie—leave their house in Big Woods, Wisconsin, and head into Indian country and on to settle on the plains of Kansas. Descriptions of all the foods they gather, butcher, and put up will make your mouth water. One of the most popular authors of the twentieth century, Wilder perfected the character of the "pioneer girl."

LITERARY MERIT

★ ★

A Little Princess by Frances Hodgson Burnett

444.

Sara Crewe is an "odd looking," pampered little girl who attends the posh Miss Minchin's School in London while her father is off seeking his fortune. When the mines he has invested in go bust and he dies, Sara is left at the mercy of nasty Miss Minchin with her "large, cold, fishy eyes, and a large, cold, fishy smile." Sara is starved and turned into a little drudge. Only her wondrous imagination keeps her sane. A wonderfully rich melodrama with a fairy-tale ending.

LITERARY MERIT

★ ★

445.

LITERARY MERIT

★ ★

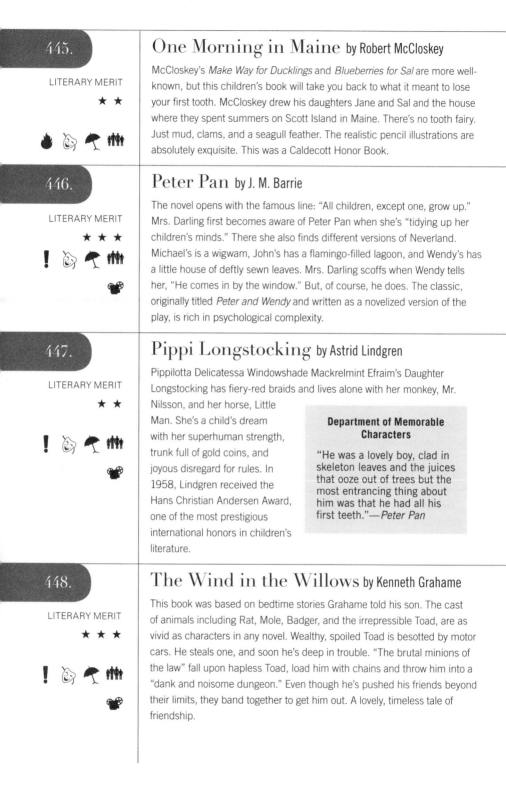

One Morning in Maine by Robert McCloskey

McCloskey's *Make Way for Ducklings* and *Blueberries for Sal* are more well-known, but this children's book will take you back to what it meant to lose your first tooth. McCloskey drew his daughters Jane and Sal and the house where they spent summers on Scott Island in Maine. There's no tooth fairy. Just mud, clams, and a seagull feather. The realistic pencil illustrations are absolutely exquisite. This was a Caldecott Honor Book.

446.

LITERARY MERIT

★ ★ ★

Peter Pan by J. M. Barrie

The novel opens with the famous line: "All children, except one, grow up." Mrs. Darling first becomes aware of Peter Pan when she's "tidying up her children's minds." There she also finds different versions of Neverland. Michael's is a wigwam, John's has a flamingo-filled lagoon, and Wendy's has a little house of deftly sewn leaves. Mrs. Darling scoffs when Wendy tells her, "He comes in by the window." But, of course, he does. The classic, originally titled *Peter and Wendy* and written as a novelized version of the play, is rich in psychological complexity.

447.

LITERARY MERIT

★ ★

Pippi Longstocking by Astrid Lindgren

Pippilotta Delicatessa Windowshade Mackrelmint Efraim's Daughter Longstocking has fiery-red braids and lives alone with her monkey, Mr. Nilsson, and her horse, Little Man. She's a child's dream with her superhuman strength, trunk full of gold coins, and joyous disregard for rules. In 1958, Lindgren received the Hans Christian Andersen Award, one of the most prestigious international honors in children's literature.

> **Department of Memorable Characters**
>
> "He was a lovely boy, clad in skeleton leaves and the juices that ooze out of trees but the most entrancing thing about him was that he had all his first teeth."—*Peter Pan*

448.

LITERARY MERIT

★ ★ ★

The Wind in the Willows by Kenneth Grahame

This book was based on bedtime stories Grahame told his son. The cast of animals including Rat, Mole, Badger, and the irrepressible Toad, are as vivid as characters in any novel. Wealthy, spoiled Toad is besotted by motor cars. He steals one, and soon he's deep in trouble. "The brutal minions of the law" fall upon hapless Toad, load him with chains and throw him into a "dank and noisome dungeon." Even though he's pushed his friends beyond their limits, they band together to get him out. A lovely, timeless tale of friendship.

...to **Clean Your Plate**

LITERARY MERIT ★

PROVOCATIVE 🔥

INFLUENTIAL !

INSPIRATIONAL 🕊

HUMOROUS 😊

BRAINY 🗽

EASY READING ☂

PAGE TURNER 📖

CHALLENGING 👓

BATHROOM BOOK 🚽

FAMILY FRIENDLY 👪

MOVIE 🎥

449.

LITERARY MERIT

★ ★

Alice, Let's Eat: Further Adventures of a Happy Eater by Calvin Trillin

In his humorous books about food, Trillin turned his beautiful, brainy wife Alice into a celebrity. She "has a weird predilection for limiting our family to three meals a day," and yet she shares his passion for food. In this volume of essays, Trillin and Alice journey to Kentucky in search of the perfect barbecued mutton, to Nebraska for a steak that looks like a softball and is so tender that you don't need a knife to cut it, and onward to other delicious destinations discovering each locale's culinary treats. There's good reason why Trillin has been called our funniest food writer.

450.

LITERARY MERIT

★ ★

American Pie: Slices of Life (and Pie) from America's Back Roads
by Pascale le Draoulec

Ah, pie! Le Draoulec is restaurant critic for the *New York Daily News* and the daughter of French immigrants. She trekked from San Francisco to New York in a Volvo with an IBRK4PIE license plate, in search of pies and stories about the people who make them. She shares with her readers the many pleasures of the pies that define America, from huckleberry pie in Montana to the elusive bumbleberry pie in Zion Canyon.

451.

LITERARY MERIT

★ ★ ★

The Art of Eating by M. F. K. Fisher

James Beard Cookbook Award 1989

This colossal volume of essays from one of America's best loved food writers is the perfect book for between-meal reading. Fisher revolutionized food writing with her funny, informal style. From the dining habits of the Elizabethans to the life-cycle of an oyster, even if you're not one of those people who live to eat, there's much to savor.

Department of Great Lines

"I have eaten several strange things since I was twelve, and I shall be glad to taste broiled locusts and swallow a live fish. But unless I change very much, I shall never be able to eat a slug."
—*The Art of Eating*

452.

LITERARY MERIT

★ ★ ★ ★

The Debt to Pleasure by John Lanchester

This is what happens when a restaurant critic turns his hand to fictionalized memoir. The protagonist is the thoroughly dislikable, food-obsessed Tarquin Winot whose goal in life is to prove that he's far more worthy than his dead brother, a celebrated sculptor. This wickedly funny, sinister tale of fraternal jealousy masquerading as a cookbook won the Whitbread First Novel Award and the Julia Child Book Award.

Eater's Digest by Lorraine Bodger

A delightful, thick compendium of short essays about food (e.g. "A moment or two with tofu") and famous foodies (meet Rex Stout and Nero Wolfe) brought to you by an award-winning cookbook writer. Find out how Sumo wrestlers get so fat, why beans give you gas, and test your food savvy. Do egg creams contain eggs? Light, frothy, and guaranteed not to fill you up.

453.

LITERARY MERIT

★

Eating My Words: An Appetite for Life
by Mimi Sheraton

This is the memoir of the award-winning cookbook writer and famed *New York Times* food critic who visited restaurants in disguise. A self-described "nitpicker and busybody," with self-effacing humor she tells of growing up in Brooklyn, memorable meals, and answers the twenty questions most frequently asked of a food critic. For foodies who've fantasized about being a restaurant reviewer.

454.

LITERARY MERIT

★ ★ ★

Home Cooking: A Writer in the Kitchen
by Laurie Colwin

This part memoir, part cookbook contains fresh, funny essays from a one-time columnist for *Gourmet* magazine. It includes the classic "Repulsive dinners: A memoir" in which Colwin recalls a triumphantly disgusting pie "in which the crust is slit so that the whole baked eels within can poke their nasty little heads out and look at the piecrust stars with which the top is supposed to be festooned." The chapters on making gingerbread and frying chicken are outstanding. She also wrote one of my favorite novels, *Happy All the Time*. Colwin died suddenly in 1992 at age forty-eight.

455.

LITERARY MERIT

★ ★

Honey From a Weed: Fasting and Feasting in Tuscany, Catalonia, the Cyclades and Apulia
by Patience Gray

Gray lived for twenty years in Italy, Spain, and Greece with a sculptor who needed to be near the stones he worked. She combines vignettes of her life with discussions of vegetables, mushrooms, weeds, herbs, fish, and meat, and the rustic recipes that use them. This is a remarkable and original book about food and a handbook on living. Published in 1986 when Gray was nearly seventy years old, it has become a cult classic among intellectual foodies.

456.

LITERARY MERIT

★ ★

457.

LITERARY MERIT

★ ★

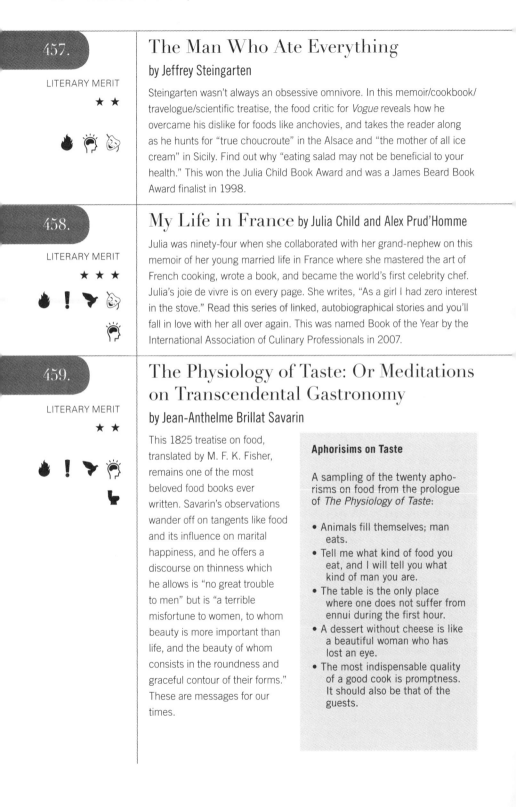

The Man Who Ate Everything

by Jeffrey Steingarten

Steingarten wasn't always an obsessive omnivore. In this memoir/cookbook/travelogue/scientific treatise, the food critic for *Vogue* reveals how he overcame his dislike for foods like anchovies, and takes the reader along as he hunts for "true choucroute" in the Alsace and "the mother of all ice cream" in Sicily. Find out why "eating salad may not be beneficial to your health." This won the Julia Child Book Award and was a James Beard Book Award finalist in 1998.

458.

LITERARY MERIT

★ ★ ★

My Life in France by Julia Child and Alex Prud'Homme

Julia was ninety-four when she collaborated with her grand-nephew on this memoir of her young married life in France where she mastered the art of French cooking, wrote a book, and became the world's first celebrity chef. Julia's joie de vivre is on every page. She writes, "As a girl I had zero interest in the stove." Read this series of linked, autobiographical stories and you'll fall in love with her all over again. This was named Book of the Year by the International Association of Culinary Professionals in 2007.

459.

LITERARY MERIT

★ ★

The Physiology of Taste: Or Meditations on Transcendental Gastronomy

by Jean-Anthelme Brillat Savarin

This 1825 treatise on food, translated by M. F. K. Fisher, remains one of the most beloved food books ever written. Savarin's observations wander off on tangents like food and its influence on marital happiness, and he offers a discourse on thinness which he allows is "no great trouble to men" but is "a terrible misfortune to women, to whom beauty is more important than life, and the beauty of whom consists in the roundness and graceful contour of their forms." These are messages for our times.

Aphorisims on Taste

A sampling of the twenty aphorisms on food from the prologue of *The Physiology of Taste*:

- Animals fill themselves; man eats.
- Tell me what kind of food you eat, and I will tell you what kind of man you are.
- The table is the only place where one does not suffer from ennui during the first hour.
- A dessert without cheese is like a beautiful woman who has lost an eye.
- The most indispensable quality of a good cook is promptness. It should also be that of the guests.

Pig Perfect: Encounters with Remarkable Swine and Some Great Ways to Cook Them by Peter Kaminsky

In this part memoir, part historical exploration of man's love affair with pork, self-described "hamthropologist" Kaminsky searches for the perfect-tasting pig. Along the way he chauffeurs twenty-three pigs from Missouri to North Carolina where he plans to turn them loose and let them dine on "hickory nuts and acorns, graze on alfalfa and peanut hay, late-summer greens" and end up tasting absolutely delicious. He traces his obsession to a "country ham epiphany" in Georgia. An odyssey for meat eaters.

LITERARY MERIT

★ ★

Roadfood by Jane and Michael Stern

461.

Read this book and you'll never eat at the rest stop on the interstate again. Husband and wife authors wander America's highways, small towns, and city neighborhoods in search of great regional meals. Included are maps and enticing descriptions of six hundred of the country's best local eateries from Maine to California. Regular revisions keep this traveler's guide up to date.

LITERARY MERIT

★

The Supper of the Lamb: A Culinary Reflection by Robert Farrar Capon

462.

First published in 1969, this book by an Episcopalian priest and self-confessed "amateur" ranges from the culinary to the theological and metaphysical. Much more than a cookbook, it's a reflection on life and on the virtues of a home-cooked meal and a well-set table. Like Julia Child, he's a proponent of cream and wine over calorie-counting, and of simple, excellent-quality ingredients over packaged food. This is a funny, wise, and moving guide to "festal and ferial" (celebratory and everyday) cooking.

LITERARY MERIT

★ ★

Tender at the Bone: Growing Up at the Table by Ruth Reichel

463.

From one-time *New York Times* food critic and editor of *Gourmet* magazine, a memoir of growing up. As a child, Reichel had to protect guests from her mother, the "queen of mold." At boarding school in Montreal, her taste buds were initiated into haut cuisine. Later she did the '60s thing—moved to Berkeley, lived in a commune, and ran a restaurant—before becoming a restaurant critic. Her powers of description are unmatched, as when she reluctantly bites into spiced pork kidneys: "It was like eating fragrant clouds."

LITERARY MERIT

★ ★ ★ ★

...to Satisfy Your Curiosity

LITERARY MERIT	★
PROVOCATIVE	
INFLUENTIAL	!
INSPIRATIONAL	
HUMOROUS	
BRAINY	
EASY READING	
PAGE TURNER	
CHALLENGING	
BATHROOM BOOK	
FAMILY FRIENDLY	
MOVIE	

464.

LITERARY MERIT

★ ★ ★

Annals of the Former World by John McPhee

Pulitzer 1999

In this book, McPhee takes a geological tour of the United States, across the continent on I-80. It includes four collected works dealing with the rocky ranges of the east and west: "Basin and Range," "Suspect Terrain," "Rising from the Plains," and "Assembling California." It also includes "Crossing the Craton" which examines the not-so-flat Midwest. Take a journey through tectonic

Department of Memorable Lines

· · ·

"Ebbets Field, where they buried the old Brooklyn Dodgers, was also on the terminal moraine. When a long-ball hitter hit a long ball, it would land on Bedford Avenue and bounce down the morainal front to roll toward Coney Island on the outwash plain. No one in Los Angeles would ever hit a homer like that."
—*Annals of the Former World*

plates, examine geological history through roadcuts and outcrops, and meet fascinating scientists, like the one who quips, "We think rocks are beautiful. Highway departments think rocks are obscene."

465.

LITERARY MERIT

★ ★

Big Bang: The Origin of the Universe
by Simon Singh

How it all began. This is an intensely readable, entertaining account of the human history of the Big Bang theory, and how it triumphed over the steady state theory. Among the surprises: A priest was one of the first to propose that the universe began at a single point in time and expanded outward from that moment. (Albert Einstein brushed him off, but later came around.) And a woman was the first to solve the problem of how to measure distances across the universe.

466.

LITERARY MERIT

★

A Brief History of Time by Stephen Hawking

"What is the nature of the universe? What is our place in it and where did it and we come from? Why is it the way it is?" Finding the answers to these simple questions, theoretical physicist Hawking tells us, is his life's work. In this book he gives the nonscientist a glimpse of the answers he's worked out thus far. This popular science book stayed on London's *Sunday Times* bestseller list for a record-breaking 237 weeks.

The Canon: A Whirligig Tour of the Beautiful Basics of Science by Natalie Angier

467.

For everyone who never "clicked with science," journalist Angier delivers on the title. This book takes the mystery out of the beautiful basics of numbers and probability, matter and energy, the origins and structure of living things, and the natural history of our planet, solar system, galaxy, and universe.

LITERARY MERIT

★ ★

The Cartoon History of the Universe
by Larry Gonick

468.

Seven comic-y volumes take the reader "from the Big Bang to Alexander the Great," guided by an Einstein-like cartoon professor and his time machine. Covertly and subversively, Gonick promotes historical and scientific literacy. Here's a history book with a blurb from the creator of *Zippy, the Pinhead*.

LITERARY MERIT

★

Coming of Age in the Milky Way
by Timothy Ferris

469.

This history of astronomy and astronomers chronicles man's gradual awakening to the vastness of the cosmos—from the ancient Greek Eudoxus who imagined the stars and planets fastened to concentric spheres, to Aristarchus of Samos who put the sun at the center of the universe nearly two thousand years before Copernicus, and on to the egocentric Galileo, the socially inept Kepler, and Newton who espoused alchemy and biblical prophecy, and finally Einstein who redefined our notions of time, space, and gravity. The book received wide acclaim, including an American Association of Physics Prize, a Pulitzer nomination, and it was named one of the best books of the year by the *New York Times*.

LITERARY MERIT

★ ★

Emotional Intelligence: Why It Can Matter More Than IQ by Daniel Goleman

470.

So how come people with high IQs do such stupid things? To find answers, psychologist Goleman examines emotional intelligence, which he says includes "being able to motivate oneself, to persist in the face of frustration, to control impulse and delay gratification, to regulate one's moods and keep distress from swamping the ability to think; to empathize and hope." Not a self-help book, this influential book was first published in 1995 and became a bestseller for educators, business managers, and people trying to get ahead in the world.

LITERARY MERIT

★

471.

LITERARY MERIT

★

Freakonomics: A Rogue Economist Explores the Hidden Side of Everything
by Steven D. Levitt with Stephen J. Dubner

Levitt teases out unexpected conclusions by drawing connections between statistics. His controversial ideas often fly in the face of conventional wisdom. For instance, why did crime decline in the 1990s? His answer: because of Roe V. Wade—fewer children were raised in broken homes and fewer unwanted children were born. Why do drug dealers still live with their mothers? Because they can't afford to pay their own rent. This bestseller was an American Bookseller Association's Book of the Year for 2006.

472.

LITERARY MERIT

★ ★

Guns, Germs and Steel: The Fates of Human Societies by Jared Diamond
Pulitzer 1998

Evolutionary biologist Diamond frames this book as an answer to the question posed to him by Yali, a local politician in New Guinea: "Why is it that you white people developed so much cargo and brought it to New Guinea, but we black people had little cargo of our own?" Diamond assembles evidence to support his argument that geography, demographics, and the environment are causal factors. An informative, provocative, and highly readable history of everyone for the last 13,000 years.

473.

LITERARY MERIT

★ ★

How Doctors Think by Jerome Groopman

This book contains fascinating and terrifying essays from a professor of medicine at Harvard Medical School and medical writer for *The New Yorker*. He shows how a "cascade of cognitive errors," not procedural errors, most often can lead to medical mistakes. The sad truth is, the same experience and expertise can lead a doctor to the correct or incorrect diagnosis. Dr. Groopman combines a physician's knowledge and a journalist's skepticism with compassion and understanding.

474.

LITERARY MERIT

★

How to Lie with Statistics by Darrell Huff

When pundits present statistics to support an argument, do you blink and swallow them at face value? Read this slim, cartoon-filled volume, first published in 1954 and the bestselling statistical text ever, and you'll swallow a little less snake oil. Maybe the book is so readable because Huff wasn't a statistician; he was an editor for *Better Homes and Gardens*.

The Know-It-All: One Man's Humble Quest to Become the Smartest Person in the World by A. J. Jacobs

475.

LITERARY MERIT

★ ★

One year when he presumably had nothing better to do, Jacobs read all thirty-two volumes of the 2002 edition of the *Encyclopedia Britannica*, covers to covers. He shows off his newly acquired knowledge whenever possible and soon even his wife is avoiding him. "Addled brain syndrome"—it's not an encyclopedia entry but Jacobs is afraid he's suffering from it as he "vacuums up the information, hour after hour." This very funny book is loaded with oddball trivia with which you, too, can annoy your friends and relatives.

Life: A Natural History of the First Four Billion Years of Life on Earth by Richard Fortey

476.

LITERARY MERIT

★ ★

Fortey goes way back, to the creation of the Earth "from debris that circled the nascent sun," and on to a toxic stew of cyanic and carbon oxides from which emerged the first photosynthesizing prokaryotic bacteria and stromatolites which pumped oxygen into the atmosphere." The senior paleontologist from London's Natural History Museum shows what evidence suggests it was like. He brings to life dinosaurs and creatures like bear-sized rodents, dragonflies with five-foot wingspans, and carnivorous kangaroos. He writes engagingly and puts the present in perspective—humans get one chapter.

Magical Mushroom, Mischievous Molds
by George W. Hudler

477.

LITERARY MERIT

★ ★

Professor Hudler's course on "Magical Mushrooms," how mold and fungi have impacted social and political structure throughout the course of history, has been one of Cornell

Did You Know It Means . . .

Formication: The sensation of ants crawling on or under the skin

University's most popular courses. In this book on his favorite topic, Hudler reveals that for much of human history, mushrooms have been viewed as the work of evil spirits, springing up as they do literally overnight. Not anymore. Here are fungi, from the exotic and tasty truffle to Phytophthora infestans which caused the Irish potato famine, to ergot which, when ingested, causes the "sensation of ants crawling over the body." An entertaining, crash-course in spore lore.

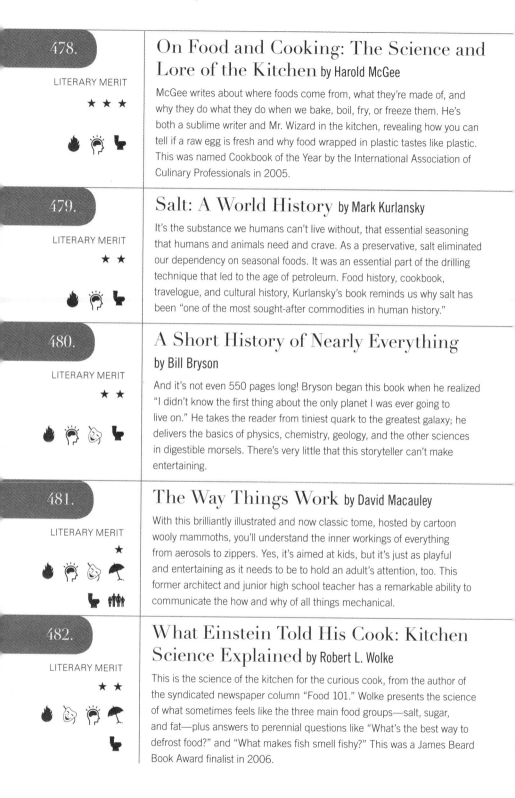

478.

LITERARY MERIT

★ ★ ★

On Food and Cooking: The Science and Lore of the Kitchen by Harold McGee

McGee writes about where foods come from, what they're made of, and why they do what they do when we bake, boil, fry, or freeze them. He's both a sublime writer and Mr. Wizard in the kitchen, revealing how you can tell if a raw egg is fresh and why food wrapped in plastic tastes like plastic. This was named Cookbook of the Year by the International Association of Culinary Professionals in 2005.

479.

LITERARY MERIT

★ ★

Salt: A World History by Mark Kurlansky

It's the substance we humans can't live without, that essential seasoning that humans and animals need and crave. As a preservative, salt eliminated our dependency on seasonal foods. It was an essential part of the drilling technique that led to the age of petroleum. Food history, cookbook, travelogue, and cultural history, Kurlansky's book reminds us why salt has been "one of the most sought-after commodities in human history."

480.

LITERARY MERIT

★ ★

A Short History of Nearly Everything
by Bill Bryson

And it's not even 550 pages long! Bryson began this book when he realized "I didn't know the first thing about the only planet I was ever going to live on." He takes the reader from tiniest quark to the greatest galaxy; he delivers the basics of physics, chemistry, geology, and the other sciences in digestible morsels. There's very little that this storyteller can't make entertaining.

481.

LITERARY MERIT

★

The Way Things Work by David Macauley

With this brilliantly illustrated and now classic tome, hosted by cartoon wooly mammoths, you'll understand the inner workings of everything from aerosols to zippers. Yes, it's aimed at kids, but it's just as playful and entertaining as it needs to be to hold an adult's attention, too. This former architect and junior high school teacher has a remarkable ability to communicate the how and why of all things mechanical.

482.

LITERARY MERIT

★ ★

What Einstein Told His Cook: Kitchen Science Explained by Robert L. Wolke

This is the science of the kitchen for the curious cook, from the author of the syndicated newspaper column "Food 101." Wolke presents the science of what sometimes feels like the three main food groups—salt, sugar, and fat—plus answers to perennial questions like "What's the best way to defrost food?" and "What makes fish smell fishy?" This was a James Beard Book Award finalist in 2006.

...*to* Indulge
Your Senses

LITERARY MERIT ★

PROVOCATIVE 🔥

INFLUENTIAL !

INSPIRATIONAL �’

HUMOROUS 😊

BRAINY 🧠

EASY READING ☂

PAGE TURNER 📖

CHALLENGING 👓

BATHROOM BOOK 🚽

FAMILY FRIENDLY 👪

MOVIE 🎥

483.

LITERARY MERIT

★ ★ ★

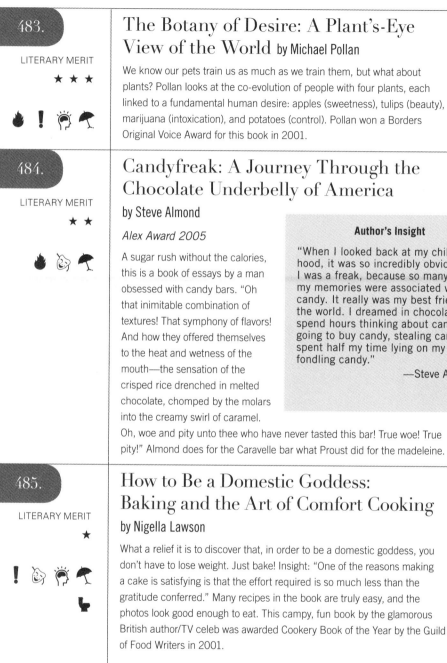

The Botany of Desire: A Plant's-Eye View of the World by Michael Pollan

We know our pets train us as much as we train them, but what about plants? Pollan looks at the co-evolution of people with four plants, each linked to a fundamental human desire: apples (sweetness), tulips (beauty), marijuana (intoxication), and potatoes (control). Pollan won a Borders Original Voice Award for this book in 2001.

484.

LITERARY MERIT

★ ★

Candyfreak: A Journey Through the Chocolate Underbelly of America

by Steve Almond

Alex Award 2005

A sugar rush without the calories, this is a book of essays by a man obsessed with candy bars. "Oh that inimitable combination of textures! That symphony of flavors! And how they offered themselves to the heat and wetness of the mouth—the sensation of the crisped rice drenched in melted chocolate, chomped by the molars into the creamy swirl of caramel.

Author's Insight

"When I looked back at my childhood, it was so incredibly obvious I was a freak, because so many of my memories were associated with candy. It really was my best friend in the world. I dreamed in chocolate. I'd spend hours thinking about candy, going to buy candy, stealing candy. I spent half my time lying on my bed, fondling candy."

—Steve Almond

Oh, woe and pity unto thee who have never tasted this bar! True woe! True pity!" Almond does for the Caravelle bar what Proust did for the madeleine.

485.

LITERARY MERIT

★

How to Be a Domestic Goddess: Baking and the Art of Comfort Cooking

by Nigella Lawson

What a relief it is to discover that, in order to be a domestic goddess, you don't have to lose weight. Just bake! Insight: "One of the reasons making a cake is satisfying is that the effort required is so much less than the gratitude conferred." Many recipes in the book are truly easy, and the photos look good enough to eat. This campy, fun book by the glamorous British author/TV celeb was awarded Cookery Book of the Year by the Guild of Food Writers in 2001.

Like Water for Chocolate by Laura Esquivel

Mexican novelist Esquivel combines magical realism, seething eroticism, and food to concoct a feast for the senses. At the center of the novel is youngest sister Tita and her excruciating wait until her older sisters are married. In 1994 it won the ABBY Award the American Booksellers Association honor for the book their members most enjoyed recommending.

Department of Great Characters

"Naked as she was, with her loosened hair falling to her waist, luminous, glowing with energy, she might have been an angel and devil in one woman. The delicacy of her face, the perfection of her virginal body contrasted with the passion, the lust, that leapt from her eyes, from her every pore."—Gertrudis, *Like Water for Chocolate*

LITERARY MERIT

★ ★ ★

A Natural History of the Senses

by Diane Ackerman

Throughout this book, Ackerman urges us to become reunited with our senses. The award-winning poet's essays should inspire you to slow down and admire, smell, caress, and taste the roses. After taking this sensualist journey through history, literature, philosophy, psychology, music, and more, you'll have a new understanding of the pain you feel when you prick yourself on a thorn. PBS put together a five-hour series inspired by this book and narrated by Ackerman, but it works much better on the page.

Department of Great Lines

"Violets smell like burnt sugar cubes that have been dipped in lemon and velvet, I might offer, doing what we always do: defining one smell by another smell or another sense."—*A Natural History of the Senses*

LITERARY MERIT

★ ★

Perfume: The Story of a Murderer

by Patrick Suskind

World Fantasy Award 1987

This novel answers the age-old question: Can a person who does not stink be possessed by the devil? It's eighteenth-century France and the city streets reek. Jean-Baptiste Grenouille is a savant sniffer, born without any odor at all. He concocts an aroma that makes him smell human—not only human but irresistible. His dream is to create the "essence absolue" of life, a perfume made from beautiful women. There's only one hitch. He's got to kill them to do it. This is a disturbing, beautiful story told within a compelling historical context.

LITERARY MERIT

★ ★ ★

489.

LITERARY MERIT

★ ★ ★

The Sixteen Pleasures by Robert Hellenga

Nuns and erotica go together in this rich, absorbing first novel. Margot Harrington is a twenty-nine-year-old librarian and book conservator, bored with her life, who ventures to Florence to help with the cleanup after the flooding in 1966. She ends up putting her skills to work at the waterlogged library of a struggling Carmelite convent. There, one of the nuns finds, bound into a prayer book, a shockingly pornographic volume, "Sixteen Pleasures"—Aretino's lost sonnets and erotic drawings, which the pope has ordered burned. But it would fetch a fortune, which could be used to save the abbey. Entrusted by the abbess with the pages, Margot lovingly restores them and embarks on a quest to find a buyer. This debut novel established Hellenga as a major literary talent.

490.

LITERARY MERIT

★ ★

The True History of Chocolate
by Sophie D. Coe and Michael Coe

The authors turn their culinary anthropologist's gaze on chocolate, aka "food from the gods." The book takes the reader from Mayan to modern chocolate production with forays into the chemistry of chocolate, its various flavors, and its use as a medicine and as an aphrodisiac. Eating it as a sweet solid is a modern invention. Meticulously researched, this is a perfect guilt-free indulgence for chocoholics.

491.

LITERARY MERIT

★ ★

Woman: An Intimate Geography
by Natalie Angier

Pulitzer-winning science writer for the *New York Times*, Angier explores female physiology and offers new theories on women's evolution. Fascinating, often provocative ("most female animals are promiscuous"), she doesn't mince words. "Flatulism dies hard," she says of post-feminist Camille Paglia's take on women's sexuality. As promised, the book is "a celebration of the female body," and one could add mind and soul.

...to **Laugh** and *Cry* at the Same Time

LITERARY MERIT ★

PROVOCATIVE 🔥

INFLUENTIAL !

INSPIRATIONAL 🕊

HUMOROUS 😊

BRAINY 💡

EASY READING ☂

PAGE TURNER 📖

CHALLENGING 👓

BATHROOM BOOK 🚽

FAMILY FRIENDLY 👪

MOVIE 🎥

492.

LITERARY MERIT

★ ★

Absurdistan by Gary Shteyngart

Misha "Snack Daddy" Vainberg is the arrogant, overweight son of the 1,238th richest man in Russia. All he wants is to be left alone so he can listen to rap music in the South Bronx with his trash-talking girlfriend, but his hoped-for visa vanishes when his gangster father murders a U.S. businessman in Russia. Snack Daddy pins his hopes on the corrupt government of Absurdistan to sell him a passport. But no sooner does he get there than he gets sucked into a civil war, staged by the country's elite. Like Borat, serious commentary lurks behind the absurdities. This outrageous novel is brimming with pessimism and intellectual incorrectness.

493.

LITERARY MERIT

★ ★ ★ ★

Behind the Scenes at the Museum

by Kate Atkinson

"I exist! I am conceived to the chimes of midnight on the clock on the mantelpiece in the room across the hall," begins this multigenerational novel. Ruby Lenox is the ebullient narrator, and this is her life and the life of members of her truly dysfunctional family in grim and gritty Yorkshire. The novel takes the reader on a wild ride, caroming through the twentieth century as Ruby uncovers her family's secrets. This enchanting, wildly funny debut novel won the Whitbread Book of the Year in 1995. Reviewers compare Atkinson's writing style to Proust and Dickens—not too shabby.

494.

LITERARY MERIT

★ ★ ★ ★

Catch-22 by Joseph Heller

Set near the end of World War II, this is a hilarious and dark satire about the absurdities of the military and the insanity of war. Yossarian is the hapless Everyman, the soldier whose one goal is staying alive when everyone is trying to kill him: Elliptical reasoning abounds. Though initial reviews of this

Department of Memorable Lines

"There was only one catch and that was Catch-22, which specified that a concern for one's safety in the face of dangers that were real and immediate was the process of a rational mind. Orr was crazy and could be grounded. All he had to do was ask; and as soon as he did, he would no longer be crazy and would have to fly more missions. Orr would be crazy to fly more missions and sane if he didn't, but if he was sane he had to fly them. If he flew them he was crazy and didn't have to; but if he didn't want to he was sane and had to. Yossarian was moved very deeply by the absolute simplicity of this clause of Catch-22 and let out a respectful whistle."—*Catch-22*

book were mixed, it quickly captured the imagination of the reading public; anti-Vietnam War bumper stickers of the time read YOSSARIAN LIVES. This is a book that touched, and still touches a nerve.

The Choirboys by Joseph Wambaugh

For the novel's ten young patrol officers in the Wilshire Division of the LAPD, "choir practice" is a euphemism for rowdy, end-of-shift drinking and carousing. These guys feel utterly authentic (Wambaugh was a former LA cop) and the incidents are so bizarre you couldn't make them up. Wambaugh perfected a darkly comic, kaleidoscopic style with multiple plots and rapid-fire action that infuses today's cop-style TV shows. It was made into a terrible movie.

495.

LITERARY MERIT

★ ★ ★

A Heartbreaking Work of Staggering Genius by Dave Eggers

496.

LITERARY MERIT

★ ★ ★

The first half of this novelistic memoir tells the story of Eggers parents' tragic death and how, just out of college, he became surrogate father

The Author Explains the Title

"Like most titles, it was a place-marker for a long time, and it kind of became too late to change it. And it made me laugh."

—Dave Eggers

to his eight-year-old brother Toph. The second half plunges into a manic struggle to get a startup magazine off the ground. The book is rife with self-conscious storytelling with pages-long footnotes of self-indulgent rants. Still it's a virtuoso performance (a 2001 Pulitzer finalist) and delivers all the promised heartbreak and genius.

A House for Mr. Biswas by V. S. Naipaul

497.

LITERARY MERIT

★ ★ ★ ★

Mr. Biswas is born "six-fingered, and the wrong way." The pundit who examines the baby says, "He will have an unlucky sneeze." And so he does. Considered Naipaul's masterwork, this dark and funny novel which evokes the writing style of the nineteenth century, tells the life story of a poor guy attempting to make a living in post-colonial Trinidad, desperately wanting his own home. Naipaul based the novel on his father's experience. In 2001 he was awarded the Nobel Prize for Literature for "having united perceptive narrative and incorruptible scrutiny in works that compel us to see the presence of suppressed histories."

It's Always Something by Gilda Radner

498.

LITERARY MERIT

★ ★

The title is a trademark line of Roseanne Roseannadanna, the character Gilda Radner played on *Saturday Night Live*. This book is Radner's poignant account of her valiant struggle with ovarian cancer. She wanted a happy ending. "Never mind," as another one of her characters might have said.

499.

LITERARY MERIT

★ ★ ★

The Little Disturbances of Man
by Grace Paley

Grace Paley tells stories but mostly she writes about people. Aunt Rose, in the collection's opening story, "Goodbye and Good Luck," reminisces about her long affair with a famous Yiddish theater actor: "I was popular in certain circles. I wasn't no thinner, only more stationary in the flesh." These eleven stories, her first published collection from 1959, give a taste of Paley's wildly funny but ultimately serious take on life. In 1993, Paley was awarded the REA Award for her contribution to the short story as an art form.

500.

LITERARY MERIT

★ ★

The Lone Ranger and Tonto Fistfight in Heaven by Sherman Alexie

This is a book of twenty-two autobiographical short stories, each a vignette of life on a Spokane Indian reservation. Meet Thomas Builds-a-Fire who tells stories, Jimmy Many Horses who jokes about his cancer, and Aunt Nezzy who makes an elaborately beaded traditional dress that's too heavy to wear. A Spokane/Coeur d'Alene Indian, Alexie writes with poetic, sometimes dark and disturbing honesty.

> **What movie was *The Lone Ranger and Tonto Fistfight in Heaven* made into?**
>
> *Smoke Signals*

501.

LITERARY MERIT

★ ★ ★ ★

Midnight's Children by Salman Rushdie

Booker Prize 1981

Two children born at midnight, at the very moment when India and Pakistan become independent nations, are switched at the hospital. One goes home to be raised by a wealthy Muslim family, the other to be raised in an impoverished Hindu household. Like the other 1,001 children born on India's day of independence, each possesses a magical power. Latin writers have no lock on magical realism, and here it serves to protest the fragmentation of a nation. This book catapulted Rushdie to worldwide readership and fame, and scholars compare this much celebrated novel to *Ulysses* for its scope and significance.

Portnoy's Complaint by Philip Roth

502.

In a tour-de-force of supine comedy, thirty-three-year-old unmarried Alex Portnoy lies on Dr. Spielvogel's couch and bares all. He is "torn by desires that are repugnant to my conscience, and a conscience repugnant to my desires." Neurotic? You should only know. Having suffered a mother who eroticized his ears, he argues that he comes by his sexual perversity and obsession with masturbation honestly. Guilt and insecurity never had it so good.

Department of Great Final Lines

"So. Now vee may perhaps to begin. Yes?"—*Portnoy's Complaint*

LITERARY MERIT

★ ★ ★ ★

🔥 ❗ 😀 🎥

The Shipping News by Annie Proulx

503.

Pulitzer 1994; National Book Award 1994
Heartbreak and humor coexist in an unforgettably bleak landscape in Proulx's bestselling novel. Quoyle, with his "great damp loaf of a body," is the ultimate self-deprecating loser. He drifts from job to job and marries badly. His wife leaves him and sells their two daughters to a pornographer. He rescues his children, moves to Killick-Claw, a harbor village in a desolate corner of Newfoundland, and reclaims his life.

LITERARY MERIT

★ ★ ★ ★

🔥 🕊 😀 👓

🎥

The Swimming Pool Library by Alan Hollinghurst

504.

This dark, erotic novel involves an unlikely friendship between elderly Lord Nantwich and the young, aristocratic, and feckless William Beckwith—British gay lifestyle in the decade before AIDS changed everything. This was a stunning debut novel for Hollinghurst who went on to win the Booker Prize in 2004 for *The Line of Beauty.*

LITERARY MERIT

★ ★ ★

🔥 😀

Tales of the City by Armistead Maupin

505.

Before there was *Sex and the City* there was sex and the other city—San Francisco. This first in a series of six books started as a 1970s newspaper serial. These are comedic, bawdy tales of sexual liberation (gay, lesbian, hetero, and everything in between) in more innocent times.

LITERARY MERIT

★ ★ ★

🔥 ❗ 😀 🎥

Tobacco Road by Erskine Caldwell

506.

Dirt-poor, uneducated sharecroppers do appalling things to each other in this dark, satirical 1932 novel. In the opening episode, Lov Bensey visits the Jeeters, his twelve-year-old wife Pearl's family, to complain that after a year of marriage Pearl still won't have anything to do with him. He torments the starving Jeeters by eating a turnip. The novel is considered a classic of Southern Gothic. Read it with *Grapes of Wrath* for searing portraits of the poor and downtrodden during the Great Depression.

LITERARY MERIT

★ ★

🔥 ❗ 😀 ⛱

🎥

507.

LITERARY MERIT

★ ★ ★

Trout Fishing in America by Richard Brautigan

He's been called the "Mark Twain of the '60s and this was his first novella. Are we really talking about trout fishing here? Well, yes and no. He wrote it while camping with his wife and daughter in 1961, but the cover features Brautigan posed in front of a statue of Ben Franklin in San Francisco's Washington Square Park. As always, Brautigan's prose is poetry and his fiction is philosophy.

508.

LITERARY MERIT

★ ★ ★ ★

White Teeth by Zadie Smith

This is a modern Dickensian saga of two families, one from Jamaica and one from Bangladesh, spanning twenty-five years. It begins with the friendship between working class Archie Jones and Bengali Muslim Samad Iqbal. It explores immigration and assimilation, roots and rootlessness. Satirical, ironic, and acerbic, this debut novel was written when Smith was only twenty-four years old and won the Whitbread First Novel Award in 2000.

...*for* **Hubris**

LITERARY MERIT ★

PROVOCATIVE 🔥

INFLUENTIAL !

INSPIRATIONAL ➷

HUMOROUS 😊

BRAINY 💡

EASY READING ☂

PAGE TURNER 📖

CHALLENGING 👓

BATHROOM BOOK 🚽

FAMILY FRIENDLY 👪

MOVIE 🎥

509.

LITERARY MERIT

★ ★ ★ ★

All the King's Men by Robert Penn Warren

Pulitzer 1947

Based on the life of Louisiana's larger-than-life Governor Huey P. Long, this novel dramatizes the rise to power of a populist Southern politician, Willie Stark, and his transformation from idealistic attorney to ruthless manipulator of people and power. The novel's narrator, Jack Burden, is not as easily corrupted. This provocative treatment of power and corruption has lost none of its punch.

510.

LITERARY MERIT

★ ★ ★

Advertisements for Myself
by Norman Mailer

This collection, first published in 1959, is a compendium of stories, essays, reviews, interviews, novel excerpts, plays and poems (including one called "The Drunk's Bebop and Chowder"). They are a potent reminder of the brilliance of this self-obsessed, angry agent provocateur of an era.

> **Department of Great Rants**
>
> "There may have been too many fights for me, too much sex, liquor, marijuana, Benzedrine and seconal, much too much ridiculous and brain-blasting rage at the miniscule frustrations of a most loathsome literary world, necrophiliac to the core—they murder their writers, then decorate their graves."—Norman Mailer, *Advertisements for Myself*

511.

LITERARY MERIT

★ ★ ★

American Prometheus: The Triumph and Tragedy of J. Robert Oppenheimer
by Kai Bird and Martin J. Sherwin

Pulitzer 2006; National Book Critics Circle 2005

This book presents a complex portrait of Oppenheimer, the physicist who led the Manhattan Project and became known as "father of the atomic bomb." Oppenheimer grew up privileged and had a brilliant career. With his famous piercing blue eyes, he possessed intense personal magnetism. But since youth he'd been frail, underweight, and intensely troubled. He fully understood the magnitude of the "evil thing," the "terrible weapon that has altered abruptly and profoundly the nature of the world." This is a great biography and a cautionary tale—the parallels to the present day are inescapable.

The Bonfire of the Vanities by Tom Wolfe

512.

LITERARY MERIT

★ ★ ★

Master of the Universe bond trader Sherman McCoy's black Mercedes takes a wrong turn in the Bronx and hits a black pedestrian. What follows is a media nightmare. Crooks, cops, a Hasidic landlord, a politically connected black minister, and a white mayor pile on to take advantage. Wolfe, a brilliant stylist and satirist, has said that the main character in this novel is New York City, and this huge bestseller certainly captured the city in a money-hungry era.

Did You Know It Means . . .

Bonfire of the Vanities: The burning of objects that tempt one to sin. In 1497 Florence the most famous of these conflagrations occurred at the behest of Dominican priest Girolamo Savonarola. In Italian, *fallò delle vanitâ.*

The Great Gatsby by F. Scott Fitzgerald

513.

LITERARY MERIT

★ ★ ★ ★

The novel was first published in 1925 and set in the Jazz Age, a giddy time in the run-up before the great stock market crash. Its characters go to any lengths to get what they want. Nick Carraway tells the story of Jay Gatsby, a millionaire famous for extravagant parties at his mansion in West Egg, Long Island. Gatsby has everything, but still yearns for Daisy Buchanan, the girl who spurned his advances years earlier because he wasn't wealthy enough. Now he is, but she's married. Nick arranges for the two to meet, and nothing good comes of it. Some would argue this is the most influential novel of the twentieth century.

The Last Hurrah by Edwin O'Connor

514.

LITERARY MERIT

★ ★ ★

Four years after "he had been inaugurated for what his opponents had fondly hoped was the last time," Boston's populist Democratic mayor Frank Skeffington announces he'll run for re-election. Skeffington sees this as his last fight to keep Boston from "reverting to Government by the Pigmies." Skeffington is based on Boston's mayor James Michael Curley, one of the last big-city Irish political bosses, who traded in corruption but understood his constituents. For readers nostalgic for old-time city politics, this 1956 classic also provides a fascinating commentary on the Irish American experience.

Lords of the Realm: The Real History of Baseball by John Helyar

515.

LITERARY MERIT

★

The author slices and dices baseball, removing the mystique and revealing another dollar-driven big business. He examines the demise of the reserve clause, the formation of the player's union, and the steady rise of players' salaries. He argues that baseball continues to thrive in spite of, not because of, managers who have consistently failed to keep their eyes on the ball.

516.

LITERARY MERIT

★ ★ ★ ★

The Poisonwood Bible by Barbara Kingsolver

In this massive, hugely successful novel set in 1959, zealous Baptist minister Nathan Price leads his wife and four daughters to the Congo village of Kilanga. Blindly self-righteous, he's obsessed only with proving himself and baptizing unwilling villagers. Meanwhile his wife, Orleanna, struggles to keep the family alive, fed, and safe from animal and human predators. "I had washed up there on the riptide of my husband's confidence and the undertow of my children's needs," she says. Their marriage, as much as the place, becomes a "heart of darkness" as the story uncoils through the eyes of their daughters. This book was a Pulitzer finalist in 1998.

517.

LITERARY MERIT

★ ★ ★

The Power Broker: Robert Moses and the Fall of New York by Robert Caro

Pulitzer 1975

He was all powerful, and the realization of his vision—a new New York connected by bridges and tunnels and roadways with public parks and playgrounds—decimated neighborhoods and relocated thousands. He justified his actions: "When you operate in an overbuilt metropolis, you have to hack your way with a meat ax." Appointed by governors and mayors, Moses parlayed his power into a virtual political machine. Theodore H. White called this massive biography "a masterpiece of American reporting."

518.

LITERARY MERIT

★ ★ ★

Primary Colors by Anonymous

When this novel was first published in 1996, there was no question that the charming, calculating, womanizing, doughnut-eating presidential candidate was a thinly fictionalized Bill Clinton, and the events were based on his 1992 primary campaign. It took a while before the anonymous author was revealed to be Washington insider, *Newsweek* columnist Joe Klein.

519.

LITERARY MERIT

★ ★

Rising Tide: The Great Mississippi Flood of 1927 and How It Changed America by John Barry

One of the worst natural disasters of the twentieth century was made much more devastating by a policy, driven by wealthy planters, to rely only on levees to contain Mississippi floodwaters. Flooding raged from Illinois and Missouri to the Gulf of Mexico. The powerful banking leaders who ran New Orleans dynamited the levee to protect the city's commerce, flooding the lower parishes. Three hundred thousand African Americans were forced into refugee camps. Read it to understand why many thought it not inconceivable that the levee breach during Hurricane Katrina was not an accident. This book won the Southern Book Critics Circle Award in 1997.

Quiz Time!

Match the historical figure to the fictional character to the actor who played him in the movies.

The man	The character	The actor
I. Huey Long	1. Frank Skeffington	a. Spencer Tracy
II. Bill Clinton	2. Jack Stanton	b. Broderick Crawford (1949), Sean Penn (2006)
III. James M. Curley	3. Willie Stark	c. John Travolta

Answers: I-3-b, II-2-c, III-1-a

...for GREED

LITERARY MERIT ★

PROVOCATIVE 🔥

INFLUENTIAL ❗

INSPIRATIONAL 🕊

HUMOROUS 😃

BRAINY 💡

EASY READING ☂

PAGE TURNER 📖

CHALLENGING 👓

BATHROOM BOOK 🚽

FAMILY FRIENDLY 👪

MOVIE 🎥

520.

LITERARY MERIT

★

Bringing Down the House: The Inside Story of Six M.I.T. Students Who Took Vegas for Millions by Ben Mezrich

This nonfiction account about a bunch of MIT students who use math and teamwork to beat the Nevada casinos reads like a thriller. Financed by shadowy investors, the kids deploy themselves in teams and spread out across the casino floor. Ultimately, greed leads to the team's undoing, and the casinos get wise and fight back. From ivory tower to seedy underworld, this is a wild ride.

Department of Odds and Ends

Card counting systems: "the simple rule of thumb preaches that low cards remaining in the deck are bad for the player, and high cards are good."
—*Bringing Down the House*

521.

LITERARY MERIT

★

Confessions of an Economic Hit Man

by John Perkins

When this book suggested that corporate interests might have undue influence over politicians and coined the term *corporatocracy* to describe that nexus, it sounded to some like warmed-over conspiracy theory. To others it had the ring of truth. Perkins argues that American corporations and government agencies employ "economic hit men" who bribe emerging economies—and he ought to know because he was one of them. Perkins exposes a shocking, secret world, and in this compelling volume confirms every paranoid thought any of us ever had. Money really does make the world go 'round. Globalization, feh.

522.

LITERARY MERIT

★ ★

Conspiracy of Fools by Kurt Eichenwald

Written like a suspense novel, this book reveals the lies, crimes, and mismanagement behind the Enron meltdown. With a cast that includes George W. Bush, Dick Cheney, and Bill Clinton, this is "corporatocracy" in action on the domestic front. If only it were fiction. This is investigative reporting at its best.

523.

LITERARY MERIT

★ ★

Den of Thieves by James B. Stewart

Michael Milken, Ivan Boesky, Martin Siegel, and Dennis Levine—during the frenzied takeover times of the 1980s, they were part of the largest insider trading ring in Wall Street history. World-class crooks, they thought they were untouchable and they almost were. In 2002, *Forbes* named this among the "20 Most Influential Business Books." It's a readable, fast-paced look at hubris on a grand scale from a Pulitzer-winning journalist.

Devil Take the Hindmost: A History of Financial Speculation by Edward Chancellor

LITERARY MERIT

★ ★

Irrational manias have accompanied many a financial boom or bust. Chancellor gives a historical perspective. From the "tulipomania" that gripped Holland in the 1600s to the Japanese real estate market euphoria of the 1980s to the Internet stock craze that climaxed in 2000, greed and hope trump logic every time. Speculation, he says, is a "Utopian yearning" in the face of the "inevitable inequalities of wealth." This entertaining, informative book was named one of six "indispensable investment classics" by *Money* magazine.

House by Tracy Kidder

LITERARY MERIT

★ ★

The yuppie homeowners want great work cheap; the builders want to do great work, too, but be well compensated; the architect wants his vision realized. One reviewer suggests that the homeowners in this nonfiction are so greedy and annoying that they deserved to have the house burn down on the day they moved in. Anyone in the building trade or about to get into a construction project would do well to read this cautionary tale book by a Pulitzer-winning author.

The Orchid Thief: A True Story of Beauty and Obsession by Susan Orlean

LITERARY MERIT

★ ★

The author headed to South Florida to investigate when she heard about John Laroche, an eccentric and charismatic plant dealer who, along with some Seminole Indians, had been caught

What movie was *The Orchid Thief* made into?

Adaptation

poaching rare orchids from Fakahatchee Strand. Laroche's dream: to make a fortune by cloning the rare ghost orchid *Polyrrhiza lindenii*. Orlean writes the true story of how she ended up following Laroche for two years, through mosquito-infested swamps and into the rarified world of orchid fanatics. When asked who was the "hero" of this book, Orlean told an interviewer it's the ghost orchid: "for both managing to drag me and half of the human population through horrible swamps to look for it, and at the same time for remaining completely elusive, to this day invisible to me, among others." A unique, fascinating read.

527.

LITERARY MERIT

★ ★ ★

She's Come Undone by Wally Lamb

"Mine is a story of craving," says the novel's narrator Dolores Price. Consuming is her way of dealing with the considerable woes of her life—abandonment, mental illness, rape, the works. She is one of those characters you'll root for, long after turning the final page. This was Lamb's debut novel, a finalist for numerous book prizes, and a *New York Times* Notable Book of 1992.

528.

LITERARY MERIT

★ ★ ★

Vanity Fair by William Makepeace Thackeray

Thackeray subtitled this "a novel without a hero" because none of the characters in this biting satire of the greed and hypocrisy of nineteenth-century England are even slightly heroic. Becky Sharp is cold, smart, and calculating, while a "good" character like her friend Miss Amelia Sedley is insufferably dull. This classic, first published in installments during 1847–1848, contains period social commentary laced with delicious melodrama.

...for HISTORICAL

LITERARY MERIT ★

PROVOCATIVE 🔥

INFLUENTIAL !

INSPIRATIONAL 🕊

HUMOROUS 🎭

BRAINY 💡

EASY READING ☂

PAGE TURNER 📖

CHALLENGING 👓

BATHROOM BOOK 🚽

FAMILY FRIENDLY 👪

MOVIE 🎥

529.

LITERARY MERIT

★ ★ ★

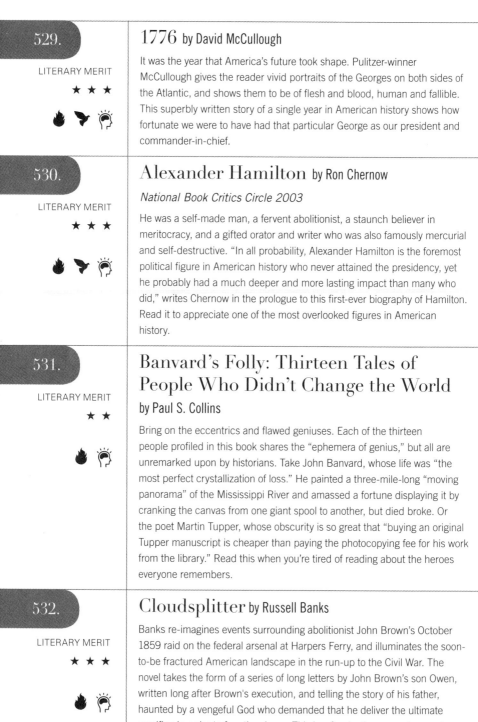

1776 by David McCullough

It was the year that America's future took shape. Pulitzer-winner McCullough gives the reader vivid portraits of the Georges on both sides of the Atlantic, and shows them to be of flesh and blood, human and fallible. This superbly written story of a single year in American history shows how fortunate we were to have had that particular George as our president and commander-in-chief.

530.

LITERARY MERIT

★ ★ ★

Alexander Hamilton by Ron Chernow

National Book Critics Circle 2003

He was a self-made man, a fervent abolitionist, a staunch believer in meritocracy, and a gifted orator and writer who was also famously mercurial and self-destructive. "In all probability, Alexander Hamilton is the foremost political figure in American history who never attained the presidency, yet he probably had a much deeper and more lasting impact than many who did," writes Chernow in the prologue to this first-ever biography of Hamilton. Read it to appreciate one of the most overlooked figures in American history.

531.

LITERARY MERIT

★ ★

Banvard's Folly: Thirteen Tales of People Who Didn't Change the World
by Paul S. Collins

Bring on the eccentrics and flawed geniuses. Each of the thirteen people profiled in this book shares the "ephemera of genius," but all are unremarked upon by historians. Take John Banvard, whose life was "the most perfect crystallization of loss." He painted a three-mile-long "moving panorama" of the Mississippi River and amassed a fortune displaying it by cranking the canvas from one giant spool to another, but died broke. Or the poet Martin Tupper, whose obscurity is so great that "buying an original Tupper manuscript is cheaper than paying the photocopying fee for his work from the library." Read this when you're tired of reading about the heroes everyone remembers.

532.

LITERARY MERIT

★ ★ ★

Cloudsplitter by Russell Banks

Banks re-imagines events surrounding abolitionist John Brown's October 1859 raid on the federal arsenal at Harpers Ferry, and illuminates the soon-to-be fractured American landscape in the run-up to the Civil War. The novel takes the form of a series of long letters by John Brown's son Owen, written long after Brown's execution, and telling the story of his father, haunted by a vengeful God who demanded that he deliver the ultimate sacrifice in order to free the slaves. This is a fascinating, complex amalgam of fact and fiction written in finely crafted prose.

Family by Ian Frazier

Frazier unearthed family diaries, letters, and documents, and crisscrossed the country (24,000 miles in a van) in search of his family's past. From the Revolutionary War to today, he presents generations of his own middle-class, Midwestern family wrapped around a history of the United States. The *New York Times* called this highly personal book a "remarkable history of an unremarkable family."

533.

LITERARY MERIT

★ ★ ★

A History of the World in 6 Glasses

by Tom Standage

Standage devotes two chapters each to the six beverages that each defined a pivotal historical period: Beer, wine, spirits, coffee, tea, and cola. Read about tea's journey from Asia to Europe, its role in the British Empire and the tea tax on the American colonies. Follow Coca-Cola from its beginnings as a nineteenth-century patent medicine through its pivotal role in the development of America's consumer culture and globalism. Standage's zippy narrative is full of fascinating tidbits of information, perfect to toss out at the next cocktail party where you're sipping Brunello di Montalcino.

534.

LITERARY MERIT

★ ★

The History of the World in 10½ Chapters

by Julian Barnes

Fictional and historical narratives intertwine in loosely connected chapters in a book that defies categorization as a conventional novel. Barnes's ironic take on history begins with a fictional account of Noah's Ark, narrated by a stowaway parasite. Fantasy animals like the hippogriff and unicorn are passengers, and Noah is "not a nice man." The next section jumps to Arabs hijacking an American cruise ship. This book, which reads more like short stories than a novel, bowled over the critics.

535.

LITERARY MERIT

★ ★ ★ ★

John Adams by David McCullough

Pulitzer 2002

"In the cold, nearly colorless light of a New England winter, two men on horseback traveled the coast road below Boston . . ." begins McCullough's masterful portrait of the second president of the United States. Always overshadowed by the presidents who bracketed him, John Adams was a revolutionary leader and primary draftsman of the American Constitution. He vied bitterly with Jefferson, then became his friend, and the two died on the same day, July 4, on the fiftieth anniversary of the Declaration of Independence.

536.

LITERARY MERIT

★ ★ ★ ★

537.

LITERARY MERIT

★ ★ ★

Julian by Gore Vidal

This is the entertaining fictional "memoir" of fourth-century Emperor Constantine's nephew, the reclusive and scholarly Julian. He became Emperor Julian "the Apostate," famous for trying to halt the spread of Christianity, and was a military genius who refused to be Constantine's puppet ruler. His devotion to restoring the gods of Hellenism led to his murder after only four years as a humane and compassionate ruler. This imaginative work is considered one of Vidal's best and richest historical fictions.

538.

LITERARY MERIT

★ ★ ★ ★

The Making of the Atomic Bomb
by Richard Rhodes

Pulitzer 1988; National Book Award 1987; National Book Critics Circle 1987

This comprehensive look at the scientific discoveries that led up to the development of the atomic bomb sets them in historical and political context. Rhodes chronicles the discoveries of the atomic nucleus and nuclear fission, the inventions of the mass-spectroscope and cyclotron, the creation of plutonium and tritium, and the triggering of a nuclear chain reaction in uranium. Included are fascinating biographical sketches of the men and women physicists who worked on the science behind the bomb. Reviewers have compared this to T*he Rise and Fall of the Third Reich* for its scope and significance. Read it to understand how science, technology, and war are lethally intertwined.

539.

LITERARY MERIT

★ ★ ★

Mayflower: A Story of Courage, Community, and War by Nathaniel Philbrick

This is a vivid account of a gruesome and morally ambiguous period in early American history. It tells how the Wampanoag Indians saved the poorly prepared Pilgrims during that first desperate winter. The Pilgrims and Wampanoags lived peacefully until 1675 when war broke out and 5,000 lives were lost. Philbrick gives both the English American and the Native American perspectives, and tells a tale of tragedy and unintended consequences.

A Midwife's Tale: The Life of Martha Ballard, Based on Her Diary, 1785–1812

by Laurel Thatcher Ulrich

Pulitzer 1991

From the pages of a real diary emerges a portrait of a midwife in eighteenth-century rural England, a busy woman whose work brought her into the loves, lives, and deaths of her neighbors. As her flax field blossomed, "scarlet fever ripened" in the nearby town. Read it to see how a hugely talented historian teases an enthralling narrative from recorded facts.

540.

LITERARY MERIT

★ ★ ★ ★

Oldest Living Confederate Widow Tells All by Allan Gurganus

By the age of 99, Lucy Marsden had witnessed the tragedy of the American South, and in this novel she tells it boldly and vividly: "My English may be ugly as a mud fence but I know what a story is." This was Gurganus's first novel, and in it he explores the twin horrors of slavery and war while celebrating the survival of the human spirit.

541.

LITERARY MERIT

★ ★ ★

The Pillars of the Earth by Ken Follett

From the author usually identified with taut espionage techno-thrillers, this novel (his most popular book) is set in the Middle Ages. Against the wishes of a bishop, the fictional town of Kingsbridge struggles to build its own cathedral and fulfill the dream of Tom Builder, a master builder, and the Kingsbridge prior Brother Phillip. Fascinating characters and multiple story lines are set against a rich historical backdrop. Follett's skill as a thriller writer makes this thick historical fiction a page turner.

542.

LITERARY MERIT

★ ★

Ragtime by E. L. Doctorow

National Book Critics Circle 1975

Doctorow intertwines the stories of three families in New Rochelle and New York City at the dawn of the twentieth century. One is white, American, and upper middle class. Another is a lower-class family of struggling Jewish immigrants. And the third is headed by an African American ragtime musician whose fine new car and good fortune earn him jealousy and violence. Real historical figures take fictional journeys (Jung and Freud take a boat together through a Tunnel of Love at Coney Island) and interact with the imagined characters of this celebrated novel.

Department of Memorable Characters

"When Mother came to the door the colored man was respectful, but there was something disturbingly resolute and self-important in the way he asked her if he could please speak to Sarah."
—Coalhouse Walker Jr. in *Ragtime*

543.

LITERARY MERIT

★ ★ ★ ★

544.

LITERARY MERIT

★ ★ ★

The Source by James Michener

This historical novel takes the reader back thousands of years to the beginning of the Jewish faith, while tagging along on a modern archaeological dig at Tell Makor. Michener imagines life in the ancient city, and traces the history of the Jewish faith from early persecution through the founding of Israel and modern conflict in the Middle East. When it was published in 1965, the *New York Times* reviewer called this "a wonderful rampage through history."

545.

LITERARY MERIT

★ ★ ★

Red Tent by Anita Diamant

Women in Biblical times gathered in the red tent, sequestered during menses and childbirth. In that private place they shared their secrets and passed along a heritage. Diamant tells the story of Dinah, a silent female character in Genesis. Dinah's mother shared her husband Jacob with three other women, and Diamant imagines a warm, loving relationship among Dinah, her mother, and her three "aunties," and the secrets they passed on to her. "They held my face between their hands and made me swear to remember." One reviewer suggested that this is what the Bible might have been like, had it been written by women.

546.

LITERARY MERIT

★ ★ ★

Wild Swans: Three Daughters of China
by Jung Chang

In this autobiographical work published two years after the demonstrations in Tiananmen Square, Chang writes of the last three generations of women in her family. Her grandmother was a warlord's concubine in the 1920s. Her mother was a young idealistic Communist organizer under Mao who married a leading party functionary. As an adolescent, Chang served in the Red Guard and worked on a peasant farm and in a factory. She captures the drama of each generation, and how women adapted to political winds of change. It was named the 1994 British Book of the Year.

547.

LITERARY MERIT

★ ★

The World Is Flat by Thomas Friedman

Globalization: Cheap telecommunications technology available worldwide lowered the barriers to international competition. Love it or hate it, read this book by the *New York Times* columnist and at least you'll understand how globalization leveled the playing field, enabling countries like India and China to compete in world markets. You won't be cheered by the statistics Friedman wrangles that show the United States lagging behind in educating engineers and the steady precipitous decline in federal funding for science and math research.

...for Hysterical

LITERARY MERIT	★
PROVOCATIVE	🔥
INFLUENTIAL	!
INSPIRATIONAL	🦋
HUMOROUS	😊
BRAINY	💡
EASY READING	☂
PAGE TURNER	📖
CHALLENGING	👓
BATHROOM BOOK	🚽
FAMILY FRIENDLY	👪
MOVIE	🎥

548.

LITERARY MERIT

★

The Alphabet of Manliness by Maddox

This triumph over good taste is definitely a guy thing, but if you find male adolescent humor irresistible then take a cruise through the alphabet with macho man Maddox. "C" is for Copping a Feel. Many of the other alphabetical subtitles are outright gross and offensive.

549.

LITERARY MERIT

★

Angus, Thongs and Full-Frontal Snogging: Confessions of Georgia Nicholson by Louise Rennison

Angus is a mad cat the size of a Labrador; thongs are underwear that go up your butt crack; snogging is kissing "with all the trimmings." Georgia is a cheeky, outrageously funny fourteen-year-old Brit. Written as diary entries, this very funny novel feels like Bridget Jones meets Monty Python.

550.

LITERARY MERIT

★

The Areas of My Expertise by John Hodgman

"History's Worst Men's Haircuts." "Seven Hundred Hobo Names." "Short Words for Use on a Submarine to Preserve Oxygen." "Nine Presidents Who Had Hooks for Hands." And more in this entirely fabricated almanac filled with utterly useless information. One shudders to think what other as-yet unexpressed pearls of wisdom are cluttering up Hodgman's brain.

551.

LITERARY MERIT

★ ★

Bridget Jones's Diary by Helen Fielding

Bridget records a lot in her diary. Gains 74 pounds; loses 72. Quits smoking at 9 a.m.; puffs "just one" at 9 p.m. Resolves to find true love even as she thrills to an affair with her charming but caddish boss. Our plucky heroine struggles through farce and adversity to reach a happy ending. This was named the 1998 British Book of the Year.

552.

LITERARY MERIT

★ ★

Gentlemen Prefer Blondes by Anita Loos

Anita Loos was a top Hollywood screenwriter and a brunette. It was on a cross-country train trip that she noticed men falling all over themselves to help a blonde starlet carry her bags while Loos struggled with her own. Like any good writer, Loos took notes. She created the blonde, beautiful, not too bright, mercenary Lorelei Lee and her non-nonsense brunette friend Dorothy Shaw (Marilyn Monroe and Jane Russell in the movie). Lorelei's great line is in the book: ". . . kissing your hand may make you feel very good but a diamond and sapphire bracelet lasts forever."

Get Shorty by Elmore Leonard

553.

Elmore Leonard gets Hollywood. His Chili Palmer is a Miami loan shark and brutal enforcer who learns that though Hollywood

Department of Great Opening Lines

When Chili first came to Miami Beach twelve years ago they were having one of their off-and-on cold winters: thirty-four degrees the day he met Tommy Carlo for lunch at Vesuvio's on South Collins and had his leather jacket ripped off." —*Get Shorty*

may be more alluring, it's just as dangerous as those mean streets. So, he shakes down a film producer and cuts himself a deal. Chili is hilariously in his element as he takes meetings and pitches ideas to studio execs. Snappy dialogue and sly wit are on every page.

LITERARY MERIT

★ ★ ★

Girl's Guide to Hunting and Fishing
by Melissa Banks

554.

This is a funny, charming collection of seven linked stories in which Jane Rosenal, a wisecracking fourteen-year-old, looks for love. Even though she knows it's ridiculous, she succumbs to advice she finds in a book *How to Meet and Marry Mr. Right* ("Play hard to get." "Don't be funny.") with hilarious results.

LITERARY MERIT

★ ★

The Hitchhiker's Guide to the Galaxy
by Douglas Adams

555.

This classic sci-fi novel coined the phrases "mostly harmless," "don't panic," and "42" (the answer to life's ultimate question). In it, Arthur Dent throws himself in front of a bulldozer that's about to destroy his house to make way for a highway (see *Watership Down*). Dent's best friend, Ford Prefect, a visitor "from a small planet somewhere in the vicinity of Betelgeuse," persuades him that the earth itself is about to be obliterated to make way for a galactic freeway. The dynamic duo hastily hitch a ride on a passing starship. No one writes with the same mirth and whimsy at the birth and death of the universe.

LITERARY MERIT

★ ★

Lucky Jim by Kingsley Amis

556.

The protagonist is a hapless academic, Jim Dixon, who considers his own scholarly research the epitome of "niggling mindlessness." He's worried about losing his job, and his bumbling department head can't or won't clue him in on his future prospects. He has a girlfriend with terrible taste in clothing and an annoying laugh. He more or less inherited her and her neuroses after her feeble suicide attempt. Every novelist should have such a felicitous first book.

LITERARY MERIT

★ ★ ★ ★

557.

LITERARY MERIT

★

! 😄 🏖 📖 🎥

One for the Money by Janet Evanovich

This mystery novel introduced out-of-work lingerie buyer Stephanie Plum to the world. Her cousin Vinnie hires her as a bounty hunter. Bringing in a fugitive turns out to be much harder than she thought, especially when the person in question is Joe Morelli, a Trenton vice cop and quintessential bad boy for whom Stephanie's got the hots. This was the series that injected a healthy dose of humor and female sex hormones into the mystery genre.

> **Department of Memorable Characters**
>
> He'd grown up big and bad, with eyes like black fire one minute and melt-in-your-mouth chocolate the next. He had an eagle tattooed on his chest, a tight-assed, narrow-hipped swagger, and a reputation for having fast hands and clever fingers."
> —Joe Morelli in *One for the Money*

558.

LITERARY MERIT

★ ★ ★ ★

🔥 ! 😄

The Sot-Weed Factor by John Barth

Set in the late seventeenth century, this is a bawdy costume drama and no-holds-barred satire of humanity. The huge cast of characters includes Ebenezer Cooke; his twin sister, Anna; and Henry Burlingame, tutor-turned-suitor to both. A highlight of the novel is the supposedly secret journal of Capt. John Smith and its version of the Pocahontas story. Barth was one of the most influential writers of the last half of the twentieth century, anchored in the firmament with the likes of Thomas Pynchon and E. L. Doctorow.

> **Did You Know It Means . . .**
>
> Sot-weed factor: Tobacco salesman

559.

LITERARY MERIT

★

🔥 😄 🏖 🚽

Texas Hold 'Em: How I Was Born in a Manger, Died in the Saddle, and Came Back as a Horny Toad by Kinky Friedman

"I never thought I'd see the day when I'd miss gun racks in the back windows of pickup trucks, but I almost do." Kinky (né Richard) Friedman, country singer turned writer, mourns his lost Texas in this hilarious essay anthology. In one, he announces his intention to become the first Jewish governor of Texas and reduce the speed limit to 54.95. Sure as all heck would make a nice change. Not for the politically correct—Friedman won NOW's Male Chauvinist Pig Award in 1974 for a song he wrote.

560.

LITERARY MERIT

★

! 😄 🏖

The Undomestic Goddess by Sophie Kinsella

For humor and light romance, suspend disbelief all ye who enter here. Meet Samantha Sweeting, a twenty-nine-year-old lawyer whose eensy little mistake costs a client of the Carter Spink law firm some 50 million pounds. She beats a hasty retreat and, in a comedy of errors, ends up with a job as housekeeper to the wealthy Geigers. In just mere weeks she's gone from boiling eggs to whipping up gourmet meals. This is chick-lit at its best.

...for **Shock**

LITERARY MERIT ★

PROVOCATIVE 🔥

INFLUENTIAL ❗

INSPIRATIONAL 🕊

HUMOROUS 😂

BRAINY 💡

EASY READING ☂

PAGE TURNER 📖

CHALLENGING 👓

BATHROOM BOOK 🚽

FAMILY FRIENDLY 👪

MOVIE 🎥

561.

LITERARY MERIT

★ ★ ★ ★

Because It Is Bitter, and Because It Is My Heart by Joyce Carol Oates

Oates looks at the brutal, unforgiving world and doesn't flinch. This novel is set in a small town in upstate New York in the '50s. Iris Courtney is a young girl who witnesses a murder. The killer, Jinx Fairchild, was trying to protect her, so she protects Jinx. She's white, the daughter of a gambling father and alcoholic mother; Jinx is black, handsome, bright, and athletic. The two are bound together, for better or for worse. This was a National Book Award finalist.

562.

LITERARY MERIT

★ ★

Blue Movie by Terry Southern

What if a great Hollywood director decided to make a high-class porn flick? Big budget. Big stars. Producer Sidney Krassman (think: Stanley Kubrick) gets the funding but there are strings. The movie can only be screened in the tiny European country of Liechtenstein. Published in 1970, this novel is crass, vulgar, funny, and yes, shocking.

563.

LITERARY MERIT

★ ★ ★ ★

The Book of Evidence by John Banville

Freddie Montgomery is an arrogant but oddly likable cad who lives in exile on a Mediterranean island. His wife and child are kidnapped when a debt he owes comes due, and Montgomery returns to Ireland to get the money to pay it off. While stealing a painting from an old friend, he brutally murders the household maid with a hammer—not because he must, but because he can. This chilling novel is told in the guise of Montgomery's courtroom deposition—but the evidence he gives is of his life, not his crime. This was a Booker Prize finalist.

Department of Odds and Ends

John Banville's *The Book of Evidence* is loosely based on a notorious true crime. Dubliner Malcolm MacArthur needed to money to support his expensive lifestyle. He murdered twenty-seven-year-old nurse Bridie Gargan with a hammer in order to steal her car and drove off with her as she was dying.

Eventually he was arrested in the home of a friend, Patrick Connelly, the Irish government's chief adviser on legal matters and with whom he was reputedly having a homosexual relationship. Because he admitted to the killing, he was sentenced to life and was never tried, protecting powerful government officials from embarrassment.

The incident gave rise to the Irish slang "GUBU" (Grotesque Unbelievable Bizarre Unprecedented).

Eight Men Out: The Black Sox and the 1919 World Series by Eliot Asinof

564.

LITERARY MERIT

★ ★

It was baseball's sordid perfect storm: naïve players, corrupt politicians, mercenary owners, crooked gamblers, and a group of eight Chicago White Sox players who were willing to throw the 1919 World Series. The Black Sox scandal—there are villains and there are victims, but only the players paid the price. This is on the *Sports Illustrated* list of Top 100 Sports Books of All Time.

Little Children by Tom Perrotta

565.

LITERARY MERIT

★ ★ ★

In this satirical novel, suburban moms and dads behave more like children than their children. Perrotta, who was once a stay-at-home dad, makes his jaundiced view of these vacuous parents evident from the novel's opening lines: "The young mothers were telling each other how tired they were. This was one of their favorite topics, along with the eating, sleeping, and defecating habits of their offspring. . . ." Ouch. Ronnie, the local predatory pedophile who's recently been released from jail, throws the neighborhood into turmoil. With characters that are hard to forget, this is a twisted, compelling look at suffocating suburban life in America.

The Monk by Matthew Lewis

566.

LITERARY MERIT

★ ★

Pious Capuchin monk Ambrosio is tempted into transgression of the carnal sort by his lovely pupil Matilda, and then by Antonia whom he rapes and kills. Turns out Matilda is one of Satan's minions who orchestrated his downfall. Written in just ten weeks when Lewis was only twenty, this novel created a sensation in 1796. This is pretty lurid stuff—the Marquis de Sade was a fan.

Montana 1948 by Larry Watson

567.

LITERARY MERIT

★ ★ ★ ★

In this coming-of-age novel, twelve-year-old David Hayden tells the story of the summer in Bentrock Montana when his sheriff father faces a horrific truth. His own brother, David's Uncle Frank, a war hero and physician, has been raping local Indian women and may have murdered one. Casting a shadow over the events is David's grandfather. With extraordinary callousness, he dismisses Uncle Frank's behavior ("You know Frank's always been partial to red meat") and positions himself squarely on the side of family loyalty instead of justice. This won several fiction prizes, and was named among the "Best Books of 1993" by *Library Journal*.

568.

LITERARY MERIT

★ ★ ★ ★

Paddy Clarke Ha Ha Ha by Roddy Doyle

Booker Prize 1993

Apparently random events of an Irish childhood, seen through the eyes of ten-year-old Patrick "Paddy" Clarke, suffuse this novel. Paddy lives in the tough, working-class neighborhood with Ma and Da and younger brother Sinbad. Paddy observes his surroundings in acute detail—wet cement, hot asphalt, fire, a beloved hot water bottle, his parents arguing—but understands little. This novel is poignant and powerful, filled with earthy humor and Irish dialect.

569.

LITERARY MERIT

★ ★

Slaves of New York by Tama Janowitz

Janowitz calls this 1986 collection of stories and brief thumbnails "modern saints" and "case histories." They convey life in lower Manhattan in the '80s from the points of view of Marley Montello, an artist who thinks very highly of himself; and of Eleanor, a diffident and neurotic jewelry designer. Can you spell SELF-OBSESSED? Shocking from the first sentence: "After I became a prostitute, I had to deal with penises of every imaginable shape and size." Janowitz, who has created a provocative persona for herself, was once featured with her pets on the cover of *Modern Ferret* magazine.

570.

LITERARY MERIT

★ ★ ★

The Virgin Suicides by Jeffrey Eugenides

This macabre debut novel opens with thirteen-year-old Cecilia Lisbon hurling herself from a window and becoming impaled on an iron fence. It's Cecilia's second try at suicide, and her four sisters follow suit. The narrators are a group of young men who love the beautiful, eccentric Lisbon girls. Twenty years later they piece together the tragedy behind their deaths. Enthralling and darkly funny.

Department of Memorable Opening Lines

"On the morning the last Lisbon daughter took her turn at suicide—it was Mary this time, and sleeping pills, like Therese—the two paramedics arrived at the house knowing exactly where the knife drawer was, and the gas oven, and the beam in the basement from which it was possible to tie a rope."
—*The Virgin Suicides*

571.

LITERARY MERIT

★ ★

Wiseguy: Life in a Mafia Family
by Nicholas Pileggi

Before Tony Soprano there was Henry Hill. Based on interviews, Pileggi writes the real-life story of the gangster who had joined the Justice Department's Federal Witness Protection Program. During his twenty-five years as a "wiseguy" Hill saw it all, and the book is a virtual oral history of New York organized crime. In this morbidly fascinating portrait, there is no redeeming justice and nothing charming about the sadistic violence of Hill's everyday world.

...*for* OUTRAGE

LITERARY MERIT ★

PROVOCATIVE 🔥

INFLUENTIAL ❗

INSPIRATIONAL 🍃

HUMOROUS 😄

BRAINY 💡

EASY READING ☂

PAGE TURNER 📖

CHALLENGING 👓

BATHROOM BOOK 🚽

FAMILY FRIENDLY 👪

MOVIE 🎥

572.

LITERARY MERIT

★ ★ ★

Ashes to Ashes: America's Hundred-Year Cigarette War, the Public Health, and the Unabashed Triumph of Philip Morris by Richard Kluger

Pulitzer 1997

This encyclopedic work chronicles the history of tobacco in America. Since the 1950s, cigarette companies knew all about the health hazards associated with tobacco. Kluger shows how they misled the public, even producing pseudo-science claims for the healthful benefits of smoking. They lulled a public all too willing to be gulled into a sense of false security.

Department of Odds and Ends

In the 1920s, Philip Morris positioned the Marlboro brand of cigarettes for women. "In case anyone missed the point, the advertisements from the first bore the prominent slogan 'Mild as May,' the drawing of an obviously female hand holding a cigarette, and a smart text saying that no less outdated than the mustache cup, the overstuffed parlor, and the lapdog was the notion that 'decent respectable women do not smoke. . . '"
—*Ashes to Ashes*

573.

LITERARY MERIT

★ ★

Barbarians at the Gate: The Fall of RJR Nabisco by Bryan Burrough, John Helyar

This is the story of the $25M leveraged buyout of RJR Nabisco Corporation, up to then the largest takeover in Wall Street history. Business and betrayals, ruthless ambition and avarice, and a gripping, penetrating look at those on and behind the scenes of a bloody corporate takeover. In 2002, *Forbes* named this number 4 on its list of "20 Most Influential Business Books."

Department of Memorable Lines

"It was the spring of 1976, and at a second-tier food company named Standard Brands, things were getting ugly."
—*Barbarians at the Gate*

574.

LITERARY MERIT

★ ★

A Civil Action by Jonathan Harr

National Book Critics Circle 1995

In 1972 there was a rash of leukemia cases in Woburn, Massachusetts, and at the same time toxic pollution was found in two of the city's water wells. This is the story of eight families that filed a lawsuit against Beatrice Foods and W. R. Grace, accusing them of dumping carcinogenic chemicals. A chilling story told in rich, vivid detail, that will leave you outraged.

Dead Man Walking: An Eyewitness Account of the Death Penalty in the United States by Sister Helen Prejean

575.

LITERARY MERIT

★ ★

Acting for Jesus Christ whom she calls "Executed Criminal," Sister Prejean became the spiritual adviser to two men convicted of murder and condemned to death. One dies repentant, the other not. In this book, Sister Prejean chronicles her experiences and makes a passionate argument that capital punishment is racist, barbaric, and fails to deter crime. Her personal experience makes a persuasive argument.

Fire on the Mountain by Edward Abbey

576.

LITERARY MERIT

★ ★

In this novel published in 1962 and inspired by real events, John Vogelin is a proud New Mexican rancher defending his property rights. The United States government wants to annex his land to the neighboring White Sands Missile Range. The story is told from the point of view of his twelve-year-old grandson. Abbey, who died in 1989, became known as an environmentalist but preferred the term *agrarian anarchist*. This work puts a human face on the issue of eminent domain.

The Gulag Archipelago: 1918–1956

by Aleksandr Solzhenitsyn

577.

LITERARY MERIT

★ ★

This is the story of one of the other holocausts of the twentieth century—the Soviet government's imprisonment and extermination of tens of millions of Soviet citizens from 1929–1953 during Stalin's

Did You Know It Means . . .

Gulag: An acronym of the central Soviet office that administered prison camps after the 1917 revolution

rule. They were incarcerated in forced labor camps scattered about the country and run by the secret police. Nobel laureate Solzhenitsyn was a survivor, and he paints a vivid, damning picture of a secret country within a country.

Krik? Krak! by Edwidge Danticat

578.

LITERARY MERIT

★ ★ ★ ★

A Haitian immigrant, Danticat came to the United States at the age of twelve. Fourteen years later, in 1995, she was a National Book Award finalist with this critically acclaimed collection of nine short stories. These powerful tales of the Haitian experience explore themes of love, loss, and longing, and deliver a scathing indictment of political oppression in lyrical prose.

579.

LITERARY MERIT

★ ★

Let Us Now Praise Famous Men

by James Agee

Photographer Walker Evans's stark portraits of sharecroppers haunt the pages of this unflinching examination of the lives of three sharecropper families during the Great Depression. First published in 1939, this kaleidoscopic book (poetry, prose, essay, photo) ignited a social conscience in America by revealing a rampant, abject poverty that had been hidden from sight. What started out as a magazine assignment for Agee from *Fortune* magazine turned into an obsession.

> **Department of Memorable Lines**
>
> "All over Alabama, the lamps are out."
> —*Let Us Now Praise Famous Men*

580.

LITERARY MERIT

★ ★ ★

The Mismeasure of Man by Stephen Jay Gould

National Book Critics Circle 1981

In this lively, controversial book, Gould takes on researchers who support biological determinism and use their research to show that social and economic differences among groups arise from inherited, inborn distinctions. He shows how biological determinism has been used to advance social agendas. He reminds us of the Supreme Court's embarrassing 1927 decision upholding the legal right of the State of Virginia to sterilize a young mother who had scored a mental age of nine on the Stanford-Binet: "Three generations of imbeciles are enough," said the revered Oliver Wendell Holmes Jr. Eminently readable, highly provocative.

581.

LITERARY MERIT

★ ★

Night by Elie Wiesel

A holocaust survivor speaks out in this deeply moving autobiography. At twelve years old, Nobel laureate Wiesel lived with his parents and sister in Sighet, a small town in the mountains of Romania. When he and his family were rounded up, they didn't even know what the word *Auschwitz* meant. Wiesel completed this book in 1956 and had difficulty finding an American publisher because it was considered too morbid and sad. Today it's considered a classic, one of the most widely read Holocaust books.

582.

LITERARY MERIT

★ ★

Outrageous Acts and Everyday Rebellions by Gloria Steinem

In this book, an undercover reporter takes a job as a Playboy Bunny. All Steinem had to do was respond to an ad and stuff her bra. This collection from one of the founders of the women's movement, first published in 1983, still feels smart and funny. Consider her musing on if men could menstruate: "Men would brag about how long and how much."

Paris Trout by Peter Dexter

National Book Award 1988

LITERARY MERIT

Paris Trout is a brutal, loud-mouthed, unapologetic bigot in the post-World War II Georgia town of Cotton Point. He murders a black girl who gets in his way while he's collecting a debt from her brother, and is stunned when he's brought to trial for the crime. Trout provides cover for the bigotry the rest of the townspeople keep hidden. This tough, unsparing novel ingnites outrage at racism and a perverted criminal justice system.

Roots by Alex Haley

Pulitzer 1977

LITERARY MERIT

Author Haley's search for his past led him back seven generations to a small village in Gambia where seventeen-year-old Kunta Kinte was kidnapped by slave traders. Haley's vision of Kinte's journey across the ocean on a slave ship is one of the most gut-wrenching pieces of prose ever written. Controversy surrounds the novel's facts, but few works can elicit outrage and horror like this one. This is a hefty, meaty page turner.

Slaves in the Family by Edward Ball

National Book Award 1998

LITERARY MERIT

An invitation to a family reunion in South Carolina sparked Ball's interest in his family's plantation and slave-holding past. He knew that his family had built its dynasty on the backs of four thousand slaves. He researched his family's meticulously documented past and traveled across America and Sierra Leone to meet the relatives and descendants of the family's slaves and to tell their stories. He struggles with a legacy of cruelty, exploitation, and intimacy in this very personal effort to come to terms with his offwn history.

Suite Française by Irène Némirovsky

LITERARY MERIT

This gripping novel about France's collaboration with the Nazis during the German occupation of France was written from 1941–1942 and anchored in unfolding events. Némirovsky was a well-known, bestselling novelist and a Russian Jew whose family had fled the Bolsheviks. The novel was lost when she was sent to Auschwitz and killed. It came to light six decades later, creating a worldwide stir when it was published. It won France's esteemed Prix Renaudot in 2004—the first time the award had been given posthumously.

Among the Banned . . .

These books are among the books most frequently requested to be banned, according to the American Library Association:

The Adventures of Huckleberry Finn by Mark Twain

American Psycho by Bret Easton Ellis

Are You There, God? It's Me, Margaret by Judy Blume

Beloved by Toni Morrison

The Bluest Eye by Toni Morrison

Brave New World by Aldous Huxley

Bridge to Terabithia by Katherine Paterson

Carrie by Stephen King

The Catcher in the Rye by J. D. Salinger

The Chocolate War by Robert Cormier

The Color Purple by Alice Walker

The Handmaid's Tale by Margaret Atwood

Harry Potter (Series) by J. K. Rowling

I Know Why the Caged Bird Sings by Maya Angelou

In the Night Kitchen by Maurice Sendak

James and the Giant Peach by Roald Dahl

Lord of the Flies by William Golding

Of Mice and Men by John Steinbeck

Ordinary People by Judith Guest

Slaughterhouse Five by Kurt Vonnegut

The Stupids (Series) by Harry Allard

To Kill a Mockingbird by Harper Lee

A Wrinkle in Time by Madeleine L'Engle

...for Hope

587.

LITERARY MERIT

★ ★

Anne Frank: The Diary of a Young Girl

by Anne Frank

She was an extraordinary, bright, spunky thirteen-year-old. Her diary, kept while she and her family hid from the Nazis, is simple, eloquent, and filled with hope. She died at Bergen-Belsen, Germany, in 1945, and her story has become part of the zeitgeist.

Department of Great Characters

"It's really a wonder that I haven't dropped all my ideals, because they seem so absurd and impossible to carry out. Yet I keep them, because in spite of everything I still believe that people are really good at heart."
—Anne Frank

588.

LITERARY MERIT

★ ★ ★

The Autobiography of Miss Jane Pittman by Ernest Gaines

This novel takes the form of tape-recorded recollections of 110-year-old Miss Jane, a woman whose life in rural southern Louisiana spanned slavery, the Civil War, Reconstruction, the civil rights movement, and black militancy in the '60s. Her eloquent narrative voice flows from one recollection to another. Critics compare Gaines's prose and characters to Faulkner's.

Author's Insight

"I read a lot of slave narratives, a lot of biographies, and a lot of history by both blacks and whites, by both Southerners and Northerners. Then I listened to rural blues and listened to sermons by ministers. . . Then I said, 'Okay, I've gotten all this in me now. Imagination must take over.'"
—Ernest Gaines on writing *The Autobiography of Miss Jane Pittman*

589.

LITERARY MERIT

★ ★ ★ ★

Black Boy by Richard Wright

Wright wrote this harrowing, at times poetic, autobiographical account of his southern childhood to "give tongue to voiceless Negro boys." He grew up outside Natchez, the son of a schoolteacher and an illiterate sharecropper. Out of poverty, abuse, abandonment, and racism he grew to become a great writer. Published in 1945, this is considered one of Wright's best books and a classic American autobiography.

Common Ground by Anthony Lukas

590.

Pulitzer 1986; National Book Award 1985;
National Book Critics Circle 1985

LITERARY MERIT

★ ★ ★

This is a gut-wrenching account of the 1970s turmoil following court-ordered busing to integrate Boston schools. Lukas bases his book on in-depth interviews with three families—the Twymons (working-class black), the Divers (middle-class white), and the McGoffs (working-class Irish). This is no good guys/bad guys story. Each family's background and situation in life color their perceptions. Ultimately, hope rises from the anger.

Imagining Argentina by Lawrence Thornton

591.

This novel is set against the backdrop of Argentina's "dirty war" in which the juntas kidnapped, tortured, and killed the country's citizens. Journalist Ceclia Rueda, who has written an impassioned editorial of protest, is kidnapped. Her grieving husband Carlos, playwright of the Argentine National Children's Theater, finds that he has a gift. He can see what happened to Argentina's disappeared. He holds weekly sessions at his home, telling his listeners the fate of their loved ones. This book about bearing witness is ultimately one of hope.

LITERARY MERIT

★ ★ ★

First, You Cry by Betty Rollin

592.

NBC News correspondent Betty Rollin was the first to write frankly and straightforwardly about breast cancer. "Fact is," she says after her mastectomy, "I'm the same car I always was, except now I have a dent in my fender." The book, which was a surprise runaway bestseller, is as uplifting as pain and heartache can be.

LITERARY MERIT

★ ★

In These Girls, Hope Is a Muscle

593.

by Madeleine Blais

LITERARY MERIT

★ ★

For five straight years they had great seasons, but the championship eluded the Lady Hurricanes, Amherst High School's girls' basketball team. Then, in their 1992–1993 season, they battled their way to become Massachusetts State Champions. Journalist Blais traveled with the team, and shows how these upper-middle-class girls found what it took to win. This book was a finalist for the National Book Critics Circle Award.

594.

LITERARY MERIT

★ ★ ★

Jubilee by Margaret Walker

Walker imagines the life of her great-grandmother, Margaret Duggans Ware Brown, born a slave in Georgia, the daughter of a "house slave" and a white plantation owner. This is the story of a strong, brave black woman, and the saga of a family torn by the Civil War, Reconstruction, and Ku Klux Klan violence. The voice is authentic and the story steeped in folk tradition. Read it with *Gone With the Wind*.

595.

LITERARY MERIT

★ ★

A Long Way Gone: Memoirs of a Boy Soldier by Ishmael Beah

This is a firsthand account of war from the point of view of a child soldier. At twelve, Beah was driven with his family from home by rebel forces during Sierra Leone's 1990s civil war. Recruited by the national army, he became a soldier. He endured a life of cocaine addiction and casual killing until he was fifteen when he was "repatriated" to life with the help of a UNICEF-sponsored rehabilitation center. He tells an eloquent, memorable tale of the journey to redemption.

596.

LITERARY MERIT

★ ★ ★ ★

Look Homeward, Angel by Thomas Wolfe

Pulitzer 1988

This autobiographical, coming-of-age story is told in lush Faulknerian prose. Like the author, his character Eugene Gant grows up in rural North Carolina and goes to Harvard. Wolfe examines life's small experiences, ordinary people, and what it means to be alive.

Department of Memorable Opening Lines

"A destiny that leads the English to the Dutch is strange enough, but one that leads from Epsom to Pennsylvania, and thence into the hills that shut in Altamont over the proud coral cry of a cock, and the soft stone smile of an angel, is touched by the dark miracle of chance which makes new magic in a dusty world."
—*Look Homeward, Angel*

597.

LITERARY MERIT

★ ★ ★ ★

No Ordinary Time by Doris Kearns Goodwin

Pulitzer 1995

In July, 1940, Eleanor Roosevelt told the Democratic Convention, "This is no ordinary time." Only Britain was engaged in the war with Hitler, but the United States was being drawn in. Goodwin tells the story of what went on inside the White House and in the nation, and of the couple, Franklin and Eleanor who, despite flaws and weaknesses, were also far from ordinary.

...for *Inspiration*

LITERARY MERIT ★

PROVOCATIVE

INFLUENTIAL !

INSPIRATIONAL

HUMOROUS

BRAINY

EASY READING

PAGE TURNER

CHALLENGING

BATHROOM BOOK

FAMILY FRIENDLY

MOVIE

598.
LITERARY MERIT
★ ★ ★

The Bean Trees by Barbara Kingsolver

Marietta "Taylor" Green has her priorities: get away from rural Kentucky and stay unencumbered. She heads west in a '55 VW. In a Tucson auto shop (Jesus is Lord Used Tires), her priorities take a radical shift when she acquires three-year-old Turtle, a silent, abandoned Cherokee child. In Tucson, both Taylor and Turtle find sanctuary. This was the extraordinary debut novel and prelude to a stunning literary career.

Author's Insight

"It probably wasn't until midway through the writing that I had a grasp of the central question: What are the many ways, sometimes hidden and underground ways, that people help themselves and each other survive hard times?"
—Barbara Kingsolver

599.
LITERARY MERIT
★ ★

Bless Me, Ultima by Rudolfo Anaya

In this novel, Antonio comes of age and must choose between his father's vaquero family and ride the plains, or his mother's farmer family and work the land. When Aunt Ultima, a *curandera* (healer), comes to live with the family, he learns to gather not only herbs but also strength and self-knowledge. One of the most influential books in Chicano literature, this is a moving tale of growing up and discovering your own identity.

600.
LITERARY MERIT
★ ★ ★ ★

The Collected Short Stories of Eudora Welty by Eudora Welty

National Book Award 1983

This volume contains the complete output from a great Southern writer and modern master of the short story. In these forty-one stories, she writes characters as diverse as a fictionalized Aaron Burr, a traveling salesman, a deaf black servant boy, and an eccentric Southern matron. One of the last stories in the book, "Where Is the Voice Coming From?" was written overnight in 1963 after Welty heard the news that Medgar Evers had been assassinated in Jackson. Her first-person narrator is the man who killed Evers.

601.
LITERARY MERIT
★ ★ ★ ★

The Color Purple by Alice Walker

National Book Award 1983; Pulitzer 1983

The heartbreaking and life-affirming story of Celie is told in diary entries and letters. At fourteen she's sexually abused by a man she thinks is her father. Her two babies are taken from her "to be with God." She's forced to marry a violent widower. And on it goes. But instead of surrendering she grows stronger. This is the ultimate tale of survival and triumph over adversity.

The Complete Stories by Flannery O'Connor

602.

National Book Award 1972

LITERARY MERIT

This volume of thirty-one stories leads with O'Connor's first published short story, "The Geranium," written in 1946 when she was twenty-one. In it, Old Dudley sits looking out his window as he does every morning, waiting for his neighbors to put a geranium on the windowsill as they do every morning. The final story, "Judgment Day," is a transformed version of the same story, written by O'Connor shortly before her death. Read this for a bird's-eye view of the greatest works of one of America's literary stars.

★ ★ ★ ★

The Five People You Meet in Heaven

603.

by Mitch Albom

LITERARY MERIT

It begins with the end: a man named Eddie, dying in the sun. It's his eighty-third birthday and he dies trying to save a little girl. "But all endings are also beginnings. We just don't know it at the time." Like Scrooge's Christmas ghosts, five people whom Eddie meets in heaven explain his life. For many readers, this has the genuine power to stir and comfort.

★

The Great Bridge: The Epic Story of the Building of the Brooklyn Bridge

604.

by David McCullough

LITERARY MERIT

The 1870s was the Age of Optimism when Americans believed anything was possible. They set their sights on the impossible, and then pulled it off. Pulitzer-winning historian McCullough vividly conveys an audacious vision—a bridge connecting Manhattan and Brooklyn—and chronicles the staggering problems to be overcome and the sheer force of will it took to pull off what, even today, seems like an engineering miracle.

★ ★

I Know Why the Caged Bird Sings

605.

by Maya Angelou

LITERARY MERIT

Poet and author Angelou grew up in Stamps, Arkansas ("How maddening it was to have been born in a cotton field with aspirations of grandeur"). She faced deep-seated racism and lynch mobs. In St. Louis, where she moved to live with her glamorous mother, she was raped by her mother's boyfriend. Traumatized, she stopped speaking. When she returned to Stamps, Mrs. Bertha Flowers threw her a "life line," and she found the courage to write. As with her poetry, Angelou inspires with her life story.

★ ★ ★

606.

LITERARY MERIT

★ ★

It's Not About the Bike: My Journey Back to Life by Lance Armstrong with Sally Jenkins

At twenty-five and already a champion bike racer, Armstrong was diagnosed with a virulent form of testicular cancer. Armstrong takes the reader through the truly awful treatment that he was required to undergo, his amazing recovery, and winning the 1995 Tour de France. It's one of the most amazing comeback stories in the history of sports.

607.

LITERARY MERIT

★ ★ ★ ★

To Kill a Mockingbird by Harper Lee

Pulitzer 1961

In this iconic twentieth-century novel, a southern town is steeped in violence and racial hatred. Attorney Atticus Finch can't convince a jury to acquit a black man who is clearly innocent of raping a white girl. The story is told from the clear-eyed viewpoint of his daughter, Scout. This is one of the best-loved novels of our time, and still has heart-wrenching power, even when you know the ending.

608.

LITERARY MERIT

★ ★ ★ ★

Midwives by Chris Bohjalian

Sibyl Danforth, a midwife in small-town Vermont, is called to deliver a baby during a snowstorm. The patient suffers a stroke and dies, and Sibyl performs emergency surgery to save the baby's life . . . but did she kill the mother in the process? She is charged with murder and brought to trial. Powerful, provocative, and loaded with moral ambiguities, this novel really makes you think. Read it with *To Kill a Mockingbird.*

609.

LITERARY MERIT

★ ★

Number the Stars by Lois Lowry

Newbery Medal 1990

In 1943 the Nazis had occupied Denmark. In this novel, a Danish family protects their ten-year-old daughter's Jewish friend and her family. It's a story of friendship, heroism, and the survival of ordinary people in extraordinary circumstances, written from the perspective of a child.

610.

LITERARY MERIT

★ ★ ★

A Prayer for Owen Meany by John Irving

The unlikely, diminutive, and endearing hero of this novel, Owen Meany, can only scream. He knows he's the "instrument of God." He knows that he will die heroically and his death will serve a great purpose. It does—but not the way you or he expect. Comic and heartbreaking, this is a story to get lost in.

What movie was *A Prayer for Owen Meany* made into?

Simon Birch

Profiles in Courage by John F. Kennedy

611.

Pulitzer 1957

Kennedy was a freshman senator in 1954 when he conceived this book, profiling eight great senators from history and highlighting that moment when each stood alone for what he believed. The profiles include John Quincy Adams as the only Federalist to vote for the Louisiana Purchase, and Sam Houston refusing to support the Kansas-Nebraska Act of 1854, which would have allowed residents of the territories to decide the slavery issue for themselves. Kennedy shows how each man paid a personal price for choosing to do the right thing.

LITERARY MERIT

★ ★

Shane by Jack Schaefer

612.

"He rode into our valley in the summer of '89, a slim man, dressed in black," young Bob Starrett tells the reader. The mysterious stranger becomes a friend and champion of the Starretts as the homesteaders clash with cattle ranchers for land and survival. The enigmatic figure of Shane inspired a generation of young men.

LITERARY MERIT

★ ★

Three Cups of Tea: One Man's Mission to Fight Terrorism and Build Nations . . . One School at a Time by Greg Mortenson

613.

Mortenson barely survived his 1993 attempt to climb K2, the world's second tallest mountain. But afterward, as he recovered in the small Pakistani village of Korphe, he found his calling. He would return and repay the villager's caring and generosity by building the town's first school. He faced daunting challenges, from raising the money to facing down enraged mullahs. In this memoir, he writes about the school that became the Central Asia Institute. Since then, he's constructed more than 50 schools across Pakistan and Afghanistan. Shows how one person really can make a difference.

LITERARY MERIT

★ ★

A Three Dog Life by Abigail Thomas

614.

Thomas's husband Richard left their apartment one night to walk their dog on Manhattan's Riverside Drive. The dog came home alone. Thomas found Richard bleeding on the street, the victim of a hit-and-run driver. Traumatic brain injury left him without short-term memory, his consciousness anchored in a painful present. With dark humor, these essays reveal how one woman finds the courage to keep on going.

LITERARY MERIT

★ ★

615.

LITERARY MERIT

★ ★ ★ ★

Their Eyes Were Watching God

by Zora Neale Hurston

This Harlem Renaissance novel, a deeply moving story steeped in the African American folklore tradition, opens at dusk in rural South Florida: "The sun was gone, but he had left his footprints in the sky." The townspeople sit "in judgment" on their porches watching Janie return from burying her husband Tea Cake. In an extended flashback, Janie tells of the pain and happiness, love and loss of her life's journey. Hurston died impoverished in 1960, was buried in an unmfarked grave, and faded from literary consciousness until 1975 when Alice Walker renewed interest in her work and revived this treasure.

> **Department of Great Opening Lines**
>
> "Ships at a distance have every man's wish on board."
> —*Their Eyes Were Watching God*

...for REDEMPTION

LITERARY MERIT	★
PROVOCATIVE	🔥
INFLUENTIAL	❗
INSPIRATIONAL	🕊
HUMOROUS	😄
BRAINY	💡
EASY READING	☂
PAGE TURNER	📖
CHALLENGING	👓
BATHROOM BOOK	🚽
FAMILY FRIENDLY	👪
MOVIE	🎥

616.

LITERARY MERIT

★ ★ ★ ★

Atonement by Ian McEwan

National Book Critics Circle 2002

It's 1935 at a bucolic English country house, and thirteen-year-old Briony Tallis tells a monstrous lie that sends her older sister Cecilia's lover Robbie to prison. McEwan dramatizes the consequences of the lie for Briony and the Tallis family. Later in life, as Briony serves as a nurse in the war and Robbie is released from prison to fight at Dunkirk, she tries to make amends. This is an unforgettable book from an author the *New York Times* reviewer called "an expert on human violence—its rules, roots, and reverberations."

617.

LITERARY MERIT

★ ★ ★ ★

Blessings by Anna Quindlen

In this sweet-edged and poignant novel, a baby girl is abandoned in a cardboard box on the steps of a magnificent estate gone to seed called Blessings. Next morning she's discovered by the new handyman, Skip, a fellow with a shady past. He's instantly

Department of Great Characters

"She made small bird noises of pleasure, then spread her arms wide, bounced slightly in Skip's arms as though she were ready to fly, then seemed to think better of it and clung to his shoulder with her starfish hands."
—The baby Faith in *Blessings*

smitten, and names her Faith. He takes the foundling in and cares for her with the help of Lydia Blessing, the elderly, isolated, embittered dowager who owns the estate. The baby nurtures them.

618.

LITERARY MERIT

★ ★ ★ ★

The Deep End of the Ocean
by Jacquelyn Mitchard

Photographer Beth Cappadora's three-year-old son Ben is kidnapped from a crowded hotel lobby when his older brother Vincent is supposedly watching him. Grief-stricken and guilt-ridden, Beth seals herself up, barely managing to go through the motions of life while Vincent acts out his own grief and guilt. Nine years later, Ben shows up on Beth's doorstep asking if he can mow their lawn. There is no pat "and then they lived happily ever after" ending to this rich, complex novel, but Beth and Vincent make a kind of peace with themselves and one another.

619.

LITERARY MERIT

★ ★ ★ ★

Falconer by Cheever

In this dark novel with a surprise, uplifting ending, convicted murderer Ezekiel Farragut ("fratricide, zip to ten, #734-508-32"), once a second-rate college professor and now a drug addict and closeted homosexual, struggles to hang onto his humanity while incarcerated at Falconer. This 1977 novel showcases Cheever at the peak of his literary powers and addressing his own demons.

Gilead by Marilynne Robinson

620.

Pulitzer 2005; National Book Critics Circle 2005

LITERARY MERIT

★ ★ ★ ★

Nearing the end of his life, Reverend John Ames writes a long letter to his young son whose very existence is an unexpected blessing. He writes of falling in love with the boy's mother, and shares memories of his father and grandfather. Then a friend's prodigal son enters Ames's life. The charming young man brings with him a terrible secret. Ames struggles, trying to understand what God would want him to do. This is a thoughtful book, beautifully written.

🔥 ! 🕊 👓

Go Tell It on the Mountain by James Baldwin

621.

In 1953, James Baldwin burst onto the literary scene with this masterpiece of autobiographical fiction. Protagonist fourteen-year-old John Deacon is the son of a fiery Pentecostal preacher in Harlem. The novel spans a single day and reveals John's moral awakening. The rocking rhythms of the prose echo a church meeting in this unflinching tale of damaged lives.

LITERARY MERIT

★ ★ ★ ★

🔥 ! 🕊

The Horse Whisperer by Nicholas Evans

622.

Teenager Grace MacLean is riding her horse Pilgrim when a forty-ton truck sweeps them off the road. Both survive, but they are physically maimed and spiritually and emotionally traumatized. Grace's self-absorbed mother moves heaven and earth to track down a legendary horse whisperer, Tom Booker, a Montana loner whose gentle touch and quiet words are said to have healing power. This plucks the same chords as *The Bridges of Madison County*.

Who played Tom Booker in the movie adaptation of *The Horse Whisperer*?

Robert Redford (he also directed the film)

LITERARY MERIT

★ ★ ★

🔥 🕊 📖 🎬

Ironweed by William J. Kennedy

623.

Pulitzer 1984; National Book Critics Circle 1983

LITERARY MERIT

★ ★ ★ ★

Francis Phelan is a prodigiously unlucky man. The novel tells how, years earlier, he threw a stone that fatally cracked a strikebreaker's skull during a rally at an Albany trolley company. So he ran from Albany. Years later, he accidentally dropped his infant son and killed him. So he ran again. Now he's hit bottom. In a final effort to reconcile with his past, he returns to Albany and roams the familiar streets with his buddy Rudy, a character who makes Eeyore look upbeat. In his exploration of a hapless Everyman, Kennedy unearths breathtaking truths.

🔥 🕊 👓 🎬

624.

LITERARY MERIT

★ ★ ★ ★

Kite Runner by Khaled Hosseini

Alex Award 2004

This story of betrayal is set against the fall of the Afghan monarchy, the Soviet invasion and the mass exodus of refugees, and the rise of the Taliban. Amir, a privileged Afghan boy, fails to defend his best friend and loyal servant Hassan when he is brutalized by local bullies. Years later, Amir and his family have fled the country but "the past claws its way out." Amir is still haunted by his own cowardice. He returns to Afghanistan to help Hassan and his family, hoping it's not too late. A blockbuster novel, this compelling human drama set in an alien land spent more than a hundred weeks on the *New York Times* bestseller list.

625.

LITERARY MERIT

★ ★ ★ ★

A Lesson Before Dying by Ernest J. Gaines

National Book Critics Circle 1993

This novel is set in segregated, rural Louisiana where Jefferson, a slow, uneducated young black man has been wrongly convicted of murder. Even the public defender calls him a "dumb animal." Jefferson's grandmother begs Grant Wiggins, a local black teacher, to teach Jefferson to read: "I don't want them to kill no hog. I want a man to go to that chair, on his own two feet." In this unforgettable human drama, the two men teach each other about human dignity.

626.

LITERARY MERIT

★ ★ ★

Plainsong by Kent Haruf

Alex Award 2000

A year in the life, the novel tells the stories of the inhabitants of a small town at the edge of the plain. There's the high school history teacher, his sons, and his wife who is sliding into despair. There's a pregnant high school girl and the kind teacher who offers her help when she's thrown out by her mother. And finally, a pair of elderly cattle ranchers. Emotionally and physically adrift, these souls are rescued by the caring of others. This is one for the heart.

> **Did You Know It Means . . .**
>
> Plainsong: Music with a single melodic line and without strict meter, and traditionally sung without accompaniment; a Gregorian chant

...*for a* **SHOT IN THE ARM**

LITERARY MERIT	★
PROVOCATIVE	
INFLUENTIAL	!
INSPIRATIONAL	
HUMOROUS	
BRAINY	
EASY READING	
PAGE TURNER	
CHALLENGING	
BATHROOM BOOK	
FAMILY FRIENDLY	
MOVIE	

627.

LITERARY MERIT
★

The 7 Habits of Highly Effective People: Powerful Lessons in Personal Change
by Stephen R. Covey

A management consultant and inspirational speaker offers sound, common-sense advice for achieving "true" personal and professional success. No instant fixes or easy answers here. "Your life doesn't just happen," Covey reminds the reader. "It is, after all, your choice."

628.

LITERARY MERIT
★

Feeling Good: The New Mood Therapy
by David D. Burns

Think something often enough and soon you begin to believe in its truth—that's why it's so hard to break free from a self-loathing cycle of depression. Dr. Burns offers practical strategies for harnessing that same thought-power to get un-depressed. This massive self-help book is based on cognitive behavioral therapy and chock-a-block with anecdotes, analysis, and no-nonsense advice.

629.

LITERARY MERIT
★

How to Stubbornly Refuse to Make Yourself Miserable About Anything: Yes, Anything! by Albert Ellis

Albert Ellis specialized in straight talk, not talk therapy. He wrote this and more than 75 books exhorting readers to stop moping around and do something about it. As in: "And you can choose to stop your nonsense and stubbornly refuse to make yourself neurotic about virtually anything. . . ." He's been called the Lenny Bruce of psychotherapy.

630.

LITERARY MERIT
★

How to Win Friends and Influence People by Dale Carnegie

First published in 1937, this is still one of the best books out there on how to get people to go your way. Carnegie shows how to make a good first impression, and how to talk to people and make yourself sound interesting. For the budding capitalist, he offers this advice: "If you want to gather honey, don't kick over the beehive."

Department of Memorable Lines

"People are not interested in you. They're not interested in me. They are interested in themselves—morning, noon and after dinner."
—*How to Win Friends and Influence People*

Learned Optimism: How to Change Your Mind and Your Life by Martin E. Seligman

631.

LITERARY MERIT
★

Pessimism and learned helplessness are states of mind that, Seligman says, you can change. He gives practical advice for how, backing up his points with research on animals and humans. Quizzes measure your perspective. This is the book that helps you look on the bright side.

Pulling Your Own Strings by Wayne W. Dyer

632.

LITERARY MERIT
★

"If you use your imagination, you will find innumerable ways to victimize yourself." Here is a practical guide to how not to. This book helps its readers recognize victimizers in the family and on the job, and avoid victimizing situations.

The World According to Mr. Rogers: Important Things to Remember by Fred Rogers

633.

LITERARY MERIT
★ ★

When TV personality Mr. Rogers said, "I'm proud of you for the times you came in second, or third, or fourth, but what you did was the best you had ever done," those of us who were children watching took heart. Keep this little book by your bedside and read the quotes and essays, songs, and poems whenever you need a pat on the back and a hug.

When Bad Things Happen to Good People by Harold S. Kushner

634.

LITERARY MERIT
★

Rabbi Kushner wrote this book as he reflected on his own experience facing his three-year-old son's fatal illness. He begins with the suffering of Job, and admits, "sometimes there is no reason." The ultimate challenge is to forgive the world for not being perfect and go on living in spite of it. This is a helpful book on getting past the worst that life can throw at you.

Author's Insight

"This a very personal book, written by someone who believes in God and in the goodness of the world, someone who has spent most of his life trying to help other people believe, and was compelled by a personal tragedy to rethink everything he had been taught about God and God's ways."
—Harold S. Kushner

Who Moved My Cheese? by Spencer Johnson

635.

LITERARY MERIT
★

Your "cheese" might be a great job, a happy family, or spiritual peace. Like a modern Aesop's fable, these allegories with a cast of mice (Sniff and Scurry) and two "little people" (Hem and Haw) demonstrate the steps and missteps we take in the maze of life, trying to find our cheese. This book provides plenty of insight with the parody.

...for a KICK IN THE PANTS

LITERARY MERIT ★

PROVOCATIVE 🔥

INFLUENTIAL !

INSPIRATIONAL 🕊

HUMOROUS 🎭

BRAINY 💡

EASY READING ☂

PAGE TURNER 📖

CHALLENGING 👓

BATHROOM BOOK 🚽

FAMILY FRIENDLY 👪

MOVIE 🎥

636.

LITERARY MERIT

★ ★

Coming Home to Eat: The Pleasures and Politics of Local Foods by Gary Paul Nabhan

What if you threw out every bit of packaged food and instead ate only foods you could hunt, gather, or that were grown within a 250-mile radius of your home? An avid gardener, agronomist, and conservation biologist, Nabhan set out to do that. He lives in the Southwest, so his diet included saguaro fruit, mesquite tortillas, wild greens, and chilies. "Think globally, eat locally," Nabhan exhorts his reader. It's a message for our time—eat right, take care of the world.

637.

LITERARY MERIT

★ ★

Mindless Eating: Why We Eat More Than We Think by Brian Wansink

Don't diet; just eat less. Hunger, this Cornell University professor argues, is a state of mind. Not only do we not really know when we're hungry, we don't know when we're full. Find out about the "200 daily decisions" that each of us unknowingly makes about eating. News flash: People eat more when there's more on the plate. This is a great antidote to all the fad diet books out there.

Did you know . . .

"People eat more when you give them a bigger container. Period. It doesn't matter whether the popcorn is fresh or fourteen days old, or whether they were hungry or full when they sat down for the movie."
—*Mindless Eating*

638.

LITERARY MERIT

★ ★

Nickel and Dimed: On (Not) Getting by in America by Barbara Ehrenreich

Alex Award 2002

"How does anyone live on the wages available to the unskilled?" Essayist and social critic Ehrenreich posed that question and took jobs as a waitress, house cleaner, and Wal-Mart sales clerk to find out. This insider's look at the extraordinary struggle to get by comes as no surprise to millions of Americans on the bottom rung of the workforce. But for the average, middle-class American, reading this is like taking a cold shower in reality.

Department of Memorable Lines

"What I would like is to be able to take a day off now and then . . . if I had to . . . and still be able to buy groceries the next day."—A low-wage earning mother of two talking about her aspirations in *Nickel and Dimed*

Stumbling on Happiness by Daniel Gilbert

639.

The book poses the question: What would you think you would do right now if you learned that you were going to die in ten minutes? Gilbert argues that your answer would probably be wrong. This not a happiness how-to book. Using research and humor, Gilbert explains why we are so bad at predicting our own futures.

LITERARY MERIT

★ ★

What Color Is Your Parachute?

640.

by Richard Nelson Bolles

Updated and revised regularly, for years this has been the go-to guide for job hunters and career changers. Bolles maps the course from figuring out what job you want to hunt, giving a great interview, and on to the secrets of successfully negotiating a salary.

LITERARY MERIT

★ ★

What to Eat by Marion Nestle

641.

James Beard Cookbook Award 2007

Nutrition has become so confusing. Tune out the food industry and the so-called experts, says Nestle, a professor of food studies at New York University. Stroll through aisles of the supermarket with her as she demystifies "wild" versus farmed, organic versus "natural" and explains whether you should worry about irradiated or genetically modified foods. Her basic advice is simple. Eat less, move more, and take it easy on junk food.

LITERARY MERIT

★ ★

Did You Know . . .

"An astonishing 320,000 edible products are for sale in the United States, and any large supermarket might display as many as 40,000 of them. You're supposed to feel daunted—bewildered by all the choices and forced to wander through the aisles in search of the items you came to buy."
—*What To Eat*

You: The Owner's Manual: An Insider's Guide to the Body That Will Make You Healthier and Younger

642.

by Michael F. Roizen and Mehmet Oz

Using the "your body is your home" analogy, the authors say, "Knowing your body gives you the power to change it, maintain it, decorate it, and strengthen it." The brain, the heart, bones and joints and muscles . . . take the 50-item "Body-Quotient Quiz" and test your body knowledge, then take a tour of your insides. Who knew your adrenals could be interesting? This is packed with fascinating trivia as well as sound advice for preserving your health and youthfulness.

LITERARY MERIT

★ ★

...*to* **March into Battle**

LITERARY MERIT ★

PROVOCATIVE 🔥

INFLUENTIAL ❗

INSPIRATIONAL 🕊

HUMOROUS 🎭

BRAINY 💡

EASY READING ☂

PAGE TURNER 📖

CHALLENGING 👓

BATHROOM BOOK 🚽

FAMILY FRIENDLY 👨‍👩‍👧

MOVIE 🎥

643.

LITERARY MERIT

★ ★

All Quiet on the Western Front

by Erich Maria Remarque

World War I. In this novel, young Paul Bäumer's teacher inspires him to join the German army. He's inducted into its realities by fellow soldier Stanislaus Katczinsky. Written by a German war veteran and first published in German in 1929, the book vividly chronicles the horrors of war and the residue of alienation it leaves as it kills the spirits of the soldiers who survive. In 1930 this was made into the first major American anti-war film. It's easy to read, but you'll need time to digest its messages.

> **Department of Memorable Lines**
>
> "To me the front is a mysterious whirlpool. Though I am in still water far away from its centre, I feel the whirl of the vortex sucking me slowly, irresistibly, inescapably into itself."
> —*All Quiet on the Western Front*

644.

LITERARY MERIT

★ ★

Band of Brothers by Stephen Ambrose

World War II. Easy Company parachute infantry regiment marched into war as ordinary servicemen. Three eventful years later, from basic training to D-Day, their achievements were extraordinary. Military historian Ambrose tells this story from the point of view of the soldiers and officers who carried out the generals' orders, revealing the heroism in soldiers' day-to-day lives.

645.

LITERARY MERIT

★ ★

The Best and the Brightest

by David Halberstam

Vietnam. How "the best and the brightest" got it wrong and led the United States into a war that couldn't be won. In this bestseller, published in 1972, Halberstam concludes: "They had, for all their brilliance and hubris and sense of themselves, been unwilling to look and learn from the past." The award-winning journalist makes his case with insider anecdotes and insightful portraits of the key players like Johnson, McNamara, Rusk, and Bundy. This classic study in how political decisions are made resonates today.

646.

LITERARY MERIT

★

Black Hawk Down: A Story of Modern War by Mark Bowden

Mogadishu, Somalia. Bowden takes apart a disaster, and examines, minute by minute, what started as a Special Forces kidnapping scheme and ended with the corpses of American soldiers being dragged through the streets of Mogadishu. It reveals both the American and the Somali points of view. The desperate, bloody retreat left eighteen Americans and at least 500 Somalis dead.

A Bright Shining Lie: John Paul Vann and America in Vietnam by Neil Sheehan

Pulitzer 1989

Vietnam. This massive book takes the perspective of army field adviser Lt. Col. John Paul Vann, one of the war's most outspoken critics, who was killed in a helicopter crash in Vietnam in 1972. Sheehan is one of the reporters to whom Vann secretly gave his insider's viewpoint. This passionate, angry book is considered the definitive expose of why America failed.

647.

LITERARY MERIT

★ ★ ★

Captain Corelli's Mandolin by Louis de Bernieres

World War II. Against a backdrop of war on a Greek island, romance blooms between Italian Captain Antonio Corelli and Pelagia Iannis, the daughter of a local physician. Corelli's treasured possession is his mandolin. Joyous and heartbreaking, this haunting novel has been compared to Dickens and Tolstoy. This won the Commonwealth Writers Prize for best book in 1993.

648.

LITERARY MERIT

★ ★ ★ ★

Dispatches by Michael Herr

Vietnam. "I went to cover the war and the war covered me," says journalist Herr of his time as a war correspondent for *Esquire* magazine. Soldiers on the way to battle "had that wild haunted going-West look that said it was perfectly correct to be here where the fighting would be the worst, where you wouldn't have half of what you needed, where it was colder than Nam ever got." In this book, Herr captures the brutality, insanity, and visceral feel of what it was like to be there.

649.

LITERARY MERIT

★ ★

From Here to Eternity by James Jones

National Book Award 1952

World War II. Jones based this novel, set in Diamond Head just before Pearl Harbor, on his own army experiences. He tells the story of two angry soldiers—Robert E. Lee Prewitt, a brilliant bugler and talented boxer who refuses to bugle or box; and Milton Anthony Warden, a frustrated sergeant who begins an affair with his commanding officer's wife. This is considered *the* great novel of World War II.

650.

LITERARY MERIT

★ ★ ★ ★

Who played Robert E. Lee Prewitt and Milton Anthony Warden in the movie adaptation of *From Here to Eternity*?

Montgomery Clift and Burt Lancaster

651.

★ ★ ★

The Guns of August by Barbara Tuchman

Pulitzer Prize 1963

World War I. They called it the Great War. Military historian Tuchman details, hour by hour, the month leading up to the war and the first month of the fighting. She tells a meticulously researched, utterly absorbing story. This is a must-read for anyone with an interest in World War I.

652.

★ ★ ★ ★

Machine Dreams by Jayne Anne Phillips

Vietnam. War as the great divider. This novel tells the intertwined stories of the Hampson family—Danner, Billy, and their parents, Mitch and Jean. At the center are Mitch's experiences in World War II and Billy's in Vietnam where, after two years, he's reported missing. From beginning to end, the book echoes with loss.

653.

★ ★ ★ ★

March by Geraldine Brooks

Pulitzer 2006

Civil War. What if the absent father in Louisa May Alcott's *Little Women,* an idealist to the core, goes off to fight in the Civil War? In Brooks's historical novel, Father March is an idealistic chaplain who ends up in a Washington hospital, sick with fever and guilt. Marmee takes up the tale, and her perspective of how and why her husband entered the war shatters what the reader has learned about him. The novel achingly recounts the heavy toll that war demands and exacts.

654.

★ ★ ★ ★

The March by E. L. Doctorow

National Book Critics Circle 2005; PEN/Faulkner Award 2005

Civil War. Doctorow imagines General William Tecumseh Sherman's march, leading 60,000 Union troops through Georgia and up into the Carolinas, cutting a 60-mile-wide swath of death and chaos. He tells the story through individual lives: the courageous daughter of a slave and slave owner, a robotically clinical military surgeon, the valiant daughter of a Southern judge, and a comedic, scheming Rebel soldier. He shows how this war was brutal and it was personal.

655.

★ ★ ★

Maus: A Survivor's Tale by Art Spiegelman

American Book Award 1990

World War II. With its black and white drawings of Jews as mice, Poles as pigs, Nazis as cats, and wartime Europe as a giant mousetrap, this helped establish the medium of the graphic novel. Spiegelman based the story on his father's experiences as a Holocaust survivor. Despite the comic-book format, the story is told with chilling realism.

The Naked and the Dead by Norman Mailer

656.

LITERARY MERIT

★ ★ ★ ★

World War II. Saturated in bitterness and disillusionment, the novel presents a realistic, compassionate depiction of an imaginary battle in the Pacific. It opens onboard a ship on the eve of battle ("Nobody could sleep.") and the story is told from the point of view of members of a fourteen-man infantry platoon. Mailer wrote this, one of the best works of his brilliant career, when he was only twenty-three. Read it with Vonnegut's *Slaughterhouse Five*.

Regeneration by Pat Barker

657.

LITERARY MERIT

★ ★ ★ ★

World War I. British army neurologist William Rivers repairs psychologically broken soldiers so they can return to the fighting. His patient is Siegfried Sassoon, an utterly sane poet whose only crime has been to speak out against the war. (A real historical figure, Sassoon spent time in a mental hospital after he'd written a letter to Parliament protesting the war's needless extension.) Barker mixes fiction and fact to create a compelling, emotionally satisfying story. Read this one with *Catch-22*.

Spartacus by Lewis Grassic Gibbon

658.

LITERARY MERIT

★ ★

Third Servile War. This historical novel, published in 1933, tells a powerful story based on sparse historical evidence of a slave uprising against the Roman Empire in 73 B.C. Led by the great gladiator Spartacus, the slaves managed to destroy legion after legion of Roman troops, inflicting five humiliating defeats upon previously undefeated forces. Then the slave army aimed for an assault upon Rome itself with devastating results. Of the captured slaves, 6,000 were crucified. Gibbon (James Leslie Mitchell) was a prolific Scots writer and a Marxist who wrote this and sixteen other novels in just seven years and died at the age of thirty-four.

A Stillness at Appomattox by Bruce Catton

659.

Pulitzer 1954; National Book Award 1954

LITERARY MERIT

★ ★ ★

Civil War. This nonfiction takes the reader from the Wilderness to Appomattox and the surrender. Through the final year of the war, Grant, Meade, Sheridan, and Lee live on the pages of this final volume of Catton's trilogy, *Army of the Potomac*. Read it to understand why Ulysses S. Grant is considered a great hero.

660.

LITERARY MERIT

★ ★ ★

Tales of the South Pacific
by James A. Michener

Pulitzer 1948

World War II. The narrator says, "I try to tell somebody what the steaming Hebrides were like and the first thing you know I'm telling about the old Tohnkinese woman who used to sell human heads." These are chronologically linked stories of a tropical paradise where the war was a war of waiting ("You rotted on New Caledonia waiting for Guadalcanal"). This was Michener's first book of fiction, written when he was in his mid-thirties and a naval historian assigned to the South Pacific. It takes the reader deep inside a war zone.

661.

LITERARY MERIT

★ ★ ★

The Things They Carried by Tim O'Brien

Vietnam. They carried letters and good luck charms from home. But more than that, "They carried the emotional baggage of men who might die." This brilliant collection of interconnected short stories tells of a fictional Alpha Company of American soldiers. An eloquent elegy to lost innocence and to those who never came back, the stories are based on O'Brien's experiences and the experiences of other soldiers.

...to Run Away from Home

LITERARY MERIT	★
PROVOCATIVE	🔥
INFLUENTIAL	!
INSPIRATIONAL	🕊
HUMOROUS	😄
BRAINY	💡
EASY READING	☂
PAGE TURNER	📖
CHALLENGING	👓
BATHROOM BOOK	🚽
FAMILY FRIENDLY	👪
MOVIE	🎥

662.

LITERARY MERIT

★ ★ ★

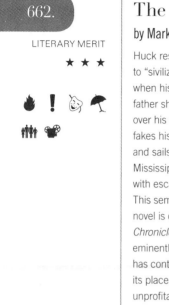

The Adventures of Huckleberry Finn
by Mark Twain

Huck resists all attempts to "sivilize" him, and when his violent, drunken father shows up to take over his rearing, he fakes his own death and sails down the Mississippi on a raft with escaped slave Jim. This seminal American novel is controversial today, as it was in its day. In 1885, the *San Francisco Chronicle* reviewer concluded, "To all readers we can commend the story as eminently readable." The *Boston Evening Traveler* demurred: "Mr. Clemens has contributed some humorous literature that is excellent and will hold its place, but his *Huckleberry Finn* appears to be singularly flat, stale and unprofitable."

> **Department of Memorable Characters**
>
> "'Now looky here; you stop that putting on frills. I won't have it. I'll lay you, my smarty; and if I catch you about that school, I'll tan you good. First you know, you'll get religion, too. I never see such a son.'"
> —Pap, Huckleberry Finn's drunken father

663.

LITERARY MERIT

★ ★ ★

Andorra by Peter Cameron

Alexander Fox is on the run from personal tragedy ("I left behind all that I needed to leave behind. Which is to say everything.") when he moves to La Plata, an idyllic spot in the tiny country of Andorra tucked into the Pyrenees. The few others living there seem inordinately interested in him, and though they seem carefree Fox discovers they, too, are on the run from grief and trouble. This is a darkly comic novel with romantic flourishes and murder mystery.

664.

LITERARY MERIT

★ ★

A Hole Is to Dig by Ruth Kraus,
illustrated by Maurice Sendak

Jennie the dog packs up her bag and leaves home. "Why is she leaving?" asks the potted plant. "Because I am discontented. I want something I do not have. There must be more to life than having everything." This is the book for the child in you, when you need to move on.

James and the Giant Peach by Roald Dahl

665.

James Henry Trotter's parents are killed by an enormous, angry rhinoceros "in full daylight, mind you, and on a crowded street." He's packed off with nothing but a pair of PJs and a toothbrush to live with odious Aunts Sponge and Spiker. Misery ensues, until a "very small old man" gives James magic crystals. By mistake, James spills them under a barren peach tree which miraculously grows a giant peach—James's salvation. Dahl writes galloping tales with huge amounts of rude outrageousness and hilarity. After you've read all of J. K. Rowling, read all of Dahl.

LITERARY MERIT

★ ★ ★

Rabbit, Run by John Updike

666.

It's 1960, and hapless Harry "Rabbit" Angstrom is a twenty-six-year-old "beautiful brainless guy" whose life peaked at eighteen when he was a high school basketball star. Now, he's spiraling downward toward mediocrity. Rabbit runs away but gets only as far as West Virginia before getting lost. He returns home and makes a series of spectacularly bad moves that ultimately lead to tragedy. He keeps running away . . . and coming back . . . and running away. This book, the first of four Rabbit novels and a novella, established Updike as a major literary talent.

LITERARY MERIT

★ ★ ★ ★

Stuart Little by E. B. White

667.

Mrs. Little gives birth to her second child, and he's no bigger than a mouse. In fact, with his "sharp nose, a mouse's tail, [and] a mouse's whiskers" he clearly is a mouse. Everyone loves him except Snowbell, the cat. Stuart's great adventure is in search of his best friend, Margalo—a bird who lived in the Boston fern plant in the Littles' living room before flying north. In this literary, lyrical chapter book for children, White showcased everything he preaches in his classic *The Elements of Style*.

LITERARY MERIT

★ ★ ★ ★

Under the Tuscan Sun: At Home in Italy

668.

by Frances Mayes

This is a memoir of buying and rehabbing an abandoned villa on the outskirts of Cortona, Italy, settling there, and the sensual pleasures that follow. "To bury the grape tendril in such a way that it shoots out new growth I recognize easily as a metaphor for the way life must change from time to time if we are to go forward in our thinking." Read this trip for the senses, and you'll want to renew your passport.

LITERARY MERIT

★ ★ ★

669.

LITERARY MERIT

★ ★ ★

Watership Down by Richard Adams

"Oh, Hazel, look! The field! It's covered with blood!" Fiver, the rabbit, senses impending danger at the outset of this allegorical novel. He convinces his fellow warren inhabitants to abandon their den just before it's annihilated by bulldozers. The intrepid rabbits search for a new home. At last they reach safety at Watership Down, but their search for mates brings them to Efrafa, a warren of docile rabbits, where they must take a courageous stand against dictatorial General Woundwort. Of course, we're not really talking bunny rabbits here, we're talking fascism. This widely acclaimed book is an Aesop's fable for our time.

670.

LITERARY MERIT

★ ★

The Wizard of Oz by L. Frank Baum

"When Dorothy stood in the doorway and looked around, she could see nothing but the great gray prairie on every side." With barely more preamble than that,

> **Did You Know . . .**
>
> The "L" in L. Frank Baum stands for Lyman.

she and Toto and the house are plucked by a tornado and deposited with a thump in the Land of the Munchkins. Dorothy gets silver (not ruby) slippers, and meets the Good Witch of the North (not Glinda), who kisses her on the forehead, bestowing a magical bruise-like mark (not a Z-shaped scar) that protects her from harm. Off she goes down the Yellow Brick Road, and when she and her companions reach the Emerald City and meet the Wizard, each must face their deepest fear. This was the first of Baum's fourteen Oz books.

671.

LITERARY MERIT

★ ★ ★

A Year in Provence by Peter Mayle

Mayle seems astonished when he announces: "We had bought a house, taken French lessons, said our good-byes, shipped over our two dogs, and become foreigners." This is a memoir of buying and rehabbing (sound familiar?) a two-hundred year old stone farmhouse in Provence with six acres planted with vines. This delightful book is the perfect introduction to goat racing and the pleasures of Provençal cooking. It will inspire you to spend time in whatever special place you've always dreamed of going.

...to

LITERARY MERIT ★

PROVOCATIVE 🔥

INFLUENTIAL !

INSPIRATIONAL 🕊

HUMOROUS 😂

BRAINY 🧠

EASY READING ☂

PAGE TURNER 📖

CHALLENGING 👓

BATHROOM BOOK 🚽

FAMILY FRIENDLY 👪

MOVIE 🎥

672.

LITERARY MERIT

★ ★ ★

The Aerialist by Richard Schmitt

A young man stumbles into a circus while looking for help pulling a stolen car from a ditch in Venice, Florida. He's immediately seduced and signs on as a lowly elephant handler. He moves up through the ranks to become a world-class tightrope walker. This debut novel is refreshingly unique, with details, dialogue, and a sense of place that feel utterly authentic. Schmitt thanks Rick Wallenda of the Flying Wallendas in his acknowledgments.

673.

LITERARY MERIT

★ ★

The Circus Fire by Stewart O'Nan

In 1944, in the middle of an afternoon circus performance with 7,000 people under the big top and a caged chute for lions and tigers blocking the main exit, a fire started. Fed by paraffin and gasoline that had been applied to the tent canvas for waterproofing, in minutes flames engulfed the crowd. O'Nan's compelling, true account of what happened shows how, in extreme circumstances, people prove who they are.

674.

LITERARY MERIT

★ ★ ★

The Circus in Winter by Cathy Day

The Great Porter Circus wintered in Lima, Indiana from 1884 to 1929, and over three generations transformed the town. For everyone who wants to know what goes on in those trailers and between the shows, this collection of eleven interrelated short stories reveals the colorful performers and their everyday lives. Perhaps these stories feel so authentic because Day grew up in a small Indiana town that was once winter quarters for several traveling circuses, and she had a great-great uncle who was an elephant trainer. This book was a finalist for the 2004 Story Prize.

675.

LITERARY MERIT

★ ★

The Circus of Dr. Lao
by Charles G. Finney

The mysterious Dr. Lao, who morphs, chameleon-like, brings his circus to the bored, jaded population of Abalone, Arizona. Instead of lions and tigers, the circus features a werewolf, a satyr, and a Medusa. The novel unwinds kaleidoscopically as tendrils of the circus ensnare the townspeople. This enthralling oddity has stayed in print since 1935.

> **Who played Dr. Lao in the movie adaptation of** *The Circus of Dr. Lao*?
>
> *Tony Randall*

Dreamland
by Kevin Baker

Gangland meets Coney Island in this sprawling debut novel, a historical fiction set in 1910. Experience early New York with all its "cigars, and oysters and roasting corn, the shady characters and the women of bad reputation." The novel takes its title from a burned-down amusement park in Coney Island, and many of the characters are based on real people. This has a glossary at the back, and you'll need it.

Author's Insight

"I was really inspired by Ric Burns's great documentary on Coney Island. . . . I saw that Coney Island was a key part of the assimilation process, a sort of blank sheet on which these people projected their greatest hopes and worst fears about life in America. Coney Island was a sort of pageant of their lives."
—Kevin Baker

The Final Confession of Mabel Stark
by Robert Hough

Mabel Stark may not be a household name, but she was the greatest female tiger trainer of her day. She got her big break because the woman who had the tiger act before her was killed. This fictionalized biography includes some pretty racy stuff about Mabel and her one true love, a 550-pound Bengal tiger named Rajah. The Canadian author picked a fascinating historical character to write about for his first novel.

Geek Love by Katherine Dunn

This creepy, hallucinogenic novel is narrated by a bald, hunchbacked, albino dwarf. It tells of Binewski's Fabulon family of sideshow freaks. Mother Lil Binewski took everything, from prescription drugs to insecticides, to ensure her children would be deformed. "What greater gift could you offer your children than an inherent ability to earn a living just by being themselves?" There are repellent and terrifying moments, as when the "freaks" convince their audience to liberate themselves by "shedding" limbs. This wildly imaginative story told in vivid prose was a National Book Award nominee.

Department of Great Opening Lines

"'When your mama was the geek, my dreamlets,' Papa would say, 'she made the nipping off of noggins such a crystal mystery that the hens themselves yearned toward her, waltzing around her, hypnotized with longing.'"
—*Geek Love*

LITERARY MERIT

★

The Life of P. T. Barnum, Written by Himself by P. T. Barnum

The great showman was his own best walking advertisement. Over the years, he crafted increasingly tame versions of this autobiography originally published in 1955. He chronicles his rise from store clerk to impresario of "humbugs." See P. T. as he saw himself.

680.

LITERARY MERIT

★ ★ ★

Water for Elephants by Sara Gruen

Alex Award 2007

Jacob Jankowski, pushing ninety and languishing in a nursing home, looks back to when he was twenty-three, getting his veterinary degree, and traumatized by his parents' sudden deaths. He jumped a train and found himself traveling with the Flying Squadron of the Benzini Brothers Most Spectacular Show on Earth. The novel tells the story of his growing love for Marlena, the beauteous equestrian wife of the hot-tempered, sadistic ringmaster, and of Rosie, the bull elephant that only he could tame. This runaway bestseller was the American Bookseller Association's "Book of the Year" for 2007.

...to Take a Trip

LITERARY MERIT ★

PROVOCATIVE 🔥

INFLUENTIAL ❗

INSPIRATIONAL 🕊

HUMOROUS 😄

BRAINY 💡

EASY READING ☂

PAGE TURNER 📖

CHALLENGING ∞

BATHROOM BOOK 🚽

FAMILY FRIENDLY 👪

MOVIE 🎥

681.

LITERARY MERIT

★ ★

Assassination Vacation by Sarah Vowell

Vowell journeys to where political assassination took place, and shows the reader how mayhem feeds our ghoulish appetites. She's a most entertaining traveling companion as she visits every site tangentially related to the murders of Lincoln, Garfield, and McKinley, mixing travelogue, history, essay, and social criticism for a truly American road trip.

682.

LITERARY MERIT

★ ★ ★

The Atlas by William T. Vollmann

In these fifty-three travel essays, wherever Vollmann goes it's another version of hell. He's shot at in Bosnia, and nearly dies researching a story on the Inuit at the magnetic North Pole. Vollmann gives the notion of a "fearless traveler" a new level of meaning. These essays are by turns sad, provocative, funny, and disturbing. The book won the PEN Center USA West Award for Best Fiction.

683.

LITERARY MERIT

★ ★

Blue Highways: A Journey into America
by William Least Heat-Moon

State highways are red, and county roads are blue on the map. Least Heat-Moon meanders along those "blue" roads for three months through small-town America after losing his wife and his job on the same day. This autobiographical

What is the name of the van that took William Least Heat-Moon on his trip along "blue highways"?

Ghost Dancing

novel, considered a masterpiece of travel writing, is as much about the people as the places.

684.

LITERARY MERIT

★ ★

Consider the Lobster: And Other Essays
by David Foster Wallace

Wallace's work is frequently hailed as "tour de force." The content in this collection is fascinating, the language original and mesmerizing but not always so easy to read. Philosopher, essayist, and teller of tall tales, he brings the same irreverence and eye for absurdity whether he's writing about the pornography industry, the cooking of lobsters, or Senator John McCain's failed 2000 run for the GOP presidential nomination.

Eat, Pray, Love: One Woman's Search for Everything Across Italy, India and Indonesia by Elizabeth Gilbert

685.

LITERARY MERIT

★ ★

Depressed, divorced, and on the rebound from a failed romance, Elizabeth Gilbert writes about how she picked herself up and took a trip to heal her soul. "I wanted to explore the art of pleasure in Italy, the art of devotion in India and,

Department of Memorable Opening Lines

"Going to Ford's Theatre to watch a play is like going to Hooters for the food."
—*Eat, Pray, Love*

in Indonesia, the art of balancing the two." A reporter for *GQ*, Gilbert packs light, eats anything, and makes friends with anybody. "I could probably make friends with a four-foot pile of Sheetrock." Read it when you need to take a break from your own humdrum day-to-day.

Even Cowgirls Get the Blues by Tom Robbins

686.

LITERARY MERIT

★ ★

This 1970s cult novel tells how Sissy Hankshaw, born with over-sized thumbs, makes the most of her "gift." She hitchhikes her way to New York where she becomes a model, and then to the Dakota Bad Lands and an all-cowgirl Robber Rose Ranch where she meets ranch boss Bonanza Jellybean. The novel is full of surprises, from funny asides to an ecstatic whooping crane migration.

Department of Memorable Characters

"Hitching proved good for her thumbs, good for her morale, good, theoretically, for her soul—although it was the mid-fifties, Ike was President, gray flannel was fashionable, canasta was popular and it might have been presumptuous then to speak of 'soul.'"
—Sissy Hankshaw

The Great Railway Bazaar: By Train Through Asia by Paul Theroux

687.

LITERARY MERIT

★ ★ ★

Theroux undertook the grand tour from London to Tokyo and back again by rail in the early 1970s. In these essays, we sit back with him and inhale the atmosphere as he writes about the characters he meets and the sights he sees from mythic trains like the Orient Express, the Khyber Pass Local, and the Mandalay Express. Experience travel through the eyes of the author many hail as the best travel writer of his generation.

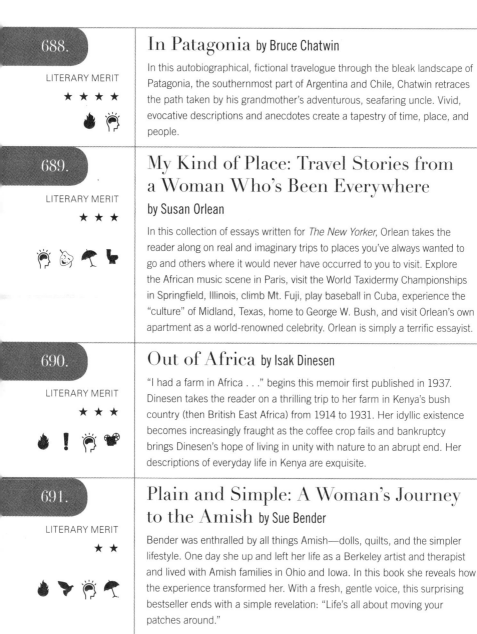

688.

LITERARY MERIT

★ ★ ★ ★

In Patagonia by Bruce Chatwin

In this autobiographical, fictional travelogue through the bleak landscape of Patagonia, the southernmost part of Argentina and Chile, Chatwin retraces the path taken by his grandmother's adventurous, seafaring uncle. Vivid, evocative descriptions and anecdotes create a tapestry of time, place, and people.

689.

LITERARY MERIT

★ ★ ★

My Kind of Place: Travel Stories from a Woman Who's Been Everywhere

by Susan Orlean

In this collection of essays written for *The New Yorker*, Orlean takes the reader along on real and imaginary trips to places you've always wanted to go and others where it would never have occurred to you to visit. Explore the African music scene in Paris, visit the World Taxidermy Championships in Springfield, Illinois, climb Mt. Fuji, play baseball in Cuba, experience the "culture" of Midland, Texas, home to George W. Bush, and visit Orlean's own apartment as a world-renowned celebrity. Orlean is simply a terrific essayist.

690.

LITERARY MERIT

★ ★ ★

Out of Africa by Isak Dinesen

"I had a farm in Africa . . ." begins this memoir first published in 1937. Dinesen takes the reader on a thrilling trip to her farm in Kenya's bush country (then British East Africa) from 1914 to 1931. Her idyllic existence becomes increasingly fraught as the coffee crop fails and bankruptcy brings Dinesen's hope of living in unity with nature to an abrupt end. Her descriptions of everyday life in Kenya are exquisite.

691.

LITERARY MERIT

★ ★

Plain and Simple: A Woman's Journey to the Amish by Sue Bender

Bender was enthralled by all things Amish—dolls, quilts, and the simpler lifestyle. One day she up and left her life as a Berkeley artist and therapist and lived with Amish families in Ohio and Iowa. In this book she reveals how the experience transformed her. With a fresh, gentle voice, this surprising bestseller ends with a simple revelation: "Life's all about moving your patches around."

The Road from Coorain by Jill Ker Conway

692.

This is a memoir of a young girl, growing up on a sheep farm in the arid and windswept Australian outback, and her departure for America. Conway experienced great tragedy before the age of eleven—her father's suicide, the accidental death of her older brother, and her mother's crushing depression. Bright and curious, she persevered. devoting herself to history and literature, and became the first woman president of Smith College. Coorain told a *New York Times* interviewer, "My book is very deliberately a story of separation—of independence and breaking away." In that she succeeds mightily.

LITERARY MERIT

★ ★ ★

The Snow Leopard by Peter Matthiessen

693.

National Book Award 1980
This is a meditative account of a seemingly fruitless odyssey. In September, 1973, a year after his wife died of cancer, Matthiessen set out on a five-week, 250-mile pilgrimage on foot across Tibet from Kathmandu, Nepal. His companions were wildlife biologist George Shaller, Sherpa guides, and Buddha. His goal: to find Himalayan blue sheep and the elusive snow leopard. In mystic prose, Matthiessen takes the reader on an arduous spiritual and physical journey.

LITERARY MERIT

★ ★ ★ ★

Travels with My Aunt by Graham Greene

694.

"I met my Aunt Augusta for the first time in more than half a century at my mother's funeral. . . ." At least narrator Henry Pulling, a retired and somewhat timid bank manager and dahlia expert, *thinks* it's his mother who just died. He and Aunt Augusta, with "her brilliant red hair, monumentally piled, and her two big front teeth which gave her a vital Neanderthal air," form an immediate and powerful bond. They travel first to Brighton Beach and on across continents to Istanbul and Paraguay. Henry learns of his aunt's fascinating and sketchy past and she teaches him how to stop fretting about dahlias and enjoy life. Witty, sophisticated, an utter delight to read.

LITERARY MERIT

★ ★ ★

What movie was *Travels with My Aunt* made into?

Auntie Mame

Two Towns in Provence by M. F. K. Fisher

695.

In this autobiography, Fisher tells how she picks up her life after her divorce from her third husband and lives alone in Aix-en-Provence in the sixties. The architecture and gardens, the views from her apartment, the cafés, the aromas, and eccentric people are vividly and lovingly rendered. This is a life, viewed through the rose-colored lens of food. The book was named one of the greatest travel books of all time by *Condé Nast Traveler*.

LITERARY MERIT

★ ★ ★

696.

LITERARY MERIT

★ ★ ★

A Walk in the Woods: Rediscovering America on the Appalachian Trail
by Bill Bryson

Bryson takes the reader on an entertaining hike along the Appalachian trail. It's a long haul, from Springer Mountain, Georgia, to Mt. Katahdin, Maine, and Bryson and his companion are singularly ill-equipped and inexperienced. Like many would-be "thru-hikers," they have the good sense to bail before things turn too ugly. In this account, there's plenty of irreverence to offend trail-fanatics, and side trips into the nature, geology, and history of the trail.

697.

LITERARY MERIT

★ ★ ★

When the Going Was Good by Evelyn Waugh

In five hilarious travel essays, Waugh's journeys take him from cruising the Mediterranean in 1929 to observing firsthand the Italian invasion of Ethiopia in 1935. He witnesses the coronation of Emperor Haile Salassie in 1930 Ethiopia, where most of the buildings planned for the event were unfinished and reporters resorted to filing imaginary stories beforehand because information was so scarce. Writing for the *New York Times*, Anatole Broyard termed this book "lapped in poetry, wrapped in the picturesque, armed with logical sentences and inalienable words."

698.

LITERARY MERIT

★ ★

Yoga for People Who Can't Be Bothered to Do It by Geoff Dyer

Not about yoga at all, this collection of eleven personal essays comprise an existential memoir chronicling Dyer's globe trotting anti-pilgrimage. Wherever he goes—Detroit, Cambodia, Libya, Paris—he hits none of the tourist destinations, and his "trips," drug-induced or otherwise, are often in his head. Hip, funny, and endlessly self-effacing, you'll end up rooting for the guy.

...to **TAKE A TRIP**
IN THE FAST LANE

LITERARY MERIT ★

PROVOCATIVE 🔥

INFLUENTIAL !

INSPIRATIONAL 🕊

HUMOROUS 😄

BRAINY 💡

EASY READING ☂

PAGE TURNER 📖

CHALLENGING 👓

BATHROOM BOOK 🚽

FAMILY FRIENDLY 👪

MOVIE 🎥

699.

LITERARY MERIT

★ ★

Around the World in Eighty Days

by Jules Verne

This novel was published in 1873, a century before the Concorde made this trip possible to do at twice the speed of sound. Banker Andrew Stuart offers a twenty-thousand-pound wager that Philias Fogg can't journey around the world in eighty days. Fogg takes the bet, and has his astonished servant, Passepartout, pack nothing but a "carpet bag, with two shirts and three pairs of stockings." Traveling by train, steamship, sledge, and elephant, they encounter natural disasters, an attack by Sioux Indians, and more to win the bet. This is a wonderful, old-timey classic from a writer who looked into the future.

700.

LITERARY MERIT

★ ★

At the Altar of Speed: The Fast Life and Tragic Death of Dale Earnhardt

by Leigh Montville

The unthinkable happened "on the final turn of the final lap of the biggest race of the NASCAR schedule." Everyone thought Dale Earnhardt, the legendary man in black, would walk away from the crash as he had countless times before. He didn't. "Crowds gathered. People cried." *Sports Illustrated* writer Montville tells the story of the charismatic man behind the megastar. It's a rags-to-riches saga and a fascinating trip into the world of car-racing (see *Sunday Money* below).

701.

LITERARY MERIT

★ ★

The Black Stallion by Walter Farley

This is the exhilarating story of young Alec Ramsay and The Black, a wild stallion, stranded together on a desert island after their ship sinks. They learn to survive by relying on one another. After their rescue, Alex secretly trains The Black for a race against champions Cyclone and Sun Raider. The author, who wrote this and thirty-three other novels about horses, spent much of his childhood hanging out in his uncle's stables.

Department of Memorable Characters

"White lather ran from the horse's body; his mouth was open, his teeth bared. He was a giant of a horse, glistening black—too big to be pure Arabian. His mane was like a crest, mounting, then falling low."
—*The Black Stallion*

The Complete Book of Running

by James Fixx

This was the book that got Americans running. At thirty-five, Fixx lost weight, quit smoking, and started to run. He encouraged the rest of us to get up off the couch, and touted the psychological and health-enhancing benefits of running. Tragically, Fixx died of a heart attack while running at age fifty-two.

702.

LITERARY MERIT

★ ★

Department of Odds and Ends

The muscular running legs on the cover photo of *The Complete Book of Running* belong to the author, Jim Fixx. He's wearing red nylon Onitsuka Tiger racing flats, shoes that became an early symbol of the running boom.

Horse Heaven by Jane Smiley

703.

This novel about racehorses and the people who own them, train them, ride them, and bet on them, is jam-packed with colorful characters. The four-legged variety range from yearlings with their futures ahead of them, like "monster" colt Epic Steam, to old hands like five-year-old Justa Bob who sees it as his job to tutor inexperienced jockeys. There's also Eileen, a terrier, and a huge cast of human characters, good and bad. Plus the hallmark of Smiley's writing: wry humor.

LITERARY MERIT

★ ★ ★ ★

The Perfect Mile: Three Athletes, One Goal, and Less Than Four Minutes to Achieve It by Neal Bascomb

704.

LITERARY MERIT

★ ★

It was common wisdom, before 1950, that no one could run a mile in under four minutes. In 1954, British medical student and amateur athlete Roger Bannister did it. Within seven weeks, Australian John Lindy, who had trained relentlessly, broke Bannister's record. Then Wes Santee, a swaggering Kansas farm boy who'd survived an abusive father, posted an even better time. Bascomb interviewed the major figures in his book and recreated their conversations and inner battles to tell a story of unlikely heroes, and of a sport in its golden age.

705.

LITERARY MERIT

★ ★

Secretariat: The Making of a Champion

by William Nack

Big Red (Secretariat) was legendary. In 1973 he won the Triple Crown. He won the Belmont Stakes by an astounding thirty-one lengths. He broke the track record at the Kentucky Derby, and every quarter mile of the mile-and-a-quarter race, he ran faster. He was on the covers of *Time*, *Newsweek*, and *Sports Illustrated*. Author Nack takes the reader through his breeding history and his life, and includes a moving account of his untimely death.

Author's Insight

"Secretariat was a chivalrous prince of a colt who was playful and mischievous—he once grabbed my notebook out of my hand with his teeth, when I was talking to his groom, Ed Sweat—and stayed the same as a stallion at Claiborne."
—Bill Nack

706.

LITERARY MERIT

★

Steam, Steel, and Stars by Tim Hensley,
photographs by O. Winston Link

This book of magnificent photographs from the 1950s captures the power of America's steam engines. To create the amazing tableau of these behemoths of the Norfolk and Western Railroad, Link needed hundreds of flashbulbs and miles of wire.

707.

LITERARY MERIT

★

Sunday Money: Speed! Lust! Madness! Death! A Hot Lap Around America with NASCAR by Jeff Macgregor

It's not just entertainment for truckers. NASCAR has become the fastest-growing American spectator sport. To find out how it happened, Macgregor and his photographer wife packed up a mobile home and drove 48,000 miles, following NASCAR for an entire year. This is a book for fans as well as the rest of us who wonder what all the shouting is about.

Department of Memorable Lines

"No matter where in America you try to hide from it, there it is, NASCAR, spooling out its story, making its case, thumping its tub, selling itself 24/7/365 on every flat surface in America."
—*Sunday Money*

...to TRIP DOWN MEMORY LANE

LITERARY MERIT ★

PROVOCATIVE 🔥

INFLUENTIAL ❗

INSPIRATIONAL 🕊

HUMOROUS 😂

BRAINY 💡

EASY READING ☂

PAGE TURNER 📖

CHALLENGING 👓

BATHROOM BOOK 🚽

FAMILY FRIENDLY 👪

MOVIE 🎥

708.

LITERARY MERIT

★ ★ ★ ★

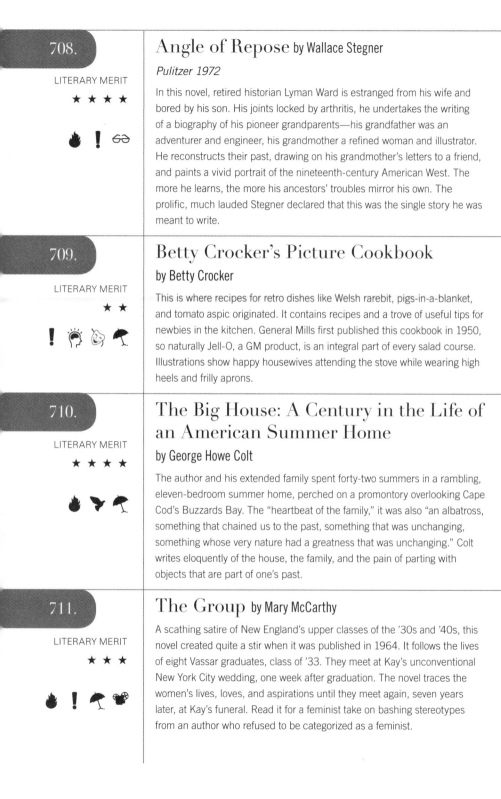

Angle of Repose by Wallace Stegner

Pulitzer 1972

In this novel, retired historian Lyman Ward is estranged from his wife and bored by his son. His joints locked by arthritis, he undertakes the writing of a biography of his pioneer grandparents—his grandfather was an adventurer and engineer, his grandmother a refined woman and illustrator. He reconstructs their past, drawing on his grandmother's letters to a friend, and paints a vivid portrait of the nineteenth-century American West. The more he learns, the more his ancestors' troubles mirror his own. The prolific, much lauded Stegner declared that this was the single story he was meant to write.

709.

LITERARY MERIT

★ ★

Betty Crocker's Picture Cookbook
by Betty Crocker

This is where recipes for retro dishes like Welsh rarebit, pigs-in-a-blanket, and tomato aspic originated. It contains recipes and a trove of useful tips for newbies in the kitchen. General Mills first published this cookbook in 1950, so naturally Jell-O, a GM product, is an integral part of every salad course. Illustrations show happy housewives attending the stove while wearing high heels and frilly aprons.

710.

LITERARY MERIT

★ ★ ★ ★

The Big House: A Century in the Life of an American Summer Home
by George Howe Colt

The author and his extended family spent forty-two summers in a rambling, eleven-bedroom summer home, perched on a promontory overlooking Cape Cod's Buzzards Bay. The "heartbeat of the family," it was also "an albatross, something that chained us to the past, something that was unchanging, something whose very nature had a greatness that was unchanging." Colt writes eloquently of the house, the family, and the pain of parting with objects that are part of one's past.

711.

LITERARY MERIT

★ ★ ★

The Group by Mary McCarthy

A scathing satire of New England's upper classes of the '30s and '40s, this novel created quite a stir when it was published in 1964. It follows the lives of eight Vassar graduates, class of '33. They meet at Kay's unconventional New York City wedding, one week after graduation. The novel traces the women's lives, loves, and aspirations until they meet again, seven years later, at Kay's funeral. Read it for a feminist take on bashing stereotypes from an author who refused to be categorized as a feminist.

The Hipster Handbook by Robert Lanham

712.

If you want to walk the walk, talk the talk, and wear the clothes, read this book—though a real hipster never would. Find out if you're "deck" or "fin." Discover that the ground zero of hipsterdom is Williamsburg, Brooklyn. Learn to discern the ten different types of kitsch-obsessed hipsters, from Tuffs to Bipsters (blue-collar hipsters).

LITERARY MERIT

★

Manhattan Transfer by John Dos Passos

713.

This is New York City in the Jazz Age, told in a series of interconnected stories. Dos Passos presents a kaleidoscopic view of the '20s, rich with unforgettable images that take the reader into skyscrapers and tenements, and into the lives of the very wealthy and the struggling immigrant poor.

> **Did You Know It Means . . .**
>
> The Manhattan Transfer: The New Jersey stop where, in the 1920s, you had to change trains to get to Penn Station.

LITERARY MERIT

★ ★ ★

Marjorie Morningstar by Herman Wouk

714.

A young Jewish girl living on Central Park West dreams of becoming a movie star. Marjorie Morgenstern, who had so much promise in summer camp and at Hunter College, changes her name, equivocates about SEX, and hooks up with a handsome cad (Noel Airman né Herman) only to end up a suburban hausfrau. This was a huge bestseller and women of a certain age have read it over and over. You'll love it too, for the first 556 pages.

> **Who played Marjorie Morningstar in the movie adaptation?**
>
> *Natalie Wood*

LITERARY MERIT

★ ★

Moon Tiger by Penelope Lively

715.

Booker Prize 1987

In this novel, Claudia Hampton is an aging historian and former war correspondent, dying of cancer. She wants to write a history of the world, but it keeps turning into recollections of her own life—love affairs, incest, childbirth, and a too-brief romantic encounter in Egypt with a British World War II tank commander. As with all Lively's novels, this meditation on the past pulls the reader in.

LITERARY MERIT

★ ★ ★ ★

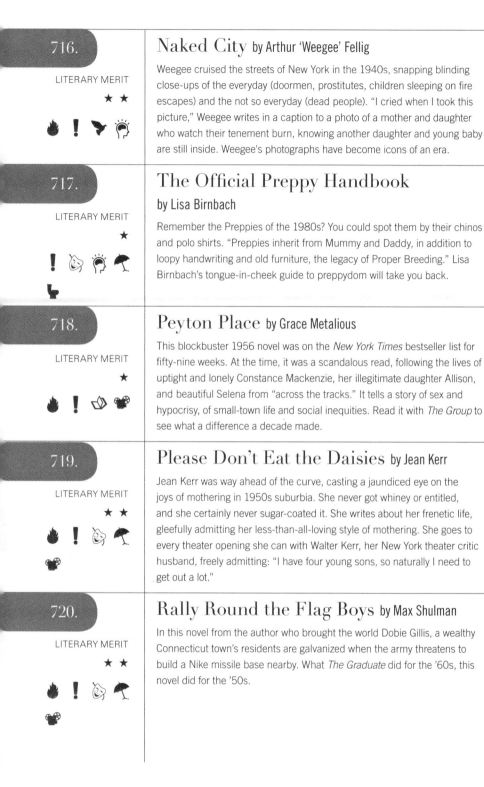

716.

LITERARY MERIT

★ ★

Naked City by Arthur 'Weegee' Fellig

Weegee cruised the streets of New York in the 1940s, snapping blinding close-ups of the everyday (doormen, prostitutes, children sleeping on fire escapes) and the not so everyday (dead people). "I cried when I took this picture," Weegee writes in a caption to a photo of a mother and daughter who watch their tenement burn, knowing another daughter and young baby are still inside. Weegee's photographs have become icons of an era.

717.

LITERARY MERIT

★

The Official Preppy Handbook
by Lisa Birnbach

Remember the Preppies of the 1980s? You could spot them by their chinos and polo shirts. "Preppies inherit from Mummy and Daddy, in addition to loopy handwriting and old furniture, the legacy of Proper Breeding." Lisa Birnbach's tongue-in-cheek guide to preppydom will take you back.

718.

LITERARY MERIT

★

Peyton Place by Grace Metalious

This blockbuster 1956 novel was on the *New York Times* bestseller list for fifty-nine weeks. At the time, it was a scandalous read, following the lives of uptight and lonely Constance Mackenzie, her illegitimate daughter Allison, and beautiful Selena from "across the tracks." It tells a story of sex and hypocrisy, of small-town life and social inequities. Read it with *The Group* to see what a difference a decade made.

719.

LITERARY MERIT

★ ★

Please Don't Eat the Daisies by Jean Kerr

Jean Kerr was way ahead of the curve, casting a jaundiced eye on the joys of mothering in 1950s suburbia. She never got whiney or entitled, and she certainly never sugar-coated it. She writes about her frenetic life, gleefully admitting her less-than-all-loving style of mothering. She goes to every theater opening she can with Walter Kerr, her New York theater critic husband, freely admitting: "I have four young sons, so naturally I need to get out a lot."

720.

LITERARY MERIT

★ ★

Rally Round the Flag Boys by Max Shulman

In this novel from the author who brought the world Dobie Gillis, a wealthy Connecticut town's residents are galvanized when the army threatens to build a Nike missile base nearby. What *The Graduate* did for the '60s, this novel did for the '50s.

Remembering Satan by Lawrence Wright

721.

LITERARY MERIT

★

Can you remember something that never happened? This is the true story of a controversial case in which Paul Ingram, a Washington State deputy sheriff, became convinced that he belonged to a satanic cult and had raped his own daughters. Journalist Wright believes mass hysteria, like the phenomenon behind the Salem witch trials, was responsible. This is an utterly fascinating, suspenseful, cautionary tale about implanted memories.

The Seven Sins of Memory: How the Mind Forgets and Remembers by Daniel Schachter

722.

LITERARY MERIT

★

Sometimes you can't remember something that happened to you. Other times you remember something that never happened at all. Psychologist Schachter calls these sins of memory omission and commission, and argues that memory malfunctions can be our psyche protecting us. Read this for an expert's eye view of the mind.

A Tree Grows in Brooklyn by Betty Smith

723.

LITERARY MERIT

★ ★ ★

At the turn of the century, Francie Nolan lives in impoverished Williamsburg where Irish and German immigrants struggle for survival. She and her brother forage in garbage, looking for something they can exchange for a few pennies at the pawn shop. Francie, with her romantic hungering for beauty, yearns for a better life. She's like this novel's repeating image, the "Tree of Heaven" that grows out of a crack in the sidewalk in front of the family home, the tree whose beauty and strength go unrecognized because it's so common.

Who played Francie Nolan in the movie adaptation of *A Tree Grows in Brooklyn*?

Peggy Ann Garner, who won a special Academy Award for her performance

Up in the Old Hotel by Joseph Mitchell

724.

LITERARY MERIT

★ ★ ★

These vivid essays about New York were written for *The New Yorker* over a period of thirty years. Mitchell portrays the city in all its eccentricities. Visit the original Fulton Fish Market or McSorley's Old Ale House before it admitted women; meet the quirky Joe Gould ("Professor Sea Gull"), marvel in his ingenious tricks for survival, and learn the truth of what's in his nine-million-word "Oral History of Our Time."

Quiz Time!

Preppy or Hipster? Identify whether
each historical figure would be a preppy
or a hipster . . .

1. Oliver Wendell Holmes Jr.
2. Marcel Duchamp
3. F. Scott Fitzgerald
4. Sitting Bull
5. Mata Hari
6. George W. Bush

Answers: 1-P, 2-H, 3-P, 4-H, 5-H, 6-P

...to Trip the Light Fantastic

LITERARY MERIT ★

PROVOCATIVE 🔥

INFLUENTIAL ❗

INSPIRATIONAL 🕊

HUMOROUS 😸

BRAINY 💡

EASY READING ☂

PAGE TURNER 📖

CHALLENGING 👓

BATHROOM BOOK 🚽

FAMILY FRIENDLY 👪

MOVIE 🎥

725.

LITERARY MERIT

★

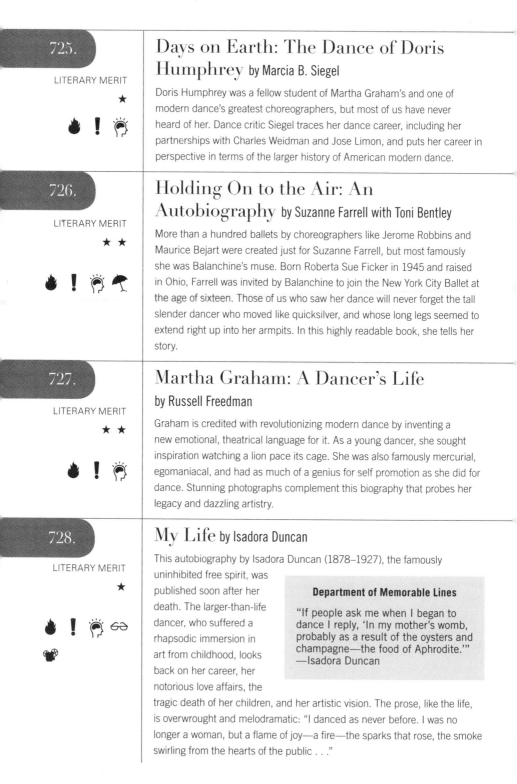

Days on Earth: The Dance of Doris Humphrey by Marcia B. Siegel

Doris Humphrey was a fellow student of Martha Graham's and one of modern dance's greatest choreographers, but most of us have never heard of her. Dance critic Siegel traces her dance career, including her partnerships with Charles Weidman and Jose Limon, and puts her career in perspective in terms of the larger history of American modern dance.

726.

LITERARY MERIT

★ ★

Holding On to the Air: An Autobiography by Suzanne Farrell with Toni Bentley

More than a hundred ballets by choreographers like Jerome Robbins and Maurice Bejart were created just for Suzanne Farrell, but most famously she was Balanchine's muse. Born Roberta Sue Ficker in 1945 and raised in Ohio, Farrell was invited by Balanchine to join the New York City Ballet at the age of sixteen. Those of us who saw her dance will never forget the tall slender dancer who moved like quicksilver, and whose long legs seemed to extend right up into her armpits. In this highly readable book, she tells her story.

727.

LITERARY MERIT

★ ★

Martha Graham: A Dancer's Life

by Russell Freedman

Graham is credited with revolutionizing modern dance by inventing a new emotional, theatrical language for it. As a young dancer, she sought inspiration watching a lion pace its cage. She was also famously mercurial, egomaniacal, and had as much of a genius for self promotion as she did for dance. Stunning photographs complement this biography that probes her legacy and dazzling artistry.

728.

LITERARY MERIT

★

My Life by Isadora Duncan

This autobiography by Isadora Duncan (1878–1927), the famously uninhibited free spirit, was published soon after her death. The larger-than-life dancer, who suffered a rhapsodic immersion in art from childhood, looks back on her career, her notorious love affairs, the

Department of Memorable Lines

"If people ask me when I began to dance I reply, 'In my mother's womb, probably as a result of the oysters and champagne—the food of Aphrodite.'"
—Isadora Duncan

tragic death of her children, and her artistic vision. The prose, like the life, is overwrought and melodramatic: "I danced as never before. I was no longer a woman, but a flame of joy—a fire—the sparks that rose, the smoke swirling from the hearts of the public . . ."

Private Domain: An Autobiography

by Paul Taylor

LITERARY MERIT

★ ★

This beautifully written autobiography is by one of today's dance greats, and the first choreographer to use natural gestures in dance. His dance career began in an offhand way when a fellow student at Syracuse University asked him to be her partner at the college's dance recital. Taylor danced with Martha Graham and others before starting his own troupe. "Trouping," he says, "builds endurance, bumpy dance roads lead to thick soles and an unnatural kind of tolerance."

Somewhere: The Life of Jerome Robbins

by Amanda Vaill

LITERARY MERIT

★ ★

Most of us know Robbins's choreography from the groundbreaking dances in *West Side Story*; balletomanes know of his long collaboration with George Balanchine, creating such classics as "Fancy Free" and "Dances at a Gathering." To dancers, though, he was a demanding, often cruel perfectionist. A

Author's Insight

Amanda Vail, on a turning point in Jerome Robbins's career: "He was offered the chance to choreograph a ballet for American Ballet Theatre in 1943 and was told to keep things modest. He went out and found an unknown young composer, Leonard Bernstein, to write the score, thus jump-starting both their careers."

man of contradictions, this biography is packed with fascinating anecdotes based on copious research and access to his papers and friends.

Quiz Time!
Match the choreographers with their dances.

1. George Balanchine
2. Jerome Robbins

3. Martha Graham
4. Isadora Duncan

5. Paul Taylor

a. "Concerto Barocco"; "Jewels"

b. "The Waterstudy Solo"; "The Three Graces"

c. "Big Bertha"; "Company B"

d. "Appalachian Spring"; "Cave of the Heart"

e. "Fancy Free"; "Dances at a Gathering"

Answers: 1-a, 2-e, 3-d, 4-b, 5-c

...to $\mathcal{S}oar$

LITERARY MERIT ★

PROVOCATIVE 🔥

INFLUENTIAL !

INSPIRATIONAL 🕊

HUMOROUS 😄

BRAINY 💡

EASY READING ☂

PAGE TURNER 📖

CHALLENGING 👓

BATHROOM BOOK 🚽

FAMILY FRIENDLY 👪

MOVIE 🎥

731.

LITERARY MERIT

★ ★

Flight of Passage by Rinker Buck

When you read this true story of the Buck brothers' flight over the Rockies, you'll marvel that they survived to tell the tale. It was all Kern's idea. Back in 1965, he announced to their father, "Rinky and I are going to fly the Cub out to California next summer." The teenagers became the youngest to fly solo across the United States, from New Jersey to California. Buck looks back and tells how they bought an old Piper Cub for $300, restored it, and then set off on a harrowing six-day journey. A riveting adventure story.

732.

LITERARY MERIT

★ ★

The Hunters by James Salter

Based on Salter's Korean War experiences, this novel tells of Captain Cleve Connell, a heroic World War II veteran fighter pilot, and his tour of duty at an Air Force base in Korea. Ultimately, there is a mission from which he does not return. Salter writes: "They had overcome him in the end, tenaciously, scissoring past him, taking him down. Their heavy shots had splashed into him, and they had followed all the way, firing as they did, with that contagious passion peculiar to hunters." The story is told in spare, powerful, elegaic prose, with an unsparing ending.

733.

LITERARY MERIT

★ ★

An Intimate Look at the Night Sky
by Chet Raymo

Organized by season, this book invites the reader to get acquainted with the night sky. Star maps, science, history, and philosophy mix with a profound appreciation of what it feels like to really see the Milky Way. This book builds understanding while destroying none of the wonder, and has the great plus of Raymo's lovely prose.

734.

LITERARY MERIT

★ ★

Jonathan Livingston Seagull by Richard Bach

This is a fable about a seagull who becomes so obsessed with flying that he's ejected from his flock. Do seagulls hang out in flocks? Never mind. Anyway, it's about not being afraid to live your dream, something we thought quite a lot about back in the '70s when this was published.

Lindbergh by A. Scott Berg
Pulitzer 1999

"For more than a day the world held its breath . . . and then the small plane was sighted over Ireland," begins this biography. Lindbergh was gifted in various disciplines, but he was also a complicated, infuriating, and private man who led a very public life until his death in 1974. Aviation pioneer, inventor, writer, master-geographer, successful businessman, Lindbergh was also a liar and a compulsive manipulator. He was accused of being both a traitor and Nazi-sympathizer. Read it to understand the many sides to this complex man, and to understand what it was about him that enthralled a generation.

735.

LITERARY MERIT

★ ★ ★

Night Flight by Antoine de Saint-Exupéry

736.

LITERARY MERIT

★ ★

First published in the 1930s, this novel is based on the author's own near-death experience as a mail pilot. In a scant hundred pages, Saint-Exupéry puts the reader in the cockpit with Fabien, trapped in a cyclone and running out of fuel over the Andes Mountains.

> **Author's Insight**
>
> "Even our misfortunes are a part of our belongings."
> —Antoine de Saint-Exupéry, *Night Flight*

Meanwhile, his boss Riviere watches the clock in the office and frets over the integrity of the flight schedule. At home Fabien's wife waits. Written before *The Little Prince*, this is the book that made Saint-Exupéry famous.

Nightwatch: A Practical Guide to Viewing the Universe by Terence Dickinson

737.

LITERARY MERIT

★

In this field guide to the stars, Dickinson, a journalist and editor of *Sky News Magazine*, gives the basics and more to amateur astronomers. Lucid, simple writing complements star charts that are intended for beginners and designed to be read outside in the dark.

The Right Stuff by Tom Wolfe
National Book Award 1980

738.

LITERARY MERIT

★ ★ ★

This book is about the first seven astronauts selected for the NASA space program, true heroes who were dedicated to accomplishing what no other person had done: fly to the moon. Wolfe casts them as characters in the exhilarating, epic tale of America's manned space program, and shows that they had the mental and physical wherewithal for flight into the unknown.

739.

LITERARY MERIT

★ ★

Seeing in the Dark: How Backyard Stargazers Are Probing Deep Space and Guarding Earth from Interplanetary Peril by Timothy Ferris

Alex Award 2003

Like a love letter to the stars, planets, and remote galaxies, this book tells how amateur backyard stargazers are reporting what they see around the world and even making discoveries of their own. Ferris says, "The universe is accessible to all, and can inform one's existence with a sense of beauty, reason, and awe as enriching as anything to be found in music, art, or poetry." Let this inspire you to turn off the lights and look up.

740.

LITERARY MERIT

★

The Sibley Guide to Birds by David Allen Sibley

If it weren't so darned big, this single volume could replace every bird guide that came before it. It covers 810 species and, with over 6,600 paintings, illustrates the diversity of each. A subset in a more portable format can be found in Sibley's field guides to Eastern North America and to Western North America. This is for when you want to know exactly what you're looking at.

741.

LITERARY MERIT

★ ★ ★

The Spirit of St. Louis by Charles A. Lindbergh

Pulitzer 1954

Once upon a time, in 1927, Lindbergh was a world-revered hero, a handsome and dashing twenty-five-year-old aviator who piloted his single-engine Ryan Monoplane, "The Spirit of St. Louis," across the ocean, completing the first nonstop solo flight from New York to Paris. In prose as memorable as the story, this book tells of Lindbergh's early life, his famous flight, and the early days of aviation. Read it with A. Scott Berg's *Lindbergh* biography to get the full story.

742.

LITERARY MERIT

★ ★

To Conquer the Air: The Wright Brothers and the Great Race for Flight by James Tobin

This race went to the inspired. While Samuel Langley sought to create the first manned flying machine with support from the U.S. War Department and the Smithsonian, the Wright brothers labored in obscurity. The Wrights framed the challenge as a problem of balance while Langley framed it as one of power. Award-winning biographer Tobin presents the reader with a fascinating history of first flight, and the efforts afterward to make it feasible.

West with the Night by Beryl Markham

Beryl Markham was a pioneer aviator and the first person to fly solo across the Atlantic Ocean. This memoir, first published in 1942, is known as much for the hypnotic, philosophical poetry of its prose as for the story of a pioneering woman who grew up in East Africa and later trained and bred horses before becoming an African bush pilot.

LITERARY MERIT

★ ★ ★

The Wild Parrots of Telegraph Hill: A Love Story . . . with Wings by Mark Bittner

744.

The eccentric Bittner, a former San Francisco street person, tells how he became famous as "the birdman of Telegraph Hill." He befriended and cared for a flock of parrots living near a house where he was staying. Bittner became as much of a tourist attraction as the cherry-headed and blue-headed characters he cared for. This is an oddball tale of urban living.

LITERARY MERIT

★

Yeager: An Autobiography by Chuck Yeager

745.

Yeager was a World War II flying ace whose buddies trusted him because "he knew the difference between being aggressive and being reckless." He became a great test pilot. In this thrilling autobiography, he tells the story of his life and how he became the first pilot to break the sound barrier.

Department of Memorable Lines

"In the midst of a wild sky, I knew that dogfighting was the thing I was born to do. . . . You were so wired into that airplane that you flew it to the limit of its specs, where firing your guns could cause a stall. You felt that engine in your bones, felt it nibbling toward a stall, throttle wide open getting maximum maneuvering performance."
—*Yeager: An Autobiography*

LITERARY MERIT

★ ★

Quiz Time!
Match the famous pilots with their planes.

1. Charles Lindbergh

2. Chuck Yeager

3. Orville and Wilbur Wright

4. Amelia Earheart

a. Flyer

b. The Electra Plane

c. Glamorous Glennis

d. The Spirit of St. Louis

Answers: *1-d, 2-c, 3-a, 4-b*

...to SET SAIL

LITERARY MERIT   ★

PROVOCATIVE   🔥

INFLUENTIAL   !

INSPIRATIONAL   🕊

HUMOROUS   😃

BRAINY   💡

EASY READING   ☂

PAGE TURNER   📖

CHALLENGING   👓

BATHROOM BOOK   🚽

FAMILY FRIENDLY   👪

MOVIE   🎥

746.

LITERARY MERIT

★ ★

The *Bounty*: The True Story of the Mutiny on the *Bounty* by Caroline Alexander

In 1789, two years after setting sail for the South Seas, the crew of the *Bounty* mutinied. History has cast Captain Bligh, who was set adrift in a long boat with some of his officers, as a villain whose cruel decisions put his crew members in danger. Alexander's research tells a very different story. Bligh's heroic adventures and near-miraculous navigation of the long boat to safety challenge our preconceptions.

747.

LITERARY MERIT

★

The Hungry Ocean: A Swordboat Captain's Journey by Linda Greenlaw

Alex Award 2000

The author was the captain of the *Hannah Boden*, the sister ship to the doomed *Andrea Gail* Sebastian Junger wrote about in *The Perfect Storm*. Here she writes of a fishing trip to the Grand Banks, and weaves it through with anecdotes from other trips. Though she's not the writer Junger is, Greenlaw ably communicates that passion for the ocean that she calls "sea fever."

748.

LITERARY MERIT

★ ★ ★

The Illustrated Longitude

by Dava Sobel, illustrated by William J. H. Andrewes

Without the ability to pinpoint their east-west location in the open sea, many ships and sailors were lost. This book tells how English clockmaker John Harrison, the "mechanical genius who pioneered the science of precision timekeeping," invented the marine chronometer, an instrument that measures time at sea and allowed sailors to calculate longitude. Wonderfully written, this conveys the importance of a gizmo as influential in its time as the computer is to our own.

749.

LITERARY MERIT

★ ★ ★ ★

In the Heart of the Sea: The Tragedy of the Whaleship *Essex* by Nathaniel Philbrick

National Book Award 2000; Alex Award 2001

In 1820, deep in the Pacific, more than a year after the whale ship *Essex* departed Nantucket, a huge sperm whale suddenly rammed it with its immense head. Then it rammed the ship a second time, sinking it. In this nonfiction, Philbrick tells the disturbing, harrowing account of the three months survivors spent in their whale boats. This is the same shipwreck that inspired Melville to write *Moby-Dick*.

Middle Passage by Charles Johnson

National Book Award 1991

In 1830, Rutherford Calhoun, a well educated, freed slave from Illinois, desperate to avoid marrying a prissy schoolmarm, stows away on a slave ship. The ship takes on a cargo of mythic Allmuseri tribesmen. It inadvertently also takes onboard their god. The patriotic former slave is caught between his loyalty to his white shipmates and his empathy for the souls in torment in the hold. The novel delivers Johnson's requirement of black literature: "a fiction of increasing artistic and intellectual growth, one that enables us as a people—as a culture—to move from narrow complaint to broad celebration."

750.

LITERARY MERIT

★ ★ ★

A Night to Remember by Walter Lord

This is *Titanic*, the book, before Leo and Kate let the wind sweep over them on the ship's bow. Published in 1955, this book presents a moment-by-moment, gripping account of the ill-fated voyage, from pre-launch hype through the last evening, from first reports of trouble to loading life boats and rescue efforts. Lord interviewed scores of survivors and tells their stories.

751.

LITERARY MERIT

★ ★ ★

The Old Man and the Sea by Ernest Hemingway

Pulitzer 1953

This novella was the last major work of fiction written by Hemingway. In it, aging Cuban fisherman Santiago struggles with a giant marlin, far out at sea. After a days-long, epic battle, Santiago emerges victorious against his "brother" marlin. He lashes his catch to the side of the boat for the trip back, only to lose the marlin to sharks that have followed behind, waiting for an easy feed. In this deeply symbolic novel, Hemingway portrays Santiago as a classic tragic hero, a courageous warrior defeated by stubborn pride.

752.

LITERARY MERIT

★ ★ ★ ★

Outerbridge Reach by Robert Stone

Middle-class, middle-aged, and dissatisfied, Owen Browne jumps at the chance to skipper a new boat in an around-the-world sailing race called the Eglantine Solo. Nevermind that he isn't up to the challenge—the boat isn't either. The effort is to be filmed by Ron Strickland, a documentary filmmaker whose claim to fame is that he makes people look ridiculous. This novel steers a disturbing course to the unexpected.

753.

LITERARY MERIT

★ ★

754.

LITERARY MERIT

★ ★ ★

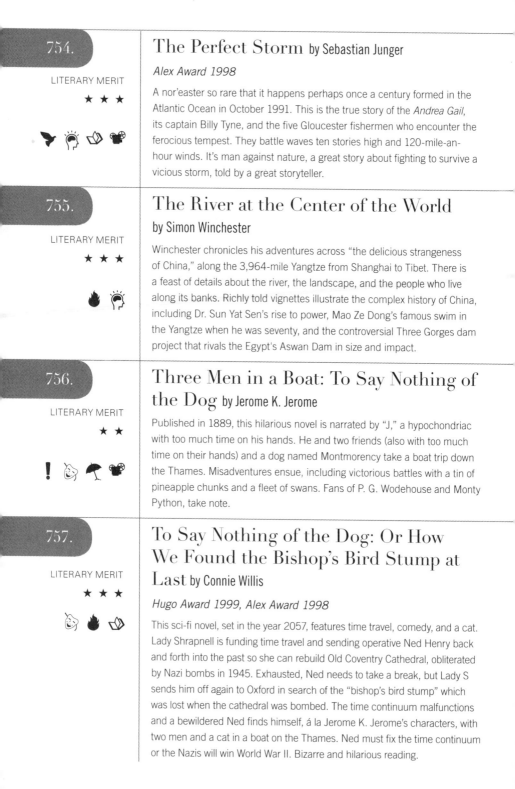

The Perfect Storm by Sebastian Junger

Alex Award 1998

A nor'easter so rare that it happens perhaps once a century formed in the Atlantic Ocean in October 1991. This is the true story of the *Andrea Gail*, its captain Billy Tyne, and the five Gloucester fishermen who encounter the ferocious tempest. They battle waves ten stories high and 120-mile-an-hour winds. It's man against nature, a great story about fighting to survive a vicious storm, told by a great storyteller.

755.

LITERARY MERIT

★ ★ ★

The River at the Center of the World

by Simon Winchester

Winchester chronicles his adventures across "the delicious strangeness of China," along the 3,964-mile Yangtze from Shanghai to Tibet. There is a feast of details about the river, the landscape, and the people who live along its banks. Richly told vignettes illustrate the complex history of China, including Dr. Sun Yat Sen's rise to power, Mao Ze Dong's famous swim in the Yangtze when he was seventy, and the controversial Three Gorges dam project that rivals the Egypt's Aswan Dam in size and impact.

756.

LITERARY MERIT

★ ★

Three Men in a Boat: To Say Nothing of the Dog by Jerome K. Jerome

Published in 1889, this hilarious novel is narrated by "J," a hypochondriac with too much time on his hands. He and two friends (also with too much time on their hands) and a dog named Montmorency take a boat trip down the Thames. Misadventures ensue, including victorious battles with a tin of pineapple chunks and a fleet of swans. Fans of P. G. Wodehouse and Monty Python, take note.

757.

LITERARY MERIT

★ ★ ★

To Say Nothing of the Dog: Or How We Found the Bishop's Bird Stump at Last by Connie Willis

Hugo Award 1999, Alex Award 1998

This sci-fi novel, set in the year 2057, features time travel, comedy, and a cat. Lady Shrapnell is funding time travel and sending operative Ned Henry back and forth into the past so she can rebuild Old Coventry Cathedral, obliterated by Nazi bombs in 1945. Exhausted, Ned needs to take a break, but Lady S sends him off again to Oxford in search of the "bishop's bird stump" which was lost when the cathedral was bombed. The time continuum malfunctions and a bewildered Ned finds himself, á la Jerome K. Jerome's characters, with two men and a cat in a boat on the Thames. Ned must fix the time continuum or the Nazis will win World War II. Bizarre and hilarious reading.

...*to* Slide Down the Rabbit Hole

LITERARY MERIT ★

PROVOCATIVE 🔥

INFLUENTIAL ❗

INSPIRATIONAL 🕊️

HUMOROUS 😄

BRAINY 💡

EASY READING ☂️

PAGE TURNER 📖

CHALLENGING 👓

BATHROOM BOOK 🚽

FAMILY FRIENDLY 👪

MOVIE 🎥

758.

Alice's Adventures in Wonderland

by Lewis Carroll

There's inspired silliness from page one as Alice chases the elusive white rabbit down the rabbit-hole. First published in 1865, this book written for children was an instant classic for all ages. Read a version with the original Sir John Tenniel illustrations; read an annotated version if you want to get all the jokes, games, tricks, and parodies; or simply read it aloud to yourself and let the language wash over you.

759.

The BFG

by Roald Dahl, illustrated by Quentin Blake

The Big Friendly Giant is one of Dahl's most benign and engaging creations. Though he snatches little Sophie from her bed, he's a "dream-maker," not a "man-gobbling cannybull." In a wildly inventive story, one of the best inventions is frobscottle, a delicious carbonated drink in which the bubbles travel down, not up, causing the imbiber to "whizzpop" instead of burp.

760.

The Didymus Contingency by Jeremy Robinson

What if you could go back to any moment in time, which would you go to? In this novel, Dr. Tom Greenbaum has discovered the secret to time travel. His wife was murdered for her Christian faith, so Greenbaum time-travels to ancient Israel to disprove Christ's resurrection. Imagine the consequences—as do a friend and an army of others who try to stop him. Christian thriller, anyone? For readers willing to suspend disbelief.

761.

The Eyre Affair by Jasper Fforde

Alex Award 2003

In the alternate reality of this novel, it's 1985 England and the Crimean War has been raging for 131 years. Thursday Next is a Special Operative in literary detection. A time-traveling V. I. Warshawski, she's on the hunt for Acheron Hades, a villain who snatches characters from literary works. When Hades kidnaps Jane Eyre from Charlotte Brontë's manuscript, *Jane Eyre* stops dead a third of the way through, having lost its point-of-view character. This book is a witty romp, a genre-buster that straddles mystery, sci-fi, and literary fiction.

Department of Great Opening Lines

"My father had a face that could stop a clock. I don't mean that he was ugly or anything; it was a phrase the Chro-noGuard used to describe someone who had the power to reduce time to an ultraslow trickle."
—*The Eyre Affair*

The Golden Compass by Philip Pullman

762.

This first novel in the His Dark Materials trilogy is a mind-bending fantasy in which twelve-year-old orphan Lyra Belacqua and her shape-shifting daemon Pantalaimon inhabit Jordan College in an Oxford of a parallel universe. Lyra's life takes a twist when she prevents her uncle's assassination and overhears a discussion about a secret entity known as "Dust." Her friend, the kitchen boy, and other children are stolen away by Gobblers. The "golden compass" can answer questions if she can only learn how to read it. This dazzling fantasy masterpiece, written for children, can be enjoyed by adults as well.

LITERARY MERIT

★ ★

The Little Prince

763.

by Antoine de Saint-Exupéry, translation by Richard Howe

LITERARY MERIT

★ ★

In this slim, poetic fantasy novel, Saint-Exupéry's plane crashes in the Sahara desert and there he meets a little prince from a tiny asteroid who asks him to draw a sheep. The boy is dissatisfied with every drawing until Saint-Exupéry draws a box: "The sheep you asked for is inside." The prince tells Saint-Exupéry of his travels through the universe in disarmingly simple and profound fables about creativity, loneliness, and grief.

Department of Odds and Ends

Antoine de Saint-Exupéry's *The Little Prince*, published in 1943, begins with a plane crash. In 1944 Saint-Exupéry and his Lockheed Lightning P-38 disappeared during a World War II spy mission for the Allies. In 2004, the wreckage of the plane, broken into hundreds of pieces, was found on the Mediterranean seabed near Provence.

Midnight in the Garden of Good and Evil

764.

by John Berendt

LITERARY MERIT

★ ★ ★

This wildly imaginative novel is based on a true crime, a murder that took place in one of Savannah's grandest mansions. Berendt revels in one outrageous character after another—a voodoo priestess, a flamboyant black drag queen, a failed inventor who "walks" flies by gluing threads to their backs. This book did for Savannah tourism what Shakespeare did for Stratford-on-Avon.

Department of Memorable Characters

"'Ooooo, child!' she said. 'You are right on time, honey.' Her voice crackled, her hoop earrings jangled. 'I am serious. I cannot tell you.' She began moving slowly toward me with an undulating walk. She trailed an index finger sensuously along the fender, feeling the hollow of each and every dent."
—Lady Chablis from *Midnight in the Garden of Good and Evil*

765.

LITERARY MERIT

★ ★

A Wrinkle in Time by Madeleine L'Engle

Newbery Medal 1963

Meg Murry is one of the most memorable little girls in young adult fiction. Smart, prickly, a sour social misfit, she illustrates what it means to "be yourself." In this much beloved book, she tries to find her scientist father. Her five-year-old brother Charles Wallace, a little genius, makes friends with three old ladies who've moved into the local haunted house. Mrs. Who, Mrs. Whatsit, and Mrs. Which have come from beyond our galaxy to confirm Mr. Murry's work on tesseracts, folds in the space-time continuum. Meg and Charles Wallace "tesser" to the "dark planet" Camazotz to save Mr. M. The novel actually begins with "It was a dark and stormy night" (which also opened Edward George Bulwer-Lytton's 1830 novel *Paul Clifford*).

> **Did You Know It Means . . .**
>
> Tesseract: A 4-dimensional, equal-sided geometric shape

...to Bend Your Mind

LITERARY MERIT ★

PROVOCATIVE 🔥

INFLUENTIAL !

INSPIRATIONAL ➤

HUMOROUS 😊

BRAINY 🧠

EASY READING ☂

PAGE TURNER 📖

CHALLENGING 👓

BATHROOM BOOK 🚽

FAMILY FRIENDLY 👪

MOVIE 🎥

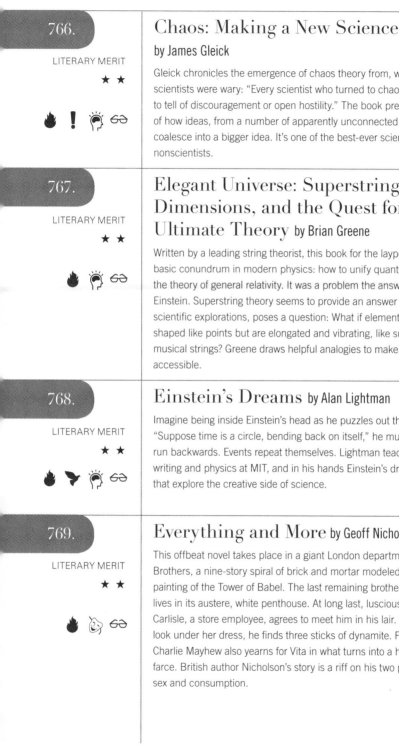

766.

LITERARY MERIT

★ ★

Chaos: Making a New Science
by James Gleick

Gleick chronicles the emergence of chaos theory from, well, chaos. Initially, scientists were wary: "Every scientist who turned to chaos early had a story to tell of discouragement or open hostility." The book presents the sociology of how ideas, from a number of apparently unconnected disciplines, coalesce into a bigger idea. It's one of the best-ever science books for nonscientists.

767.

LITERARY MERIT

★ ★

Elegant Universe: Superstrings, Hidden Dimensions, and the Quest for the Ultimate Theory by Brian Greene

Written by a leading string theorist, this book for the layperson explains a basic conundrum in modern physics: how to unify quantum mechanics and the theory of general relativity. It was a problem the answer to which eluded Einstein. Superstring theory seems to provide an answer that, like all good scientific explorations, poses a question: What if elementary particles aren't shaped like points but are elongated and vibrating, like submicroscopic musical strings? Greene draws helpful analogies to make this content accessible.

768.

LITERARY MERIT

★ ★

Einstein's Dreams by Alan Lightman

Imagine being inside Einstein's head as he puzzles out the nature of time. "Suppose time is a circle, bending back on itself," he muses. Or time might run backwards. Events repeat themselves. Lightman teaches creative writing and physics at MIT, and in his hands Einstein's dreams are fables that explore the creative side of science.

769.

LITERARY MERIT

★ ★

Everything and More by Geoff Nicholson

This offbeat novel takes place in a giant London department store, Haden Brothers, a nine-story spiral of brick and mortar modeled on Bruegel's painting of the Tower of Babel. The last remaining brother, Arnold Haden, lives in its austere, white penthouse. At long last, luscious young Vita Carlisle, a store employee, agrees to meet him in his lair. When he gets a look under her dress, he finds three sticks of dynamite. Furniture porter Charlie Mayhew also yearns for Vita in what turns into a highly entertaining farce. British author Nicholson's story is a riff on his two preoccupations: sex and consumption.

Fifth Business by Robertson Davies

Dunstable Ramsay is a fusty history professor, retiring after a forty-five-year teaching career at a Canadian boys' school. Disgusted by the newspaper report of him as a doddering schoolmaster, he writes a lengthy

The Author Explains the Title

"Those roles which, being neither those of Hero nor Heroine, Confidante nor Villain, but which were nonetheless essential to bring about the Recognition or the denouement, were called the Fifth Business in drama and opera companies organized according to the old style; the player who acted these parts was often referred to as Fifth Business."
—Robertson Davies

LITERARY MERIT

★ ★ ★ ★

autobiographical letter to set the record straight. His story begins with a badly aimed snowball that results in the premature birth of Paul Dempster who will grow up to be the world's greatest magician. The first in the Deptford trilogy, this novel has been called the Canadian *Citizen Kane*.

Flatland: A Romance of Many Dimensions
by Edwin A. Abbott

LITERARY MERIT

★

This fantasy about a two-dimensional world was first published in 1880. The narrator, a Square, tells the reader: "I call our world Flatland, not because we call it so, but to make its nature clearer to you, my happy readers, who are privileged to live in Space." All is well, as long as the geometric shapes who inhabit Flatland think their world is all there is. But things get dicey when the narrator discovers the existence of the third dimension. Abbott published the book under the pseudonym A. Square. Originally a satire on Victorian society, today this mind-bending oddity particularly appeals to those with a mathematical, analytical bent.

Gödel, Escher, Bach: An Eternal Golden Braid by Douglas R. Hofstadter

LITERARY MERIT

★ ★ ★

Pulitzer 1980
On the surface, the book appears to be an exploration of the symbols of mathematics, art, and musical composition. In the introduction to the twentieth anniversary edition, Hofstadter clarifies: This book is "a very personal attempt to say how it is that animate beings can come out of inanimate matter. What is a self, and how can a self come out of stuff that is as selfless as a stone or a puddle?" But don't be put off. This is a playful, imaginative book. Each chapter presents a dialogue between characters like the Tortoise and Achilles who talk about concepts that are then treated in depth.

773.

LITERARY MERIT

★ ★ ★

Gravity's Rainbow by Thomas Pynchon

National Book Award 1974

The novel opens: "A screaming comes across the sky." It's a launch of V-2 rockets over London in 1944. Turns out the rockets hit precisely where and when US Army Lt. Tyrone Slothrop gets an erection. "Complex." "Bonecrushingly dense." "Brilliant." "Impenetrable." Those are just some terms readers have used to describe this novel from an author who is one of the most influential of our time.

> **Department of Odds and Ends**
>
> In 1974 the Pulitzer Prize committee unanimously recommended the prize be given to Thomas Pynchon's *Gravity's Rainbow*. The Pulitzer Prize Board rejected it as "obscene," "overwritten," and "unreadable."

774.

LITERARY MERIT

★ ★ ★ ★

House of Leaves by Mark Z. Danielewski

A man explores a house that, according to blueprints, is larger inside by exactly one-quarter inch than it is outside. Rooms lead to rooms lead to other rooms, and the house seems to be growing from within, toward the ever-elusive dark at the end of the hallway. The house echoes the text of this 700-page opus with its footnotes and footnoted footnotes, making this gripping novel itself an Escher landscape. Danielewski's writing has been compared (favorably) to Thomas Pynchon and J. G. Ballard, and by any measure is a tour de force.

775.

LITERARY MERIT

★ ★ ★

The Illustrated Man by Ray Bradbury

The narrator meets a wanderer whose body is covered with vivid tattoos. At night the "pictures move" and predict the future. These tattoos provide a framing device for eighteen sci-fi short stories. In "Marionettes, Inc.," a man unhappy in his marriage decides to replace himself with a robot so he can leave his wife, only to discover that, for quite some time, he's been living with a robot version of her. Read this collection to experience one of the greatest science fiction writers of our time.

776.

LITERARY MERIT

★ ★ ★ ★

Infinite Jest by David Foster Wallace

Part philosophical quest, part comedy routine, this novel is hefty (over a thousand pages) and widely praised (compared to works by Thomas Pynchon and John Irving). It features hundreds of characters and a baroque narrative with more than four hundred footnotes. The "Infinite Jest" of the title is a movie so mesmerizing that anyone who watches it loses all desire to do anything else. The novel tells of the movie's effect on recovering addicts at a Boston halfway house and on students at a nearby tennis academy.

Neuromancer by William Gibson

Nebula Award 1984; Hugo Award 1985

Cyberspace cowboy Case lives in a dark world where people are absorbed by technology in a massive "consensual hallucination." Case uses the digital matrix to scam and plunder. He gets caught and his ability to access the matrix is burnt out of him. The plot twists, and twists again as wealthy, mysterious ex-army officer Armitage saves Case and arranges for his rehabilitation; then it's revealed Armitage is not what he seems to be. This early-early cyberpunk novel won the trifecta of science-fiction—the Nebula, the Hugo, and the Philip K. Dick Award.

LITERARY MERIT

★ ★ ★

Mr. Tompkins in Wonderland by George Gamow

Physicist Gamow worked with Niels Bohr on the development of quantum mechanics and participated in the Manhattan Project. For this charming book, he invented Mr. Tompkins, "the little clerk of a big city bank," whose dreams and adventures provide a vehicle for illustrating relativity, atomic structure, and quantum mechanics. For every non-physicist out there who'd like a painless lesson in physics.

LITERARY MERIT

★

Outlander by Diana Gabaldon

Time travel and historical fiction combined with a good, ol' fashioned bodice ripper. In one timeline, it's 1945 and combat nurse Claire Randall is back from the war and so is her husband. On a trip together, she touches an ancient stone and suddenly she's catapulted to 1743 war-torn Scotland. There she's an outlander, has a lover, and her fate is linked with Clan MacKenzie, the hunky Jamie Frasier, and the forbidden Castle Leoch. This first of a wildly successful series has legions of fans and spawned its own subgenre.

LITERARY MERIT

★ ★

The Puttermesser Papers by Cynthia Ozick

Like Walter Mitty, Ruth Puttermesser invents a life to fulfill her wishes and dreams. In this comic novel, Ruth is a brilliant, pedantic, funny Jewish lawyer in Manhattan's civil service. However, she loses her job when a new boss fires her so he can replace her with a friend. But a golem makes her mayor of New York and helps her transform the city into a cultural and intellectual utopia. Yet each fulfilled desire brings new pain. Anyone who reads and yearns will identify with its protagonist.

LITERARY MERIT

★ ★ ★

781.

LITERARY MERIT

★ ★ ★

Sexing the Cherry by Jeanette Winterson

Jordan is a young, seventeenth-century adventurer and naturalist who travels through space and time. His adoptive mother is smallpox scarred giantess Dog Woman, who breeds dogs for fights and races in Hyde Park. The author has an original and poetic voice, and the story she tells is a bawdy, imaginative, horrifying feminist fairy tale for adults.

782.

LITERARY MERIT

★ ★ ★

Stranger in a Strange Land by Robert A. Heinlein

Hugo Award 1962

Valentine Michael Smith is born during the first manned mission to Mars. A quarter century later, the ship is recovered along with Smith, its only survivor. He returns to earth, a true innocent. The government tries to keep him under wraps because, through a legal fluke, he owns Mars. A nurse spirits him off to the estate of Jubal Harshaw, a wealthy free-thinking writer. Philosophically, this novel is a paean to the '60s—if you grok my meaning. A great sci-fi novel and an American Bookseller Association's "Book of the Year," it broke through to a wider audience and has become an enduring classic.

783.

LITERARY MERIT

★ ★ ★

The Wind-up Bird Chronicle
by Haruki Murakami

In this swirling, dream-like tale set in suburban Tokyo, Toru Okadu is a laid-back young man, a World War II Japanese Army veteran. He's lost his job, his wife has left him and so has his cat. He consults sister psychics who visit him in his dreams, and spends his days obsessed with death. Moving and magical scenes intertwine, and reality and dreams become indistinguishable as he descends to the bottom of a dry well where he passes through the stone wall into a dark hotel room where a woman seduces him. Ultimately, Okadu must face his own action and inaction in the Japanese Army in World War II. Murakami is one of Japan's most celebrated novelists, and this is his most ambitious book so far.

...to Get Philosophical

LITERARY MERIT ★

PROVOCATIVE 🔥

INFLUENTIAL !

INSPIRATIONAL 🕊

HUMOROUS 😃

BRAINY 🗽

EASY READING ☂

PAGE TURNER 📖

CHALLENGING 👓

BATHROOM BOOK 🚽

FAMILY FRIENDLY 👪

MOVIE 🎥

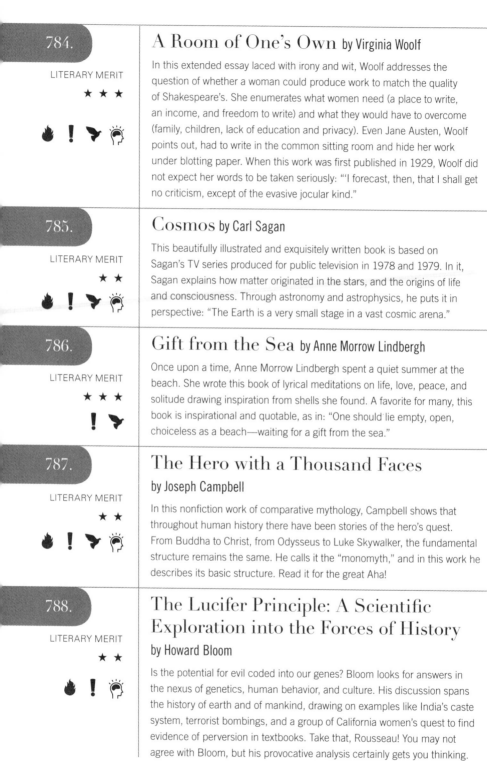

784.

LITERARY MERIT

★ ★ ★

A Room of One's Own by Virginia Woolf

In this extended essay laced with irony and wit, Woolf addresses the question of whether a woman could produce work to match the quality of Shakespeare's. She enumerates what women need (a place to write, an income, and freedom to write) and what they would have to overcome (family, children, lack of education and privacy). Even Jane Austen, Woolf points out, had to write in the common sitting room and hide her work under blotting paper. When this work was first published in 1929, Woolf did not expect her words to be taken seriously: "'I forecast, then, that I shall get no criticism, except of the evasive jocular kind."

785.

LITERARY MERIT

★ ★

Cosmos by Carl Sagan

This beautifully illustrated and exquisitely written book is based on Sagan's TV series produced for public television in 1978 and 1979. In it, Sagan explains how matter originated in the stars, and the origins of life and consciousness. Through astronomy and astrophysics, he puts it in perspective: "The Earth is a very small stage in a vast cosmic arena."

786.

LITERARY MERIT

★ ★ ★

Gift from the Sea by Anne Morrow Lindbergh

Once upon a time, Anne Morrow Lindbergh spent a quiet summer at the beach. She wrote this book of lyrical meditations on life, love, peace, and solitude drawing inspiration from shells she found. A favorite for many, this book is inspirational and quotable, as in: "One should lie empty, open, choiceless as a beach—waiting for a gift from the sea."

787.

LITERARY MERIT

★ ★

The Hero with a Thousand Faces
by Joseph Campbell

In this nonfiction work of comparative mythology, Campbell shows that throughout human history there have been stories of the hero's quest. From Buddha to Christ, from Odysseus to Luke Skywalker, the fundamental structure remains the same. He calls it the "monomyth," and in this work he describes its basic structure. Read it for the great Aha!

788.

LITERARY MERIT

★ ★

The Lucifer Principle: A Scientific Exploration into the Forces of History
by Howard Bloom

Is the potential for evil coded into our genes? Bloom looks for answers in the nexus of genetics, human behavior, and culture. His discussion spans the history of earth and of mankind, drawing on examples like India's caste system, terrorist bombings, and a group of California women's quest to find evidence of perversion in textbooks. Take that, Rousseau! You may not agree with Bloom, but his provocative analysis certainly gets you thinking.

Murphy's Law by Arthur Bloch

789.

We all know the law: "If anything can go wrong, it will." This little book of pithy revelations about negative outcomes is where it came from. Read it to nurture your inner pessimist.

LITERARY MERIT
★

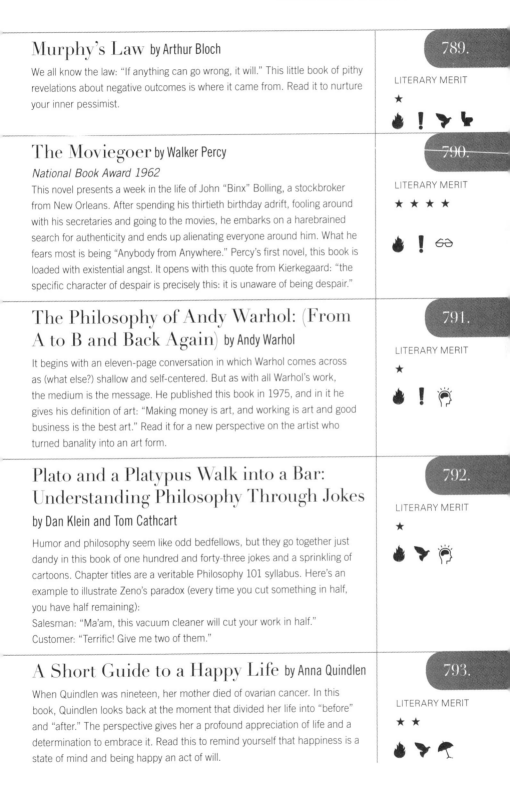

The Moviegoer by Walker Percy

790.

National Book Award 1962
This novel presents a week in the life of John "Binx" Bolling, a stockbroker from New Orleans. After spending his thirtieth birthday adrift, fooling around with his secretaries and going to the movies, he embarks on a harebrained search for authenticity and ends up alienating everyone around him. What he fears most is being "Anybody from Anywhere." Percy's first novel, this book is loaded with existential angst. It opens with this quote from Kierkegaard: "the specific character of despair is precisely this: it is unaware of being despair."

LITERARY MERIT
★ ★ ★ ★

The Philosophy of Andy Warhol: (From A to B and Back Again) by Andy Warhol

791.

It begins with an eleven-page conversation in which Warhol comes across as (what else?) shallow and self-centered. But as with all Warhol's work, the medium is the message. He published this book in 1975, and in it he gives his definition of art: "Making money is art, and working is art and good business is the best art." Read it for a new perspective on the artist who turned banality into an art form.

LITERARY MERIT
★

Plato and a Platypus Walk into a Bar: Understanding Philosophy Through Jokes

792.

by Dan Klein and Tom Cathcart

LITERARY MERIT
★

Humor and philosophy seem like odd bedfellows, but they go together just dandy in this book of one hundred and forty-three jokes and a sprinkling of cartoons. Chapter titles are a veritable Philosophy 101 syllabus. Here's an example to illustrate Zeno's paradox (every time you cut something in half, you have half remaining):
Salesman: "Ma'am, this vacuum cleaner will cut your work in half."
Customer: "Terrific! Give me two of them."

A Short Guide to a Happy Life by Anna Quindlen

793.

When Quindlen was nineteen, her mother died of ovarian cancer. In this book, Quindlen looks back at the moment that divided her life into "before" and "after." The perspective gives her a profound appreciation of life and a determination to embrace it. Read this to remind yourself that happiness is a state of mind and being happy an act of will.

LITERARY MERIT
★ ★

LITERARY MERIT

★ ★ ★

The Unbearable Lightness of Being
by Milan Kundera

This novel of existential angst is set in Prague on the eve of the "Velvet Revolution." Physician Tomas escapes with his wife Tereza to Zurich after Russian tanks roll in. He loves Tereza, but he also loves making love to other women, including his favorite mistress Sabina. Tereza leaves Tomas, and he follows her to Prague, knowing he'll be punished for his vocal stance against Communism. This is a novel that asks the big questions: What is the nature of love? Is it better to live silently under oppression or protest? What is a life well-lived?

LITERARY MERIT

★ ★

Zen and the Art of Motorcycle Maintenance: An Inquiry into Values
by Robert M. Pirsig

A cross-country motorcycle trip frames the narrative, and philosophy is introduced slowly, mixed with memoir and biography. "Zen is nothingness," Pirsig would later say. "If you talk about it you are always lying, and if you don't talk about it no one knows it is there." Rather than analyze, he'd rather "just enjoy watching the wind blow through the trees." Published in 1974, this best-selling philosophy book ever searches for the meaning of life and offers solutions to the anxieties of a generation.

...*to* STRIKE
IT RICH

LITERARY MERIT ★

PROVOCATIVE

INFLUENTIAL !

INSPIRATIONAL

HUMOROUS

BRAINY

EASY READING

PAGE TURNER

CHALLENGING

BATHROOM BOOK

FAMILY FRIENDLY

MOVIE

796.

LITERARY MERIT

★ ★

Blink: The Power of Thinking Without Thinking by Malcolm Gladwell

Leaping to conclusions—sometimes it's a good thing, sometimes it's not. Gladwell argues that the science of "leaping well" can be learned. "The power of knowing, in that first two seconds, is not a gift magically given to a fortunate few. It is an ability we can all build for ourselves." The key, he says, is "thin slicing"—picking up on patterns based on a narrowly constrained range of experience. This book will teach you how to make better snap decisions, and revolutionize how you think about how you think. For his insightful writing about social issues, Gladwell received the American Sociological Association's Award for Excellence.

797.

LITERARY MERIT

★ ★

Buffett: The Making of an American Capitalist by Roger Lowenstein

Little Warren grew up in Omaha, the son of parents who were "skilled at business and loath to spend a dollar." The man who would grow up to be a billionaire stock market wizard didn't fall far from the family tree. This biography tells of his difficult childhood and the investment philosophy that led him to become Coca-Cola's biggest individual stockholder by investing in the soft drink he'd delivered as a kid. Well written and thoughtful, this is an outstanding biography on a fascinating subject.

798.

LITERARY MERIT

★ ★

A Fool and His Money: The Odyssey of an Average Investor by John Rothchild

Rothchild chronicles the year he took off from financial writing to learn how to invest. He studied the markets, asked questions, observed professionals, and invested a modest sum (he sold an old Renault and a twice-used sailing dinghy).

> **Department of Odds and Ends**
>
> Here are a few glossary definitions from *A Fool and His Money*. Read them and weep.
>
> - **Average investor:** Born loser
> - **Successful investor:** Liar
> - **Long-term average investor:** Patient fool
> - **Short-term average investor:** Impatient fool
> - **Conservative investment:** A gamble in drag

He didn't get rich, but he earned wisdom and shares a gold mine of sound advice for how not to lose your shirt. For instance, "If you think it's right it's wrong, and vice versa."

Liar's Poker: Rising Through the Wreckage on Wall Street by Michael Lewis

LITERARY MERIT

★ ★

This smart, funny book reveals Lewis's meteoric rise, starting in 1985, from lowly trainee, or Geek, at Salomon Brothers to institutional bond salesman, or Big Swinging Dick. It's survival of the fittest in an every-man-for-himself environment. *Forbes* named this among 2002's "20 Most Influential Business Books."

The Millionaire Next Door: The Surprising Secrets of America's Wealthy
by Thomas J. Stanley and William D. Danko

LITERARY MERIT

★

The authors analyze surveys and twenty years of research, and their portrait of today's millionaires will surprise you. They're well educated, they drive older cars, are often self-employed, and—most of all—they're skinflints when it comes to spending their hard-earned cash. They live well below their means. How else do you think they've become PAWS (prodigious accumulators of wealth)? This persuasive book argues that there is no shortcut—for most of us it's save, save, save.

Did You Know It Means . . .

Adequate net worth: Multiply your age times your realized pretax annual household income from all sources except inheritances. Divide by ten. This simple rule of thumb tells you how much wealth you should have accumulated, according to *The Millionaire Next Door*.

The Richest Man in Babylon by George S. Clason

LITERARY MERIT

★

Why Babylon? Because it was reputedly one of the wealthiest nations ever, as well as a center of science and education. This slim volume of "Babylonian parables," originally published in 1926, illustrate Clason's "Seven Rules for a Lean Purse." The book is lean, too, without an ounce of bluster in it. The message is basically the same: First make it, then save it.

...to **Get Wasted**

LITERARY MERIT ★

PROVOCATIVE 🔥

INFLUENTIAL !

INSPIRATIONAL 🕊

HUMOROUS 😂

BRAINY 💡

EASY READING ☂

PAGE TURNER 📖

CHALLENGING 👓

BATHROOM BOOK 🚽

FAMILY FRIENDLY 👨‍👩‍👧

MOVIE 🎥

802.

LITERARY MERIT

★ ★ ★

Angels by Denis Johnson

Jamie Mays leaves her husband in a trailer park in Oakland, California, and is on a Greyhound bus with her two kids when she meets ex-Navy man Bill Houston (complete with tattoos and wraparound sunglasses). The two bounce between bus stations and cheap hotels, fueled by booze and desperation, and end up in an even more dangerous place—with Houston's family. Obscenity and poetry mix. This was a first novel from one of the most interesting and provocative writers today. Johnson told the *New York Times*, "My ear for the diction and rhythms of poetry was trained by—in chronological order—Dr. Seuss, Dylan Thomas, Walt Whitman, the guitar solos of Eric Clapton and Jimi Hendrix, and T. S. Eliot."

803.

LITERARY MERIT

★ ★

Edie by Jean Stein

Edie Sedgwick, the socialite whom Andy Warhol turned into a superstar, was all aristocratic glitz and glamour on the outside but nothing sustainable inside. At twenty-eight, she died of a drug overdose. This tapestry of reminiscences brings Edie's life into sharp perspective—a cautionary tale for Lindsay, Paris, and Britney.

804.

LITERARY MERIT

★ ★ ★

The Electric Kool-Aid Acid Test by Tom Wolfe

Wolfe chronicles the drugged-out adventures of novelist Ken Kesey (*One Flew Over the Cuckoo's Nest*) and his followers, the Merry Pranksters, as they bound across the country in a psychedelically painted, 1939 International Harvester schoolbus named "Further." These guys are the link between the beats and the hippies. This is a classic of literary journalism, and a book that captures a seminal moment in history.

805.

LITERARY MERIT

★ ★

Fear and Loathing in Las Vegas
by Hunter S. Thompson

Before he flamed out on drugs, journalist Thompson wrote this whacked-out autobiographical novel that appeared in *Rolling Stone* in 1971. It opens with protagonist Raoul Duke tearing down the highway to Vegas to cover a motorcycle race for a sports magazine with attorney Dr. Gonzo. The trunk of their huge, rented red convertible "looked like a mobile police narcotics lab" with its "galaxy of multi-colored uppers, downers, screamers, laughers" plus booze. Hallucinations, paranoia, and car wrecks mark their trip. This book made Thompson and his style of "gonzo" journalism famous.

Department of Memorable Lines

"Every now and then when your life gets complicated and the weasels start closing in, the only real cure is to load up on heinous chemicals and then drive like a bastard from Hollywood to Las Vegas."
—*Fear and Loathing in Las Vegas*

Fight Club by Chuck Palahniuk

806.

In this brutal novel of disaffected youth, the nameless narrator is a disillusioned insomniac who gets off on crashing support group meetings. He meets Tyler Durden, self-styled "guerilla terrorist of the service industry." Durden's "Project Mayhem" consists of subversive pranks like spitting into customer's soup and splicing porno into family films. Durden starts the Fight Club, and gets young men to pay to beat each other up—only it's an initiation ritual into Durden's larger plans for mayhem. A compulsively readable, angry, no-holds-barred book, it has become a cult classic.

LITERARY MERIT

★ ★

Ham on Rye by Charles Bukowski

807.

"This is presented as a work of fiction and dedicated to nobody," read the words on an otherwise empty dedication page of this autobiographical novel. The story begins, "The first thing I remember is being under something." Henry Chinaski (initials HC, like Holden Caulfield of *The Catcher in the Rye*) is under a table, it's Germany, and he's two years old. Then, two people are screaming and he's afraid of both of them. Disturbing and often written with raw vulgarity, the novel takes us through a childhood overshadowed by an abusive, alcoholic father, and on to life as a failing college student and alcoholic fledgling writer who would become one of the great writers of the beat generation.

LITERARY MERIT

★ ★

Naked Lunch by William S. Burroughs

808.

More a collection of loosely related anecdotes and hallucinations than a novel, this work chronicles a narcotic addict's descent into hell. Mostly it concerns drugs—buying them, taking them, sex acts and perversions performed while on them, the paranoia of getting caught, and medical interventions that attempt to control addiction. Not recommended for readers with delicate sensibilities, but an intriguing trip for readers made of stronger stuff.

LITERARY MERIT

★ ★ ★

On the Road by Jack Kerouac

809.

On a cross-country road trip, the narrator, Sal Paradise, finds beatitude. Supposedly Kerouac wrote this novel in a single burst of coffee and Benzedrine-fueled inspiration. The *New York Times* proclaimed it "the most beautifully executed, the clearest and the most important utterance yet made by the generation." Kerouac, the apotheosis of "beat," died at forty-seven from alcoholism.

LITERARY MERIT

★ ★ ★

810.℗

LITERARY MERIT

★ ★ ★

Trainspotting by Irvine Welsh

This disturbing collection of connected stories is set in working-class Leith, Edinburgh, Scotland where trains haven't stopped at the central station for decades. Mark Renton is a young junkie who wants to get clean. His friends are as wounded as he. Life is dull, violent, and hopeless, yet the novel is wildly funny. Welsh is a controversial writer for, among other things, his misogynistic portrayal of women. For the reader who craves an adrenaline rush.

811.

LITERARY MERIT

★

Valley of the Dolls by Jacqueline Susann

In this blockbuster novel, first published in 1966, three women try to make it in New York. Aspiring actress Anne Wells is a WASP Radcliffe graduate (think Grace Kelly), dancer/singer Neely O'Harar is hoofing it with a third-rate vaudeville act (think Judy Garland), and beautiful but needy Jennifer North is acting bit parts (think Marilyn Monroe). It's a trashy novel that captured the hypocrisy and chaos of the drugged-out '60s.

> **Who played Jennifer North in the movie adaptation of *Valley of the Dolls*?**
>
> Sharon Tate

812.

LITERARY MERIT

★ ★

Whiskey: The Definitive World Guide

by Michael Jackson

This is the guide to storing it, serving it, mixing it into cocktails or serving it straight up. Jackson takes the reader on a lavishly illustrated journey around the world, from grain through fermentation to glass. Learn how to "nose and taste." This won the James Beard Book Award in 2006.

...*to* Get Sober

LITERARY MERIT ★

PROVOCATIVE 🔥

INFLUENTIAL !

INSPIRATIONAL 🕊

HUMOROUS 😂

BRAINY 💡

EASY READING ☂

PAGE TURNER 📖

CHALLENGING 👓

BATHROOM BOOK 🚽

FAMILY FRIENDLY 👪

MOVIE 🎦

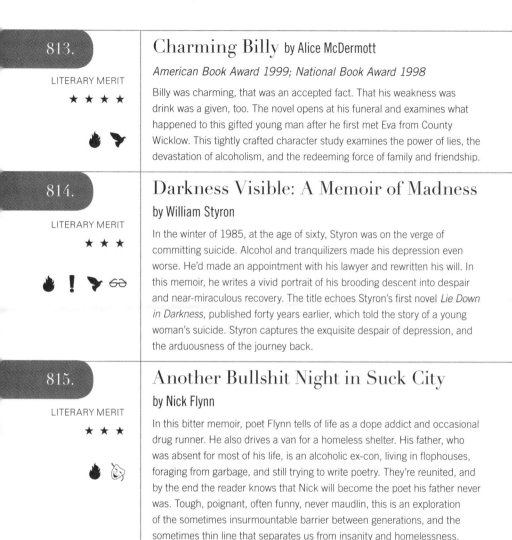

813.

LITERARY MERIT

★ ★ ★ ★

Charming Billy by Alice McDermott

American Book Award 1999; National Book Award 1998

Billy was charming, that was an accepted fact. That his weakness was drink was a given, too. The novel opens at his funeral and examines what happened to this gifted young man after he first met Eva from County Wicklow. This tightly crafted character study examines the power of lies, the devastation of alcoholism, and the redeeming force of family and friendship.

814.

LITERARY MERIT

★ ★ ★

Darkness Visible: A Memoir of Madness
by William Styron

In the winter of 1985, at the age of sixty, Styron was on the verge of committing suicide. Alcohol and tranquilizers made his depression even worse. He'd made an appointment with his lawyer and rewritten his will. In this memoir, he writes a vivid portrait of his brooding descent into despair and near-miraculous recovery. The title echoes Styron's first novel *Lie Down in Darkness*, published forty years earlier, which told the story of a young woman's suicide. Styron captures the exquisite despair of depression, and the arduousness of the journey back.

815.

LITERARY MERIT

★ ★ ★

Another Bullshit Night in Suck City
by Nick Flynn

In this bitter memoir, poet Flynn tells of life as a dope addict and occasional drug runner. He also drives a van for a homeless shelter. His father, who was absent for most of his life, is an alcoholic ex-con, living in flophouses, foraging from garbage, and still trying to write poetry. They're reunited, and by the end the reader knows that Nick will become the poet his father never was. Tough, poignant, often funny, never maudlin, this is an exploration of the sometimes insurmountable barrier between generations, and the sometimes thin line that separates us from insanity and homelessness.

The Broken Cord: A Family's Ongoing Struggle with Fetal Alcohol Syndrome

by Michael Dorris

National Book Critics Circle 1989

Dorris was twenty-six when he adopted a little Native American child, "Adam," who turns out to have overwhelming behavioral, emotional, and developmental problems that no amount of nurturing can overcome. Part Native American himself, Dorris took a long time to unravel the cause. This was an important book—the first to explore Fetal Alcohol Syndrome. Among the many sad footnotes to this book, Dorris's adopted son died at age twenty-three after a hit-and-run accident in 1991. Dorris himself committed suicide in 1997 at the age of fifty-two.

816.

LITERARY MERIT

★ ★

Drinking: A Love Story by Caroline Knapp

Once a columnist for the *Boston Phoenix*, Knapp writes this moving, soul-baring memoir about her struggle with alcoholism. She began using it as a teenager as "liquid armor," and drank for twenty years, even as she held down a job and convinced herself and others around her that she didn't have a problem.

817.

LITERARY MERIT

★ ★

Smashed: Story of a Drunken Girlhood

by Koren Zailckas

Zailckas writes vividly of her first taste of alcohol at fourteen—forbidden, thrilling, and liberating—and of her alcohol poisoning two years later. At twenty-two she wakes up and doesn't know where she

818.

LITERARY MERIT

★ ★

Department of Memorable Lines

"Alcohol is a manipulative bitch. If she were a person, I think she'd be a tele-marketer or a used-car saleswoman, the type of woman who could persuade you to do just about anything. . . . Drunk, I can seduce myself into any course of action."
—*Smashed*

is. She gives up drinking. Throughout the narrative, she weaves statistics and research that show binge drinking is a troubling trend among today's young women.

819.

LITERARY MERIT

★ ★

When the Sacred Ginmill Closes
by Lawrence Block

Former New York cop Matthew Scudder looks back ten years to when he was in a very dark place. Divorced from his wife, estranged from his kids, living in a seedy hotel, he spent his time drinking in Manhattan bars and doing favors for his cronies in the face of mounting danger. This is a terrific mystery novel about betrayal.

...to *Suffer*

820.

LITERARY MERIT

★ ★ ★

The Bookseller of Kabul by Åsne Seierstad

Norwegian journalist Seierstad spent four months living with Afghan bookstore owner Shah Mohammed Rais and his family. Though Rais is intellectual and dedicated to preserving Afghan literary culture, he's a tyrant by Western standards. He sends his wife of sixteen years off to Pakistan to make room for a sixteen-year-old second wife. He forces his twelve-year-old son to work long hours selling candy in a dank booth in a hotel lobby. He treats his nineteen-year-old sister as a household slave. For the reader, this is a rare, intimate look inside an unhappy Afghan family. Seierstad's subject is not so pleased—Rais sued her for invasion of privacy.

821.

LITERARY MERIT

★ ★ ★ ★

The Grapes of Wrath by John Steinbeck

Pulitzer Prize 1940

The anger and outrage Steinbeck felt when he visited migrant labor camps in northern California in the late 1930s inspired him to write this, considered his best novel. Its portrait of the dispossessed Joad family's move from the Oklahoma Dust Bowl to California migrant labor camps and their struggle to survive in the face of ruthless agricultural

> **Department of Memorable Opening Lines**
>
> "To the red country and part of the gray country of Oklahoma, the last rains came gently, and they did not cut the scarred earth."
> —*The Grapes of Wrath*

economics struck a chord. Detractors accused Steinbeck of being a Communist and exaggerating the conditions. Eleanor Roosevelt came to his defense, and the controversy led to changes in labor laws.

822.

LITERARY MERIT

★ ★ ★

The Man Who Loved Children
by Christina Stead

This novel is a classic tragedy of ordinary people in a horrifyingly dysfunctional family. Henny Pollit is the angry, unpredictable, cruel mother. Her charismatic, hyperactive husband Sam alternately baby-talks and abuses their six children. The story is told from the point of view of eldest daughter Louisa, who struggles to break free. This book was first published in 1940 and then rediscovered in the late 1960s. Read it to discover a major twentieth-century Australian writer.

Misery by Stephen King

823.

Author Paul Sheldon meets a good Samaritan from hell, nurse Annie Wilkes, his "number-one" fan. After a car accident near her home, she holds him hostage. She forces him to rewrite the book in which he killed off her favorite character, Misery Chastain. This is a great horror novel and a fascinating meditation on the symbiotic author-reader relationship.

LITERARY MERIT

★ ★ ★

The Scarlet Letter
by Nathaniel Hawthorne

824.

LITERARY MERIT

★ ★ ★

Department of Memorable Characters

Hester Prynne has given birth to a child from an adulterous affair. She's publicly harangued and forced to wear the scarlet letter "A," but refuses to name her lover. She raises her daughter, doing good works. But still she's shunned by the community while her former lover suffers a living hell. First published in 1850 and one of America's first psychological novels, it sets rigid, seventeenth-century Puritan morality against passion and individualism.

"The scarlet letter was her passport into regions where other women dared not to tread. Shame, Despair, Solitude! These had been her teachers—stern and wild ones—and they had made her strong, but taught her much amiss."
—Hester Prynne

The Swallows of Kabul by Yasmina Khadra

825.

LITERARY MERIT

★ ★ ★

In this novel, written by a former Algerian army officer using a pseudonym to evade military censors, Taliban-ruled Kabul is a grim place. Public laughter is a criminal offense and the streets are ruled by jailers. Mohsen Ramat, once a well-to-do shopkeeper, and his beautiful wife Zunaira, a former teacher, have lost everything. Mohsen nearly loses his humanity as well when he finds himself participating in the public stoning of an adulterous woman. There he crosses paths with Taliban prison-keeper Atiq Shaukat, a man numbed by war and hardship, whose wife is dying. This compassionate novel offers rich insights into the complexities of life in the Muslim world.

Theory of War by Joan Brady

826.

LITERARY MERIT

★ ★ ★ ★

Brady bases this novel, a chilling tale of a white child sold by his father into slavery, on her grandfather's experiences. Narrator Mallory Carrick, the stand-in for Brady, interviews her alcoholic, forgetful great-uncle to learn how her grandfather survived. This won the 1993 Whitbread Book of the Year award.

827.

LITERARY MERIT

★ ★ ★ ★

The Tin Drum by Günter Grass

This novel is framed as the autobiography of Oskar Matzerath written from a mental hospital in the early 1950s. His memory begins with his own birth, when he was gifted a "glass demolishing scream." At three he receives a tin drum and determines "that I would never under any circumstances be a politician, much less a grocer; that I would stop right there, remain as I was—and so I did; for many years I not only stayed the same size but clung to the same attire." Refusing to grow up is the only way Oskar survives the Nazi era. The novel presents a horrifying, clear-eyed, insider's view of a corrupt, brutal World War II Germany. The furor this work created when it was published in 1959 still reverberates today.

828.

LITERARY MERIT

★ ★ ★

Train by Pete Dexter

From an author whose works are steeped in sex and violence, this novel is propelled forward by a double murder and rape aboard a seventy-two-foot yacht docked at Newport Beach. The murderers, black men who caddy at a posh Brookline golf club, are killed, execution-style, by ruthless police detective Miller Packard. Packard ends up marrying the widowed rape victim. Into the story walks Lionel "Train" Walker, a seventeen-year-old black caddie at the Brookline golf club. Packard recognizes Train's extraordinary talent and starts betting on him in matches with golf hustlers. When Train moves into Packard's guest cottage, he becomes enmeshed in a volatile triangle. This book is a provocative, unsettling exploration of racism.

829.

LITERARY MERIT

★ ★ ★ ★

World of Our Fathers: The Journey of the East European Jews to America and the Life They Found and Made by Irving Howe

National Book Award 1977

This nearly eight-hundred-page book tells the history of Jewish immigrant life, from the Old Country, through the arduous voyage, to resettlement in ghetto tenements on New York's Lower East Side. It details the struggle to make a living, to create labor unions, settlement houses, and synagogues. It examines the development of Catskill retreats, and the flourish and decline of Yiddish culture. A fascinating social anthropology of Jews in America.

...*to* Suffer (No) Fools

LITERARY MERIT ★

PROVOCATIVE 🔥

INFLUENTIAL ❗

INSPIRATIONAL 🕊

HUMOROUS 😄

BRAINY 🧠

EASY READING ☂

PAGE TURNER 📖

CHALLENGING 👓

BATHROOM BOOK 🚽

FAMILY FRIENDLY 👪

MOVIE 🎥

830.

LITERARY MERIT

★ ★ ★

Airships by Barry Hannah

This is a collection of wickedly funny short stories from a talented southern writer who can pitilessly dispatch a character, as in: "She had a certain smile that would have brought her the world had the avenue of regard been wide enough for her." Or: "Her husband was an intellectual in real estate." This collection won the Arnold Gingrich Short Fiction Award.

831.

LITERARY MERIT

★ ★ ★

Candide by Voltaire

Considered a comic masterpiece, this 1759 novel relates the misadventures of Candide, a hapless and, today we would say, clueless youth. Despite misfortune atop misfortune (he's beaten, banished, separated from the woman he loves), Candide declares this to be "the best of all possible worlds" in which "things cannot be otherwise, for, everything being made for an end everything is necessarily for the best end." Voltaire published the work anonymously because it attacked the hypocrisy of the church, popular philosophy, and other established institutions of his time. It still resonates today.

832.

LITERARY MERIT

★ ★ ★ ★

The Corrections by Jonathan Franzen

National Book Award 2001

The tortured relationships among the five adult members of the Lambert family are grist for this realistic family saga. Patriarch Alfred is losing his grip on reality courtesy of the drugs he takes for Parkinson's. His wife Enid, with her frazzled niceness, wants "one last Christmas" family gathering. Oldest son Gary is an unhappy, married banker. Middle sister Denise is a chef, rebounding badly from failed relationships. And youngest son Chip, a failed teacher and writer, is in Lithuania floundering around when he's hired to produce a profit-making Web site for a failed nation. "Corrections"—therapy and drugs and vacation cruises—do little to stop the decay. This is character-based fiction at its best, and a satiric look at life in America.

833.

LITERARY MERIT

★

The Darwin Awards by Wendy Northcutt

This series of annual books celebrates individuals who, "By removing themselves from the gene pool . . . give their all for the good of the rest of us." Winners are selected from submissions to the Darwin Awards Web site. Celebrate the twenty-seven-year-old motorcycle enthusiast killed speeding down Meridian Avenue in Tacoma, steering with his feet. Or the inebriated Austrian who tried to enter his house through the kitchen window, got stuck, and drowned in his kitchen sink.

The Dilbert Principle by Scott Adams

834.

LITERARY MERIT

★

This is a book of business advice from the anti-business creator of cartoon character Dilbert. Adams worked for Pacific Bell for years where he labored in a cubicle and learned, firsthand, the Dilbert Principle: "The most ineffective workers are systematically moved to the place where they can do the least damage: management." If nature operated this way, he observes, you'd see "a band of mountain gorillas led by an 'alpha' squirrel. And it wouldn't be the most skilled squirrel; it would be the squirrel nobody wanted to hang around with." Sequester this book in your cubicle and dip into it when you're feeling mad as hell and not going to take it anymore!

Doubt: A History: The Great Doubters and Their Legacy of Innovation from Socrates and Jesus to Thomas Jefferson and Emily Dickinson by Jennifer Hecht

835.

LITERARY MERIT

★ ★

In this celebration of history's great religious doubters, Hecht reasons there are believers who "refuse to consider the reasonableness of doubt," just as there are doubters who "refuse to consider the feeling of faith." She's squarely on the side of the doubters, and includes offbeat figures like the Islamic philosopher and physician Abu Bakr al-Razi (854–925) and Annie Besant, a social activist who wrote a "Gospel of Atheism" in 1876. This somewhat scholarly, completely fascinating, meticulously researched social history will get you thinking.

The Emperor's Children by Claire Messud

836.

LITERARY MERIT

★ ★ ★

Set in the months before and after 9/11, this satirical comedy of manners tells the intersecting stories of three entitled young New Yorkers who met at Brown University. All are obsessed with their own under-achievement. Danielle Minkoff is a TV documentary producer. Julian Clarke is a struggling freelance book reviewer. The beautiful Marina Thwaite is a writer who fails to live up to her legacy as the daughter of a legendary liberal journalist. September 11 arrives and destabilizes their world. This is a big, highly readable, compassionate comedy of manners.

837.

LITERARY MERIT

★ ★ ★ ★

Excellent Women by Barbara Pym

British novelist Barbara Pym is one of those excellent authors whose work is often compared to Jane Austen. Her comedy of manners masquerades under a veneer of gentility. First published in 1952, this novel tells the story of witty, self-deprecating, contented British spinster Mildred Lathbury. She keeps herself busy with friends, good works, and church jumble

> **Department of Memorable Lines**
>
> "I suppose an unmarried woman just over thirty, who lives alone and has no apparent tie, must expect to find herself involved or interested in other people's business, and if she is also a clergyman's daughter then one might really say that there is no hope for her."
> —*Excellent Women*

sales. Exotic new neighbors move in and Mildred finds herself enmeshed in a messy love triangle. The book raises the radical possibility that a woman might be better off alone.

838.

LITERARY MERIT

★

Flim-Flam! Psychics, ESP, Unicorns, and Other Delusions by James Randi

Randi has made a career of debunking myths. From Arthur Conan Doyle and his taste for fairies to UFOs to spoon-bending Uri Geller, Randi exposes the smoke and mirrors. What worries him is scientists who've climbed aboard what he calls the "paranormal bandwagon." As a magician and escape artist, he knows how easy it is to create an illusion, and how much people want to believe. This is a great primer in skepticism and one of the movement's early classics before Penn and Teller picked up the gauntlet.

839.

LITERARY MERIT

★

The Hidden Persuaders by Vance Packard

Before psychology got its pop, Vance Packard examined how the media manipulates our perceptions and gets us to crave the products they're pushing. This book, published in 1957, alerted us to the effects of subliminal messages. With a wealth of examples, Packard shows us how ad campaigns exploit our every vulnerability.

840.

LITERARY MERIT

★

Innumeracy: Mathematical Illiteracy and Its Consequences by John Allen Paulos

Paulos is dismayed, nay, angered by how many of us are innumerate (unable to understand fundamental notions of numbers and chance). It's not just unfortunate, it's dangerous. Innumeracy makes us vulnerable to pseudoscience and explains why we're not fazed by a government that spends "more than a quarter of a trillion dollars each year on ever smarter weapons for ever more poorly educated soldiers."

On Politics: A Carnival of Buncombe

841.

by H. L. Mencken

LITERARY MERIT

★ ★

Mencken's famously opinionated and controversial columns for the *Baltimore Evening Sun* earned him a national reputation. This volume contains a collection of seventy political pieces that combine biting sarcasm with plain talk. In the lead essay, he says of the candidates in the 1920 presidential race: "They are all extremely wary, and all more or less palpable frauds." Read insights that are as fresh today as when they were first penned.

The Peter Principle by Laurence J. Peter

842.

LITERARY MERIT

★

The Peter Principle says that each employee rises within a hierarchy to his level of incompetence. Great salesmen become mediocre managers. Great teachers turn into lousy principals. Peter's advice: Practice creative incompetence to avoid the ultimate promotion. It's a great book to remind us all not to take ourselves too seriously.

Department of Odds and Ends

On incompetence, from *The Peter Principle:*
"In a hierarchy every employee tends to rise to his level of incompetence."
"Work is accomplished by those employees who have not yet reached their level of incompetence."
"Some problems are so complex that you have to be highly intelligent and well informed just to be undecided about them."

Pride and Prejudice by Jane Austen

843.

LITERARY MERIT

★ ★ ★

This is a genteel comedy of manners in which the quick-witted but prejudiced Elizabeth Bennet finally finds her match in the prideful Mr. Darcy, while Elizabeth's mother Mrs. Bennet bustles about in her muddled determination to make "appropriate" matches for her girls. Austen wrote this in less than a year when she was just twenty-one-years of age and published it in 1813. If you haven't read this classic, you're in for a treat.

Department of Memorable Opening Lines

"It is a truth universally acknowledged, that a single man in possession of a good fortune must be in want of a wife."
—Pride and Prejudice

844.

LITERARY MERIT

★ ★

Surely You're Joking, Mr. Feynman!: Adventures of a Curious Character
by Richard P. Feynman

In this scientist's coming-of-age memoir, Nobel laureate Feynman tells of collaborating with Einstein and Bohr on atomic physics, trading gambling tips with Nick the Greek, and his forays into safe cracking, hypnotism, and topless bars. He's smart, funny, and a consummate entertainer.

845.

LITERARY MERIT

★

Yes, We Have No Neutrons: An Eye-Opening Tour Through the Twists and Turns of Bad Science by A. K. Dewdney

This irreverent work exposes eight cases where science went wrong. Read about the cold fusion fiasco, the terminally elusive N-ray, the saga of the media-hyped biosphere, and the flawed search for extraterrestrial intelligence. Weep when you hear of millions of dollars poured down the drain pursuing such ill-conceived studies. This irreverent Canadian professor of computer science takes pokes at scientists (sorcerers) and would-be scientists (apprentices) whose pride and ambition prevent them from recognizing fatal flaws in their work.

...to Survive

LITERARY MERIT ★

PROVOCATIVE 🔥

INFLUENTIAL !

INSPIRATIONAL ➤

HUMOROUS 😄

BRAINY 💡

EASY READING ☂

PAGE TURNER 📖

CHALLENGING 👓

BATHROOM BOOK 🚽

FAMILY FRIENDLY 👪

MOVIE 🎥

846.

LITERARY MERIT

★ ★

Alive: The Story of the Andes Survivors

by Piers Paul Read

In 1972, a plane carrying forty-five people, including a Uruguayan rugby team, crashed and came to rest in a valley of snow high in the Andes. Thirty-two survived the initial crash, but only sixteen emerged from the mountains nine weeks later. They survived the only way they could. Journalist Read interviewed survivors and tells a gripping tale of endurance against all odds.

847.

LITERARY MERIT

★ ★ ★ ★

Bitter Grounds by Sandra Benitez

American Book Award 1998

In this saga, we follow three generations of women from two families who survive after losing most of their relatives in war-torn El Salvador. The rich family owns a coffee plantation, the poor family works there. Benitez writes the novel based on suffering she knows firsthand—four of her friends were killed during the war and her brother-in-law was kidnapped and later fled the country. The story packs a powerful emotional punch.

848.

LITERARY MERIT

★ ★ ★

The Book Thief by Markus Zusak

Death narrates this novel, set in World War II Germany. Liesel Meminger is the thief of the title. She can't even read when she steals *The Gravedigger's Handbook* at her little brother's funeral, where she meets Death. After her mother disappears, Liesel is put in foster care in the cozy home of Rosa and Hans Hubermann. From there, she watches Jews being sent to Dachau and must march with Hitler Youth. She uses a stolen copy of *Mein Kampf* to save the life of a young Jewish man. Other stolen books form the backbone of the story. This moving book was an American Bookseller Association's 2007 Book of the Year.

849.

LITERARY MERIT

★ ★ ★

A Childhood: The Biography of a Place

by Harry Crews

This 1978 memoir chronicles the author's first six years, growing up dirt-poor in rural southern Georgia during the Depression when "there wasn't enough cash money in the county to close up a dead man's eyes." The characters are right out of Walker Evans's photos. Crews's father worked himself to death at thirty. His mother married his father's abusive brother, fled, and then returned to work the farm herself. To escape, Crews created his own imaginary reality from photographs in the Sears Roebuck catalog, just as he would later create imaginary worlds in wonderfully bizarre Gothic novels. These earliest memories are hard to forget.

Deliverance by James Dickey

Four southerners, pals from the suburbs with romantic visions of testing their manhood, embark on a three-day whitewater canoeing and camping trip through the Georgia wilderness. The narrator says in anticipation, "I had a good feeling about this trip. After so much shooting at paper images of deer, it was exciting to think of encountering a real one." Deer turn out to be the least of the challenges of this nightmare trip. This is a classic adventure story, a dark exploration of what it means to be a man, and a vivid portrayal of the great outdoors.

LITERARY MERIT

★ ★

The Glass Castle by Jeannette Walls

Alex Award 2006

It's a wonder that the author and her siblings survived their parenting. This memoir tells how they were hurtled from one bleak, dusty, Southwestern mining town to another by an exuberant, paranoid alcoholic father and artist mother who was an "excitement freak." Walls drank ditch water, survived being thrown from a moving car, and at four was so good with Dad's six-shooter that she "could hit five out of six beer bottles at 30 paces." Most amazing is the evenhanded tenderness with which Walls treats her execrable parents.

LITERARY MERIT

★ ★ ★

The Good Earth by Pearl S. Buck

Pulitzer 1932

This novel tells the story of farmer Wang Lung and his complex relationship with the land. Hardship drives him to the city to beg, but he refuses to sell his land. Through hardwork

> **Who played Wang Lung in the 1937 movie adaptation of *The Good Earth*?**
>
> Paul Muni

and determination, he grows wealthy and becomes the kind of decadent landowner he once despised. Nineteenth-century China comes alive in this classic by a woman who spent much of her life there.

LITERARY MERIT

★ ★ ★

The Great Influenza: The Epic Story of the Deadliest Plague in History by John M. Barry

More devastating than World War I, the 1918 influenza epidemic killed an estimated 50 to 100 million people worldwide, most within a 12-week period. People set off for work, feeling fine, and were dead by the end of the day. City hospitals quickly filled and bodies stacked up in morgues as undertakers ran out of coffins. Read about the disease's mutation from animal- to human-carried, its raging outbreak, the political expediency that hampered adequate response, and the scientists who unlocked its secrets.

LITERARY MERIT

★ ★

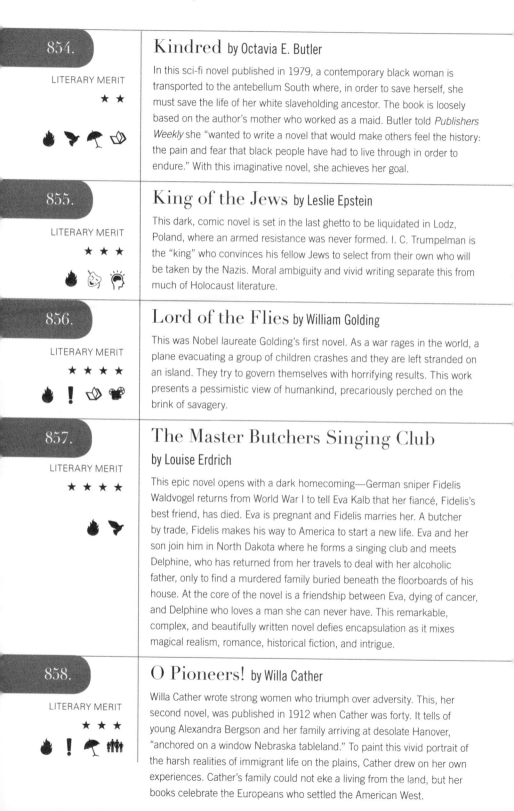

854.

LITERARY MERIT

★ ★

Kindred by Octavia E. Butler

In this sci-fi novel published in 1979, a contemporary black woman is transported to the antebellum South where, in order to save herself, she must save the life of her white slaveholding ancestor. The book is loosely based on the author's mother who worked as a maid. Butler told *Publishers Weekly* she "wanted to write a novel that would make others feel the history: the pain and fear that black people have had to live through in order to endure." With this imaginative novel, she achieves her goal.

855.

LITERARY MERIT

★ ★ ★

King of the Jews by Leslie Epstein

This dark, comic novel is set in the last ghetto to be liquidated in Lodz, Poland, where an armed resistance was never formed. I. C. Trumpelman is the "king" who convinces his fellow Jews to select from their own who will be taken by the Nazis. Moral ambiguity and vivid writing separate this from much of Holocaust literature.

856.

LITERARY MERIT

★ ★ ★ ★

Lord of the Flies by William Golding

This was Nobel laureate Golding's first novel. As a war rages in the world, a plane evacuating a group of children crashes and they are left stranded on an island. They try to govern themselves with horrifying results. This work presents a pessimistic view of humankind, precariously perched on the brink of savagery.

857.

LITERARY MERIT

★ ★ ★ ★

The Master Butchers Singing Club
by Louise Erdrich

This epic novel opens with a dark homecoming—German sniper Fidelis Waldvogel returns from World War I to tell Eva Kalb that her fiancé, Fidelis's best friend, has died. Eva is pregnant and Fidelis marries her. A butcher by trade, Fidelis makes his way to America to start a new life. Eva and her son join him in North Dakota where he forms a singing club and meets Delphine, who has returned from her travels to deal with her alcoholic father, only to find a murdered family buried beneath the floorboards of his house. At the core of the novel is a friendship between Eva, dying of cancer, and Delphine who loves a man she can never have. This remarkable, complex, and beautifully written novel defies encapsulation as it mixes magical realism, romance, historical fiction, and intrigue.

858.

LITERARY MERIT

★ ★ ★

O Pioneers! by Willa Cather

Willa Cather wrote strong women who triumph over adversity. This, her second novel, was published in 1912 when Cather was forty. It tells of young Alexandra Bergson and her family arriving at desolate Hanover, "anchored on a window Nebraska tableland." To paint this vivid portrait of the harsh realities of immigrant life on the plains, Cather drew on her own experiences. Cather's family could not eke a living from the land, but her books celebrate the Europeans who settled the American West.

Persepolis by Marjane Satrapi

Alex Award 2004

This graphic novel/memoir of growing up in Iran has black-and-white drawings that ache with innocence. Satrapi's great-grandfather was Iran's last Qajar emperor. At six, she led a privileged, liberated life with her intellectual parents in Tehran. Their lives changed after the 1979 revolution that deposed the Shah. In her own coming-of-age story, she tells how she found respite from grim reality in a fantasy world where she is a prophet talking directly to a God whom she imagines as a Karl Marx look-alike, "though Marx's hair was a bit curlier." At fourteen, dressed in a chador, she flees alone to Vienna. In 2003, this won Spain's Fernando Buesa Peace Prize. Read it with *Waiting for Snow in Havana.*

859.

LITERARY MERIT

★ ★

The Pianist: The Extraordinary True Story of One Man's Survival in Warsaw, 1939–1945 by Wladyslaw Szpilman

"I began my wartime career as a pianist in the Café Nowoczesna, which was in Nowolipki Street in the very heart of the Warsaw Ghetto," begins this memoir. Published soon after the war but suppressed by the Communist authorities, the book depicts life in Poland under Nazi occupation. Near the war's end, a German soldier saved Szpilman's life. But his family perished. No self-pity or polemics here, just a vivid, understated narrative that barely masks bitterness and rage.

860.

LITERARY MERIT

★ ★ ★

Poor People by William T. Vollmann

Vollmann writes of his travels throughout the world, seeking out people who eke out a living at the edge of subsistence. His goal: to see the impoverished and to understand poverty. Lyrical prose, photographs, interviews, philosophy, and statistics paint an indelible picture.

861.

LITERARY MERIT

★ ★ ★

Refuge: An Unnatural History of Family and Place by Terry Tempest Williams

Naturalist Williams writes of personal tragedy and natural disaster. Grieving over cancer deaths of women in her family caused by nuclear weapons testing, she witnesses disaster along the shores of the Great Salt Lake. Water levels rise, threatening to obliterate sanctuaries that are home to herons, owls, and snowy egrets. She traces the nexus between ourselves, the people who nurture our lives, and the places that surround us. There are mournful echoes here of Rachel Carson's *Silent Spring.*

862.

LITERARY MERIT

★ ★ ★

863.

LITERARY MERIT

★ ★ ★ ★

Schindler's List by Thomas Keneally

Booker Prize 1982

German Otto Schindler saved 1,300 Jews from certain death. This novelistic nonfiction tells how he did it while winning lucrative military contracts, which were fulfilled using Jewish slave labor. Schindler was a charmer, a cunning businessman, and a notorious philanderer with a lust for the good things in life. But by the end of his life, his "munitions factories" were producing nothing and he had no fortune. He had created an elaborate mechanism for saving lives. A gripping, inspiring story, despite the moral ambiguities.

864.

LITERARY MERIT

★ ★ ★ ★

Stones from the River by Ursula Hegi

In this stunning novel of war-torn Germany, Trudi Montag is an outcast because she's a dwarf. It's a chaotic time—one neighbor erects a statue of Hitler in his front yard and another is killed trying to tear it down—as Trudi and her father sequester fleeing Jews. The unforgettable Trudi, often compared to Oskar of Günter Grass's *The Tin Drum*, searches for love and acceptance but finds only despair.

865.

LITERARY MERIT

★ ★ ★ ★

This Boy's Life by Tobias Wolff

This grim, candid, and often funny memoir begins, "It was 1955 and we were driving from Florida to Utah, to get away from a man my mother was afraid of and to get rich on uranium." Wolff battles his divorced mother's abusive boyfriend, and then a cruel, neurotic stepfather who paints the entire house, including the piano and the Christmas tree, white. He runs off to Alaska where he survives by kiting checks and stealing cars before reinventing himself. Fortunately for us, he found his foothold in writing.

866.

LITERARY MERIT

★ ★

What Is the What: The Autobiography of Valentino Achak Deng by Dave Eggers

This fictional autobiography is based on the true account of survival of one of Sudan's "Lost Boys." Deng was one of 20,000 boys caught in the crossfire between the Sudanese government and rebel forces. His trek across hundreds of miles to hoped-for safety in Ethiopia was fraught with danger as he dodged soldiers, bombs, crocodiles, and lions. Many died along the way. After years in refugee camps, Deng came to America. Though there is no happy-ever-after ending, this remains a testament to the resilience of the human spirit.

867.

LITERARY MERIT

★ ★ ★

Winter Wheat by Mildred Walker

In the '50s and '60s, Walker was one of America's most popular novelists, and this is one of her best. It tells the story of Ellen Webb who grows up on an arid, dry-land wheat farm. The harvest is good the year she goes off to college and falls in love. Like the land, love alternately rewards and disappoints.

...to **Trust No One**

LITERARY MERIT ★

PROVOCATIVE 🔥

INFLUENTIAL ❗

INSPIRATIONAL 🕊

HUMOROUS 😄

BRAINY 💡

EASY READING ☂

PAGE TURNER 📖

CHALLENGING 👓

BATHROOM BOOK 🚽

FAMILY FRIENDLY 👪

MOVIE 🎥

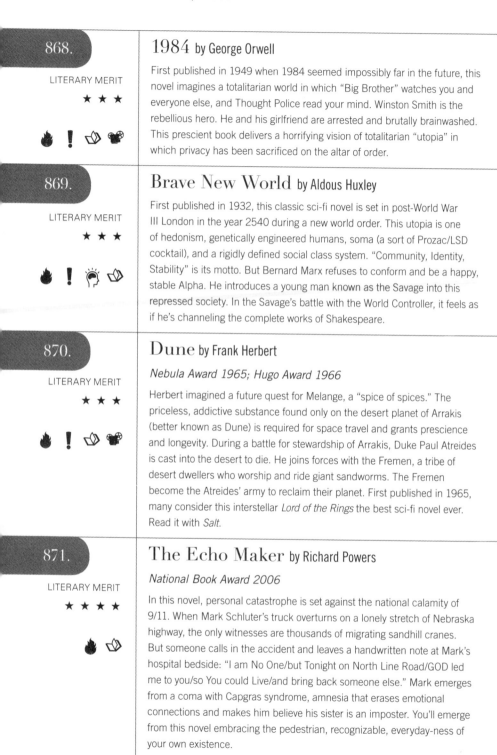

868.

LITERARY MERIT

★ ★ ★

1984 by George Orwell

First published in 1949 when 1984 seemed impossibly far in the future, this novel imagines a totalitarian world in which "Big Brother" watches you and everyone else, and Thought Police read your mind. Winston Smith is the rebellious hero. He and his girlfriend are arrested and brutally brainwashed. This prescient book delivers a horrifying vision of totalitarian "utopia" in which privacy has been sacrificed on the altar of order.

869.

LITERARY MERIT

★ ★ ★

Brave New World by Aldous Huxley

First published in 1932, this classic sci-fi novel is set in post-World War III London in the year 2540 during a new world order. This utopia is one of hedonism, genetically engineered humans, soma (a sort of Prozac/LSD cocktail), and a rigidly defined social class system. "Community, Identity, Stability" is its motto. But Bernard Marx refuses to conform and be a happy, stable Alpha. He introduces a young man known as the Savage into this repressed society. In the Savage's battle with the World Controller, it feels as if he's channeling the complete works of Shakespeare.

870.

LITERARY MERIT

★ ★ ★

Dune by Frank Herbert

Nebula Award 1965; Hugo Award 1966

Herbert imagined a future quest for Melange, a "spice of spices." The priceless, addictive substance found only on the desert planet of Arrakis (better known as Dune) is required for space travel and grants prescience and longevity. During a battle for stewardship of Arrakis, Duke Paul Atreides is cast into the desert to die. He joins forces with the Fremen, a tribe of desert dwellers who worship and ride giant sandworms. The Fremen become the Atreides' army to reclaim their planet. First published in 1965, many consider this interstellar *Lord of the Rings* the best sci-fi novel ever. Read it with *Salt*.

871.

LITERARY MERIT

★ ★ ★ ★

The Echo Maker by Richard Powers

National Book Award 2006

In this novel, personal catastrophe is set against the national calamity of 9/11. When Mark Schluter's truck overturns on a lonely stretch of Nebraska highway, the only witnesses are thousands of migrating sandhill cranes. But someone calls in the accident and leaves a handwritten note at Mark's hospital bedside: "I am No One/but Tonight on North Line Road/GOD led me to you/so You could Live/and bring back someone else." Mark emerges from a coma with Capgras syndrome, amnesia that erases emotional connections and makes him believe his sister is an imposter. You'll emerge from this novel embracing the pedestrian, recognizable, everyday-ness of your own existence.

Fahrenheit 451 by Ray Bradbury

Guy Montag is a fireman in a dystopian future—he burns books in a society that suppresses critical thinking. One night he meets Clarisse McClellan, a liberated idealist who causes him to ask questions. She's killed, and he begins to steal books and burn televisions to stop the mindlessness. Soon, they really *are* out to get him. This may have been written during the paranoia of the '50s, but it has a frightening resonance today.

Did You Know It Means . . .

Fahrenheit 451: The temperature at which paper burns

872.

LITERARY MERIT

★ ★ ★

I Am the Cheese by Robert Cormier

At the end of the children's game, the cheese stands alone. In this scary suspense novel, young Adam Farmer is very much alone, too. He's been in a psychiatric hospital, suffering from amnesia. As he rides his bike toward a Vermont hospital, determined to find his father and discover the truth about his past, excerpts from taped interviews with his psychiatrist and a terrible secret are revealed. Picked as a *School Library Journal* Best Book of the Year, this is a beautifully crafted psychological thriller to which any age can relate.

873.

LITERARY MERIT

★ ★

I, Robot by Isaac Asimov

Nine stories about Positronic Robots comprise Asimov's first published collection. The stories are framed as chief robopsychologist Dr. Susan Calvin's reminiscences of her life's work—"To you, a robot is just a robot. But you haven't worked with them. You don't know them. They're a cleaner, better breed than we are." Asimov's famous "Three Laws of Robotics" first appeared here. This book is a great introduction to Asimov, perhaps the greatest sci-fi writer of the twentieth century, who is credited with coining the term *robotics*.

874.

LITERARY MERIT

★ ★ ★

Slaughterhouse-Five by Kurt Vonnegut

Billy Pilgrim, "tall and weak, and shaped like a bottle of Coca-Cola," has a problem. He's "unstuck in time" and can't control where he's going next. Vonnegut's sci-fi novel jumps back and forth in time to tell Pilgrim's story. He's kidnapped by aliens from the planet Tralfamadore and educated there, "where everything was beautiful, and nothing hurt." He also survives the bombing of Dresden (Vonnegut drew on his own experiences in World War II). His life ends with his assassination. Absurd, hilarious, heartbreaking, and profound.

875.

LITERARY MERIT

★ ★ ★ ★

876.

LITERARY MERIT

★ ★ ★

Snow Falling on Cedars by David Guterson

Fairness and forgiveness are the subjects of this riveting courtroom drama, set in 1954 on San Piedro Island in the Puget Sound. Japanese American Kabuo Miyomoto stands accused of killing a fellow fisherman in a land dispute. While Kabuo was interred in a prison camp, he lost his land to the family of the man he killed. Ishmael Chambers is a journalist who covers the trial for the local newspaper. He was once Kabuo's high school classmate, and lost his arm fighting in the war. He also loves Kabuo's wife. This intricately plotted bestseller was an American Bookseller Association's 1996 Book of the Year.

877.

LITERARY MERIT

★ ★ ★ ★

The Tortilla Curtain by T. Coraghessan Boyle

Delaney Mossbacher, a wealthy Californian and self-proclaimed "liberal humanist" with an "unblemished driving record and a freshly waxed Japanese car with personalized plates," almost runs down Cándido Rincón, "a dark little man with a wild look in his eye." Rincón and his family are barely scratching out an existence in the canyon outside the gated community where Mossbacher and his family live. In this novel that engages the reader in the ongoing human drama of immigration, real people from opposite worlds collide.

Quiz Time!

Match these terms from the *Dune* universe to their definitions.

1. Melange

2. Foldspace

3. Shai-Hulud

4. Arrakis

5. Mentats

6. Bene Gesserit

a. Enormous, virtually indestructible sandworms

b. Females with superhuman physical sensory and deductive powers

c. A spice; the most valuable commodity in the universe

d. Wrinkles in space that enable instantaneous travel across vast distances

e. A planet nearly devoid of water

f. Humans who can perform complex, computer-like computations

Answers: *1-c, 2-d, 3-a, 4-e, 5-f, 6-b*

...to Grieve

LITERARY MERIT ★

PROVOCATIVE 🔥

INFLUENTIAL ❗

INSPIRATIONAL 🕊

HUMOROUS 😀

BRAINY 🧠

EASY READING ☂

PAGE TURNER 📖

CHALLENGING 👓

BATHROOM BOOK 🚽

FAMILY FRIENDLY 👪

MOVIE 🎥

878.

LITERARY MERIT

★ ★ ★

About Alice by Calvin Trillin

She was Trillin's beloved wife, the mother of his children, and they traveled together and ate. She died much too soon. This is an endearing and heartbreakingly funny paean to Alice, who had "a weird predilection for limiting our family to three meals a day," and who thought that if you didn't go to every performance of your child's school play, "the county would come and take the child."

879.

LITERARY MERIT

★ ★ ★

Among the Dead by Michael Tolkin

Caught in traffic and delayed by saying his farewells to his mistress, Frank Gale misses the plane that was supposed to take him on a healing vacation with his wife and child. The plane crashes. Tolkin takes this premise and turns it on its head by making Gale a despicable, self-centered, conniving, heartless SOB. Gale's first questions on learning of the crash: How much money will the airline pay him for his loss? He decides to "create his grief for public consumption." Then, among the debris, authorities find his letter to his wife, confessing to his affair. Gale gets the media maelstrom he deserves, not the one he sought to create.

880.

LITERARY MERIT

★ ★ ★ ★

Angela's Ashes by Frank McCourt

Pulitzer 1997; National Book Critics Circle 1996

There's far more humor and honesty than bitterness and resentment in this bestselling memoir of a horrific childhood. Frankie's beloved father drank the family's money so his mother was reduced to begging. Three of his siblings died in infancy. The family couldn't afford sheets or blankets. The family returns to Limerick from Brooklyn and things get even worse. By age eleven, Frankie is the chief breadwinner. Amid the suffering he discovers poetry and girls.

881.

LITERARY MERIT

★ ★ ★ ★

As I Lay Dying by William Faulkner

Seems like every novel with lyrical prose, stream of consciousness, and multiple narrators is dubbed "Faulknerian." Read this 1930 novel to find out why that's a good thing. It tells of the Bundren family's trek to Jefferson, Mississippi, to fulfill the family matriarch's wish to be buried in her hometown. It's an arduous journey. Rains flood the main bridges, and a bridge they attempt to cross collapses. Along the way, the reader takes on each family member's point of view—including Addie herself, as her body decomposes in the heat.

Being Dead Is No Excuse: The Official Southern Ladies Guide to Hosting the Perfect Funeral by Gayden Metcalfe with Charlotte Hays

882.

LITERARY MERIT

★

This is an outrageously funny exposé of the etiquette of a southern funeral. Read about the ins and outs of a tasteful sendoff. Where to be fashionably buried. How to look your best during your last rites. Above all,

> **Did You Know . . .**
>
> The Top Ten Foods for a Southern Funeral: fried chicken, stuffed eggs, Virginia's Butter Beans, tomato aspic, Can't-Die-Without-It Caramel Cake, homemade rolls, banana nut bread, Aunt Hebe's Coconut Cake, Methodist Party Potatoes, and tenderloin.
> —*Being Dead Is No Excuse*

learn the essential foods to be served to mourners when they finally get back to the house. "Chief among these is tomato aspic with homemade mayonnaise—without which you practically can't get a death certificate."

The Child in Time by Ian McEwan

883.

LITERARY MERIT

★ ★ ★

In this novel, Stephen Lewis is a children's author grieving over the loss of his three-year-old daughter, Kate, snatched literally out from under his nose at a supermarket. Stephen continues through life numb, devastated, his memory flashing back to his own boyhood or to the day of Kate's disappearance. What happened will never be explained, but as Stephen comes to realize, "Without the fantasy of her continued existence he was lost, time would stop." A profound sense of loss pervades this novel which won the Whitbread Prize.

Death Be Not Proud by John Gunther

884.

LITERARY MERIT

★ ★

This is a father's love story for his terminally ill son. Gunther's son, Johnny, died of a brain tumor at the age of seventeen. Gunther writes movingly about "a long, courageous struggle between a child and Death." The reader is left with the portrait of a vital, intelligent, level-headed young man who wished he could have spared his parents the pain of his illness.

Howl and Other Poems by Allen Ginsberg

885.

LITERARY MERIT

★ ★ ★ ★

This collection of poems from the great Beat poet was published in 1956. It includes "Howl," a lament for his friend Carl Solomon that begins, "I saw the best minds of my generation destroyed by/madness, starving hysterical naked/dragging themselves through the negro streets at dawn/looking for an angry fix." Its repetitions are at times reminiscent of a Gregorian chant; at other times, its cadences echo the rhythms of jazz. A masterwork of the twentieth century, no one had heard anything like it before.

886.

LITERARY MERIT

★ ★ ★ ★

Last Orders by Graham Swift

Booker Prize 1996

Four older men meet at an east London pub, as they have for years. Their friend Jack Dodds has asked them to scatter his ashes in the sea at Margate. They drive to lay their friend to rest and, with echoes of Faulkner's *As I Lay Dying*, each character remembers his own life as well as Dodds's. A beloved friend is evoked through their flickering interplay. The novel's title plays on a pub's call for "last orders" before closing for the night.

887.

LITERARY MERIT

★ ★ ★

The Memory Keeper's Daughter

by Kim Edwards

The novel opens with a winter storm that blankets 1964 Kentucky in snow as Norah Henry goes into labor. Her husband, David, an orthopedic surgeon, realizes he can't make it safely to the hospital. So he brings her to his own medical clinic to deliver the child. Two babies are born—a healthy son and a daughter with Down syndrome. To protect his wife, David asks his nurse, Caroline Gill, to take the baby girl to a home. He tells his wife that the second baby died. Caroline, who secretly loves David, can't give the baby away. Instead, she takes her as her own and moves away. Norah mourns her lost child, and her husband's lie corrodes the family. This is a riveting story about choices we make to protect the people we love.

888.

LITERARY MERIT

★ ★

Necessary Losses: The Loves, Illusions, Dependencies, and Impossible Expectations That All of Us Have to Give Up in Order to Grow by Judith Viorst

"We begin life with loss," begins Judith Viorst's book of essays about the psychology of loss. She argues that losses, conscious and unconscious, shape our lives. By learning to deal with the end of childhood, with change, and with death, we learn to become functioning adults. This book has helped many readers deal with losses that are an integral part of life.

Ordinary People by Judith Guest

889.

LITERARY MERIT

★ ★ ★

This novel explores what happens when very bad things happen to ordinary people. The Jarretts are a wealthy, middle class family. The story opens in the painful aftermath of a freak boating accident that kills their outgoing older son Buck. His quieter brother, Conrad, has just been released from a psychiatric hospital after being treated for a suicide attempt. Life goes on, in a manner of speaking, but Mrs. Jarrett grows more and more distant, hardening herself, while her son tries to open up. This is an emotional and moving story about the redemptive power of love.

Department of Odds and Ends

Ordinary People was the first unsolicited manuscript in twenty-six years to be accepted for publication by Viking Press.

Sepharad by Antonio Muñoz Molina

890.

LITERARY MERIT

★ ★ ★

This book contains seventeen stories of Sephardic Jews, dislocated from Spain. In the original Spanish, the book is subtitled "A Novel of Novels," and it presents a network of interlinked stories memorializing lives that Molina fears otherwise will "fade from memory as if they had never existed." Margaret Sayers Peden's English translation won the 2004 PEN/ Book-of-the-Month Club Translation prize.

The Solace of Open Spaces by Gretel Ehrlich

891.

LITERARY MERIT

★ ★ ★

The author is a poet who moved from the East to a small Wyoming farm where she found solace, peace, and inspiration in its wide-open spaces, exquisite and harsh landscape, and quirky inhabitants. This book of essays, a testimony to the healing power of nature, explores her present and her past and tells how the move helped her deal with the death of the man she loved.

A Tale of Love and Darkness by Amos Oz

892.

LITERARY MERIT

★ ★ ★

Bear witness to the birth of a nation in this moving memoir of childhood. Oz examines his family's past against the backdrop of Israel's emergence as a nation. He tries to come to terms with defining moments in his life—his mother's suicide three months before his bar mitzvah and his rift with his scholarly, conservative father. He shows what it was like to grow up in an atmosphere of fear, in the shadow of so much loss, and dramatizes the moment when an entire neighborhood stood in silence around a single radio to hear that the UN had voted to create two independent states in Palestine.

893.

The Year of Magical Thinking by Joan Didion

National Book Award 2005

In December 2003, Didion's only daughter died from a runaway pneumonia infection. After returning from the hospital, Didion's husband, author John Gregory Dunne, died so suddenly of a massive heart attack that Didion at first mistook the event for a failed joke. As the initial numbness wore off, she realized, "Widows did not throw themselves in the burning raft out of grief. The burning raft was instead an accurate representation of the place to which their grief (not their families, not the community, not custom, their grief) had taken them." This unsparingly honest, often funny and surprising memoir of grief never reaches for cliché or banality.

...to *Turn On*

LITERARY MERIT ★

PROVOCATIVE 🔥

INFLUENTIAL !

INSPIRATIONAL 🕊

HUMOROUS 😊

BRAINY 🧠

EASY READING ☂

PAGE TURNER 📖

CHALLENGING 👓

BATHROOM BOOK 🚽

FAMILY FRIENDLY 👪

MOVIE 🎥

894.

LITERARY MERIT

★ ★

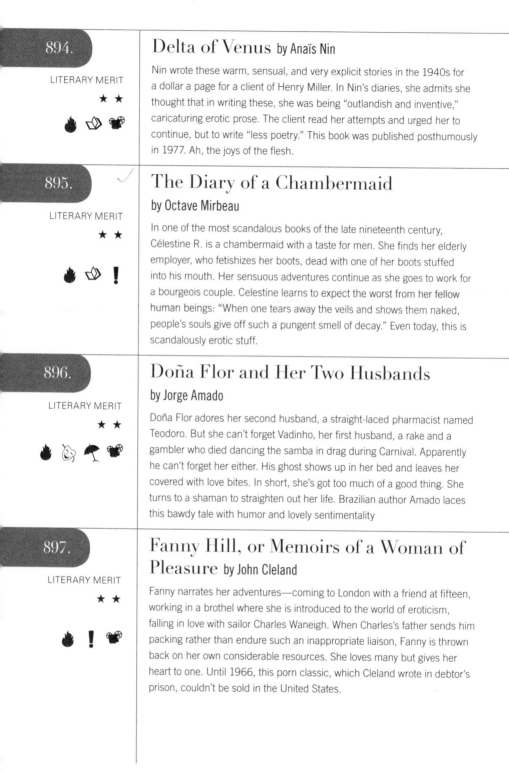

Delta of Venus by Anaïs Nin

Nin wrote these warm, sensual, and very explicit stories in the 1940s for a dollar a page for a client of Henry Miller. In Nin's diaries, she admits she thought that in writing these, she was being "outlandish and inventive," caricaturing erotic prose. The client read her attempts and urged her to continue, but to write "less poetry." This book was published posthumously in 1977. Ah, the joys of the flesh.

895. ✓

LITERARY MERIT

★ ★

The Diary of a Chambermaid
by Octave Mirbeau

In one of the most scandalous books of the late nineteenth century, Célestine R. is a chambermaid with a taste for men. She finds her elderly employer, who fetishizes her boots, dead with one of her boots stuffed into his mouth. Her sensuous adventures continue as she goes to work for a bourgeois couple. Celestine learns to expect the worst from her fellow human beings: "When one tears away the veils and shows them naked, people's souls give off such a pungent smell of decay." Even today, this is scandalously erotic stuff.

896.

LITERARY MERIT

★ ★

Doña Flor and Her Two Husbands
by Jorge Amado

Doña Flor adores her second husband, a straight-laced pharmacist named Teodoro. But she can't forget Vadinho, her first husband, a rake and a gambler who died dancing the samba in drag during Carnival. Apparently he can't forget her either. His ghost shows up in her bed and leaves her covered with love bites. In short, she's got too much of a good thing. She turns to a shaman to straighten out her life. Brazilian author Amado laces this bawdy tale with humor and lovely sentimentality

897.

LITERARY MERIT

★ ★

Fanny Hill, or Memoirs of a Woman of Pleasure by John Cleland

Fanny narrates her adventures—coming to London with a friend at fifteen, working in a brothel where she is introduced to the world of eroticism, falling in love with sailor Charles Waneigh. When Charles's father sends him packing rather than endure such an inappropriate liaison, Fanny is thrown back on her own considerable resources. She loves many but gives her heart to one. Until 1966, this porn classic, which Cleland wrote in debtor's prison, couldn't be sold in the United States.

The Joy of Sex by Alex Comfort

898.

"The starting point of all lovemaking is close body contact," Dr. Comfort counsels his readers in the preface. First published in 1972, the frank content of this sex manual was a revelation to its first generation of readers. The author became the Dr. Spock for couples. The book looks a whole lot less daring now, but still uncovers all the basics.

LITERARY MERIT

★

Lady Chatterley's Lover by D. H. Lawrence ✓

899.

Constance Chatterley is married to a wealthy aristocrat whose war wounds have left him impotent. She has an affair with Mellors, a gamekeeper, and becomes pregnant. The novel was banned for its adulterous love affair and explicit language, and from 1928 until 1959 unexpurgated versions were confiscated. In 1959, attorney Charles Rembar defended the novel's publication and the Supreme Court decision revolutionized obscenity laws by introducing the redeeming-social-value test for obscenity. No longer banned, this novel celebrates the power of good sex between a man and a woman.

LITERARY MERIT

★ ★ ★

Lolita by Vladimir Nabokov ✓

900.

This novel tells the sad story of middle-aged Humbert, Humbert and his doomed obsession with twelve-year-old Lolita. When Lolita's mother dies, the pair set off on a cross-country trip. Humbert indulges his fantasies. Between Graham Greene naming this novel one of the three best he'd read that year and a conservative Scottish newspaper editor calling it "the filthiest book I have ever read," sales soared. Today it is acclaimed as a great literary masterpiece of the twentieth century.

> **Department of Great Opening Lines**
>
> "She was Lo, plain Lo, in the morning, standing four feet ten in one sock. She was Lola in slacks. She was Dolly at school. She was Dolores on the dotted line. But in my arms she was always Lolita."
> —*Lolita*

LITERARY MERIT

★ ★ ★ ★

A Sport and a Pastime by James Salter

901.

The subject is sex and the narrator is a voyeur. The place is (where else?) France. Philip Dean is a thirty-four-year-old American who dropped out of Yale and is traveling on borrowed money. He drops by and stays with a dissolute group of friends near Paris where he meets Anne-Marie, and the narrator imagines them living an erotic dream. Ultimately, reality invades. This book is considered a tour de force of erotic realism.

LITERARY MERIT

★ ★ ★

902.

LITERARY MERIT

★ ★ ★

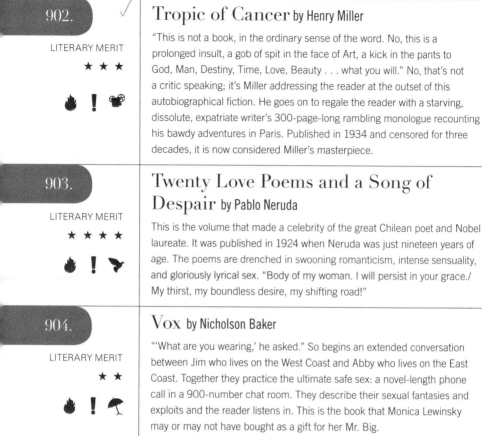

Tropic of Cancer by Henry Miller

"This is not a book, in the ordinary sense of the word. No, this is a prolonged insult, a gob of spit in the face of Art, a kick in the pants to God, Man, Destiny, Time, Love, Beauty . . . what you will." No, that's not a critic speaking; it's Miller addressing the reader at the outset of this autobiographical fiction. He goes on to regale the reader with a starving, dissolute, expatriate writer's 300-page-long rambling monologue recounting his bawdy adventures in Paris. Published in 1934 and censored for three decades, it is now considered Miller's masterpiece.

903.

LITERARY MERIT

★ ★ ★ ★

Twenty Love Poems and a Song of Despair by Pablo Neruda

This is the volume that made a celebrity of the great Chilean poet and Nobel laureate. It was published in 1924 when Neruda was just nineteen years of age. The poems are drenched in swooning romanticism, intense sensuality, and gloriously lyrical sex. "Body of my woman. I will persist in your grace./ My thirst, my boundless desire, my shifting road!"

904.

LITERARY MERIT

★ ★

Vox by Nicholson Baker

"'What are you wearing,' he asked." So begins an extended conversation between Jim who lives on the West Coast and Abby who lives on the East Coast. Together they practice the ultimate safe sex: a novel-length phone call in a 900-number chat room. They describe their sexual fantasies and exploits and the reader listens in. This is the book that Monica Lewinsky may or may not have bought as a gift for her Mr. Big.

...*to* **Turn Off**

LITERARY MERIT ★

PROVOCATIVE 🔥

INFLUENTIAL !

INSPIRATIONAL ➤

HUMOROUS 😊

BRAINY 💡

EASY READING ☂

PAGE TURNER 📖

CHALLENGING 👓

BATHROOM BOOK 🚽

FAMILY FRIENDLY 👪

MOVIE 🎥

905.

LITERARY MERIT

★ ★

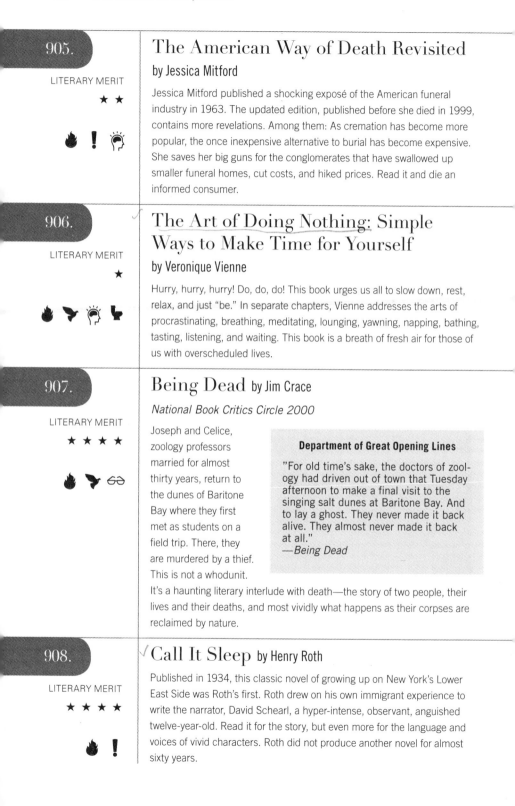

The American Way of Death Revisited
by Jessica Mitford

Jessica Mitford published a shocking exposé of the American funeral industry in 1963. The updated edition, published before she died in 1999, contains more revelations. Among them: As cremation has become more popular, the once inexpensive alternative to burial has become expensive. She saves her big guns for the conglomerates that have swallowed up smaller funeral homes, cut costs, and hiked prices. Read it and die an informed consumer.

906.

LITERARY MERIT

★

The Art of Doing Nothing: Simple Ways to Make Time for Yourself
by Veronique Vienne

Hurry, hurry, hurry! Do, do, do! This book urges us all to slow down, rest, relax, and just "be." In separate chapters, Vienne addresses the arts of procrastinating, breathing, meditating, lounging, yawning, napping, bathing, tasting, listening, and waiting. This book is a breath of fresh air for those of us with overscheduled lives.

907.

LITERARY MERIT

★ ★ ★ ★

Being Dead by Jim Crace

National Book Critics Circle 2000

Joseph and Celice, zoology professors married for almost thirty years, return to the dunes of Baritone Bay where they first met as students on a field trip. There, they are murdered by a thief. This is not a whodunit.

Department of Great Opening Lines

"For old time's sake, the doctors of zoology had driven out of town that Tuesday afternoon to make a final visit to the singing salt dunes at Baritone Bay. And to lay a ghost. They never made it back alive. They almost never made it back at all."
—*Being Dead*

It's a haunting literary interlude with death—the story of two people, their lives and their deaths, and most vividly what happens as their corpses are reclaimed by nature.

908.

LITERARY MERIT

★ ★ ★ ★

Call It Sleep by Henry Roth

Published in 1934, this classic novel of growing up on New York's Lower East Side was Roth's first. Roth drew on his own immigrant experience to write the narrator, David Schearl, a hyper-intense, observant, anguished twelve-year-old. Read it for the story, but even more for the language and voices of vivid characters. Roth did not produce another novel for almost sixty years.

Coming into the End Zone: A Memoir

909.

by Doris Grumbach

LITERARY MERIT

★ ★

She hates getting old. In this diary, written during the seventieth year of her life, Grumbach looks squarely into her own future as she is surrounded by young friends dying of AIDS. Her journal includes a curmudgeonly list of "things I now actively dislike." This is a thoughtful, honest memoir, bitter and cranky at times. This was written in 1989, and somehow, in the interim, seventy has ceased to look all that old.

✓ ## Dracula by Bram Stoker

910.

LITERARY MERIT

★ ★ ★

Young attorney Jonathan Harker journeys through the Carpathian Mountains to Count Dracula's crumbling castle. It's a terrifying coach trip, powerfully foreshadowing what's to come. Dogs howl and wolves bay as they drive deep into the forest. Harker has come to give the Count legal advice, but soon he's a prisoner. After an encounter with three female vampires, he barely escapes with his life. But more than Harker, Count Dracula desires Lucy, the spunky friend of Harker's fiancée Mina, and Mina herself. With its luscious language, this novel seethes with sexuality.

✓ ## How We Die: Reflections on Life's Final Chapter by Sherwin B. Nuland

911.

LITERARY MERIT

★ ★ ★

National Book Award 1994
The sad truth: "we rarely go gentle into that good night." Dr. Nuland, a professor of surgery who teaches bioethics at Yale University, sets out to "demythologize" death. He reveals the graphic details of the most common pathways: old age, cancer, AIDS, Alzheimer's, accidents, heart disease, and stroke. At one point, he holds in his palm a fibrillating heart (like "a wet, jellylike bagful of hyperactive worms.") He argues that by knowing what we'll face, by understanding that death is a natural part of life, we can go through it with dignity and without false expectations. It's a noble and worthy goal.

✓ ## I Am Legend by Richard Matheson

912.

LITERARY MERIT

★ ★

Robert Neville is the last living human in a world populated by vampires. By day he works diligently to kill as many of "them" as he can; by night he barricades himself at home. First published in 1954 with action that takes place in 1976, this has become the gold standard for vampire novels. Matheson also wrote the famous *Twilight Zone* episode "Nightmare at 20,000 Feet"—William Shatner played the passenger who looks out the window from his seat on a passenger jet and sees a creature on the wing, staring back at him.

913.

LITERARY MERIT

★ ★

On Death and Dying by Elisabeth Kübler-Ross

Dr. Kübler-Ross worked with dying patients for two years before she wrote what would become a classic handbook on dying. She identifies the five stages of dying—denial and isolation, anger, bargaining, depression, and acceptance—and the defense mechanisms we use to cope. She acknowledges the sustaining role of hope. This book changed the way the world looks at terminally ill patients, and paved the way for hospice care.

914.

LITERARY MERIT

★ ★

Stiff: The Curious Lives of Cadavers

by Mary Roach

Alex Award 2004

We've been inured to gore by programs like *CSI*, so why not enjoy this compelling look at what happens to a body when its use-by date has expired. Roach reveals how cadavers have served humanity over the years—as space shuttle crash dummies, to test the first guillotines, and as guinea pigs for surgical procedures. Roach tells her story with macabre humor and a historian's eye for fascinating detail.

915.

LITERARY MERIT

★

The Stupids Die

by Harry G. Allard, illustrated by James Marshall

The Stupids picture books are a bracing change from the treacly stuff often offered up for youngsters. In this one, the lights go out and Stanley Q. Stupid and his family think they've died and gone to heaven. Turns out they're in Cleveland. The hilarious illustrations are full of sly jokes, too. Kids who love this series will grow older and adore the books of Roald Dahl and Lemony Snicket.

...to Revel in Words

LITERARY MERIT ★

PROVOCATIVE 🔥

INFLUENTIAL !

INSPIRATIONAL 🕊

HUMOROUS 😊

BRAINY 💡

EASY READING ☂

PAGE TURNER 📖

CHALLENGING 👓

BATHROOM BOOK 🚽

FAMILY FRIENDLY 👪

MOVIE 🎥

916.

LITERARY MERIT

★ ★

The American Language by H. L. Mencken

With this book, published in 1921, Mencken set out to capture "English, as it's spoken by the masses of the plain people of this fair land." He used the term *Americanisms*, coined by John Witherspoon, to refer to English words that are peculiarly American. Here you'll find the origin of *palooka*, *belly-laugh*, and *high-hat*. Mourn colorful terms that have faded like *infanticipating* (expecting), *shafts* (legs), and *Reno-vated* (contemplating divorce).

917.

LITERARY MERIT

★ ★ ★

Bird by Bird by Anne Lamott

Lamott recalls her older brother struggling to write a report on birds for school, overwhelmed by the task, and her father's advice: "Bird by bird, buddy, just take it bird by bird." She offers the anecdote and much more sound advice ("good writing is about telling the truth") in a warm, funny, wise, and practical guide for the budding writer.

918.

LITERARY MERIT

★ ★ ★

The Book of Nonsense
by Edward Lear

This delightful book of limericks was first published in 1846. Take, for example, "There was a Young Person of Crete,/Whose toilette was far from complete;/She dressed in a sack,/Spickle-speckled with black,/That ombliferous person of Crete." Lear's original illustrations are as much fun as the text.

919.

LITERARY MERIT

★ ★ ★ ★

A Coney Island of the Mind
by Lawrence Ferlinghetti

The poems in this book echo the jazz beat of its era. First published in 1958, the poems are infused with poignant memories ("In the pennycandystore beyond the El/is where I first/fell in love/with unreality"), surreal imagery ("Don't let that horse eat that violin"), and angry polemic ("we come we conquer all/but all the while/real standard time ticks on"). This is a slim volume to read, and then reread aloud to yourself with jazz accompaniment.

920.

LITERARY MERIT

★ ★ ★

Eats, Shoots, and Leaves: The Zero-Tolerance Approach to Punctuation
by Lynne Truss

The title, among other things, made this grammar book a runaway bestseller—it's actually from a definition of *panda* with a misplaced comma that fractures its (not *it's*) meaning. A Miss Manners of the semicolon, Truss says, "Part of one's despair, of course is that the world cares nothing for the little shocks endured by the sensitive stickler." She calls for rules buttressed by common sense. This was named the 2004 British Book of the Year.

An Exaltation of Larks by James Lipton

921.

Another book with a great title, this one revels in the English terms that have been used over the ages to describe a group of "whatever beast, fish, fowl, or insect designated." A superfluity of nuns. A murmuration of starlings. A leap of leopards. A cowardice of curs. Lipton wanders through science, history, and literature to assemble this word-lover's lexicon.

LITERARY MERIT

★ ★ ★

Just So Stories by Rudyard Kipling

922.

In these classic children's stories, we find out about the first armadillo, and how the whale got his throat. But it's the language that transports. Of the whale, Kipling writes, "He ate the starfish and the garfish, and the crab and the dab, and the plaice and the dace, and the skate and his mate, and the mackerel and the pickerel, and the really, truly, twirly-whirly eel."

LITERARY MERIT

★ ★ ★ ★

Max Perkins: Editor of Genius by A. Scott Berg

923.

National Book Awards 1978
Max Perkins invented the profession of book editing. His first acquisition for Scribners was F. Scott Fitzgerald's *The Beautiful and the Damned*. He worked on the manuscripts of Ernest Hemingway, Thomas Wolfe, and other great authors whom he often coddled as well as edited. Through fascinating anecdote, this biography paints a portrait of the life of a man of letters and of the literary giants of his time.

LITERARY MERIT

★ ★ ★

The Moons of Jupiter by Alice Munro

924.

Canadian author Munro is considered by many to be one of this century's best short-story writers. This early collection of eleven stories is an excellent introduction to her work. Her extraordinary storytelling takes on mortality, self-delusion, and loves and relationships in the lives of ordinary women. In the title story, as the narrator waits for her father to undergo heart surgery, she ponders how her relationship with her estranged daughter Nichola changed when Nichola was suspected of having leukemia as a child. Munro's stories make the everyday profound.

LITERARY MERIT

★ ★ ★ ★

925.

LITERARY MERIT

★ ★

The Mother Tongue: English and How It Got That Way by Bill Bryson

"More than 300 million people in the world speak English and the rest, it seems, try to," journalist Bryson notes at the start of this fascinating, entertaining, and thoroughly informative book on the history of the English language and all its glorious quirks.

Department of Odds and Ends

Spellings in English are treacherous and opportunities for flummoxing abundant, says Bill Bryson in *The Mother Tongue*. Which words in this list he presents are misspelled?

1. supercede	5. concensus
2. conceed	6. afficianado
3. procede	7. grafitti
4. idiosyncracy	

Answer: They all are.

926.

LITERARY MERIT

★ ★ ★

On Writing: A Memoir of the Craft
by Stephen King

"This is a short book because most books about writing are filled with bullshit," says King in the forward of this nearly 300-page work. The first part, subtitled "C.V.," is a memoir of King's writing life. His "earliest memory is of imagining I was someone else." The second part, subtitled "On Writing," reveals the gritty, often messy details of how he writes. Aspiring writers love it for the image of a wad of rejection letters so thick that King had to use a spike to nail them to his office wall.

927.

LITERARY MERIT

★ ★ ★

On Writing Well by William Zinsser

Zinsser takes the romantic hoo-hah out of writing and tells it like it is. Writing is hard and lonely. The words seldom just flow. Rewriting is the essence of writing. It's a craft, not an art. Most of all, "there isn't any 'right' way to do such personal work." This is a terrific guide to writing clear, strong prose: Hold the adjectives, hold the adverbs, hold the excess.

928.

LITERARY MERIT

★ ★ ★

Oxymoronica: Paradoxical Wit and Wisdom from History's Great Wordsmiths by Mardy Grothe

Oxymoronic wit depends on contradictions and paradoxes, like this from Oscar Wilde: "The suspense is terrible. I hope it will last." This book compiles 1,400 examples, from Confucius to Shakespeare to Woody Allen. Great for dipping into when you need a little pick-me-up.

The Professor and the Madman: A Tale of Murder, Insanity, and the Making of the Oxford English Dictionary by Simon Winchester

LITERARY MERIT

★ ★ ★

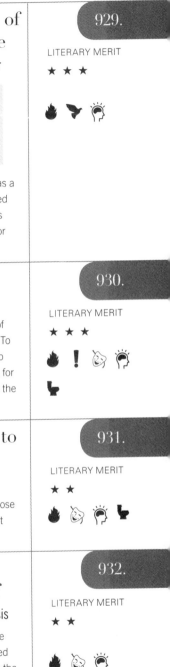

"Twelve tombstone-sized volumes" comprised the original OED. It took seventy years to complete, and this story of its creation and the unlikely friendship it spawned reads like a gaslight thriller. Its editor, Professor

Did You Know It Means . . .

Portmanteau word: A word formed from the parts of other words

James Murray, was a teacher and philologist. Dr. William Charles Minor was a volunteer who contributed 10,000 words to the volumes. After Minor turned down Murray's many invitations to visit, Murray discovered why: Minor was an inmate at Broadmoor Hospital for the Criminally Insane, incarcerated for murder.

The Unabridged Devil's Dictionary
by Ambrose Bierce

LITERARY MERIT

★ ★ ★

Ambrose Bierce published this satirical classic back in 1911. Here's one of his 1,600 subversive definitions: "Abroad: At war with savages and idiots. To be a Frenchman abroad is to be miserable; to be an American abroad is to make others miserable." Many of his definitions shade over into profound, for example: "Religion: A daughter of Hope and Fear, explaining to Ignorance the nature of the Unknowable."

Woe Is I: The Grammarphobe's Guide to Better English in Plain English
by Patricia O'Connor

LITERARY MERIT

★ ★

This guidebook to good grammar is actually a fun read. It addresses all those gnarly problems that one encounters the minute one endeavors to commit thoughts to paper—like that-or-which, it-or-it's, and who-or-whom.

Word Freak: Heartbreak, Triumph, Genius, and Obsession in the World of Competitive Scrabble Players by Stephen Fatsis

LITERARY MERIT

★ ★

Fatsis takes the reader deep inside the world of Scrabble tournaments. He enters contests himself, at first as an interested journalist. Soon he's turned into another Scrabble-obsessed nut. Meet the quirky Scrabble elite, learn the tricks of the game, and find out where you can hang out in Greenwich Village and find a pick-up game. Read this for one of the odder trips you'll ever take.

Quiz Time!
Match the authors and the nonsense
words they invented.

1. Edward Lear

2. Lewis Carroll

3. Kurt Vonnegut

4. J. K. Rowling

5. Dr. Seuss

6. Roald Dahl

a. wampeter, granfalloon,
   karass

b. frabjous, vorpal, whiffling,
   uffish, brillig, slithy, gyre,
   borogoves

c. squitch, thneed, sneetch,
   grinch, gack, Bar-ba-Loot

d. frobscottle, swishfiggler,
   snozzcumber, Oompa-
   Loompas, disgusterous

e. scroobious, meloobious,
   borascible, slobaciously,
   himmeltanious, flumpetty,
   mumbian

f. pensieve, muggle, animagus,
   bludger, patronus, mud-
   blood, obliviate, splinch

Answers: 1-e, 2-b, 3-a, 4-f, 5-c, 6-d

...to Revel in Wit

LITERARY MERIT ★

PROVOCATIVE 🔥

INFLUENTIAL !

INSPIRATIONAL 🕊

HUMOROUS 😄

BRAINY 💡

EASY READING ☂

PAGE TURNER 📖

CHALLENGING 👓

BATHROOM BOOK 🚽

FAMILY FRIENDLY 👪

MOVIE 🎥

933.

LITERARY MERIT

★ ★ ★

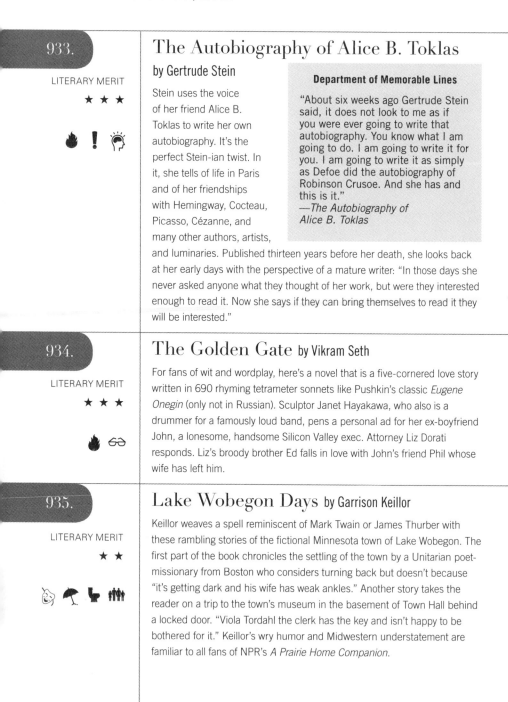

The Autobiography of Alice B. Toklas

by Gertrude Stein

Stein uses the voice of her friend Alice B. Toklas to write her own autobiography. It's the perfect Stein-ian twist. In it, she tells of life in Paris and of her friendships with Hemingway, Cocteau, Picasso, Cézanne, and many other authors, artists, and luminaries. Published thirteen years before her death, she looks back at her early days with the perspective of a mature writer: "In those days she never asked anyone what they thought of her work, but were they interested enough to read it. Now she says if they can bring themselves to read it they will be interested."

Department of Memorable Lines

"About six weeks ago Gertrude Stein said, it does not look to me as if you were ever going to write that autobiography. You know what I am going to do. I am going to write it for you. I am going to write it as simply as Defoe did the autobiography of Robinson Crusoe. And she has and this is it."
—*The Autobiography of Alice B. Toklas*

934.

LITERARY MERIT

★ ★ ★

The Golden Gate by Vikram Seth

For fans of wit and wordplay, here's a novel that is a five-cornered love story written in 690 rhyming tetrameter sonnets like Pushkin's classic *Eugene Onegin* (only not in Russian). Sculptor Janet Hayakawa, who also is a drummer for a famously loud band, pens a personal ad for her ex-boyfriend John, a lonesome, handsome Silicon Valley exec. Attorney Liz Dorati responds. Liz's broody brother Ed falls in love with John's friend Phil whose wife has left him.

935.

LITERARY MERIT

★ ★

Lake Wobegon Days by Garrison Keillor

Keillor weaves a spell reminiscent of Mark Twain or James Thurber with these rambling stories of the fictional Minnesota town of Lake Wobegon. The first part of the book chronicles the settling of the town by a Unitarian poet-missionary from Boston who considers turning back but doesn't because "it's getting dark and his wife has weak ankles." Another story takes the reader on a trip to the town's museum in the basement of Town Hall behind a locked door. "Viola Tordahl the clerk has the key and isn't happy to be bothered for it." Keillor's wry humor and Midwestern understatement are familiar to all fans of NPR's *A Prairie Home Companion*.

Leaving Home: A Memoir by Art Buchwald

Pulitzer-winning humorist Buchwald was a Marine, grew up in a foster home, and struggled with depression. It's hard to line those descriptors up with a man the world knew as a great comedic writer. In his trademark casual, conversational style, Buchwald tells the story of his troubled childhood. "People ask what I am really trying to do with humor. The answer is, 'I'm getting even.'" As with all great clowns, his heartbreak and humor are closely allied.

936.

LITERARY MERIT

★ ★ ★

The Portable Dorothy Parker by Dorothy Parker

This compendium of the great American wit's short stories, essays, and poems is filled with zingers and one-liners that made her one of the most famous diners at the fabled Algonquin Hotel's Round Table. She's clever, ever quotable, and often very wise.

Author's Insight

"Wit has truth in it . . . wise-cracking is simply calisthenics with words."
—Dorothy Parker

937.

LITERARY MERIT

★ ★ ★

Rootabaga Stories by Carl Sandburg

Sandburg wrote these gloriously silly stories for his young daughters. Meet the Potato Face Blind Man and Eeta Peeca Pie; visit the Village of Liver-and-Onions; and take a ride on the Zigzag Railroad where "Sometimes the open-and-shut of the steam hog's nose choked and spit pfisty-pfoost, pfisty-pfoost, pfisty-pfoost." Simply gorgeous wordplay.

938.

LITERARY MERIT

★ ★ ★ ★

Shopgirl: A Novella by Steve Martin

Mirabelle is a shy, cautious shopgirl in a dead-end job: "When you work in the glove department at Neiman's, you are selling things that nobody buys anymore." Her boyfriend is a monosyllabic slacker she met at the laundromat. Into her life walks a crass, handsome, wealthy older man. This is not the gut-splitting ha-ha humor you might expect from the standup comic, but a novella imbued with subtle wit and great heart.

939.

LITERARY MERIT

★ ★ ★

Side Effects by Woody Allen

These seventeen essays were first published in *The New Yorker* during the 1970s, in the innocent early days of Allen's career. In "Remembering Needleman," Allen eulogizes his friend, a fusty professor: "Who would have thought that while Needleman would be watching the demolition of a building on his lunch hour, he'd be tapped in the head by a wrecking ball?" In another comic masterpiece, "The Kugelmass Episode," a man enters his friend's time machine and meets and beds Emma Bovary. This book is a potent reminder of Allen's prodigious talent.

940.

LITERARY MERIT

★ ★

941.

LITERARY MERIT

★ ★ ★

! 🤭 👪 🎥

Thank You, Jeeves by P. G. Wodehouse

There's plenty of slapstick in this novel when Jeeves the butler and Bertrand "Bertie" Wooster go their separate ways over Bertie's incessant banjolele playing. They end up on Lord "Chuffy" Chuffnell's estate; Jeeves must serve Chuffy, and Bertie is banished to a remote rental cottage. Chuffy, who is as always impoverished, enlists Jeeves's help in his attempt to convince a visiting millionaire to front the cash to turn his estate into a psychiatric hospital. Romantic liaisons, fortuitous and otherwise, complicate the plot. Monty Python meets the Marx Brothers.

Who played Bertie Wooster and Jeeves in the movie adaptation of *Thank You, Jeeves*?

David Niven and Arthur Treacher

942.

LITERARY MERIT

★ ★ ★

🔥 ! 🤭

Westward Ha!
by S. J. Perelman, illustrated by Al Hirschfeld

Perelman, who wrote scripts for the Marx Brothers and regularly published witty essays in *The New Yorker*, penned these hilarious essays in the 1940s as he traveled from Hollywood to the Far East. "The whole sordid business began on a bleak November afternoon a couple of years ago in Philadelphia, a metropolis sometimes known as the City of Brotherly Love but more accurately as the City of Bleak November Afternoons." This is an excellent introduction to the man who was an influential and supremely gifted wit and writer.

943.

LITERARY MERIT

★ ★

🕊 ! 🤭 ☂

🚽 👪

Where the Sidewalk Ends by Shel Silverstein

"If you are a dreamer, come in. . . ." Silverstein invites the reader at the start of this collection of one hundred and thirty poems. Who can resist "Ickle Me, Pickle Me, Tickle Me Too," or "Me-Stew," or "Recipe for Hippopotamus Sandwich"? This is a wonderfully irreverent collection from a great humorist and illustrator who understood kids.

...to Revel in Art

LITERARY MERIT ★

PROVOCATIVE 🔥

INFLUENTIAL !

INSPIRATIONAL 🕊

HUMOROUS 😄

BRAINY 💡

EASY READING ☂

PAGE TURNER 📖

CHALLENGING 👓

BATHROOM BOOK 🚽

FAMILY FRIENDLY 👪

MOVIE 🎥

944.

LITERARY MERIT

★ ★ ★

De Kooning: An American Master

by Mark Stevens and Annalyn Swan

Pulitzer 2005

This biography of the great abstract expressionist painter, written by the husband and wife team of art critic and journalist, tells of an outsider who called art theory "baloney." Born in 1904, De Kooning grew up poor in Amsterdam. He started his career as an interior decorator, went to art academy, and sailed to America as a stowaway. He lived a bohemian life of binge drinking and squalor in Greenwich Village. It wasn't until 1950 that his work began to be recognized. Very much a romantic hero, De Kooning cut a dashing, handsome figure in the art world, and created a vast body of work and a lasting legacy.

945.

LITERARY MERIT

★ ★

Diane Arbus: An Aperture Monograph

by Marvin Israel, Doon Arbus, and Diane Arbus

This 1972 book, of and about the photographs of Diane Arbus, was published a year after her suicide. The collection of eighty-one black-and-white photographs focus on what interested Arbus most, people in unguarded moments and revealing often painful, often hilarious, truths. The book contains revealing excerpts from tapes of Arbus discussing her work. Read it to appreciate the womann who transformed the way we see.

Author's Insight

"I really believe there are things nobody would see if I didn't photograph them." —Diane Arbus

946.

LITERARY MERIT

★ ★ ★ ★

Girl in Hyacinth Blue by Susan Vreeland

What if there were an undiscovered Vermeer masterpiece, a portrait of "a young girl wearing a short blue smock over a rust-colored skirt [sitting] in profile at a table by an open window?" This book of eight interconnected stories traces the provenance of the fictional painting through generations, starting in contemporary America and going back to seventeenth-century Holland. This beautifully written historical fiction reads like a mystery novel.

The Girl with the Pearl Earring

by Tracy Chevalier

Alex Award 2001

The young servant girl of the novel's title is hired by the great painter Vermeer to clean his studio. She becomes his assistant and the subject of his most celebrated painting. When Vermeer meets her, she is chopping vegetables and arranges them in a circle. She explains to Vermeer that she separated them as she did because "the colors fight when they are side by side, sir." Vermeer recognizes a kindred spirit. Read it to appreciate an author who paints with words and brings the characters in Vermeer's luminous paintings to life.

LITERARY MERIT

★ ★ ★ ★

Michelangelo and the Pope's Ceiling

by Ross King

When Michelangelo Buonarroti was persuaded by Pope Julius II to paint the ceiling of his grand tomb in the Sistine Chapel, the artist was an accomplished sculptor. He knew little about painting and even less of the challenge of fresco. Set against the upheavals of sixteenth-century Rome, this nonfiction tells how Michelangelo and his assistant spent four years doing it. (They painted standing on scaffolding, not lying on their backs.) The results stunned contemporary audiences. Vasari wrote, "There is no other work to compare with this for excellence, nor could there be." With this vastly entertaining book, King captures Michelangelo's day-to-day world and its tempestuous personalities.

LITERARY MERIT

★ ★ ★

The Music Lesson by Katharine Weber

Yet another Vermeer-inspired book. In this one, art scholar Patricia Dolan, still grieving over her young daughter's tragic, accidental death, is swept off her feet by firebrand Irishman Michael O'Driscoll, a distant cousin. She abandons her life and moves to a remote Irish seaside cottage. Alone there, her only company is a great Vermeer painting (*The Music Lesson*) stolen in an IRA-inspired plot. Ironically, the book she is reading is John Banville's *Book of Evidence*. Ultimately she must choose between art and politics. This very modern story reads like a psychological thriller.

LITERARY MERIT

★ ★ ★

> **Department of Great Characters**
>
> "In her contemplative isolation, the woman looks up from her music and regards us, and she asks us to take a position, she commands us to exist, to see ourselves."
> —The model of Vermeer's painting, *The Music Lesson*

...to **SAVE THE WORLD**

LITERARY MERIT ★

PROVOCATIVE

INFLUENTIAL !

INSPIRATIONAL

HUMOROUS

BRAINY

EASY READING

PAGE TURNER

CHALLENGING 👓

BATHROOM BOOK

FAMILY FRIENDLY

MOVIE

950.

LITERARY MERIT

★ ★

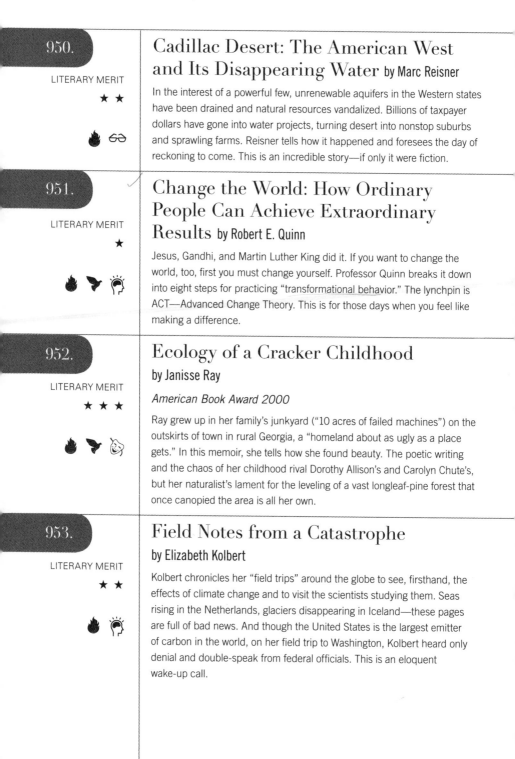

Cadillac Desert: The American West and Its Disappearing Water by Marc Reisner

In the interest of a powerful few, unrenewable aquifers in the Western states have been drained and natural resources vandalized. Billions of taxpayer dollars have gone into water projects, turning desert into nonstop suburbs and sprawling farms. Reisner tells how it happened and foresees the day of reckoning to come. This is an incredible story—if only it were fiction.

951.

LITERARY MERIT

★

Change the World: How Ordinary People Can Achieve Extraordinary Results by Robert E. Quinn

Jesus, Gandhi, and Martin Luther King did it. If you want to change the world, too, first you must change yourself. Professor Quinn breaks it down into eight steps for practicing "transformational behavior." The lynchpin is ACT—Advanced Change Theory. This is for those days when you feel like making a difference.

952.

LITERARY MERIT

★ ★ ★

Ecology of a Cracker Childhood
by Janisse Ray

American Book Award 2000

Ray grew up in her family's junkyard ("10 acres of failed machines") on the outskirts of town in rural Georgia, a "homeland about as ugly as a place gets." In this memoir, she tells how she found beauty. The poetic writing and the chaos of her childhood rival Dorothy Allison's and Carolyn Chute's, but her naturalist's lament for the leveling of a vast longleaf-pine forest that once canopied the area is all her own.

953.

LITERARY MERIT

★ ★

Field Notes from a Catastrophe
by Elizabeth Kolbert

Kolbert chronicles her "field trips" around the globe to see, firsthand, the effects of climate change and to visit the scientists studying them. Seas rising in the Netherlands, glaciers disappearing in Iceland—these pages are full of bad news. And though the United States is the largest emitter of carbon in the world, on her field trip to Washington, Kolbert heard only denial and double-speak from federal officials. This is an eloquent wake-up call.

How the Irish Saved Civilization

by Thomas Cahill

In this thoroughly engaging account, Cahill tells how Christian monks and scribes copied books being destroyed by continental barbarians after the fall of the Roman Empire, and ensured that the texts survived the Dark Ages. Cahill also sets himself on a mission to correct the image of the Irish as "wild, feckless, and charming, or morose, repressed, and corrupt, but not especially civilized."

954.

LITERARY MERIT

★ ★

An Inconvenient Truth by Al Gore

Dismissed by George W. Bush during the 1992 presidential campaign as "ozone man," Gore presents a hit-the-high-spots introduction to global warming and an impassioned warning about global climate change. He outlines staggering consequences—from violent weather, drought, and fire, to melting ice sheets and flooding—and asks his reader to consult the daily news, not a crystal ball, to see if he's right. He was awarded the Nobel Peace Prize for his work on climate change.

955.

LITERARY MERIT

★ ★

Ishmael: An Adventure of the Mind and Spirit by Daniel Quinn

The novel's unnamed narrator answers a personal ad ("Teacher seeks pupil") and meets Ishmael, a learned gorilla who teaches telepathically. They engage in a series of Socratic dialogues examining the history and philosophy of mankind. Ishmael argues that humanity belongs to the planet, not the other way around, and for our world to survive we must become "givers" instead of "takers." A bit heavy-handed, but still this delivers a much-needed message for our time.

956.

LITERARY MERIT

★ ★

The Monkey Wrench Gang

by Edward Abbey, illustrated by R. Crumb

The "eco-raiders" in this novel are four redneck, beer-swilling, gun-toting slobs who are out to put a stop to the desecration and development of the desert of the American west. Their target: the Glen Canyon Dam that plugs up the Colorado River. Published in 1975, the illustrations are as memorable as the text.

957.

LITERARY MERIT

★ ★

958.

LITERARY MERIT

★ ★

! 🐦

Mountains Beyond Mountains
by Tracy Kidder

This is the true story of how one man can make a difference. Paul Farmer is a physician obsessed with public health. A specialist in infectious diseases, he truly believes problems can be solved and "the only real nation is humanity." Dr. Farmer lives his beliefs, and author Kidder traces his life story as he follows him into the Haitian hills, Siberian prisons, and Cuban clinics. A truly inspiring story.

959.

LITERARY MERIT

★ ★

🔥 ! 🐦

Silent Spring by Rachel Carson

With this nonfiction, biologist and writer Carson took on the chemical industry. Her interest was sparked by a 1958 letter from a friend, telling of massive bird deaths on Cape Cod after DDT sprayings. She could find no magazine interested in assigning her the story, but she spent four years writing it anyway. In the book's most haunting chapter, "A Fable for Tomorrow," all life in a nameless town has been "silenced" by DDT. As a result of the publicity the book generated, laws banning DDT were passed and the environmentalist movement was born.

960.

LITERARY MERIT

★

🔥 !

Unsafe at Any Speed: The Designed-in Dangers of the American Automobile
by Ralph Nader

Once upon a time, not so long ago, dashboards were made of metal and seat belts were considered exotic, expensive add-ons. With his focus on the unsafe features of the Corvair, Nader goaded American automobile companies into spending money on safety. Within a year of the book's publication, Congress passed the Motor Vehicle Safety Act. This was the seminal book on consumer safety, back when only industrial titans wanted to shut this author up.

...to Defy Expectations

LITERARY MERIT	★
PROVOCATIVE	🔥
INFLUENTIAL	❗
INSPIRATIONAL	🕊
HUMOROUS	😊
BRAINY	💡
EASY READING	☂
PAGE TURNER	📖
CHALLENGING	👓
BATHROOM BOOK	🚽
FAMILY FRIENDLY	👪
MOVIE	🎥

961.

LITERARY MERIT

★ ★ ★

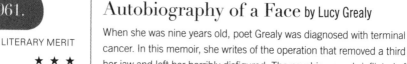

Autobiography of a Face by Lucy Grealy

When she was nine years old, poet Grealy was diagnosed with terminal cancer. In this memoir, she writes of the operation that removed a third of her jaw and left her horribly disfigured. The psychic wounds inflicted after were even worse. Imbued with great wit, this memoir is neither self-pitying nor magically uplifting. (Footnote: Grealy endured a total of thirty-eight operations. She died of an apparent heroin overdose at the age of thirty-nine. Her friend, author Ann Patchett, wrote about Grealy's struggles in *Truth and Beauty*.)

962.

LITERARY MERIT

★ ★

Bee Season by Myla Goldberg

The novel's appealing protagonist, eleven-year-old Eliza Naumann, is a quiet underachiever compared to her scholarly father and brilliant lawyer mother. She finally gets their attention and bumps her talented brother off his pedestal when she sweeps her school spelling bee. Her father guides her through mystical texts as they practice for the national competition, and soon spellings come to her as if by magic. The closer she gets to apotheosis, the more her family falls apart. Coming of age and religious mysticism make a fascinating combination.

963.

LITERARY MERIT

★ ★ ★ ★

Charlotte's Web by E. B. White

Fern Arable reproaches her father as he stands over the littlest pig in the litter with an axe: "The pig couldn't help being born small, could it? If I had been small at birth, would you have killed me?" This is the timeless tale of a smart little pig, and the feisty young girl and maternal spider who believe in him. For an overdose of inspiration, read this and then watch *Rocky*.

964.

LITERARY MERIT

★ ★

The Diving Bell and the Butterfly: A Memoir of Life in Death by Jean-Dominique Bauby

In 1995, Bauby, then editor of *Elle* magazine in Paris, suffered a massive stroke. He survived, mentally aware but physically "locked in," only able to move an eyelid. Using eye movements and a blinking code, he managed to dictate this brief, poignant, and sad memoir, transforming pain into creativity.

Department of Memorable Lines

"'You can handle the wheelchair,' said the occupational therapist, with a smile intended to make the remark sound like good news, whereas to my ears it had the ring of a life sentence."
—*The Diving Bell and the Butterfly*

The Chocolate War by Robert Cormier

965.

This 1974 novel is set at all-boys Trinity Academy which turns out to be its own "Lord of the Flies" island.

Department of Odds and Ends

Robert Cormier's son inspired the writing of *The Chocolate War* when he refused to sell the chocolates at his school's annual sale.

LITERARY MERIT

★ ★ ★

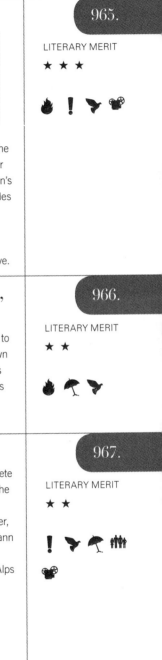

Lowerclassmen are tyrannized by the Vigils, a gang of upperclassmen led by Archie Costello. The Vigils are, in turn, tyrannized by corrupt adults. As part of a hazing ritual, for ten days young Jerry Renault refuses to participate in powerful Brother Leon's pet project, a scheme to sell chocolates. When the days are up, Jerry decides to continue his boycott. Brother Leon enlists the Vigils to bend Jerry to his will, and the result is a classic standoff between an individual and a mob. The poster Jerry hangs inside his locker says it all: "Do I Dare Disturb the Universe." This is a courageous book about standing up for what you believe.

Expecting Adam: A True Story of Birth, Rebirth, and Everyday Magic by Martha Beck

966.

LITERARY MERIT

★ ★

Sometimes life has a way of altering one's priorities. That's what happened to Beck and her husband when Beck became pregnant with a baby with Down syndrome. Throughout her pregnancy, Beck experiences visions and hears the baby speaking to her from the womb. Little Adam is born and continues to be himself, not at all the person Beck and her husband were expecting. This book tells a heartfelt story imbued with great warmth and humanity.

Heidi by Johanna Spyri

967.

LITERARY MERIT

★ ★

In this classic children's book published in 1880, Heidi's ambitious Aunt Dete schleps the ever-cheerful, rosy-cheeked, five-year-old orphan halfway up the Alps and palms her off on Grandfather. He's a curmudgeonly recluse, and there's a lovely transformation as Heidi humanizes him. But three years later, Aunt Dete returns and grabs Heidi back. She wants the money the Sesemann family of Frankfurt will pay for providing a companion for their paralyzed daughter, Clara. You may remember the story, but the descriptions of the Alps will feel like an infusion of fresh goat's milk and Alpine air.

968.

LITERARY MERIT

★ ★ ★

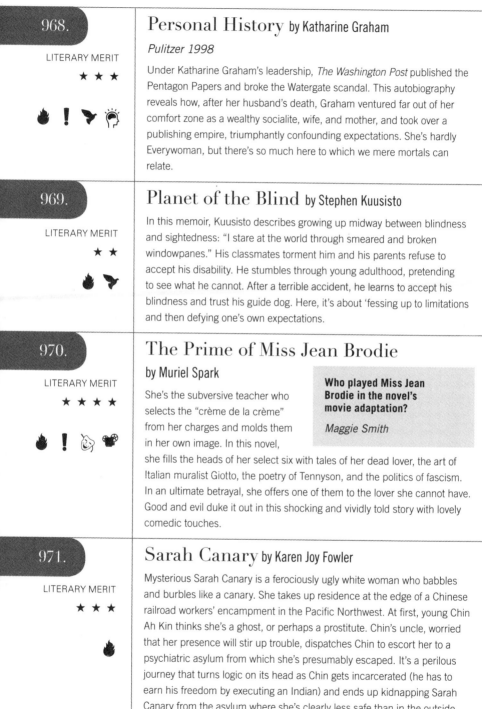

Personal History by Katharine Graham

Pulitzer 1998

Under Katharine Graham's leadership, *The Washington Post* published the Pentagon Papers and broke the Watergate scandal. This autobiography reveals how, after her husband's death, Graham ventured far out of her comfort zone as a wealthy socialite, wife, and mother, and took over a publishing empire, triumphantly confounding expectations. She's hardly Everywoman, but there's so much here to which we mere mortals can relate.

969.

LITERARY MERIT

★ ★

Planet of the Blind by Stephen Kuusisto

In this memoir, Kuusisto describes growing up midway between blindness and sightedness: "I stare at the world through smeared and broken windowpanes." His classmates torment him and his parents refuse to accept his disability. He stumbles through young adulthood, pretending to see what he cannot. After a terrible accident, he learns to accept his blindness and trust his guide dog. Here, it's about 'fessing up to limitations and then defying one's own expectations.

970.

LITERARY MERIT

★ ★ ★ ★

The Prime of Miss Jean Brodie

by Muriel Spark

She's the subversive teacher who selects the "crème de la crème" from her charges and molds them in her own image. In this novel,

Who played Miss Jean Brodie in the novel's movie adaptation?

Maggie Smith

she fills the heads of her select six with tales of her dead lover, the art of Italian muralist Giotto, the poetry of Tennyson, and the politics of fascism. In an ultimate betrayal, she offers one of them to the lover she cannot have. Good and evil duke it out in this shocking and vividly told story with lovely comedic touches.

971.

LITERARY MERIT

★ ★ ★

Sarah Canary by Karen Joy Fowler

Mysterious Sarah Canary is a ferociously ugly white woman who babbles and burbles like a canary. She takes up residence at the edge of a Chinese railroad workers' encampment in the Pacific Northwest. At first, young Chin Ah Kin thinks she's a ghost, or perhaps a prostitute. Chin's uncle, worried that her presence will stir up trouble, dispatches Chin to escort her to a psychiatric asylum from which she's presumably escaped. It's a perilous journey that turns logic on its head as Chin gets incarcerated (he has to earn his freedom by executing an Indian) and ends up kidnapping Sarah Canary from the asylum where she's clearly less safe than in the outside world. Fowler, whose talent shines in this, her first novel, went on to write the hugely popular *Jane Austen Book Club*.

Seabiscuit: An American Legend

972.

by Laura Hillenbrand

LITERARY MERIT

★ ★ ★ ★

This is the astonishing true story of an owner, a trainer, a jockey, and a horse, not one of them with the apparent makings of a winner. Owner Charles Howard, who started with a bicycle repair shop and ended up a millionaire car dealer, hires a "mysterious, virtually mute mustang breaker," Tom Smith. Smith urges Howard to buy Seabiscuit, a "smallish, mud-colored animal with forelegs that didn't straighten all the way," an also-ran with the temperamental disposition of his legendary sire, Man O'War. Red Pollard, a down-on-his-luck jockey, becomes his rider. From 1936 to 1940, Seabiscuit took a rapt nation "through anguish and exultation." Like her subjects, Hillenbrand is an unlikely winner—she wrote this bestseller while she was bedridden with chronic fatigue syndrome so bad that at times she had trouble rolling over in bed.

The Story of My Life by Helen Keller

973.

Helen Keller, born in 1880, was nineteen months old when she suffered a fever that left her blind and deaf. Cosseted by her family, she became a little hellion until teacher Anne Sullivan came into her life and brought her the power of language. When she was a student at Radcliffe College, Keller wrote this biography of the first twenty-two years of her life—it really does live up to the hype.

LITERARY MERIT

★ ★

Thinking in Pictures: And Other Reports from My Life with Autism by Temple Grandin

974.

Grandin is the autistic woman Oliver Sacks describes in *An Anthropologist on Mars*. In this memoir, Grandin, an animal welfare expert who teaches at Colorado State University, ably picks up where Sacks leaves off. She reveals how her thoughts come to her in pictures, and how she needs to be held but is intensely afraid of being touched. She describes how she invented a "squeeze machine" which allowed her to control the strength and duration of a hug. For a woman who thinks in pictures, she gives the reader an eloquent insider's view of autism.

LITERARY MERIT

★ ★

The Wet Engine by Brian Doyle

975.

Nine years before writing this book, Doyle's wife gave birth to twin boys. One was entirely normal, but the other was missing a chamber in his heart. At five months and again at eighteen months, little Liam had open-heart surgery. Doyle writes about Liam, his surgeon, his family, and dozens of others with heart-related stories in a moving meditation on the meaning of love.

LITERARY MERIT

★ ★

...*to* Reinvent Yourself

LITERARY MERIT ★

PROVOCATIVE 🔥

INFLUENTIAL ❗

INSPIRATIONAL 🕊

HUMOROUS 😃

BRAINY 🧠

EASY READING ☂

PAGE TURNER 📖

CHALLENGING 👓

BATHROOM BOOK 🚽

FAMILY FRIENDLY 👪

MOVIE 🎥

976.

LITERARY MERIT

★ ★

The Adventures of Pinocchio by Carlo Collodi

Much longer, more complex, and darker than the fairy tale versions, this novel first published in the 1880s tells a picaresque tale of growing up poor and Italian. Pinocchio starts out life as a stick of wood. When carpenter Master Anthony strikes the stick with an axe, it cries out. Master Anthony gives the stick to impoverished Gepetto who makes it into a marionette. No sooner has Gepetto fashioned a mouth than Pinocchio sticks out his tongue. An aggressive, rebellious child, he runs away, but it's Gepetto who ends up imprisoned. Finally Pinocchio meets the Talking Cricket who tells him if he doesn't shape up, he'll become a jackass. Pinocchio becomes angry and kills the messenger. Throughout the novel, Pinocchio changes—from stick of wood to wooden puppet to watchdog to donkey, and finally to a boy. One assumes Collodi was turning over in his grave when this wonderful, rich story got Disney-fied.

977.

LITERARY MERIT

★ ★ ★

Alice Adams by Booth Tarkington

Pulitzer 1922

When we first meet Alice, she's daydreaming and posturing before the mirror, "clasping her hands

Who played Alice Adams in the movie adaptation?

Katherine Hepburn

behind her neck, and tilting back her head to foreshorten the face in a tableau conceived to represent sauciness, then one of smiling weariness, then one of scornful toleration, and all very piquant." This is Alice's painful essence, a self-conscious young woman, desperate to rise above her shabby background and be what she is not. The novel, written with pathos and infused with humor, gave the world an enduring literary character.

978.

LITERARY MERIT

★ ★ ★ ★

The Amazing Adventures of Kavalier & Clay by Michael Chabon

Pulitzer 2001

Young Sam Clay, son of a psychiatric nurse and a vaudeville muscleman, dreams of literary glory as he toils as a clerk for a novelty wholesaler. His cousin, Josef Kavalier, a veteran magician who used his Houdiniesque talents to escape Nazi-held Prague, yearns for enough

Do You Know . . .

The characters Kavalier and Clay are reminiscent of partners Jerry Siegel and Joe Shuster who created Superman and signed over the rights to their creation for a paltry sum while the publishers made a fortune off it.

money to free the family he left behind. Inspired by the greatest dreams and darkest fears, together they create masked superhero comic characters and go on to build a comic empire. This sprawling and enthralling novel is saturated with real events and historical figures from the golden age of the comic-book industry.

The Bone People by Keri Hulme

Booker Prize, 1985

Set in New Zealand, this novel tells of despairing artist Kerewin Holmes who can no longer create art. She builds herself a tower on the beach and spends her days there, dreaming and drinking. Into her life come a mute, silver-haired little boy, shipwrecked and rescued by locals, and his embittered adopted Maori father. This unusual and riveting novel is woven through with dreams, myth, magic, the world of the dead, and the traditions of ancient cultures. When it was published in 1984, it became the most successful novel in New Zealand's publishing history.

979.

LITERARY MERIT

★ ★ ★

Catch Me If You Can

by Frank W. Abagnale and Stan Redding

For years he impersonated, swindled, and counterfeited. He conned his way into piloting a Pan Am passenger jet. He pretended to be a pediatrician, a hospital supervisor, a government attorney, and a college professor. In this astounding autobiography, Abagnale (a high-school dropout) reveals the amazing, true story of how he pulled it off.

980.

LITERARY MERIT

★

Cindy Sherman: A Play of Selves

by Cindy Sherman

This volume is organized as a four-act "play." Artist/photographer Sherman presents assemblages of photographs of herself, utterly transformed into various personas, and relates the tale of a young woman who overcomes self-doubt. This is an early work of a provocative, influential artist, and puts a new spin on the notion of self-transformation.

981.

LITERARY MERIT

★

David Copperfield by Charles Dickens

Poor David suffers a truly Dickensian childhood. His father dies, and his mother remarries brutish Mr. Murdstone. David is sent off to boarding school with a ruthless headmaster. His mother dies and his stepfather consigns him to work at a grim London factory. David escapes and walks to Dover to find his eccentric aunt who christens him "Trot." Published in 1850, this novel gave birth to an enduring array of characters: David's faithful nurse Peggotty, eccentric Aunt Betsy Trotwood, evil headmaster Mr. Creakle, and of course the dissolute Mr. Micawber and the villainous Uriah Heep. Dickens' writing is still held up as a standard for storytellers.

982.

LITERARY MERIT

★ ★ ★

983.

LITERARY MERIT

★ ★ ★

Dr. Jekyll and Mr. Hyde by Robert Louis Stevenson

Framed as a detective story, this timeless novella, which first appeared in 1886, tells a harrowing tale of a man who is not what he seems. Attorney Gabriel John Utterson investigates his friend Dr. Henry Jekyll's mysterious liaison with the reputedly murderous Edward Hyde. This quintessential battle of good and evil within a single human being has inspired legions of mad-scientist characters.

984.

LITERARY MERIT

★ ★ ★ ★

Final Payments by Mary Gordon

"My father's funeral was full of priests," the novel opens, and at last thirty-year-old Isabel Moore's eleven years of caring for her invalid and intensely religious Catholic father come to an end. She's free to live her own life, to find personal and sexual fulfillment—but first she has to free herself from the guilt crippling her spirit. Gordon wrote about reinventing herself in this first novel, which established her as one of America's pre-eminent novelists.

985.

LITERARY MERIT

★ ★

Flowers for Algernon by Daniel Keyes

Nebula Award 1966

Based on an award-winning short story, this novel and cautionary tale is written in the guise of Charlie Gordon's diary. Charlie is an engaging simpleton with an IQ of 68 who wants, more than anything, to become smart. He agrees to be subjected to an experimental operation that's been proven successful on a white mouse named Algernon. At first, Charlie's operation seems to have achieved the called-for miracle. He's smart, but intelligence brings anguished realizations. Then, Algernon's sudden deterioration bodes ill for Charlie. This book will inspire you and break your heart at the same time.

986.

LITERARY MERIT

★ ★ ★

Frankenstein, or the Modern Prometheus by Mary Wollstonecraft Shelley

Dr. Viktor Frankenstein longs to infuse "life into an inanimate body." When he succeeds, he recoils from the creature he's created. The novel opens with the doctor's rescue from an iceberg where he's been fleeing his own creation. On the ship, he relates his story. By the end, the reader is not sure who has humanity: the doctor himself and by extension the rest of us, or the monster. Shelley was only twenty-one in 1818 when this iconic novel was published anonymously.

Fried Green Tomatoes at the Whistlestop Café by Fannie Flagg

987.

LITERARY MERIT

★ ★

This tale within a tale is a rollicking read of love, loss, triumph, and transformation. Unhappy housewife Evelyn Couch becomes inspired by the stories eighty-six-year-old Cleo Threadgood tells about volatile tomboy Idgie Threadgood, gentle and unhappy Ruth Jamison, and the Whistlestop Café with its colorful characters who drop in for buttermilk biscuits, red-eye gravy, and Big George's barbecue. The stories inspire Evelyn to transform herself into "Towanda!"

Great Apes by Will Self

988.

LITERARY MERIT

★ ★ ★

Painter Simon Dykes wakes up from a drunken stupor to find his world is run by chimpanzees. His girlfriend is a chimp, and Simon himself is growing hairier by the moment. He's treated by a psychiatric team of chimps for his delusion that he's human, and for the even more bizarre notion that humans are the evolutionarily successful primates. Distinguished psychologist/chimp Dr. Zak Busner journeys with Simon to Africa to one of the world's remaining populations of wild humans, hoping to find answers. This brilliant, outrageous, and satirical novel is written in lush, literary prose.

Heat: An Amateur's Adventures as Kitchen Slave, Line Cook, Pasta-Maker, and Apprentice to a Dante-Quoting Butcher in Tuscany by Bill Buford

989.

LITERARY MERIT

★ ★

Buford starts his adventures as a home cook, trying to pull off a birthday dinner party for a friend. Celebrity chef Mario Batali, who is invited to the gathering, saves Buford's roast. Determined to learn, Buford endures a voluntary stint working in the kitchen of Batali's New York restaurant, Babo's. There he screws up grilled branzini, butchers carrots, mangles fennel, and endures abject humiliation. But he learns. Interspersed with an insider's view of a pulsating world-class restaurant is the intriguing story of chef Batali's rise to stardom.

How the Garcia Girls Lost Their Accents
by Julia Alvarez

990.

LITERARY MERIT

★ ★

The novel takes a look back with vivid vignettes at the pains and pleasures of four sisters, growing up between two worlds. Carle, Sandi, Yolanda, and Fifi are born in the Dominican Republic and flee to the United States after their father is involved in a failed coup. They are neither quite at home being Hispanic in the United States or being emigrants visiting their homeland. A lovely, funny, serious book about that complicated process of finding one's own identity—read it with Amy Tan's *The Joy Luck Club* and Jamaica Kincaid's *Annie John*.

991.

LITERARY MERIT
★

I'm Good Enough, I'm Smart Enough, and Doggone It, People Like Me!
by Al Franken

Stuart Smalley—remember him from *Saturday Night Live*? His "diary," like the earnest memoir/self-help books it satirizes, overflows with platitudes including solemn vows to "let go of past mistakes," "believe in me," and "bounce back." In 2007, Franken got serious and launched a run for the U.S. Senate seat for Minnesota. The book title makes the ultimate campaign slogan. Besides, who says an actor can't run for office?

992.

LITERARY MERIT
★ ★ ★ ★

The Impressionist by Hari Kunzru

Pran is half English, half Indian. He can come across as either, depending on the image he wants to convey, and morphs to suit the occasion. Often his survival depends on it. His picaresque adventures take him to a brothel where he is forced to dress as a girl, to Bombay where he's fought over by a minister and his estranged wife, and to deepest Africa where he's part of an ethnographic expedition. Read it to appreciate the absurdity of a world in which people are judged by their race. This book was awarded a literary prize by Britain's *Daily Mail*, but Kunzru rejected it for what he called the newspaper's "hostility towards black and Asian British people."

993.

LITERARY MERIT
★ ★ ★ ★

Invisible Man by Ralph Ellison

National Book Award 1953

The novel's nameless narrator is a gifted black man who grows up in a black southern community. His orating talent and achievements as high school valedictorian get him a scholarship to a Southern Negro college; his naiveté as he gives a rich, white trustee a campus tour gets him thrown out. His prospects are sabotaged and he spirals down. Only by finding his voice does he shed his invisibility. When first published in 1952, this angry, impassioned novel shook the country. It still packs a wallop.

994.

LITERARY MERIT
★ ★ ★

Kitchen by Banana Yoshimoto

"I love even incredibly dirty kitchens to distraction—vegetable droppings all over the floor, so dirty your slippers turn black on the bottom." This is the voice of the novella's young narrator, college student Mikage Sakurai. After the abrupt death of the grandmother who raised her, Mikage realizes she is alone in the world. She's rescued from a deep depression by Yuichi Tanabe when he invites her to live with him and his mother. Terrified of loneliness and comforted by the hominess of the Tanabe kitchen, Mikage accepts. Eventually, roles are reversed and it's Mikage who keeps Yuichi from descending into despair. This much-lauded, bestselling first novel won a raft of 1987–1988 literary prizes in Japan. It explores personal and sexual identity, and is said to capture the frustration and angst of Japanese youth.

Mary Reilly by Valerie Martin

995.

In the final scene of Robert Louis Stevenson's *Dr. Jekyll and Mr. Hyde,* a housemaid is briefly mentioned, standing outside Dr. Jekyll's laboratory and weeping. In Martin's novel, the story is retold from that maid's viewpoint. The reader watches the orderly household disintegrate as the ungentlemanly Mr. Hyde takes it over, and Mary Reilly's concern for her kind master turns into love and a willingness to risk all to save him. This fresh take on a classic tale was nominated for Nebula and World Fantasy awards.

LITERARY MERIT

★ ★

Memoirs of a Geisha by Arthur Golden

996.

Disguised as a memoir of one of Japan's most celebrated geishas, this tour de force is written by a man. It tells of Satsu, a fisherman's daughter, being sold into slavery. She's taken to Kyoto and transformed into the intoxicatingly beautiful geisha Sayuri. For years, she works to pay back the price of her purchase, and along the way acquires a generous tutor and a dangerous rival. This book, filled with fascinating details of geisha life, tells an unforgettable story.

LITERARY MERIT

★ ★ ★ ★

The Metamorphosis by Franz Kafka

997.

The first line of this novella, published in 1915, says it all: "One morning, as Gregor Samsa was waking up from anxious dreams, he discovered that in bed he had been changed into a monstrous verminous bug." He's oddly unconcerned as he checks the messy room and the weather, and laments his traveling salesman job, but he has a tough time getting out of bed and soon realizes he can no longer speak. Initially his family cares for him, but gradually he's seen as a burden his relatives are eager to squash. This is a nightmarish, comedic masterpiece from the consummate pessimist of the twentieth century.

LITERARY MERIT

★ ★ ★

Praisesong for the Widow by Paule Marshall

998.

American Book Award 1984

Avey Johnson, a wealthy, recently widowed African American woman, takes a Caribbean cruise with two friends and finds herself surrounded by memories—a marriage that took her from Harlem to an affluent New York suburb, her strivings for success that cost her personal happiness, and her childhood and the ways of her people. Finally she's able to embrace the person she's been all along. This is a novel about reconnecting with and embracing a cultural heritage.

LITERARY MERIT

★ ★ ★

999.

LITERARY MERIT

★ ★ ★ ★

Sacred Country by Rose Tremain

Six-year-old Mary Ward realizes that inside she's really a boy. It's 1952 and small-town Suffolk, England, isn't ready for this kind of news bulletin. The novel takes Mary from rural Suffolk to the 1960s' swinging London, through a sex-change operation and transformation into "Martin," and on to a new life, singing in Nashville. This moving, often funny novel, shortlisted for the Booker Prize, asks the reader to examine hard questions of identity and self.

1000.

LITERARY MERIT

★ ★ ★

She Got Up Off the Couch: And Other Heroic Acts from Mooreland, Indiana
by Haven Kimmel

Haven Kimmel's 268-pound mother Delonda rules from a couch in the den. One Friday, at 5:55, she got up ("I knew that what I was witnessing was no less than a miracle"). This sequel to *A Girl Named Zippy* tells the story of a mother who triumphantly transforms herself as her daughter comes of age. The writing and the voice are captivating.

1001.

LITERARY MERIT

★ ★ ★

The Talented Mr. Ripley by Patricia Highsmith

Tom Ripley, the charming sociopath narrator of this black comedy, starts out as a small-time scam artist. He impersonates an IRS agent, collecting money he tells his marks they owe the government. He's recruited by wealthy, ailing shipbuilder Herbert Greenleaf to find his son, Dickie, and convince him to return home from Europe. Ripley finds Dickie all right, kills him as if it's nothing more than chopping down a tree, and assumes his identity. In this one, Highsmith revels in tormenting her readers with moral ambiguity.

About the Author

Hallie Ephron, Ph.D. is a critically acclaimed writer. Her fiction has been praised by *Publishers Weekly* for its "adrenaline-pumping prose" and by the *Sun Sentinel* for "rapid-fire pacing" and "crisp writing." Her book on mystery writing was an Edgar Award finalist, and she teaches at writing workshops throughout the country. An award-winning book review columnist for the *Boston Globe*, Ephron knows her literature.